EUROPEAN INTEGRATION IN SOCIAL
AND HISTORICAL PERSPECTIVE

EUROPEAN INTEGRATION IN SOCIAL AND HISTORICAL PERSPECTIVE

1850 to the Present

Edited by
Jytte Klausen
and
Louise A. Tilly

ROWMAN & LITTLEFIELD PUBLISHERS, INC.
Lanham • Boulder • New York • Oxford

ROWMAN & LITTLEFIELD PUBLISHERS, INC.

Published in the United States of America
by Rowman & Littlefield Publishers, Inc.
4720 Boston Way, Lanham, Maryland 20706

12 Hid's Copse Road
Cummor Hill, Oxford OX2 9JJ, England

British Library Cataloguing in Publication Information Available

Library of Congress Cataloging-in-Publication Data

Klausen, Jytte.
    European integration in social and historical perspective : 1950
to the present / Jytte Klausen and Louise A. Tilly.
        p.   cm.
    Includes bibliographical references and index.
    ISBN 0-8476-8500-4 (alk. paper) ISBN 0-8476-8501-2 (pbk: alk. paper)
        1. European federation.   2. Europe—Economic integration.
    I. Tilly, Louise.   II. Title.
    JN15.K57   1997
    341.242′2—dc21   97-16722
                                                            CIP

ISBN 0-8476-8500-4 (cloth: alk. paper)
ISBN 0-8476-8501-2 (pbk.: alk. paper)

Printed in the United States of America

∞ ™ The paper used in this publication meets the minimum requirements of
American National Standard for Information Sciences—Permanence of Paper for
Printed Library Materials, ANSI Z39.48–1984.

Contents

v

Tables

Preface

This book is the result of a collaborative research project and extended discussions among the contributors, and between contributors and editors. As sociologists, political scientists, and historians, we brought different scholarly traditions and methodologies to the project, but found a common ground in our desire to use historical inquiry to get perspective on current political developments in Europe. It is our hope that this interdisciplinary approach to historical comparative political studies will stimulate new questions about European integration and new approaches to its study.

Most of the authors had the privilege of meeting for one weekend in New York, at the Center for Studies of Social Change, of the Graduate Faculty of the New School for Social Research. We are grateful to Dieter Dettke and the Friedrich Ebert Foundation in Washington, D.C., for making this project possible. We also want to thank the Florence Gould Foundation; the Council for European Studies, Columbia University; and the Center for West European Studies, the East and Central Europe Project, and Dean Judith Friedlander of the Graduate Faculty, all at the New School for Social Research, for support at various stages. We are particularly indebted to those who have served as commentators, including Aristide Zolberg, Charles Tilly, and Eric Hobsbawm. We also want to extend our thanks to Stanley Hoffmann, Jeffrey Anderson, and to our editor, Susan McEachern.

Abbreviations

BEC	British Employers' Confederation
CDU	Christlich Demokratische Union (Christian Democratic Union)
CEE	Central and Eastern European Countries
CEEP	European Confederation of Public Sector Employers
CGB	Christlicher Gewerkschaftsbund (Christian Trade Union Confederation)
CGT	Confédération génerale du travail (General Confederation of Trade Unions)
CSU	Christlich Soziale Union (Christian Social Union)
DGB	Deutscher Gewerkschaftsbund (German Trade Union Confederation)
EC	European Community
EEC	European Economic Community
ECOSOC	Economic and Social Committee
ECSC	European Coal and Steel Community
EFTA	European Free Trade Association
EFTUC	European Federation of Free Trade Unions in the European Community
EISs	European industrial committees
EP	European Parliament
ETUC	European Trade Union Confederation
ETUI	European Trade Union Institute
EU	European Union
EURATOM	European Atomic Community
EWCs	European works councils
FBI	Federation of British Industries
FRG	Federal Republic of Germany
FDP	Freie Demokratische Partei (Free Democratic Party)
GDR	German Democratic Republic

ICFTU	International Confederation of Free Trade Unions
IALL	International Association for Labor Legislation
ILO	International Labor Office (or International Labor Organization)
ITSs	International trade sectariats
ITUCs	Interregional trade union councils
LO	Landsorganisationen (Swedish Trade Union Confederation)
NFAEL	National Federation of Associated Employers of Labour
OECD	Organization for Economic Cooperation and Development
OPEC	Organization of Petroleum Exporting Countries
SAF	Svenska Arbetsgivareföreningen (Swedish Employers Confederation)
SAP	Socialdemokratiska Arbetareparti (Swedish Social Democratic Party)
SEA	Single European Act
SPD	Sozialdemokratische Partei Deutschlands (Social Democratic Party)
TGWU	Transport and General Workers Union
TNC	Transnational corporation
TUC	Trades Union Congress
UNICE	Union of Industrial and Employer Confederations of Europe
U.K.	United Kingdom

Chronology

1648	Peace of Westphalia ends Thirty Years' War.
1713	Treaty of Utrecht signed.
1789–1795	French revolution overturns Old Regime.
1791–1799	First French Republic.
1792–1799	Revolutionary wars fought.
1799–1802	Napoleonic Wars fought.
1803–1814	
1814	Bourbon Restoration in France.
1815	Congress of Vienna held. Battle of Waterloo fought.
1830	Revolution in France brings in July Monarchy.
1848	European revolutions overturn monarchies. Nationalist constitutionalist movements lead to creation of parliaments in, among other places, Frankfurt and Prague.
1848–1852	Second French Republic established.
1849–1871	Italy unified.
1852–1870	Second French Empire (Bonapartism rules).
1866–1871	Germany unified.
1870–1871	Franco-Prussian War fought.
1870–1940	Third French Republic, established based on a parliamentary form of government.
1871	Deutsches Reich (Wilhelmine German Empire) founded.
1900	International Association for Labour Legislation created.
1913	Reichs- und Staatsangehörigkeitsgesetz introduces German citizenship based on descent.
1914–1918	World War I fought.
1919	Versailles peace conference meets.
1919–1933	Weimar Republic established and governs.

1920–1921	Hyperinflation occurs in Germany and most other industrialized countries.
1929	Collapse of Wall Street sets off Great Depression.
1932	Swedish Social Democrats ascend to power. Except for six weeks in 1936, they stay in power for next 44 years.
1933	Adolf Hitler appointed chancellor of Germany.
1933–1945	Nazi dictatorship endures.
1935	Nuremberg Laws formally deny citizenship to all Germans with at least one Jewish grandparent.
1938	Anschluss. Germany invades Austria.
1939	Finno-Russian Winter War fought.
March 1939	Germany invades Czechoslovakia.
September 1939	Germany invades Poland. United Kingdom declares war against Germany. British Expeditionary Force lands in France.
December 1939	P. A. Hansson invites three other parties to join Swedish Social Democrats in a national government.
1939–1945	World War II fought.
April–May 1940	Germany invades Denmark and Norway, then Holland, Belgium, and France.
May 1940	Winston Churchill invites British Labour Party to join Conservative Party in a national government.
June 1940	British Expeditionary Force evacuated from Dunkirk.
1940–1942	Collaborationist Vichy regime set up in unoccupied parts of France.
1941	Japan bombs U.S. Navy unit stationed at Pearl Harbor.
1944	United Nations conference at Bretton Woods produces International Monetary Fund and agreement on principles of postwar monetary system. J. M. Keynes represents Britain.
April 1945	Upon Allied occupation of Austria, Social Democrat Karl Renner forms provisional government. In Germany, Admiral C. Doenitz replaces Hitler as chancellor.
May 1945	War with Germany ends.
July–August 1945	At Potsdam Conference, Allied Powers negotiate agreement on postwar settlement.
August 1945	Labour Party forms new government. War with Japan ends.
September 1945	European Payments Union established, easing international currency transactions.
1946	Bank of England nationalized as part of Labour gov-

	ernment's reform program. Fourth French Republic resumes Third Republic's constitution.
January 1947	Labour government nationalizes coal industry.
June 1947	General Marshall announces European Recovery Program in commencement speech at Harvard University.
July–August 1947	U.K. sterling briefly made freely convertible with dollars.
June 1948	Economic controls lifted and currency reform instituted in "Bizonia," the U.K.- and U.S.-controlled zones of Germany. Berlin blockade begins. Ends 11 months later.
July 1948	Military governments of Germany's three Western Zones accept in principle a Basic Law (Grundgesatz) specifying future political organization for those zones.
April 1949	North Atlantic Treaty signed and NATO (North Atlantic Treaty Organization) founded.
May 1949	French, U.K., and U.S. military governors give final approval to Basic Law. Article 116 of Basic Law defines German citizenship in ethnolinguistic terms. Simultaneously, they also agree to an Occupation Statute that gives them control over foreign policy and various oversight powers. Occupation Statute expires in 1952.
October 1949	Federal Republic of Germany (FRG) founded, German Democratic Republic (GDR) founded.
1950–1954	Korean War fought.
1951	European Coal and Steel Community established.
February 1951	U.K. Labour government nationalizes steel industry.
October 1951	After election in United Kingdom, Labour government resigns.
1952	Equalization of Burdens Law provides internal settlement of German war debts and reparations.
1954	Food rationing ends in United Kingdom.
1956	Egypt seizes Suez Canal, starting "Suez crisis."
1957	Treaty of Rome creates European Communities.
1958	European Monetary Agreement replaces European Payments Union. U.K. sterling made convertible with other currencies, with some restrictions.
1959	European Economic Community begins.
1959–1973	FRG recruits temporary labor (Gastarbeiter) from Mediterranean countries.
1961	Berlin Wall built, finalizing separation of West and East Germany.
1963	EEC concludes association agreement with Turkey,

	with provisions for free mobility of labor, services, and goods.
1967	GDR changes East German citizenship law, introducing GDR citizenship.
1971	Bretton Woods monetary system collapses.
1973–1974	Oil-producing countries, through OPEC, impose embargo on some European countries in retaliation for their support for Israel. Price hikes on crude oil follow. Many Western countries forced to ration oil and gasoline.
1978	EC enters into cooperation agreements with Algeria, Tunisia, and Morocco.
1986	Single European Act projects "Europe 1992."
1989	With East German revolution, communist regime collapses. Communist regimes collapse in other Eastern and Central European states.
1989	Maastricht Treaty signed.
1990	Germany unified.
1990	Communist parties defeated in free elections in Czechoslovakia, Hungary, and Poland. Economic reform starts.
1990–1993	Severe economic crisis occurs in postcommunist countries. Privatization of state-owned property begins.
1991	EC concludes association agreements with Poland, Hungary, and Czechoslovakia.
1992	Czechoslovakia divided into two independent states, Czech Republic and Slovak Republic.
1993	Social Democratic and Agrarian Parties win Polish national election. Freedom of services within EU starts. Germany ratifies Maastricht Treaty on European Union. German asylum law restricted by amendment to Basic Law's Article 16.
1994	Socialist Party wins Hungarian national election. Populist coalition wins Slovak national election.
1996	Czech minority government accedes to power, relying on support from Social Democratic Party. EU member states agree on regulating working conditions, social rights, and wages of transnational contract workers.

Introduction

1

European Integration in a Social and Historical Perspective

Jytte Klausen and Louise A. Tilly

Between 1914 and 1989, the national state was the predominant frame for interest group mobilization and for protective policies configured as a cluster of political, social, and economic rights. Citizenship was the operative criterion for entitlement, and as the warfare state made way for the welfare state after 1945, the emphasis shifted from one of shared hardship to one of shared prosperity. Fifty years have passed since the end of World War II, and we still speak of the "postwar period" as a continuous stretch of time. In the absence of any event to punctuate time that rivals the importance of the war and its conclusion, we have little choice but to use this imprecise language. Likewise, we speak of the time between the end of World War I and the beginning of what became World War II as the "interwar period." We also speak, equally imprecisely, of the period before 1914 as the "prewar period." Hence, our chronology is punctuated by the advent of major wars. The question is whether the real impact of the beginning and end of wars reflects the importance that our periodization implies. This book will affirm that it does. Both world wars represented major strategic events that caused a reorganization of state-society relations and gave birth to a powerful, but now challenged, state-centered international order.

The book also posits the somewhat controversial proposition that the "postwar order" has come to an end. We have chosen the collapse of the Soviet Union and the reunion of Eastern Europe with its Western counterpart in 1989–1991, along with the conclusion of yet another war, the cold war, as another of our markers. By necessity, this last demarcation point represents more of a retrospective assessment of significant change than a confident assertion of new beginnings. We have numerous other candidates for the position of "markers of time passed." The oil crisis in 1973–1974

3

and the signing of the Maastricht Treaty, which committed the signers to the creation of a European political union, are candidates for end markers, but neither has in fact brought about concerted and collective change on the scale of war and its associated reordering of the international state-system. There is a coherence to what Eric Hobsbawm (1994) has called "the short twentieth century," running from 1914 to 1991, based upon the rise of the nation-state as the dominant form of public authority and of class (or collectivism) as the dominant form of political and social organization. Posed as a contrast to the short twentieth century, the late nineteenth century and the years up to the beginning of World War I present us with a natural comparison to the present fin de siècle. Both the first and the last decades of this century have the virtue of being—in the case of the first, temporary—liberal international orders, characterized by energetic international trade activity and a kind of societal openness that only comes with peace. Fifty years have passed since 1945 without a major war. It is in this particular "slice" of history that the state-centered order created by the World War I, World War II, and the cold war stands out as an interregnum characterized by strong state and social, economic, and political enclosure.

European Integration as a Social Process

When we refer to European integration, we do so not in the common usage of the formation of EU institutions and the development of policy coordination among the fifteen member states.[1] We are not primarily concerned with the "core" issues of European integration and have in fact detached the concept of integration to some extent from its common meaning. We speak here not of the formal process of integration as represented by deliberate collective decisions rationalized and codified by treaties or other forms of agreement among national states. We focus instead on the multiple social processes that have promoted the integration of economic, political, and social life within the larger European framework. In contemporary perspective, these processes include EU institution building (including representative fora, elections, and citizenship), European reunification and its demographic implications, the creation of Europe-wide interest representation, the emergence of transnational product and labor markets, and intra-European migration, to mention some of the primary currents of change. We consider European integration an aggregate outcome of diverse social, economic, and political processes that are stimulated by EU institution building but not entirely determined by such. In a long historical perspective, European integration has been a contingent outcome of autonomous processes, occasionally nourished, and periodically checked, by national elites.

European integration did not begin with the Treaty of Rome (1957), nor will it be brought to a halt by failures to produce new treaties or other formal agreements. As in the past, it can be halted almost overnight by historical events like those that set off the process of closure early in the century: wars, depressions, and demographic risks ranging from mass migration to epidemics.

We extend the chronology of the processes of European integration and social and political mobilization from the 1850s to the present, seeing it as a continuous process interrupted by war and by a period of international order built upon enclosure within rigid state boundaries. In the second half of the nineteenth century and the first decade of this century, political and economic change proceeded in contradictory directions. Within national states, nationalist and exclusionary policies sought to promote the national interest, to institutionalize citizenship, and to define nationality. But economic development and the social and structural changes that went along with it involved nonstate actors whose construction of economic and social institutions (international labor unions, cross-national business alliances, and reform organizations, for example) contested the monopoly of the state on the exercise of policy-making authority and provided an alternative path to self-regulatory capacity. One consequence was a blurring of boundaries between political and extrapolitical institutions similar to that we see today in the context of European integration, reinforced by internationalization and declining statism.

Conceptualized as a *social* process, then integration has proceeded in response to transborder movements of people, trade, jobs, and investment, and only indirectly in response to international conventions or, more recently, EU policy making. The authors of this book examine primarily such second-order causal factors that form the microfoundations for political, economic, and social integration. In principle, these range from business practices and consumer habits to voting behavior and geographic mobility patterns at the microlevel. The long historical view provided by Gary Marks in this book demonstrates that there was no simple process of state formation leading to greater and greater state power, multiplying functions, and national differentiation. As Marks argues, there has been no single master plan for the evolving Euro-state, just as there was none for the construction of the national state.

The nineteenth-century process of defining and implementing citizenship (with its related political and civil rights and exclusion of noncitizens) and nationality illustrates the importance of conjunctural factors for the state-formation process. Not only did the meaning of citizenship vary from state to state; it has also varied within states in response to social and political conflicts caused by particular citizenship policies (described in this book, in the case of France, by Michael Offerlé and Gérard Noiriel and in the case of Germany, by Christiane Lemke.)

The authors of this book are concerned both with the micro-foundations of the contemporary process of European integration (essay in part 3) and with the theoretical and historical precedents that we see in the internationalism of the pre-1914 system (essays in part 1) and in national state building or state mobilization (essays in part 2), which Gary Marks so provocatively compares with European integration. The claim of comparability is controversial because it directs our attention to possible parallels between historically disparate mechanisms and events, but several authors provide a good deal of evidence for at least rough parallels between the progress and hesitations in state building and those in integration. In both these processes, state capacities are linked through defining the relationship between subjects (citizens) and states. The stronger the control states exercise over this relationship, the weaker the prospects of a strong internationalism. In democratic states, state competencies are often the product of what Marks terms "perverse" processes. Competence is expanded and enhanced, not in relation to the designs of rulers, but in response to concessions to claims made by interest groups and to the mobilization for war as well as for peace.

Citizenship

Citizenship has been defined in practices and codified by specific acts of states; it has no existence outside embedded rights and obligations except as a normative hteory. Unanticipated consequences may follow when social categories, like citizenship, change more slowly than the political construction of borders and the flows of trade, capital, or labor. As citizenship is defined and implemented, distributional conflicts may ensue over the precise implications of the exclusionary and inclusionary aspects of rights and obligations. Appeals to norms of equality and inclusion and to the basic humanity of all individuals are yet another use of the language of citizenship as a metaphor for claim making. States respond to such appeals in calculated and opportunistic fashion.

Modern conceptions of citizenship are so indelibly linked, both theoretically and empirically, to a state-system consisting of sovereign national states that we can decouple nationhood and citizenship only with great difficulty. The evolution of a multitiered system of political authority with a complicated layering of competing and complementary competencies between the Europe-wide institutions of the EU and the national institutions of the member states (and in some instances, even regional institutions that circumvent the national state in dealings with EU institutions) forces us to consider different anchors and criteria for citizenship. In this respect, we disagree with the claims of Yasemin Soysal (1994, 1); no state can extend citizenship in practice to all claimants on the basis of principles of universal personhood.

In retrospect, we can see that, together, the national state and citizenship provided a frameowrk conducive to political mobilization and collective action aimed at increasing the range of protective rights associated with belonging to a national polity. The small Scandinavian welfare states are examples of how far national political mobilization could drive egalitarian policies. They emply the capstone of "golden age" welfare capitalism: the marriage between socialism and liberal democracy that held forth as long as the Keynesian commitment to full employment held, roughly from 1947 to 1973. The perception that European integration threatens such national gains has acquired wide appeal, by no means limited to Scandinavia; it is, however, no coincidence that opposition to membership in the European Union (EU) has been particularly fierce there (Featherstone 1988).

The history of citizenship is more contentious than the story of the small generous welfare states suggests. It is often forgotten that the promise of "social citizenship" dates back to the 1942 Beveridge Report published during World War II, in a context that cannot be separated from wartime mobilization and the contemporary sufferings of the British people (United Kingdon 1942).[2] As part of the monumental *History of the Second World War,* edited by W. K. Hancock, the sociologist Richard Titmus (1950) wrote a detailed report on teh expansion of social service during the war. From the mass of detail emerges as clear conclusion: when Beveridge extended the promise of "social citizenship" to the British people, he was not making new promises. Worried that workers would not stay in the factories and on their jobs, but would flee to safter locations, on the outbreak of war Parliament passed the Personal Injuries (Emergency Provisions) Act, providing workers with a universal guarantee of relief in the case of injury. A broad expansion of social services followed, causing Titmus to conclude,

> The State was assuming new, and in many respects wide, responsibilities for the well-being of individual members of society. From its initial pre-occupation with the cruder manifestations of total war, expressed in such defensive policies as removing the injured to hospital, the frightened to safety, and the dead to mortuaries, the Government was to turn, under the pressure of circumstances and the stimulus of a broader conception of social justice, to new fields of constructive welfare policies. (p. 95)

Recent work by Susan Pedersen (1990) and a collection of essays edited by Richard Wall and Jay Winter (1988) have pointed to the importance of World War I in building prototypes of child welfare and family allowance policies, in France and the United Kingdom in particular. Several essays of this book show how the concept of citizenship and its administration owe more to the mobilization for war in the early parts of the period than to the mobilization for social inclusion in the later. This leaves us to ponder the transparency of T. H. Marshall's famous articulation (1950) of the principles of modern citizenship as a "trinity" of civil, political, and social rights. Marshall's much-cited essay has assumed a central role in analyses and discussions of the modern welfare state and the meanings of citizenship.[3] He divided citizenship into three complementary parts—civil, political, and social citizenship—originating in different centuries. If the gift of the eighteenth and nineteenth centuries to humankind was civil and political rights, then the twentieth century's gift was social rights. Marshall dealt with the first two categories of citizenship summarily. Political rights, for example, were plainly typified as the "right to participate in the exercise of political power." He devoted his energy instead to expanding upon "social citizenship," by which he understood the following: "The right to share to the full in the social heritage and to live the life of a civilized being according to the standards prevailing in the society" (pp. 10–11)[4] By incorporating social rights in the status of citizenship, "a universal right to real income which is not proportional to the market value of the claimant" is created (p. 47). The cryptic reference to "market value" assimilates a taste of Marxism to Marshall's theory by offering a distinction between a person's "citizen value" and the person's capacity to earn a living in capitalist labor markets. The exact aim of his trinity has never been clear; is it a historical theory or a normative, political theory? As the former it is clearly flawed, and as the latter it is deficient, as it takes the existence of a bounded redistributive community as unproblematic.

Logically, there is a close fit between theories of justice based upon citizenship and an international order constructed of sovereign states deviding the world's territory and populations in an exhaustive and mutually exclusive fashion based upon ascription of national identification. Empirically, the imposition of a rigid taxonomy of national citizenship on a fluid and far more complex reality required the development of new enforcement technologies and raised difficult questions regarding belongs and exclusion.[5] In stable states with stable borders, citizenship may be acquired automatically by place of birth or parents' origin. Wars, the ends of wars, rearranged borders, migration, and different types of state failure—including not only the failure to provide political security and civil protection but also failure to provide economic opportunity—expose the coercive aspects of constructing citizenship as national identity.

In his study of medieval constitutionalism, Brian Downing (1992) links military strategies for resource mobilization to the willingness of rulers to grant protective rights to subjects and suppliers. At its most rudimentary stage, the exchange between rulers and subjects consisted of land for military service, but it evolved into "a network of mutual obligations" linking together lords, officeholders, and the rulled (p. 23). Military technology evolved to encompass conscription and the creation of national armies, and also a tradition of constitutional rights preserving fundamental citizenship rights for those who bore arms. Once entire populations were enrolled as soldiers, the public ceased to be subjects and became citizens, a process described in the French case by Noiriel and Offerlé in chapter 4. (The alternative, coercive mobilization, and its twentieth-century counterpart, fascism, are not discussed by Downing.)

Twentieth-century wars were "total wars"; the "home front" was indistinguishable from the "military fronts." In his study of the consequences of World War II for the American presidency and the U.S. Constitution, the political scientist Edwar Corwin (1947, 4) spoke of the emerging "functional totality" as

the political ordered participation in the war effort of all personal and social forces, the scientific, the mechanical, the commercial, the economic, the moral, the literary and artistic, and the psychological.

Corwin argued that the effects of "total war" cannot be confined to wartime but will spread into peacetime. He was concerned that the concentration of presidential power and the rollback of federalism that the war effort had wrought would never recede, a conclusion that today seems exaggerated. The war legacy did not fix postwar social and political organization in stone; it merely shaped the institutions that social and political actors strove to appropriate and to change. We may ask if, on balance, the expansion of protective rights in exchange for support for the war has been themore enduring legacy. The question, in our view, points to an interesting, and unachieved, research program. Aside from a brief flurry of mostly historical research in the immediate postwar years, historians, sociologists, and political scientists have only recently begun to rethink the links between the warfare and the welfare state. Susan Pedersen's work on gender relations and the reordering of state-society relations in the course of war comes to mind (1990, 1993).

Downing's "exchange" (1992, 275) posits a theory about the relationship not only between rulers and the ruled but also between social organization on the one hand and military strategy and geopolitical contexts on the other. Similar ideas have ifnormed the work of a diverse group of people, including "realists" like Samuel Huntington (1964) and Stephen Krasner (1983) but also those more inclined to assign causal importance to domestic social relations in shaping states' actions in the international realm, like John Ruggie (1983) and Susan Strange (1996). Downing's departure differs by suggesting a somewhat counterintuitive connection between freedoms, rights, and state power: the more of the latter, the more of the former. In his theory, the concentration of state power associated with conscription (in contrast to professional armies) and the rigid regulation of national communities associated with popular mobilization for military purposes are connected to enhanced social and political rights. This connection was clearly articulated by U.K. labor leaders when, at the onset of war in 1940, they called for mobilization to "win the war of peace."

In a speech to a special conference of trade union executives on 25 May 1940, Ernest Bevin, Minister of Labour in the wartime national government and foreign minister in the 1949–51 Labour governments, appealed to the unions for collaboration. Individualism had to make way for discipline and solidarity. The reward would be socialism, not just at home but "throughout the world."

> I have to ask you virtually to place yourselves at the disposal of the State. We are Socialists, and this is the test of our Socialism. It is the test whether we have meant the resolutions which we have so often passed. . . . But this I am convinced of: if our Movement and our class rise with all their energy now and save the people of this country from disaster, the country will always turn with confidence forever to the people who saved them. (Bevin 1941, 51)

At what was perhaps the darkest moment of the war for the British, the link between military mobilization and new social rights was unequivocally made.

We have conceptualized citizenship as an outcome of a critical historical transformation linked to the process of defining the state, rights, and representation. It is also linked in a complex fashion to collective mobilization and institution building, for together these provided a means by which (1) states could expand territorial control; and (2) individuals could make claims against the state. Our working hypothesis conceives of European integration as a process driven by the differentiation of national modes of representation and constructing rights associated with supranationality, thus revising the concept of citizenship. A possible result of this process may be the devolution of citizenship rights from the level of the national state, a level typical of the twentieth century, in two directions: to supranational institutions and to subnational ones, urban or regional.

The Return to a Liberal Order

The collapse of communism in 1989 undid the European state-system that had been constructed by the postwar settlements of 1917 and 1945. In

1961, the construction of the Berlin Wall had made it physically impossible to pass from East to West Berlin and extremely difficult to cross the boundaries within the divided and "frozen" state system. Overnight, the wall crumbled in 1989. Its collapse suddenly allowed families to reunite and goods and people to travel and ended the communist challenge to capitalism and liberalism. It also reopened old questions about access to markets and to jobs, and the distribution of wealth, welfare, and growth between the West on the one hand and the postcommunist economies of Eastern and Central Europe on the other. As the chapter by Martin Potůček illustrates, the postcommunist heritage is one of state failure, not state expansion, as was the case for the post-1945 welfare states. The derelict state of postcommunist economies and societies is an impediment to the mobilization of the state capacities needed to create a comprehensive welfare state. Postcommunist state development takes place in contexts of unimpeded transborder mobility—of people, trade, and capital—with few of the controls that were available to the postwar states and with a very different endowment of public sentiments with respect to the prospects of capitalist development.

In a liberal order, there is, inevitably perhaps, a mismatch among the reach of political, social, and economic systems. This, then, is where the authors of this book agree in finding reason for concern. As Carl Strikwerda writes, integration can be derailed at any time, irrespective of the economic benefits to be derived, if no mechanisms are found for allocating the advantages of economic integration and ameliorating the disadvantages. The success of economic integration cannot be assured in the absence of social integration.

As others have pointed out, the construction of European citizenship is uniquely shaped by the constitutional foundations of the European Union. It is, as Chiara Saraceno shows in her chapter in this book, based upon the citizen-as-worker and upon the EU elite's skillful manipulations of the European Commission's and the ECJ's competencies with respect to labor market regulation. The key sources of EU competencies with respect to individual rights are mobility rights in connection with labor markets, based mostly upon Articles 117 and 118 of the Treaty of Rome. A case in point is the Social Protocol, which became part of the constitutional framework for European integration when it was attached to the Maastricht Treaty. At the time of its inception, it was presented as a "Bill of Social Rights" for an integrated European labor market.[6]

Because of the constitutional constraints, EU citizenship policy is being developed in the context of three areas of policy: immigration, industrial relations, and gender equality in labor markets. (Each of the three is discussed in part 3, immigration by Thomas Faist, industrial relations by Jelle Visser and Bernard Ebbinghaus, and gender equality by Chiara Saraceno.)

The absence of competence to impose direct taxation places another limita-tion on the development of a "social dimension" to Europe-wide institu-tion building. EU action relies upon administrative rule making as the chief means of policy development and upon the European Court of Justice and the national administrations of the member states for implementation and enforcement (Mancini 1991, 185–91). While European citizenship already has a "social dimension," it does not establish the Euro-state as the anchor in a redistributive state-community. Europe-wide social rights are, in sum-mary, founded upon regulation rather than redistribution and tied to a transnational labor market rather than to a national community.

The chapters that follow recognize the opportunistic and coercive origins of citizenship and see the new possibilities for internationalism and revision of the confining state-system of the interregnum of 1914–1989, although they also have concerns about the implications for the national welfare state and the actors who have benefited from it. A paradox lies at the heart of the achievements of the democratic national state with all its trappings of redistributive and protective rights. Social inclusion for the members of the state-community presupposes the exclusion of nonmembers.[7] Liberal the-ory provides no theoretical justification for the restriction of political and welfare rights to members of particular state-communities. Political theorist Stephen Holmes asks, "Why should someone starve, [for example] because he or she happens to live on the wrong side of a political frontier?" Once we recognize the arbitrariness of political frontiers, the answer obviously is that there is no justification, on moral grounds or on the grounds of rights, for such exclusion. Holmes indicts liberalism as "wholly unable to draw territorial boundaries or separate insiders from outsiders in a principled way" (1995, 39). Nevertheless, it is only in liberal democratic national states that the definition of legal equality has produced "citizenship" and comprehensive redistributive and protective rights in pursuit of social, po-litical, and even economic equality. Socialism achieved these ends only after abandoning its nineteenth-century internationalist aspirations and adapting the class struggle to the electoral competition of liberal democracy.

Migration

Susan Strange has argued that national policy choice has become so con-stricted by the internationalization of trade that politics has lost its meaning. Government controls over national economies have become emasculated to a point where neoliberal policies represent the only choice; there are no alternatives (1995). Labor is the last factor of production to adjust to inter-nationalization, and the spectacle of British bricklayers hanging out in pubs in Berlin after work becomes the ultimate sign of the subversion of the "national." Like Strange, the authors in this book have regarded labor migration as a test of the national principle of organization. It is, so to speak, a "dependent" variable that can be interpreted as a measure of closure and, conversely, also of openness. By that measure, however, the twentieth-century interregnum of national states exercising territorial control in an exclusive fashion is still with us.

Transborder migration is still less significant than it was prior to the imposition of passport laws and restrictive migration laws in the closing decade of the nineteenth century and particularly—and more definitively—during and after World War I (Eichengreen and Hatton 1988). Elaborate filing systems for legal-administrative categories of immigrants cause spurious distinctions to be made based upon country of origin and, in effect, also cultural and religious differences. In his chapter, Thomas Faist contradicts the pictures of the past decades as one of progressive ratcheting up of internationalization by pointing out that migration among the EU member states has declined since the 1970s. Strange reacts to the presence of U.K. bricklayers in Berlin, and declares it to be evidence of the impotence of states. But she confuses a change in the pattern of migration with its epiphany. In fact, as argued here by Faist, labor migration has receded and taken on new forms, more similar to those characteristic of the late nineteenth century described by Moch in chapter 6—the temporary movement of "cheaper hands" across borders in an integrated European labor market. In the 1960s and 1970s, internal European migration was defined almost exclusively in North-South terms, with Italy and Portugal being the countries of emigration. Today, the pattern has shifted to one of a center-periphery relationship, with British and Finnish construction workers joining Polish and Czech workers as migrant workers in the growth centers of Europe.

Despite the recent increase in the importance of contract work, one of the overriding differences between European migration at the close of the twentieth century and that of a hundred years earlier is—aside from levels of magnitude—a change in the family status of immigrants. In the late nineteenth century, immigrants were typically male young adults. Today, single adults are a minority (Hatton and Williamson 1991, 7). Family status matters a great deal to policy. It is the Turkish families of second- and third-generation immigrants barred against assimilation by rigid citizenship laws (in Germany, as in Turkey) that have become perhaps the most powerful symbol of the unfairness of citizenship law. While the young single adult approximates the "cheaper hands" image of labor as a mobile factor of production as described by Moch, the immigrant family represents a wholly different bundle of economic and social needs. In the case of the single adult (of whom the contract worker is a subcategory), labor market mobility may represent a realistic means for opportunity and inclusion. Not so

in the case of the migrant family, whose presence inevitably challenges
definitions of rights, from education to social rights, tied to national identity.

Ironically, labor migration has exposed the limitations and exclusionary
aspects of rights and citizenship anchored in the national state by challenging national identity as a criterion for access to the economic privilege that
working in high-wage areas represents. But it is also the immigrant family
that challenges the liberal image of the worker-as-citizen. Immigrants are
not disembodied hands looking for work. Immigrant families are dependent
in equal measure on the welfare state as a vehicle of social inclusion and on
political representation of their interests for protection in the formation of
policy.

Forms of Representation

It may be clear from the context, but is nevertheless worth stating explicitly,
that we consider rights obtained by means of formal citizenship to constitute only a subset of a broad range of political, social, and economic rights.
"Citizenship" implies membership in a state-community and defines the
relationship between the individual and the state. Rights and representation
through citizenship are not necessarily "better" than rights obtained by
other means, such as those assigned on group basis and guaranteed by
nonstate actors. Representation as a citizenship right assigns primacy to the
state-community, but if it ceases to be a primary actor, the state's relative
importance is depreciated correspondingly. Representation as citizenship is
based upon the exercise of what Reinhard Bendix called the "plebiscitarian
principle," which became a revolutionary principle when it sought concessions from elites that based their power upon control over the national
state. The plebiscitarian principle has assumed special importance in democratic theory, but in reality it has always been complemented by other
forms of representation. In the European context, group-specific activities,
rights, and duties have historically played an important role and continue
to constitute another channel of interest representation. This represents
what Bendix called the "functional principle" deriving from the traditions
of the *Ständestaat* (1977, 90).

As principles of distributive justice and democratic legitimacy, electoral
representation and group-based representation diverge with respect to
qualifying criteria and implications. Trade unions, business associations, and
other types of comprehensive and inclusive organizations have continued
this tradition via what has become known as "neocorporatism." The relative importance of neocorporatist representation compared to that facilitated by the electoral channel of representation varies from country to

country, and from issue area to issue area. Neocorporatist representation is often a matter of contention and condemnation, but this does not diminish its importance. Its endurance is illustrated by its mobilization as a channel of representation within the context of EU policy making. Some of the chapters in this book suggest, however, that the continued importance of neocorporatist representation is predicated on its transformation. The "pillared" system of hierarchical functional representation that sustained national welfare-state corporatism does not work well in the new EU institutions, and it is being replaced by adaptable networks of issue-specific and group-specific interest representatives.

The plebiscitarian principle of representation implies a notion of the basic equality of all qualified citizens; there is no such presumption involved in group-based representation. When, however, citizenship can be obtained only as a birthright and not by choice or commitment alone, the principle of universality implied by liberal theory is breached in an equally troubling fashion. Both the appeal of and the cause for concern about extensive reliance upon group representation are that it violates one set of principles of liberal democratic ideals while accommodating another. The violation lies in its rejection of equality among citizens. In the group-based channel of representation, the capacity to mobilize membership and resources on the basis of particularistic characteristics and interests is what counts. Group-based representation, in contrast to the electoral representation of citizens, is tied to belonging to a particular group, often defined simply by occupation and work, which of course usually reflect a conscious choice of action and are rarely limited by birthright. Therein, then, lies the appeal. As a citizen-as-worker, even a nonnational is entitled to representation and social protection. The question is, how much does it still matter that he or she is excluded from other rights?

Largely by accident, the liberal conception of citizenship has been reborn in the context of the EU. Judith Shklar (1991, 99) argues that the right to work—by which she means "a comprehensive commitment to providing opportunities for work to earn a living wage"—has had a place of primacy in the American conception of citizenship. Today, European citizenship has become defined in terms of equal mobility rights, establishing for the first time a transnational norm for equal access to opportunity and the right to work. Hence, European citizenship has shifted from the statist definitions inflicted by state mobilization and nationhood to one encompassing more of the liberal ideal of autonomy embraced by Shklar. It is a conceptualization of citizenship fitting to a country of immigrants, like the United States. If the EU is becoming that, the shift is a logical one here too.

If citizenship loses its meaning of membership in particular state-communities, a diffusion of rights and representation among various collectivities, communities, and authorities may replace it. In this fluid state of affairs, individuals can enjoy protective rights and exercise civic rights and obligations in relationship to a varied range of regulatory authorities, representative institutions, and self-regulating communities or associations. The basic modes of organization and principles of representation may vary, and few of them may conform to the ideals of the liberal constitutional democracies.

Important issues that arise in this connection concern the history of the "democratic deficit." This term usually refers to the weakness of formal channels for democratic representation in the policy-making process of the EU. It may seem anachronistic to characterize the institution building of past regimes with a term that has gained meaning only in recent decades. We argue, however, that there are appropriate comparisons to be made. Looking back at the history of codification and institutionalization of various rights (protective as well as representational ones), rights and representation have flowed from the mobilization of state power and regulatory authority, not the other way around. In that sense, it is appropriate to talk about a "democratic deficit" as endemic in state building. The concentration of power and authority precedes, rather than succeeds, the granting of rights and representation.

Some Central Puzzles

The chapters that follow present pieces of an answer to three central puzzles. The first is the possibility of the liberal ideal of citizenship. Can social rights be constructed as both nondiscriminatory and universal and still be meaningful? Does social citizenship—which (albeit articulated by postwar British reformers) can be traced back to John Stuart Mill and nineteenth-century ideals—presuppose a closed international system of states that is inescapably antithetic to other important liberal ideals, such as unencumbered social and geographical mobility and the universalist thrust? Our answers have been somewhat at variance. Strikwerda strikes a decidedly more optimistic tone than Visser and Ebbinghaus, understandable when one considers that few social actors benefited more from "golden age" capitalism than the trade unions discussed by the latter. We may conclude that the shift to a liberal international order may well have divergent implications for different social actors. We count business and women's organizations (the Scandinavians exempted) among the "winners," and trade unions as "losers."

A second puzzle regards the balance between protective impulses and support for internationalization. In the tradition of Karl Polanyi, some scholars have argued that, in popular democracies, the protective instincts of society will always dominate, and rule out a social organization of markets congruous with liberal principles. This idea was articulated strongly twenty years ago by the sociologist Fred Hirsch in *Social Limits to Growth* (1976). Hirsch not only spoke of the "depleting moral legacy of capitalism" but also argued for protectionism as a moral instrument. With the expansion of democracy, fairness norms would inevitably be applied to new ground, including the functioning of markets. Protectionism would be needed because certain types of economic organization are inherently predatory on society. Hirsch underestimated the importance of domestic sources of support for increased economic openness and for "open societies." There has always been, as Strikwerda's contribution makes clear, significant domestic support for European integration and transborder mobility. These principles are, so to say, the "natural" way, not in the sense of predominance, but rather the way things would be if nothing else got in the way. Border life has always accommodated itself to frontiers with surprising fluidity. Workers, like goods and capital, have long moved across national borders looking for opportunity, except when prevented by states from doing so. The mobilization of internationalist and nationalist impulses can take place in parallel processes. Hence, popular support for the Single European Act, which anticipated the creation of a unified European economic "space," has been significant, while the objective of a political union held out by the Maastricht Treaty has been widely unpopular. Our thesis regarding the existence of dual circuits for nationalist and internationalist responses to European integration may help explain why increased economic openness and integration have been associated with more restrictive immigration policies, but it also raises a question to which we have no answer. Is the urge to curb immigration and restrict the benefits of generous welfare states and economic development the beginning of a wave of ideological and xenophobic mobilization, or is it simply a rational—and temporary—reaction to social friction in times of unemployment? Or is it both? Our authors oscillate between pessimistic and optimistic prospects for the future of a unified Europe, Gary Marks representing the optimistic camp and Eric Hobsbawm the pessimistic one.

The third puzzle regards theory building. In our account, state building is an events-driven process, and state society relations are in large part shaped by the big events that cast the international order. This raises a methodological issue: if state formation is events-driven, it is also contingent, apt to proceed in spasms. There is no predetermined end point or any particular internal logic discernible to the clever observer. A historical theory of citizenship is almost inevitably a disappointment to the political theorist looking for predictable progress or guarantees regarding social justice. Time is an important dimension of a causal theory of state building, and as Marks says, fifty years is a short time in the history of states. We focus, in this book, on the effects of war on state-society relations, the equivalent of a "big bang" theory of state formation. We can speculate about the kinds of events that drive integration or protectionism, those that likely enhance social autonomy and political rights and those that restrict either, but we cannot predict them. We do argue that international crises are independent variables shaping social organization, but that does not mean that they fix state-society relations until another "big bang" comes along to unsettle things. Nor does it mean that minor events have no implications for the state system and for state capacities. The prospects for monetary integration were strengthened (some may say they were diminished, however) by the experience of currency instability in the aftermath of the collapse of the dollar. Later, in November 1992, they were further strengthened by George Soros's windfall from a monetary regime that forced states to use public money to sustain their currencies against the onslaught of private speculators, in one of the largest transfers of taxpayers' money to private individuals ever.[8] German unification on the heels of the collapse of the Soviet Union is another recent example of the large-scale changes wrought to the state-system by endogenous historical events. Beginning with demobilization, the thread of history, running from 1945 to 1995, is one of disappointment for planners and their ambitions regarding public control. On balance, we have witnessed a gradual restoration of private power, not vice versa.

The authors of the chapters in this book—historians, political scientists, and sociologists—share methods and approaches connecting historical research and contemporary practice. In this we emulate the aspirations of Marc Bloch and Lucien Febvre, when they launched their *Annales d' histoire économique et sociale,* to work with social scientists by drawing on history to better understand the present (Müller 1992). We have tried to respond to questions about contemporary problems in the light of the past, in hopes of producing new knowledge that will contribute to our search for answers to these problems. We do this at the risk of a charge of "reinventing" the past through anachronistic inferences about parallels between past and present. In response, we have proceeded with caution and attention to empirical historical contexts. What we have gained in this fruitful cooperation among historians, sociologists, and political scientists are illuminating social historical perspectives on the last decades of political and economic change in Western and Central Europe.

About This Book

This book consists of three parts organized thematically and preceded by this introductory chapter, in which the editors place the parts and the individual chapters within the larger context of the book. In a second introductory chapter, Gary Marks compares contemporary institution building within the framework of the EU to the processes of European state formation.

Part 1, "Historical Perspectives on Defining and Implementing Citizenship in the State-Formation Process," contains four chapters on what Strikwerda calls the "troubled origins" of the modern national state. Chapters by Strikwerda, Noiriel and Offerlé, Lemke, and Moch all examine aspects of pre–World War I citizen and group mobilization for state power. Strikwerda analyzes the attempts at international coordination by voluntary agreement that were brought to an abrupt end by the mobilization for, and outbreak of, war. Noiriel and Offerlé reflect on the nineteenth-century codification of French citizenship law, the accompanying development of technologies of state power through voting, and the operationalization of the principle of nationality. Lemke writes of some of the German national, and European, contexts of debates about citizenship and migration. Moch compares the European international labor market of the early twentieth century (and the scale of the period's labor market migration, which makes today's transborder mobility look insignificant) with patterns in the closing years of the same century.

Part 2, "The Social Process of Developing Group Representational Institutions in Nineteenth- and Twentieth-Century European States," includes comparative chapters by Michael Hanagan and Jytte Klausen that span almost the entire time frame of the book. The theme in this case is the importance of preexisting labor market institutions and internal politics in shaping national trajectories of states' use of trade unions and employer associations in economic planning and labor market regulation. Hanagan compares the political ramifications of nineteenth-century labor market institutions in France with those in the United Kingdom; Klausen, the failure of U.K. economic reform in the post–World War II years with Swedish and German reforms. Both chapters raise important questions regarding the relationships among self-regulation, government planning, and the foundations for trade union rights. Martin Potůček discusses the prospects of efforts in Eastern and Central European countries to construct welfare states, and those countries' failure to implement Marshallian "social citizenship" in the years since the collapse of their communist regimes. All three chapters raise questions about whether the particular concentration of state capacities needed for state-centered coordination of the economy is even possible in the absence of the particular transformations of state-society relations brought on by economic autarky and war mobilization.

Part 3 considers "Citizenship and Group Representation at the Transnational Level." Chapters by Thomas Faist, Bernhard Ebbinghaus and Jelle Visser, and Chiara Saraceno examine changes that have taken place in the wake of the events of 1989, the collapse of communism, and the declaration of a European Union. Faist looks at some of the fissures in the content of "social citizenship" that have opened in response to worker immigration from East and Central Europe to seek jobs in the West. Ebbinghaus and Visser discuss labor's efforts to institutionalize group representation at the level of Europe. Saraceno writes about the complex process of "add on" citizenship produced by the new opportunities for women's groups to bypass recalcitrant national governments and appeal directly to the EU for rights and representation. The afterword, by E. J. Hobsbawm, presents his fin de siècle reflections on the prospects and meaning of European union for Europeans.

The chronology at the front of this book helps readers place the particular discussion in historical context. It begins with the 1648 Peace of Westphalia and ends with the 1996 decision by the European Union to guarantee contract workers migrating between member states nationally prevailing wages and social rights. The former event put an end to the Thirty Years' War and signaled the beginning of an international system based on sovereign nation-states. The latter signals the need of the still-important nation-state—acting as a member of a union of states—to protect national actors and prevent national standards from eroding. The chronology lists major events that have shaped the European state-system, as they relate to events discussed in the chapters that follow. It does not pretend to be an exhaustive listing of all major events in Europe between 1648 and today.

Notes

1. Twelve states (Belgium, Denmark, France, Germany, Greece, Ireland, Italy, Luxembourg, Netherlands, Portugal, Spain, United Kingdom) were party to the Maastricht Treaty (1989). Three states have become full members since then, and Poland and the Czech Republic have become associated members.

2. This report is commonly known as the Beveridge Report. The concept of "social citizenship" was immortalized after the war by T. H. Marshall in his essay titled, "Citizenship and Social Class," (1950) reprinted many times. Recent critical scholarship on Lord Beveridge and his famous report has stressed the importance of personal calculation, as well as the importance placed by the government upon the need for an uplifting message with respect to the future. See Hills, Ditch, and Glennerster 1994; Barnett 1995.

3. Marshall has been particularly influential in interpretations of Scandinavian welfare-state development. See Korpi 1983; Esping-Andersen 1985, 1990; Hernes 1987.

4. For a detailed criticism of Marshall's theory, see Klausen 1995b, 1996.

5. International relations theory has been struggling to redefine realist theory, which, like the conceptions of citizenship based upon national sovereignty, needs

to take into account the shift to a different kind of regime. See Ruggie 1993; Koslowski and Kratochwill 1994.

6. The European Council passed the Social Charter at its meeting in Strasbourg on 8–9 December 1989. The charter was first proposed and endorsed by the EC Economic and Social Committee in March 1989 and then forwarded to the council by the European Commission. When it was attached to the Maastricht Treaty in 1992, the United Kingdom refused to endorse it.

7. The more generous definitions of "social citizenship" are particularly vulnerable to this critique. It can be argued that fiduciary concerns alone precipitate the need for entitlement policing of generous benefits and, hence, strict immigration policies (Klausen 1995b, 263).

8. On the occasion of the publication of an EC Monetary Committee report on the crisis, European Commission President Jacques Delors acquitted the monetary regime and blamed the governments of the participating countries: "If there were currencies that had to leave the system or change their parities, that was due to the fundamentals of their economies and not to the malfunctioning of the EMS." (Eurecom 1993, 2).

2

A Third Lens: Comparing European Integration and State Building

Gary Marks

The creation of a European polity over the past four decades has been a sui generis experiment in interstate coordination and supranational institution building. While the European Union is a new kind of political form, scholars have sought to gauge its particularities and understand its dynamics by comparison. This chapter lies squarely in that tradition, one that goes back to the earliest attempts to analyze the European integration.

Comparison, but with what? Given the exceptional character of European integration, the question has no single answer. European integration does not fit neatly into any class of political phenomena, though it shares interesting commonalities with several.

Two lenses have been used to gain comparative insight. The first treats the European Union as an international regime. Like the United Nations, the General Agreement on Trade and Tariffs, or the North American Free Trade Association, the EU can be conceived as an organization created, sustained, and dominated by national governments. Conceptualizing the EU as an international regime focuses attention on intergovernmental bargaining and allows scholars to inquire into the factors that lead to coordination among national governments (Moravcsik 1991, 1994; for a critique, see Sandholtz 1996). Why do national governments create international regimes, and what functions does the European Union fulfill?

A second lens treats European integration as the development of a federal constitutional order—a *domestic* regime. From this standpoint, the European Union has been compared to a variety of existing federal regimes, including those in Switzerland, Canada, Germany, and the United States (Sbragia 1992; Cappelletti, Seccombe, and Weiler 1986; Scharpf 1992).[1] Here the focus has been on institutional arrangements that link constituent governments to the center. What is the role of constituent territorial units in central decision making, and how are they constrained by the center? How are constituent territorial units represented in EU institutions?

In this chapter, I conceive of the EU as a domestic regime, but from a slightly different angle. Here I conceive of the European Union as an emerging polity, as a set of institutions performing basic functions of governance, and compare it to the process of polity creation that preceded it, namely state building.[2] What is at stake in both episodes is the structuration of legitimate authority. My concern is with the underlying dynamics of political change. In what respects are state building and European integration intended or unintended outcomes of decision making? Are these processes driven by conceptions of how best to structure authority, or are they more oriented to particular policies? How can one characterize the distribution of authority as a result of state building and European integration? What, in short, does the experience of state building in Western Europe tell us about European integration?

The State and the European Union as Artifacts

The building of modern states in Western Europe took from two centuries to about seven centuries, depending on what features one includes under the process. For example, one might stick with a minimal definition focusing on monopoly of the legitimate means of coercion based in national court systems within a given territory. Thus, the formative period in which a pluralistic state-system emerged from the variegated, multilevel, and multicephalous feudal order with its diffuse, overlapping secular and religious loyalties would be from the twelfth to the fourteenth centuries (Strayer 1970). At the other extreme, one might examine the consolidation of the state in its distinctive modern form, that is, one consolidated in a fixed territory; served by specialized personnel; organized along functionally differentiated lines; and based ideally, though infrequently in practice, on a common nationality. This would take us up to the eighteenth or even the nineteenth century (Finer 1975, 1990; Rokkan 1975, 567; Tilly 1975b). By contrast, the period from the foundation of the European Coal and Steel Community to the present is less than fifty years, a fact that throws into sharp relief both the extraordinary pace of change in recent decades and the necessarily tentative nature of our attempts to draw conclusions about a process that may well be in its infancy.

European integration has certainly been the result of self-conscious political creativity, and it could be argued that this lies at the root of the comparative speed with which an impressively broad and diverse set of institutions has been put in place. But in this respect, state building is no different. Gianfranco Poggi (1990, 95) describes the modern state as "an artificial, engineered institutional complex rather than one that has developed spontaneously by accretion." Along these lines, we speak of the process of state building, of "the will" to create the state, of the modern state as a "deliberately erected framework," a "made" reality.

What is different, however, is the diversity, coherence, and sheer number of powerful actors who have to be mobilized, negotiated with, cajoled, or defeated in the process of power redistribution and institutional creation. Modern states were created by monarchs who had to struggle for predominance in societies in which loyalties were diffuse and coercive power was thinly spread among shifting coalitions of entrenched and geographically disparate baronies. Moreover, monarchs lacked effective means of interest aggregation and political coordination. Racheting up the state's resource base, the perennial challenge of state builders, had to be pursued in a drawn-out struggle to build coalitions among diverse and independently powerful constituencies which themselves bore the brunt of additional taxes.

The context of institution building is totally different today. States have dominated political life in Western Europe over the past several centuries, and it is difficult to escape the conclusion that they will play a vital role, though not necessarily a dominant one, in any hypothesized future political order. At the same time, however, states have introduced a capacity for dynamic institutional change that exceeds that available in previous centuries. European integration, and in particular the latest spurts of institutional creativity, the Single European Act (1986) and the Maastricht Treaty (1992), were achieved because, not in spite, of the existence of state executives able to bargain authoritatively in international fora and set the terms, if not dictate the outcomes, of their respective domestic debates concerning ratification.

The Absence of a Master Plan

Given that the European Union is a consciously constructed set of institutions, it is tempting to draw a parallel between it and the creation of modern constitutional political systems, particularly federal systems such as the American or the German. But there is an essential difference. The European Union is not patterned on any blueprint for a workable system of government. Unlike the U.S. Constitution or the Basic Law, the Treaty of Rome did not try to settle fundamental questions of governance according to some overall plan based on principles such as protection of minorities, justice, equality, and political stability. This is not to deny that European integration has taken place within an ongoing debate among alternative conceptions of the European polity, encompassing, for example, a "Europe of the Regions" in which states would wither away, a federal Europe combining member states, or a free-trade Europe composed of sovereign states. But these conceptions have not dictated the process of integration. They are used as normative guidelines for future development or to describe what has already taken place. In its practice, European integration has been open-ended in a way that has escaped those who have thought in terms of grand architectural plans or final destination.

The European Union is the outcome of formal treaties setting out institutional competencies in a legalistic framework. But such treaties are not like the founding constitutions of existing democracies. The treaties are simply agreements among member states to achieve specific ends by creating particular institutions and institutional relationships at the European level. Instead of having its constitutional birth in a single founding moment, the European Union has been created step by step in the same way that a building plan is revised by placing successive transparencies over an initial design. The result is a dense and convolved polity whose current institutions are molded on past ones and in whose present structure one can still see the remains of past treaties.

This is nowhere more apparent than in the changing and convoluted terminology of the European Union and its institutions. The current name for the European polity is just the most recent, and almost certainly not the last, of some six names that have been adopted in official documents over the past twenty years: Common Market; European Economic Communities; European Economic Community; European Communities; and European Community. While the Maastricht Treaty creates an entirely new term (the European Union), two previous terms (European Community and European Communities) are still used in formal legal parlance to refer to the prior structure that is nested inside the new one. There are corresponding nuances in the terminology of decision-making bodies. The Council of Ministers, which is now termed the Council of the European Union (the term "Ministers" has been dropped), becomes the Council of the European Communities when it acts as a legislative body. Of course, such nuances are lost on all but the most legally minded participants in the Euro-polity. In the absence of a constitution with a fixed, or at least relatively stable, political terminology, many active participants, to say nothing of mass publics, are confused about the formal designations of major European political institutions.[4]

European integration resembles state building in its lack of a master plan. As noted above, state building was a conscious process of political engineering. Yet it was not engineering according to some external master plan. There was no attempt to set out a constitution specifying, once and for all, the scope and responsibilities of the state with respect to its monopoly of legitimate coercion, its centralization of territorial administration, its extent of resource extraction, and so forth. The features we associate with the state emerged out of a series of struggles, domestic and external, undertaken by state builders (usually, but not exclusively, monarchs) to expand their armies, extract more resources from their subject populations, develop new and more efficient administrations for this purpose, and find additional resources to undermine or repress the popular resistances that all of the above engendered (Tilly 1975a).

By and large, the state was created as an instrument for purposes that were not intrinsically state oriented. If some other institutional mix available under the particular circumstances of European feudalism had been better suited to the creation of large and well-equipped armies and the capacity to fund them at short notice, the modern state would quite likely (though it is not provable) never have been established.

The State and the European Union as Means-Rather Than Ends-Oriented

A corollary of this is that both the state and the European Union are goal-oriented institutions rather than ends in themselves. This is perhaps the main reason why it is so difficult to describe the outcome of either state building or European integration as a static system organized around some coherent set of political principles. The conventional defining characteristic of the state, its monopoly of legitimate coercion within a fixed territory, does not tell us much about what the state really is or what it does. When one goes beyond this elemental characteristic to other features relating to the degree of centralization, the type and scope of state regulation, or of resource extraction, one finds very wide variations across states and across different policy areas within states. In explaining such variations, political scientists analyze such factors as technocratic influences on policy making across program areas, patterns of contestation among policy actors, class relations, and social democratic participation in government, rather than the essential character of the state or its formal political goals.

The European Union, conceived in terms of its essential political structure or its final destination, is similarly elusive. Notions of federalism, intergovernmentalism, and so forth, have influenced the development of the EU, but they have not determined it. In practice, the institutions of the EU have been created to achieve discrete, diverse, contested, and contingent goals (Lindberg and Sheingold 1970, ch. 4).[5] The result is an immensely complex and variegated structure, or (more precisely) set of structures, that reflect the logics of individual policy arenas and the consequences of their intricate connections. When one describes these structures from the standpoint of governance, one finds an impressive scope of variation, ranging from a European superstate in trade-barrier regulation or competition, to a weakly coordinated intergovernmentalism in most areas of foreign policy.

In recent years, there have been some very interesting attempts to apply the concept of federalism to the European Union, highlighting member-state governments as decisive actors in determining the composition of the major decision-making bodies at the European level (Sbragia 1993). As in the German federal system (but not in the American), the member states are represented as autonomous institutions (rather than territorial constituencies) at the heart of the European polity. As in other federal systems, territorially defined political units structure the European polity. But federalism has not served as the architectural principle of the EU. National governments in the member states have greater powers of self-determination than constituent units in any existing federal state, and while territorial units within the same federal regime tend to have similar subnational political systems, the domestic political systems of the member states vary greatly. The territorial units of the European Union are more heterogeneous than in any federal polity.

One of the principal functions of the EU is to supply collective goods to its constituents—diverse publics, subnational groups, and above all, state executives. As for program areas within the state, the institutional structure of provision in each program area within the EU reflects the character of individual programs and the distribution of power more than it reflects the EU's constitutional structure. The overall shape of the European Union is the result of the accretion of numerous bargains about specific policies and their institutional frameworks. Hence, one can say that the EU, like the modern state, has been created self-consciously with respect to its *parts,* but not to its *whole.*

The development of the European Union as a result of the Single European Act (SEA) and the Maastricht Treaty can be conceived of as an interstitial process.[6] It has taken place largely as a by-product of goals that had little to do with the uniting of Europe itself (Sandholtz and Zysman 1992; Moravcsik 1992). The critical lowest common denominator in the rounds of negotiation that led up to the SEA was the desire to create a more integrated European market in the expectation that this would tap previously unexploited sources of economic productivity. The growth and reorganization of the EU-administered cohesion policy were, as I have argued elsewhere, a by-product of this initiative (Marks 1992, 1993; Pollack 1995). Key actors, including Prime Minister Thatcher, embraced the SEA because it was an obvious and effective means towards limited goals, not because they favored the creation of a European polity, per se, as an outcome.

The Maastricht Treaty sets out a detailed plan to deepen and extend coordination in monetary policy and in several other areas, including the environment, social policy, cohesion and structural policy, trans-European transport and communications networks, national borders, immigration, voting at the local and European levels, educational and cultural exchange, research and technological development, law enforcement, and foreign policy.[7] While institutional reform of the four major institutions of the European polity (particularly the European Parliament and European Court of Justice) is featured in the treaty, the relevant provisions specify incremental reforms based on existing competencies. The logic of the treaty is that of policy-oriented problem solving in which institutions are means to solve problems rather than goals in themselves.

Similarly with state building. While some actors, including monarchs and state officeholders, actively favored centralizing the capacity for resource extraction, most other actors, including powerful segments of the landed aristocracy, merchants, and clerics, found themselves going along for diverse reasons that had little to do with any desire to build the state as an intrinsic goal. And if they did resist the centralizing impetus, they were drawn into the political arena of the territorial state to fight the process. Centralized states arose because they served the interests of powerful actors who wished to wage war more effectively, extract resources from society, consolidate their authority, and provide for an environment hospitable to expansion of their resource base.

State Building and European Integration as Perverse Processes

Neither the development of the state nor that of the EU has been driven by abstract conceptions of how best to organize decision making. Indeed, one might make a case for a perverse theory positing that state building and European integration have taken place *despite* the doctrines of those in power, rather than *because* of them. Monarchs often saw themselves as defending the feudal order and traditional local privileges that were being undermined in the process of state building and of the imposition of centralized authority. In the nineteenth and twentieth centuries, many of the most politically influential supporters of particular pieces of labor market and welfare regulation—on the left as well as the right—did so despite their basic belief that state regulation was inferior to either communal self-regulation or the market. In many instances, the state's role grew not because those in power thought this to be an intrinsic good but because ruling groups set aside their opposition to the principle of state regulation for specific, usually ad hoc reasons. For example, the extension of state responsibility for welfare in Victorian England clearly contravened the dominant dogma of laissez-faire. Many of the steps towards the modern state were taken not because they led in that direction but despite the fact that they did so.

The same may be said of European integration. One of the puzzles of the EU is to explain its emergence and consolidation in the absence of widespread support for shifting authority to the European level. While some influential political leaders such as Jean Monnet or Walter Hallstein favored creating a supranational polity, they realized that they were in a minority and could not achieve their goals by appealing to an emergent European identity. Their challenge was to create a European polity in the absence of "Europeans." Their strategy, and the strategy of integrationists who followed them, was to mobilize support for concrete projects. Integrationists downplayed the decisional implications of their proposals and emphasized, instead, the substantive (usually economic) benefits of particular proposals that had as their by-product the piecemeal creation of a European polity (Wallace 1982, 64–65). The key for integrationists was not to convince opponents of the virtues of creating a European polity but to shift the debate to practical matters having to do with reaping collective benefits. Before the Maastricht era, integrationists' main opposition came from recalcitrant political leaders, above all de Gaulle in the mid-1960s and Thatcher in the late 1980s, whose commitment to national sovereignty trumped the political benefits of further integration.

Episodes of retrenchment notwithstanding, the consolidation of the EU across wide policy spaces in the absence of support for a supranational Euro-polity testifies to the primacy of policy making over institutional choice. But this primacy is not written in stone. In recent years, institutional choice has itself become the subject of intense debate, and in the wake of the Maastricht Treaty, substantive policy issues no longer determine political institutions.

This is a fundamental change, though nobody predicted it. The Maastricht Treaty itself provides few, if any, clues to the response it has generated. Like the Single European Act, the Maastricht Treaty is a shopping list of ad hoc substantive provisions that happen to coexist within the same document. The logic of these reforms (many still not fully enacted) is one of piecemeal political negotiation rather than constitution building. They bear the mark of bargaining among twelve state executives under the decision rule of unanimity. The treaty provides for (1) policy initiatives at the European level (monetary union, plus new competencies in several other areas, including the environment, social policy, communications, and law enforcement); (2) a series of ad hoc institutional reforms designed to facilitate these new policy making responsibilities (e.g., a higher threshold for blocking certain types of legislation in the Council of Ministers; creation of a European Monetary Institute, and eventually a European central bank);

(3) side payments to gain the acquiescence of recalcitrant state executives (e.g., a further large increase in the structural funds; a new cohesion fund; a variety of derogations exempting states from certain provisions of the treaty); and (4) a set of institutional reforms to put the side payments into effect (e.g., reform of the structural funds; a new cohesion fund administration). In this complex and dense melange of specific proposals, one finds only the barest mention of principles of decision making. The Maastricht Treaty refers to the concept of "subsidiarity" just three times, and each reference is vague enough to allow for competing interpretations.[8]

The reception to this agreement has opened a new era for the EU, for instead of technocratic discussion of policy outcomes, the 1992 debate over whether to ratify Maastricht turned on issues of decision making: the advisability of shifting authority to Brussels; whether national sovereignty was at risk and what to do about it; and how democratic the decision making in the European Union is, and how democratic it should be. Previously, state retrenchment had taken place under the temporary influence of rogue leaders. In the post-Maastricht era, the fate of the European Union has become subject to a far-reaching and highly politicized debate in the member states. For the first time, party positions on the European Union count in party competition, and outsider parties, particularly on the extreme right, have exploited resistance to integration to boost their electoral fortunes in domestic elections. Over the past two years, in response to the Maastricht Treaty, discussion of European issues has become more widely disseminated to the popular press and among political parties, particularly when at least one party in a country believes it may gain electoral support by raising the salience of European issues.[9] In some countries, European integration has become a vital issue in party competition. It dominated debate at the annual conference of the British Conservative Party in 1995. And it features strongly among a variety of extreme right-wing parties across Western Europe. No longer can state executives determine institutional reform as a technocratic by-product of substantive policy objectives.

The Democratic Deficit

The EU is not a constitutionally constructed polity. It has been assembled piecemeal to facilitate particular policies. Democracy, the master principle of constitutional creation in the twentieth century, has remained in the background. Nevertheless, there is within the EU a wide variety of representative institutions, organized along diverse principles: direct representation in the European Parliament; functional interest representation in the Economic and Social Committee; and regional (and local) government representation in the Committee of the Regions. But up to the present, by far the most influential has been indirect state-based territorial representation in the Council of Ministers and the European Council (Sbragia 1993). It is noteworthy that after the Council of Ministers, the two most important decision-making institutions are the European Commission and the European Court, neither of which has representational legitimacy. The EU is a labyrinthine polity with multiple principles of governance. In no other Western polity is the principle of direct representation so weakly articulated.

While the European Parliament (EP) has the formal power to sack the commission, its power over the composition of the political executive of the EU stops there. It is unable to influence the choice of commissioners by member-state executives, and if it were to take the unprecedented step of rejecting the commission as a whole, it would be faced with a new commission, once again selected by member-state executives, which it would then have to reject for a second time or swallow whole. Furthermore, the EP, even under the new codecision procedure initiated under the Maastricht Treaty, cannot enact legislation by simple majority, as can directly elected legislatures in member states. The EP is the junior partner of the European Council, which is, in effect, an indirectly elected upper chamber representing member-state executives.[10]

The weak formal position of the EP by comparison to national legislatures reflects the contrasting logics of European integration and state building. The liberal democratic state is an *outcome* of state building, but it is the point of *departure* for European integration. Liberal democratic states— above all, state executives legitimated by directly elected national legislatures—are the prime actors in the new European polity. In its origins, the EU was an international organization and therefore not subject to constitutional principles that apply to its constituent polities. If member states are democratic and the EU is the creature of the member states, why, it was asked, should the EU replicate direct democratic channels that already exist in individual countries. So the debate about democracy in the EU has turned on conflicting conceptions of the Euro-polity rather than on the intrinsic merits of democracy. The democratic deficit—that is, the weakness of representative democracy in the EU—is rooted in the institutional genesis of the EU as an offspring of national institutions that claim exclusive sovereignty in their respective territories.

In this respect, the logic of European integration is very different from that of state building. Western European states developed in a context of overlapping, ill-defined, and contending claims to legitimate authority on the part of monarchies, empires, city-states, fiefdoms, and the church. Democracy in the process of state building has its origins in the compromises forced on state builders (in most cases, monarchs) as they squeezed taxes from nobles, burghers, and bishops, usually in time of war or preparation for war. The balance of power among these estates, and between them and the monarchy, varied across Western Europe, but from the late eighteenth century, monarchs across Western Europe were confronted with middle-class demands for liberal freedoms and citizenship. The state came to be seen as an instrument for purposeful reform, and as the role of state control grew, pressures for participation intensified. To explore the links between state building and democratization would take us far beyond this essay. But the connection is clear: the creation of the modern state in Western Europe went hand in hand with the creation of territorial, (in most cases) national communities and demands for participation in sovereign parliaments.

In the EU, authority is shared among national and supranational institutions. The chief representative institutions are the Council of Ministers and the European Council, and these are dominated by national governments. But over the past decade, the European Parliament has become an influential player. Beginning with the election of 1979, representatives to the EP were directly elected rather than being selected by national parliaments. The Single European Act gave the EP an influential role in amending legislation, and this role was enhanced under the Maastricht Treaty.

The European Union was never intended to be a polity resembling existing liberal democracies, but as it takes over competencies that were once performed exclusively by national governments, demands for direct democratic accountability have intensified. Given the powerful drive towards democracy in national states in the nineteenth and twentieth centuries, and the unquestioned legitimacy of the principle of direct representation in Western democratic polities, it is natural to ask if we may be observing a ratchetlike process at the European level.

However, the pressures for democratization are dissimilar. The struggle for democracy in Western European states mobilized millions of people in trade unions and political parties. Democracy was the outcome of protracted political struggle among entrenched groups and classes. In the EU, by contrast, there has been little social mobilization on this issue, and no struggle. The principle of democracy is conceded by all sides: disagreement has hinged on whether this principle should apply to the European Union.

In recent years, the issue has become more salient as the stakes have grown. The EU is regarded no longer as merely a mechanism for achieving particular policy goals but as a set of authoritative institutions worth fighting over.

One dimension of conflict pits neoliberals against social democrats on the shared assumption that the greater the role of direct democracy in the EU, the more scope there will be for authoritative control over European markets. Rather than centralize regulation at the European level, neoliberals have sought to limit regulation by mutually recognizing, rather than harmonizing, national rules in product, labor, and capital markets. Neoliberals wish to constrain supranational authority and weaken interest group influence in order to insulate markets from political regulation.[11] Social democrats, in contrast, believe that the European Parliament has a positive role to play in aggregating demands for a "peoples' Europe," that is, a Europe characterized by overarching citizenship rights, commitment to social welfare, and positive market regulation. They are supported, particularly in the richer member countries, by organized labor, which has been hurt by the creation of Europe-wide markets in the absence of Europe-wide social regulation. Trade unions and many others on the Left wish to counter the market-opening thrust of European integration with supranational institutions capable of regulating markets at the European level.

A second dimension of conflict is between nationalists and integrationists. Those who believe that national states are the ultimate political communities view the European Parliament as a threat to national parliaments and sovereignty. Nationalists view the EU as a service organization to facilitate interstate bargains, and oppose any shift of democratic sovereignty to the supranational level. Today, this view is found mainly on the political Right, but it has also led some on the Left to oppose European integration because they fear that hard-won legacies of democratic struggle in individual countries will be lost if the EU takes on additional competencies. On the other side, those who want deeper political integration in Europe view the strengthening of the European Parliament as a necessary condition to their long-term goal. According to integrationists, if the EU is to become a legitimate arena for decision making on a range of vital issues, then it must become as democratic as the national polities it is supplanting. From the integrationists' standpoint, democracy and integration are interdependent: more integration, in turn, makes it imperative to strengthen the powers of the EP; a strengthened parliament will lead to increased pressure for integration.

From Exclusive to Nested Identity

The development of the modern state over the last two centuries was interwoven with the rise of nationalism and the attempted assimilation of ethnoterritorial minorities through the imposition of national symbols, language, culture, and state-funded education. The identification of state and nation was reinforced by recurrent international conflict. The logic of such conflict demanded ever more intense mobilization of communal solidarities to fight and fund wars that pitted entire societies against each other—culminating in the total wars of the twentieth century. In this context, national identity was pressed into an all-or-nothing phenomenon. Exclusive, belligerent nationalism consumed every part of an individual's being, including his or her identity, and in time of war, made absolute claims on the lives of citizens.

European integration, by contrast, has been accompanied by a weakening of exclusive nationalism and by the first signs of what might be described as *nested* identity, that is, multiple, coexisting identities with local, regional, and supranational territorial communities, alongside an identity with the nation. Surveys reveal an increasing number of individuals who simultaneously maintain strong attachments to more than one level of community. A survey by Eurobarometer in November 1991 (European Commission 1991) found on average that individuals report as strong an attachment to regional and local communities as to their country. Only in Denmark, Ireland, and the United Kingdom was attachment to country stronger than attachment to region, while the two were evenly matched in Greece, Italy, and Portugal. Around 30 percent of those surveyed in the twelve countries professed their attachment to the European Union to be as strong as (or stronger than) their attachment to their country. In general, nested identities are stronger among younger Europeans, among the more educated, and among those who have more positive attitudes to the European Union.

The EU is becoming a territorially diverse polity rather than an international regime determined by national governments. However, it is already evident that the pattern of cleavages in this Euro-polity is different from that in the member countries. Cleavages based on social class, religion, and environmental/lifestyle issues are far less important than they are in individual states, for at the European level they are accompanied by a major new cleavage—one based on territorial identity—that arises in the course of political integration. A paradox of European integration is that national and regional identities become more, not less, salient as the peoples of Europe are brought into closer political proximity. Instead of melding particular identities in a new European mold, the EU internalizes rivalries and conflicts that were once played out in relations among national governments. A French automobile worker may feel himself to be, first and foremost, a worker inside France, but also a Frenchman in Europe. Eleven transnational political "parties" exist in the European Parliament, but they are not cohesive. Members of the EP inject their national standpoints into many of the most important issues that face them. As the Euro-polity domesticates international relations, so national rivalries will be played out among interest groups and political parties in addition to national governments.

Centripetal State Building vs. Centrifugal European Integration

From the thirteenth to the twentieth centuries, the overall direction of power redistribution and the locus of power creation in the process of state building were towards the center. The monopolization of legitimate authority, the creation of a secular hierarchical system of justice, the deepening and widening of taxation—all pressed decision making towards the national level. This development was greatly intensified as nationalism rose across Europe and as centralized extraction, provision of welfare, and control of various sectors of the economy came to be identified with the interest of the nation as expressed by the state.

After almost forty years of European integration, scholars dispute the underlying direction in which the European Union has developed and should develop, an uncertainty that reflects the existence of wide variations in authority relations across policy areas and the aconstitutional character of European integration. At this point in time, three alternative outcomes have been hypothesized: (1) a European superstate; (2) a reinforced preeminence of states and state executives; or (3) a polity characterized by multilevel governance in which decision making is fragmented across subnational, national, and supranational levels of government. Which is it to be?

Does the telescopic vantage point adopted in this chapter provide any additional leverage in coming to grips with this fundamental question? At the outset, one should recognize that because state building and European integration are successive historical episodes, they cannot be viewed as independent cases of political structuration. It would be impossible to conceive of European integration without the prior establishment of states, for state executives have played a decisive role in European integration. It is, therefore, not surprising that the institutions of the EU have been and are being shaped by state executives. While states developed in a context of dispersed power and diffuse loyalties, the EU is being created in a context where power is focused in preexisting states having impressive reserves of loyalty, extensive organizational and financial resources, deep-rooted and powerful (though, in several cases, multiple and contested) national identities, and an undiluted monopoly of legitimate coercion within their respective territories (Hoffman 1966). Moreover, central state executives are powerfully positioned in the decision-making process of the European Union. State executives dominate the Council of Ministers, and they determine the composition of the most important supranational institutions, the European Commission and the European Court. State executives shape the outlines of the European polity through the European Council, which is an intergovernmental organization that exists outside of the formal framework of the EU, and through intergovernmental treaties that empower states as the only recognized legal actors representing their respective territories.[12]

This cluster of functions supports the thesis that the EU consolidates state executives, but the situation is ambiguous because it can be interpreted as revealing the point of institutional departure for the European Union rather than its dynamic properties. Given the strength of states after World

War II, any major restructuring of European political life would, presumably, have to give existing states pride of place even if it were to engender fundamental change in relations of authority over time. [13]

When one looks at the practice of policy making as distinct from the high politics of treaty making, there are many signs of such change. State executive domination of policy is diluted in several policy areas. Research into structural policy, for example, reveals a fragmented pattern of decision making involving the commission and subnational governments, alongside state executives (Marks 1992, 1993).[14] Instead of state control or the centralization of decision making at the European level, one finds a centrifugal process in which policy competencies have been spun away from state executives both up to EU institutions and down to regional actors. New policy networks link subnational governments directly to supranational European institutions. State executives no longer monopolize the representation of domestic interests in international relations (Marks, Hooghe, and Blank 1994; Marks, Nielsen, Salk, and Ray 1994).

The conception of the European Union as a multilevel polity is consistent with the empowerment of subnational government in several European countries since World War II. The spin-off of decision making away from the state over the past decades has been just as visible in the shift down to the subnational level as in that up to the European level (Rosenau 1990; Goldsmith 1993).[15] Governments across Western Europe have experimented with ways to deconcentrate administration and decentralize decision making to mollify ethnolinguistic minorities, to bring policy provision closer to policy receivers, to cushion demands on the state, and to reduce the central tax burden (Keating 1988, ch. 8; Sharpe 1988, 1989). Over the last three decades, Belgium has been transformed from a unitary into a federal polity; Italy, France, and Spain, previously highly centralized political systems, have created a comprehensive layer of regional government; and Greece, and to a more limited extent Portugal, have moved tentatively in the same direction, partly in response to the financial advantages of participation in the EU's structural policy. Only Germany, which is a federal polity in a culturally homogenous society, has moved steadily in the opposite direction. Ireland remains highly centralized, though there are pressures for the creation of regional government. And in the United Kingdom, successive Conservative governments have restricted the autonomy of subnational governments and resisted demands for devolution, though such demands are unlikely to dissipate in the future.

Although state executives remain strongly entrenched in the EU and play the major role in determining the basic institutional setup, there are some strong reasons for believing that the trend over the past several years is towards a multilevel polity in which competencies are shared across institutions stretching both above and below the state (Leibfried and Pierson

1996; Scharpf 1994; Marks 1993). In some respects, the structuration of authority in this polity has more in common with feudalism than with the state system. Both the feudal and the European political orders are characterized by multiple spheres of legitimate authority and by a corresponding propensity for individuals to have nested, rather than exclusive, political identities. Table 2.1 describes basic characteristics of the feudal political order, the state order that followed it, and an emergent poststate order exemplified in the emerging Euro-polity.

It is worth stressing that there is nothing inexorable about the development of a poststate order in Europe. The dynamic of European integration is not an objective process divorced from the political projects of the participants, and the future of the EU has now become the subject of polarized debate. Because it is the project of creative political actors, the EU is liable to be molded in innovative and unpredictable ways. State building, in which innovation was constrained by the dictates of systemic, often coercive, competition, the shape of the European polity is, as I argue in the next section, not as tightly coupled to its international environment.

The Systemic Contexts of State Building and European Integration

Both state building and European integration are driven by competition and learning. That is to say, the dynamics of state building and of European integration are to be found beyond the individual societies in which the particular forms of the state and the European Union developed. But the logic of political development appears different in the two cases.

The state developed in an international system of multiple diverse, and contending national states, city-states, and city-empires. Competition, often violent competition, among these units shaped the kinds of political structures that could feasibly be sustained.[16] In this scenario, institutional development can be understood in terms of Darwinian political-economic competition, enhanced by learning oriented, above all, to capacity for war making. The state did not develop autonomously in each political unit, but as a result of the interaction of those units.

European integration has also been profoundly influenced by its international context. The European Union originated in the 1950s in a window of opportunity created by the absence of great power rivalries among Western European countries, by the cold war, and by the horrendous experience of World War II. The "1992" market-opening reforms were a response to the weakening competitive position of strategic Western European industries and the rise of East Asian economies, particularly that of Japan. But the development of the EU appears far less tightly coupled to its international

Table 2.1. Typology of Political Orders in Western Europe

	Feudal order	State order	Post-state-order
Constituent units	Multiple overlapping kingdoms, fiefdoms, duchies, city-states, principalities, etc., alongside universalistic church	Limited number of sovereign states, each containing a nested layer or layers of territorially differentiated, nonoverlapping subnational governments	Limited number of states alongside a variety of overlapping supranational and international organizations formed by states and subnational groups
Principles of integration	Multiple, nested secular obligations alongside transterritorial loyalty to church	Exclusive, territorially defined identification with individual states and their constituent nations	Multiple, nested identification with communities at diverse levels of aggregation
Decisional locus	Multiple, autonomous spheres of secular and ecumenical competencies alongside traditional rights and immunities	Singular, hierarchical structure of decision making within each sovereign state, modified in some cases by federalism	Multiple, shared competencies among national, subnational, and supranational governments

environment than was that of the state. Rulers who failed to meet the demands of war making and resource extraction faced coercive removal from office. European integration appears less constrained. The institutional form of the EU is determined by neither violent confrontation nor the pressures of adopting lessons from struggles among other, similar regimes.[17] European integration is an open-ended, noncoercive process that, unlike state building, lacks unambiguous criteria of success and failure.

In recent years, there have been renewed signs of institutional diffusion with the establishment of the North American Free Trade Agreement and a variety of regional regimes in South America, Africa, Asia, and the former Soviet Union. The European Union offers several possible models for emulation: a supranational polity diminishing the possibility of war among its constituent states; an integrated market enhancing economic welfare; a regional trading bloc able to exert considerable leverage in trade negotiations; a potential monetary, political, and defense union with superpower ambitions. There are already signs that the perceived benefits of European integration have precipitated similar efforts elsewhere. If this is the case, then the logics of European integration and state building may not be so dissimilar after all: both may be driven by competitive mobilization, by an attempt to increase relative political power vis-à-vis contending political units.

States Were Created in War; the European Union in Peace

The most important sources of state building have to do with funding and conducting war. The coalescence of states in the critical fourteenth century was a direct response to the changing scale of warfare. Innovative organization and the drilling of infantry reduced the effectiveness of traditional heavy cavalry and greatly increased economies of scale in conducting war. Siege cannon practically eliminated the castle as a means of defense and opened up additional economies of scale. Armies became larger; feudal barons were denied the possibility of effective resistance behind the walls of their castles unless they made huge new investments; and the invention of new intensive and extensive sources of taxation became a matter of survival in relations among increasingly centralized monarchies (Bean 1973).[18]

One can see a similar causal dynamic in the development of the modern state as a response to total war in the twentieth century. The first such total war involved an unprecedented mobilization of human and material resources. Recruitment of millions of soldiers, provision of arms and munitions on a vast scale, rationing of scarce commodities, and an intensified need for legitimacy and cooperation of organized labor—all led national governments to assume direct control of key sectors of industry, to regulate the labor market as never before, and to set up an array of authoritative decision making institutions to bring diverse areas of the economy and society under centralized control. The terms used to describe this development usually refer to some form of socialism (for example, "state socialism," "war socialism," and "wartime collectivism"). But the dynamic of change was not class conflict or social democratic rule but total warfare. Although much of the apparatus of wartime control was eventually dismantled in peacetime, the experience of total war reinforced the identification of state and nation, racheted up permissible limits of taxation, revealed new possibilities for state intervention in diverse fields of human affairs, and decisively broadened conceptions of the proper responsibilities of the state (Hobsbawm 1992).

Given the powerful impetus towards the centralization of decision making in the state as a consequence of war, it is not surprising that European integration and the general process of diffusion away from the national state has taken place during a period of extended peace in Europe. A dominant characteristic of European integration has been diversity of levels, styles, and arenas of decision making.

On the basis of past experience with war, one may wonder if this mosaic is a peacetime luxury that would be compressed into a new centralized state order under wartime conditions. The question is, of course, a matter of speculation, but it is possible to imagine a potential reimposition of national state domination in the efforts of some governments to defend their "sovereignty" by framing issues in sharply nationalistic terms, or even to imagine a world divided into a limited number of mutually exclusive, intensely competitive, and potentially combative spheres of influence of which the European Union would be one. One may gain a taste of the latter possibility in the competitive creation of trading blocs in Europe, North America, and Asia and in the mobilization of national xenophobias, particularly those between the United States and Japan. Under this scenario, European integration would no longer be a misnomer; integration would take place in the historical mold of state building, guided by the centripetal logic of war and taxation and by the solidification of new identities in the process.

Notes

1. Peter Katzenstein's conceptualization (1987, 1997) of Germany as a "semi-sovereign state" provides an interesting point of departure for comparisons with the EU.

2. James Caporaso (1996) has written a suggestive article that captures differences between the EU and the Westphalian state.

3. The fact that the Basic Law was conceived as a temporary constitution for the western portion of a divided Germany reinforces the contrast between regime building and European integration.

4. Correspondence with Neil Nugent. This is a recipe for confusion and cannot help the EU's quest for legitimacy. In the matter of names, constancy is itself a virtue. After the response to Maastricht, it may safely be predicted that intangible as well as financial costs of terminological change will be factored more fully into treaty proposals. Experts themselves are liable to slip up. I cannot resist recounting that at a recent conference a prominent scholar tried to update terms in midsentence, and found himself referring to the European "Communion."

5. In this context, Haas speaks of the "autonomy of functional contexts" (1961, 376) and "asymmetrical overlapping" (1971, 31).

6. This idea is applied to state building by Mann (1986, 436).

7. The best overview of the Maastricht Treaty and its implications is provided by Schmitter (1996).

8. The three mentions are the following (my italics):

Article A: "This Treaty marks a new state in the process of creating an ever closer union among the peoples of Europe, *where decisions are taken as closely as possible to the citizen.*" [Subsidiarity is here defined without mentioning the term.]

Article B: "The objectives of the Union shall be achieved as provided in this Treaty and in accordance with the conditions and the timetable set out therein *while respecting the principle of subsidiarity as defined in Article 3b of the Treaty establishing the European Community.*"

Article 3b: "The Community shall act within the limits of the powers conferred upon it by this Treaty and of the objectives assigned to it therein. *In areas which do not fall within its exclusive jurisdiction, the Community shall take action, in accordance with the principle of subsidiarity, only if and insofar as the objectives of the proposed action cannot be sufficiently achieved by the Member States and can therefore, by reason of the scale or effects of proposed action, be better achieved by the Community.*"

9. Peter Lange and Louise Davidson-Schmich (1995) make this point, though they argue that elections for the EP have not, in general, become more focused on European issues since 1977.

10. On the intermeshing of power in the EU, see Marks, Hooghe, and Blank 1994. The EP has more influence over legislation than it is usually given credit for. See Tsebelis 1994 for a revealing analysis of the power of the EP under the codecision rules that preceded Maastricht.

11. Mancur Olson (1984) argues along these lines.

12. This line of argument is developed in Moravcsik 1994.

13. Alan Milward (1992) takes a different view. He points out that most states in Europe collapsed under German aggression between 1938 and 1940, and claims that the "rescue of the nation-state from this collapse, which appeared to mark the end of [the nation-state's] long domination of European history, is the most salient aspect of Europe's post-war history" (p. 4). However, the collapse of states in Europe only lasted as long as the coercive domination of the Third Reich. Once Germany had been defeated, political life once again was organized in states. Hitler swept individual states away but did little to delegitimize the idea of the nation-

state as the ultimate form of political organization. Little effort was needed to rescue the idea of the nation-state, and the rescue of individual states was achieved by Allied force of arms between 1940 and 1945. The exceptions were Eastern Europe, where German hegemony was replaced by forty-four years of Soviet hegemony, and West Germany, where a state built on a divided nation suffered, initially, from a deficit of legitimacy.

14. For a wide-ranging overview of issues and evidence, see Majone 1994b.

15. This is the point of sharpest disagreement between the view developed here and that of Michael Mann (1993, 118), who claims that "even if [the state] were declining in the face of . . . supranational forces . . . , it is still gaining at the expense of the local, the regional, and especially the private forces."

16. Essentially, as Charles Tilly (1989, 582) points out, the city-state and city-empire were doomed once national states effectively mobilized their populations into mass armies.

17. Perhaps it would be well to emphasize that the contrast I am drawing between state building and European integration does not rest on an assumption that states were uniquely determined by the logic of their interaction. Even if one were to apply a framework of biological evolution to the development of the state, it would not in principle be possible to predict institutional outcomes from initial conditions, just as it would not be possible to predict the course of a species' adaption from knowledge of its biological make-up and its environment.

18. Charles Tilly (1985, 178), though critical of Bean's historical analysis, observes, "After 1400 the European pursuit of larger, more permanent, and more costly varieties of military organization did, in fact, drive spectacular increases in princely budgets, taxes, and staffs." For an overview of contending approaches to state building, see Ertman 1994.

I

Historical Perspectives on Defining and Implementing Citizenship in the State Formation Process

This part discusses some of the historically contingent aspects of nineteenth-century state building and the ways in which we find reasons to draw parallels between, on the one hand, contemporary and, on the other, late-nineteenth- and early-twentieth-century conflicts between nationalism and internationalism. The significant break between the nineteenth-century fluidity of transborder life and the rigid border controls of the twentieth century occurred in 1914. Mobilization for war occasioned an expansion of the power techniques already associated with the implementation of citizenship. Selected individuals designated as "citizens," and hence members of particular state-communities, accumulated new rights and channels for influencing government. In the same process, however, the systematic codification of rights and obligations between the individual and the national state also led to social enclosure, through a process of inclusion and exclusion of who was a citizen and who was not, a process that shored up state power.

Carl Strikwerda demonstrates the continuing openness in the nineteenth century of borders and the high degree of inter-European trade and investment. He shows that in the boom in the third quarter of the century, two antithetical trajectories appeared. One, an integrationist path based on international and transnational regulation of labor standards and trade, can be conceived as an early, but ultimately failed, precursor to the European Community and, later, the EU. The other led to mobilization for war, strong state controls, and a closure of borders and transborder activities that has only been relaxed in the last decades by the conscious effort to reintegrate European trade and labor markets.

Strikwerda presents us with a "revisionist" interpretation of the origins of World War I, arguing that there was "an impressive degree of convergence among economies during the late nineteenth century" and that politicians, not business, were to blame for the mobilization of nationalist and imperialist impulses. V. I. Lenin famously advanced the thesis that capital was responsible for imperialism, a thesis that subsequently informed official Soviet scholarship on the origins of World War II. Serious Marxist scholarship, represented by Eric Hobsbawm (1987), did not succumb to similar reductionism. At the same time, Western scholars have been inclined to discount the importance of international economic activity as a brake on the nationalist impulse. Strikwerda makes a strong argument for the possibility of the counterfactual outcome: the eventual victory of internationalizers over nationalists. In doing so, he points to one of the central paradoxes of twentieth-century political development, namely, the disjuncture between the universalist aspirations of liberal political theory, dating back to the efforts of John Stuart Mill, and the statist reality of liberal democracy. The liberal idea of citizenship is in principle a global theory of justice emphasizing the universality of the human condition, but liberal democracy has only been realized in the context of the nation-state. Socialism, too, did not succeed until it gave up its internationalist aspirations and adapted the class struggle to the framework of the sovereign nation-state. Hence, our only models for international social citizenship derive from efforts, described by Strikwerda, to create international agreements with social clauses. It is of interest to note that analogous efforts today have focused on the development of a convention against child labor and of a social clause to the World Trade Organization that will replace the postwar trade organization GATT.

In the introduction to this book, we outlined our thesis regarding the correspondence between, on the one hand, the expansion of protective rights and formal guarantees of individual autonomy for citizens and, on the other, concentrations of state power. The contributions by Leslie Moch and by Gérard Noiriel and Michel Offerlé support this argument. Noiriel and Offerlé provide us with a detailed study of what they, in the tradition of Michel Foucault, speak of as citizenship "technologies," namely, the practices and administrative means by which the exercise of citizenship becomes possible. Only in the last decades of the nineteenth century did states begin to formalize citizenship and nationalist policies, which required the development of accounting techniques for distinguishing between citizens and noncitizens. Noiriel and Offerlé show how, in the case of France, the practical problems of implementation shaped policy. Pragmatic concerns often shaped the conception of who should be counted as a citizen and who should not. Again, the importance of the link to military mobilization is demonstrated: concerns that foreign workers exempt from military service would appropriate jobs and enjoy other benefits—including the ability to marry and establish families—at the expense of citizens informed in part the willingness to adopt a territorial definition of citizenship. With the outbreak of war, security concerns would later inform more restrictive definitions of citizenship qualifications, consigning French policy to an oscillating course between the territorial principle and the ethnic principle. Noiriel and Offerlé also show us how the development of new administrative capacities enhanced the power of the centralized state, with secondary implications for voting rights.

France and Germany offer the clearest cases of the historical path-dependence of citizenship policies, which diverged early and are still distinct in their underlying principles. Christiane Lemke shows how the German "nation" was constructed on ethnic principles, based on a common culture and language that did not coincide with a single political unit. In place of Marshall's somewhat teleological perspective, which optimistically postulates ever-expanding realms of citizenship as an accompaniment to capitalist development, Michael Mann (1988) argues that there have been five trajectories in the development of citizenship as a tension tamer for class struggle. Mann emphasizes that the expansion of citizenship has, above all, been shaped by the ruling class; the specific character of citizenship norms, by the strategies through which political and military elites have coped with change and the challenge of holding on to power. Finally, Mann also argues that the longevity and durability of regime strategies have hinged upon geopolitical variables, in particular victory in world wars, and not on "internal efficiency," by which he presumably means the fit between rules and domestic social interests.

Interestingly, Mann proceeds to discuss national trajectories in the evolution of political rights exclusively in the context of domestic class relations. The disjuncture between the original theses and the subsequent argument is particularly conspicuous in the discussion of Wilhelmine Germany, in which Mann focuses exclusively on regime responses to the threat of working-class mobilization (p. 199). (Mann also neglects to make a clear distinction between policy and constitutional rules.) It would appear that Mann's original theses have found a belated footing in Lemke's contribution to this book, which explicitly links the peculiar histories of German citizenship norms to the rise and fall of German imperial ambitions and fortunes in war. Hence, Lemke also sustains Mann's presumption that geopolitical variables are more important than domestic political contestation in shaping the central ingredients in national conceptions of citizenship.

The thesis regarding the link between a liberal international order and transborder mobility is supported also by the last chapter in part 1, written by Leslie Moch. Moch's study of the vast, still unmatched population flows in the period before World War I demonstrates the tendency of open markets and labor mobility to counteract definitions of social rights based upon a narrow conception of the state-community as an inclusive unit of social organization and protective policies. Moch sees an inevitable conflict between immigration policies that treat foreign labor as a factor of production, or as disembodied, "cheaper hands," and the social and political needs of both migrant and domestic labor for inclusive organization and interest representation.

In the post-1945 years, the development of the generous welfare state militated against the development of an international social dimension. Faced with a choice between international trade liberalism and the development of a generous welfare state, the European Left and labor saw no choice. The Swedish economist, Gunnar Myrdal, put things straight when he argued that the postwar welfare state and internationalism were antinomies and that the welfare state was bound to be the victorious party. "It cannot be helped," he said, "that everywhere national integration [in the welfare state] is now bought at the cost of international disintegration" (1960, p. 131). No nation could reasonably be asked to compromise national economic development in order to sustain the realization of liberal ideals regarding internationalization and free trade. Four decades later, Myrdal's confident prediction has been proven false, as we resume discussion of how to reconcile social guarantees with economic openness. Moch's analysis is also resumed in the final chapters of this book, which discuss new labor market legislation promulgated by the European Union, legislation that not infrequently has turned out to be more favorable to immigrants and to women than that at the national level.

3

Reinterpreting the History of European Integration: Business, Labor, and Social Citizenship in Twentieth-Century Europe

Carl Strikwerda

The Difficult Road toward Integration

Although it has had its successes, the movement for unity among European countries has also experienced a complex set of setbacks. When the European Community was created in 1959 as a customs union, many people believed that increasing trade among countries would lead to a genuine United States of Europe within a few decades. The literature on economic integration strengthened this belief by arguing that industrialization has an almost inevitable tendency to create larger and larger markets that span national boundaries (El-Agraa 1982; Robson 1980). By the 1980s, it was clear that this goal was far from being achieved. National governments still kept in place hundreds of policies and regulations that prevented genuine integration of the economics of the various European states. Even the new goal of a truly integrated European Community by 1993, set in 1985 by Community President Jacques Delors, has also been only partially achieved as of 1997.[1]

This persistence of national policies is nowhere as clearly demonstrated as in the area of social welfare. The dream of many Europeans, particularly in the labor movement, is that a united Continent will not only stimulate economic growth and create a new European political citizenship but offer "social citizenship" as well. According to this ideal, the creation of a new Europe should entitle all workers to equal rights within it. Those in advanced social welfare states should retain all their social and economic rights, while those in less advanced countries would win greater rights.

Workers should gain by unity, not lose. Using Marshall's famous typology, Western states developed into full political communities by offering, in chronological order, first civil, then political, and finally social citizenship. If a united Europe is someday to be a true political community, it, too, must move to deepen its notion of citizenship to include social and economic rights (Marshall 1950; 1973, 71–122). One of the most important questions which arises from the history of European integration is why "social citizenship," along with genuinely transnational markets, has not emerged more fully.

Understanding why economic integration and social citizenship have encountered so many roadblocks requires taking a new look at the conventional history of European unity. For decades, the history of European integration has emphasized the actions of political decision makers at the top of society and the changes in a generalized public opinion. According to this line of argument, Schuman, Adenauer, and De Gasperi laid the foundations of unity in the late 1940s, helped by a popular skepticism about nation-states, which had arisen in reaction to the world wars. Similarly, scholars have usually attributed the slow progress of the European Community in the 1960s to 1980s to the opposition of such leaders as de Gaulle and Thatcher, or to the underlying residual power of nationalism within European populations.

This conventional approach to the history of integration also assumes a clear scenario about the last hundred years of European history. From this perspective, the late nineteenth and early twentieth centuries are a period of rising nationalism and economic protectionism, with the only sign of an alternative being the hapless peace movement. World War I showed the folly of nationalism, but the attempts at international cooperation in the interwar era were not strong enough to produce any lasting effects. It required another world war, decolonization, and Europe's loss of position to the two superpowers before integration began to take hold. The movement toward unity that began with the European Coal and Steel Community, EURATOM, and the Treaty of Rome was, according to most accounts, a radical break with the nationalist past (Kitzinger 1963; Laurent 1989).

In contrast to that approach, this chapter suggests a new focus and a new periodization for the history of European integration. To understand fully integration's successes and setbacks, a new explanatory framework is needed that looks within a longer time frame, at factors relatively neglected by many earlier scholars. For a new perspective, it is important to examine the actions of mobilized social groups, such as business and labor, within states and to include the whole sweep of European history from the late nineteenth century to the present. In the pre-1914 era, business and labor participated in an unusually integrated economy and began creating an unparalleled kind of internationalism. States encouraged this integration and internationalism by eliminating barriers to integration and refusing to intervene in the economy within countries. After 1914, much of the integration and internationalism disappeared, but the state in almost every country took on important powers for the first time. The social welfare state, as beneficial as its effects were for many poorer citizens, was closely tied in many countries with the decline of international economic ties. During the post-1945 period, the European community cautiously rebuilt a small degree of integration, but given the increase in state power, internationalism failed to expand. The challenge for European integration in the future, one could argue, is to encourage internationalism once again without losing the gains made in social welfare in the last half of the twentieth century.

To make this argument, it is necessary to examine, in sequence, the era before 1914, the interwar years, and the period after 1945. Within each period, we need to look at the forces making for economic integration and at the nature of social citizenship, that is, the degree to which social welfare was seen as an international or national concern. Finally, this story can help us point out the process by which integration or disintegration occurs, in particular the enormous role of the state as the arbiter of economic change.

The Pre-1914 Economy: Nationalist or Internationalist?

The deeply rooted conventional view of Europe before 1914 argues that a rising tide of protectionism forestalled cooperation between rival nation-states and encouraged hostilities.[2] As economic historian Sidney Pollard (1981, 59) writes, "In the forty years or so before the First World War, the tendencies that were breaking up the economic unity of Europe were getting stronger in relation to those that made for continuing integration." Similarly, M. S. Anderson (1993, 193) argues, "From the 1870s onwards Europe's political frontiers were becoming, for the first time, also well-defined economic ones." Most continental countries adopted higher tariffs against foreign goods, thus abandoning the free-trade policies of the mid-nineteenth century (Bairoch 1993, 24–28; Gourevitch 1977, 281–92). Behind this concern for protecting home markets lay suspicion of foreigners. The reactionary Action française writer Léon Daudet (1901, 1) claimed that German goods and business investments in France represented "Jewish-German espionage." Even the United Kingdom, which clung to free trade, experienced campaigns against "Made in Germany" (Williams 1897).

Recent research on prewar economic history casts doubt on this view of an increasingly nationalist economy. Tariffs remained much lower than they had been before the 1860s or were to be again until the 1960s. In continental Europe, excluding continually protectionist Spain and Russia, tariffs in the late nineteenth century only rose from an average of 9.4 to 13.9 percent. This was much lower than the 25 percent reached after World War I (Liepmann 1938, 383–401; Bairoch 1993, 40). Nor did tariffs or nationalist agitation in Europe have a significant effect in dampening international trade; trade between France, Germany, the United Kingdom, and Russia was at all all-time high and increasing steadily in the last few years before World War I (Ashworth 1974; Poidevin 1969; Bairoch 1989). The freedom to seek work and to establish businesses in other countries was greater in this period than in any other period of European history (Strikwerda 1993b).

Nowhere was this more true than in the industry that was the fastest-growing and most vital for national security, the iron and steel industry. By 1913 German and Belgian interests owned perhaps as much as 35 percent of the iron ore fields in French Lorraine, the largest source of iron ore in Europe, and probably 40 percent of those in Luxembourg. French, Belgian, and Luxembourgian capital owned almost 20 percent of the production of the German steel cartel, the Stahlwerksverband, while three of the six largest Ruhr members of the cartel—Gelsenkirchener, Deutsch-Luxembourg, and Thyssen—had become heavily committed to investments in France, Belgium, or other countries (Tubben 1930). The Thyssen concern, for example, contained the second largest steel company in Belgium, coal mines and metallurgical firms in Germany, and a set of French companies, one of which was building the largest steel mill in France on the eve of the war (Treue 1966). Even Krupp, the German armaments maker that writers have seen as the quintessential nationalist firm, in 1914 had subsidiaries in Russia and Spain, joint ventures with U.K. and French firms, and investments in Brazil, Africa, and the South Pacific (Krupp-Archiv n.d.). On the eve of World War I, all the nations in continental Western Europe that produced iron, coal, or steel were becoming interdependent. Through economic integration, Europe had the potential to eliminate the advantage the United States supposedly had through its abundant natural resources. Gavin Wright (1990) has pointed out that, considered as a continent, Europe was no less well endowed; the real U.S. advantage lay in the absence of political boundaries dividing different regions. Nor were iron and steel exceptional. In chemicals, Swiss and German firms, as well as the Belgian firm Solvay, had operations throughout Europe (Hohenburg 1966; Haber 1958). The largest German zinc producer, based in Silesia, had operations in Belgium, Hungary, and Sweden, while the Continent's largest zinc firm, the French-Belgian multinational Vieille-Montagne, had over thirteen thousand employees scattered in Germany, Belgium, France, the United Kingdom, Italy, Algeria, Tunisia, Spain, and Sweden.[3]

Historians have nonetheless discounted this internationalized economy because they have doubted that it had real effects strong enough to overcome the supposed rising tide of economic nationalism. New research by economists, however, demonstrates that there was an impressive degree of convergence among economies during the late nineteenth century. As Jeffrey Williamson and his associates argue, continued economic growth and the ease of migration raised wages in sending countries as much as 10 percent above what they would have been without migration (Hatton and Williamson 1992, 1994). Similarly, despite all the arguments about tariffs and economic nationalism, the economies of France, Germany, and the United Kingdom were becoming more integrated, and at a faster rate, than they would be at any other time in history until the 1960s. By 1914, business cycles in the three countries increasingly coincided (van der Wee 1986). The growing integration of European economies, furthermore, did not simply run on its own. The international gold standard survived as an essential framework because liberal government officials in various countries worked together to maintain financial stability (Gallarotti 1995; Eichengreen 1990). A whole range of international agreements—on railroads, telegraphy, shipping, and postal systems—provided a critical institutional foundation. Most historians have treated these agreements as products of the economic growth of the nineteenth century, but as Craig Murphy (1994) argues, it is equally true that these agreements enabled economic growth to reach new levels.

Just as business moved easily, so, in the years before World War I, did workers move between states ever more freely until, for the only time in modern history, a large part of the world formed virtually a single labor market. Governments still retained the right to expel foreigners as vagrants and political undesirables, but the large majority of immigrants looking for work crossed borders freely (Caestecker 1994, 99–131). In Europe, the one major exception was German restrictions on Polish workers from outside the Reich, but even here the demand for labor eventually forced the Germans to encourage Poles to come (Olsson 1992). The multinational firms in heavy industry expanded on the Continent precisely along with the growth of labor migration. In 1912, in French Lorraine, where Belgian and German investment dominated in heavy industry, immigrants made up 57 percent of the population. Two-thirds of the industrial workforce was Italian (Vignes 1913). When French companies controlled by the German magnate August Thyssen built blast furnaces in Normandy, they employed a polyglot workforce that included Italians, Greeks, and Moroccans (Gutehoffnungshütte 1913). A large share of the workforce of Ougrée-Marihaye, the largest Belgian steel producer and a large-scale investor in France and Luxembourg, had long been nonnative, including both Germans and Dutch-speaking Flemings from northern Belgium (Wautelet 1975, 79). Ruhr industrialists who invested in France had long employed Poles.

The same was true for French firms that went multinational. Acieries de

Longwy, which formed a partnership with the Röchling firm in the Saar, had a workforce in France that was over 85 percent non-French—Belgians, Germans, Italians, and Swiss (Merrheim 1908; Kellenbenz and Schneider 1977). Of a French-owned coal mine near Aachen, Germany, Victor Cambon (1914, 25) noted, "Very few of the workers are Germans; one finds a mélange of Poles, Hungarians, Belgians, Dutch, Italians, and Swiss." Nor was this foreign labor cheap. During the economic boom before the war, the United States and Argentina were often competing with Europe for the same workers. French labor contractors were outraged when a trainload of Italians whom they had hired stopped en route in Metz, in German Lorraine, and German recruiters lured away the entire contingent (Vignes 1913).

Internationalism: From the Economy to Policy

Although it has been relatively neglected by scholars, this economic integration before 1914 helped create bonds between interest groups in different countries. Business leaders, labor activists, and reformers in different countries forged ties with their counterparts across borders. Most important, along with the strong nationalism of the period, an equally strong internationalism emerged, a sense of internationalism that, in turn, influenced how leaders saw the prospects for social welfare policy.

The continental iron and steel industry again provides a good example of how shared economic ties influenced internationalism. Because the Luxembourg and Lorraine mines and steel mills lay right on the French, German, and Luxembourg borders, and because all of these establishments relied on immigrant labor, a large floating pool of Italian, Belgian, German, and French workers moved back and forth across the border.[4] The floating labor pool forced French, German, and Luxembourg firms to adopt similar wage scales and working conditions to attract workers (Bonnet 1962; Moine 1989). The French Comité commercial franco-allemand and the German Deutsch-Französischer Wirtschaftsverein worked actively with both countries' parliaments and consular officials for freer trade, lower railroad rates, and more uniform laws. In 1909, these two groups brought together members of the Chamber of Deputies and the Reichstag from Lorraine, mayors of towns on both sides of the border, and the two nations' railroad directors to plan a new railroad line between French and German Lorraine (Germany 1908, 1910; "La percée des Vosges" 1909, 2; Poidevin 1969). Even more striking, when implementation of the eight-hour day began to be discussed seriously, French, Belgian, and German representatives considered an international agreement to lower hours simultaneously (Rust 1973).

Labor internationalism before World War I has often been dismissed as an ignominious failure since it failed to stop the move toward war (Joll 1974; Haupt 1972; Mommsen 1979; van Holthoon and van der Linden 1988). But while the top leadership and rank-and-file of the various national labor movements may not have overcome nationalist tendencies, some local leaders whose interests clearly spanned borders made important contributions to building genuine labor internationalism. The coal miners in the Dutch province of Limburg belonged to the German Christian coal miners federation, while the iron and steelworkers in Luxembourg were members of the German Socialist metallurgists' union federation. In both cases, these workers had been recruited by the German federations because the industries over the borders had become closely linked to Germany (Jurriens 1981; Steil 1992). One of the industries in which unions in different countries worked most closely together was shipping, partly because the shipowners were organized in international cartels (Aldcroft 1968). Both German and U.K. transport workers' unions organized locals in the Netherlands. In one of the few cases of a genuine international strike, longshoremen in the United Kingdom, Belgium, and the Netherlands struck together in the summer of 1911 (Boezee 1991).

This cooperation is all the more impressive when one sees that the continental unions had to organize an extremely diverse workforce. In Antwerp, the busiest port on the Continent, labor newspapers came out in four languages—Dutch, English, Dano-Norwegian, and German. In the French *département* of the Nord, on the border with Belgium, where thousands of Flemish workers migrated and commuted across the border, French and Belgian unions, both Catholic and Socialist, cooperated in several instances (Strikwerda 1993a). When German metallurgists organized workers in the Luxembourg plants of the multinationals, they worked with French and Italian unionists in order to reach Italians who drifted back and forth across the border; union publications came out in three languages—French, Italian, and German (Luxembourg n.d.). In 1911, the Belgian metallurgical unions in Liège reorganized themselves after sending a study mission to learn German union methods (Centrale des métallurgistes de Belgique 1913, 8). German leaders, although they failed to recruit Poles into their unions, reached out to Italian immigrants more than did union leaders in any other country (Del Fabrio 1989; Lorwin 1929, 112; Kulczycki 1994, 105–212). Within the Second International, too, there were more concrete attempts to organize immigrant workers and to organize cooperation between national union federations than earlier scholars have suggested (Forberg 1987). Although less well-organized than the Germans, French unionists, rubbing shoulders with numerous immigrants, also participated in some significant attempts to create international ties between labor movements (Thorpe 1989).

Internationalism and Social Citizenship

From the perspective of European integration, the most interesting aspect of the internationalization of business and labor in the pre-1914 era was the accompanying developments in social welfare. The welfare states of the twentieth century had yet to emerge, and national governments did not appear to be the exclusive hope for workers in the pre-1914 era. Instead, many unions, municipalities, employers, and industrial associations provided benefits or protected workers (Bliss 1910; Spencer 1984). The partisans of international labor policy sought, through bilateral agreements, to solve the problems that workers faced from unrestricted capitalism within countries. International agreements were designed to undercut the argument that it was dangerous to burden the nation's industry with regulations that foreign competitors did not bear (Francke 1909). The highly integrated world economy also made international agreements appear more practical. At the same time, the international sphere had a certain mystique for nineteenth-century activists. Just as "national" in the days of liberal nationalism sometimes connoted a larger notion of the common good above that of party, interest, or faction, so "international" signified that reformers appealed to a higher level of judgment. A truly international order to which states would agree would necessarily have to be based on higher principles than those petty, short-sighted goals to which politics within states often descended. Around 1900, the emerging organizations that represented labor or other disadvantaged groups could still consider the international realm one in which their interests were at stake and in which they could win significant gains (Lange and Schou 1954; Anderson 1993; Lyons 1963; Strikwerda 1991).

The achievements of the movement for international labor agreements before 1914 were modest, but they nonetheless raised high hopes. Two meetings, the Berlin Conference on Labor of 1890 and the conference on labor legislation in Brussels in 1897, led in 1900 to the creation in Paris of the International Association for Labor Legislation (IALL). Almost all industrial countries created national associations or chapters of the IALL, all of which, like the umbrella organization, were devoted to publicizing the need for global regulations (Lowe 1918). Besides regular world congresses held up until 1914, the IALL created the International Labor Office (ILO), based in Switzerland. Privately financed, the world congresses and the ILO were still able to get some governments to subsidize their work (Miller 1921; Lowe 1935, 112–390). The IALL and its close ally, the Association internationale pour la lutte contre le chômage, tackled many practical concerns: hours of work, judicial disputes, shipping regulations, women's employment, and border controls (IALL 1901; Lazard 1911; Lyons 1963). Only two relatively modest international agreements actually resulted.

Known as the Bern conventions, one banned the use of dangerous white phosphorus in the manufacture of matches; the other prohibited the night work of women.

On the eve of the war, activists were working on two more substantial agreements that would have established a ten-hour day for women and prohibited night work for young people. These, too, might well have been adopted if the war had not intervened. None of these agreements, however, was seen even by proponents as important in itself. They established the legal principle and practicality of international labor agreements and could be used, it was hoped, to coax governments into further action. It is significant that all of these agreements began, as labor legislation within most countries had, by protecting women and young people. (Match production disproportionately hired women.) By beginning with the supposedly least debatable targets for protection, the movement could appeal to common notions of civilized behavior. The IALL and its affiliates could also claim that their publications, lobbying, and conferences had contributed to the small wave of bilateral labor agreements enacted in the last years before the war. Germany, Denmark, Italy, Belgium, France, the Netherlands, the United Kingdom, and Austria-Hungary all signed agreements guaranteeing reciprocity for accident insurance (Lowe 1935; Mahaim 1933).

Most important, all the signs of internationalism before World War I grew up alongside a sense of nationalism and citizenship that was still open. As with the foregoing observations on the international economy, the argument that internationalism and nationalism co-existed may seem wrong headed. Every textbook and virtually every leading historian of the period tells us that the pre–World War I era was one of conservative nationalism (Hobsbawm 1990). The rising tide of nationalism is unmistakable, but it was not necessarily the wave of the future. Few observers predicted that tensions over national minorities—in Ireland, Alsace-Lorraine, Prussian Poland, or the Slavic lands of Austria-Hungary—would lead to dismembering any of the major states. The most radical expectation in almost all the areas of explosive nationalist tension was autonomy or home rule (Silverman 1972; Sundhausen 1992). Radical nationalism among the ethnic majorities was concentrated in small groups, such as the Action française and the Pan-Germans, that rarely exercised political influence. All the campaigns led by radical nationalists against foreign penetration of national economies hardly made a dent in the rise of international trade, foreign investment, or immigration. The much larger, mainstream nationalist revival of the early twentieth century was a mixture of patriotic and cosmopolitan elements. U.K., German, and French leaders wanted greater "national efficiency" or greater social solidarity, but they were often open to adopting foreign models to achieve this (Searle 1971).

Meanwhile, much of the internationalism of the late nineteenth century was not opposed to nationalism or to the nation-state per se. Instead, advocates of international cooperation were what might be called "liberal nationalists." They saw nation-states as communities that protected rights and saw agreements between nation-states as additional guarantors of rights. The leading international jurist Louis Olivi argued that a convention between states protecting the human rights of immigrants would be an appropriate complement to national legal codes. The distinction that international law makes in the later twentieth century between states as sovereign entities and international bodies or agreements as limiting state sovereignty was less clear in the view of many observers in the late nineteenth century. As Louis Olivi (1897, 426) argued,

> The State enjoys and ought to enjoy a sovereign independence, except where it is limited by the nature of things, individual human rights, the rights belonging to other states and collectivities, and the superior rights of the international collectivity.

In many ways, the internationalists of the late nineteenth century were continuing the tradition, which went back in Western civilization to the Renaissance, and farther back to the Stoics, of appealing to the law of civilized communities, the *jus gentium,* which states were supposedly putting, imperfectly, into practice. Ernest Mahaim (1912, 2–7) in a famous set of lectures on international labor law in Paris in 1912, argued that international legal reformers sought to derive from accepted laws of justice or human rights (*droits*) principles for positive law or the law of states (*lois*).

Nor was this view so utopian as it might seem. The legal framework governing international ties between states was more open than commonly assumed. As the international economic regime just described makes clear, in the late nineteenth century, passports were virtually unknown, migration was astonishingly free, and the right to set up businesses or own property in foreign countries was widely enjoyed (Kern 1983, 11–16, 230–231). Much of this occurred without treaties. The reason why this tradition of legal internationalism has been ignored is that international jurists in the nineteenth century dealt almost exclusively with the legal problems arising from foreign relations, that is, diplomacy and war. The whole web of relations between the legal systems of different countries was considered part of the relations between societies, or simply part of Western civilization. Before 1914, the formally designated body of "international law" was often narrowly concerned with declarations of war, diplomatic immunity, and the rights of neutrals (Hall 1895). But in actual practice, national courts, even in continental European countries, applied "customary international law" so that many citizens in different Western countries worked within similar de facto legal frameworks (Masters 1932).

Within this legal tradition, citizenship in national communities was not necessarily so exclusive that it forbade appeal to international standards. Nor was national citizenship clearly limited to political rights granted by, and duties to, the sovereign state. The state itself might be considered legitimate in part because it upheld natural human rights (*les droits de gens*). Agreements between states were not necessarily an alternative to national legislation. They might also be a logical extension of national sovereignty; that is, they might be seen as guaranteeing the rights of citizenship. In other words, "social citizenship" was still being defined, and it could be either national or international, or both. At the top, between states, agreements could help secure it. Even though international labor laws came slowly, many other agreements set a precedent. Between 1900 and 1909, there were 119 new international organizations founded, and an astonishing 112 more were created between 1909 and 1914 (Lyons 1963, 14). In the years before World War I, the leading social reformers, labor activists, and government administrators met frequently in international congresses on the eight-hour day, home production, women's employment, and child welfare. The welfare states that were beginning to be planned in these years formed part of an ongoing international discourse that embraced most of Europe and the United States as well (Lyons 1963).

The idea that international laws would secure rights in conjunction with national ones was more comprehensible because national governments were only beginning to intervene to secure social welfare (Pedersen 1993). Many labor reformers and union leaders still believed that national policies were a major goal, since, in theory, national-level standards would be more just and egalitarian than local or sectoral ones. But this did not preclude them from desiring or working for international standards. Instead, they hoped national and international laws would come at the same time. This is one reason the international labor law movement designed model codes; they hoped that nations would adopt similar codes more or less simultaneously, even if an international agreement was not yet in effect. An international agreement would supplement national laws and pull the last recalcitrant states along. Despite the vehemence of conservative or militarist nationalism, the projects of international labor law and of international cooperation between labor organizations had strong foundations in European traditions. That they failed was not inevitable. Nor should their failure mean that citizens planning for the twenty-first century cannot claim them as a precedent for their own future.

The Impact of World War I

World War I marks a decisive break in the history of European integration as it does in world history. As the classicist and international activist Gilbert

Murray wrote in 1921 (p. vii) in disbelief, "Things are done now, in time of peace, which would have been inconceivable before 1914." Abruptly, during World War I, governments sequestered the property of foreigners, imposed passport and visa controls, and introduced or restricted the issuance of work permits. Most of these legal powers were not undone after the war. Indeed, they became a foundation and precedent for further action in the Great Depression. What is more, many of these restrictions continued right down to the 1960s and, in some cases, though amended, almost to the present. The legal tradition that the European Community is trying to unravel at present goes back to the protectionism of the interwar years (Kunz 1968). The destruction of much of the economic integration of the pre–1914 era meant that the foundation for internationalism was gone. Most European societies redefined themselves in a more nationalistic fashion. Social citizenship, in other words, came to be defined as a set of rights confined within the nation-state and almost completely defined by the nation-state alone. The result has been to make it much more difficult for workers to see their interests as international. Just as important, the nation-states acquired a much larger clientele determined to keep their position and to preserve the existing national governments and the policies they enforced.

Thus, World War I destroyed much of the economic integration, labor internationalism, and open notions of citizenship on which cooperation between different countries depended. As a telling sign of the explosion of nationalism caused by the war, one-third of the international organizations created in the late nineteenth century disappeared during the hostilities and their aftermath (Murphy 1994, 82). The multinational connections in the iron and steel industry on the Continent disappeared or stagnated. Germany lost all its foreign holdings, and the Belgians and French soon found that they could not expand their own. The Germans never revived the holdings they lost in Belgium, Luxembourg, and Alsace-Lorraine; surviving multinationals like Ougrée-Marihaye nearly went bankrupt; and the French eventually sold off many of the holdings they had acquired in Luxembourg and the Saar after the war (Bariéty 1977; Bussière 1984). The European and International Steel Cartels finally gave continental heavy industry a precarious stability, but they were rarely more than truces between the various national cartels (Nocken 1983; Barbezat 1989). Aside from some expansion in automobiles and food processing, multinational investment in Europe shrank in importance by comparison with investment in the rest of the world (Dunning 1983).

World War I greatly restricted migration and redefined the legal status of migrants. The United Kingdom introduced an Aliens Act in 1914, which remained in effect after the world war (Brown 1926). By the 1920s, writes Colin Holmes (1988, 114) the "liberal procedures of the Victorian Age and indeed of the years between 1905 and 1914 belonged to a different and vanished world." As the International Labor Office noted, "During the war the possession of a passport issued by the national authorities, with a visa of the representatives of the country to which the traveller intended to go, became compulsory for all international travelling" (ILO 1922, 163). In 1916, the French government created an identity card that had to be carried by all of the new immigrant workers who had come to the country to work because of the wartime labor shortage. The following year, the card was imposed on all foreigners. Not until the 1950s did French workers who were citizens have to carry a card. The requirement of a visa or an identity card became the lever that operated the restrictive mechanisms many countries imposed on foreign workers. Workers who were recruited through official labor agencies and who followed regulations once they were working in the host country obtained visas or cards. Those who were not recruited officially or who did not follow regulations, did not receive visas or cards and thus were vulnerable to expulsion. The net effect of the regulations imposed on immigrant workers was that those workers became a special category of laborer within the nation's workforce. As Eugene Kulischer (1948, 251) wrote, the foreign worker became a "modern coolie," allowed into the country for a specific amount of time under special regulations.

Even Germany, which had set a precedent for regulating foreign workers through its pre–World War I restrictions on the Poles, made major changes as a result of the war (Herbert 1990). For the first time, German law established the principle that foreigners were to be recruited only if no native workers could be found (Bade 1987). In Germany, "immigrant" (*Einwanderer*), too, became legally redefined. An immigrant was no longer a "foreign" worker or businessperson residing in Germany who sought to become a German citizen but an ethnic German from other countries who wished to "return" to Germany (ILO 1922, 242; Lemke ch. 5 below).

Some nations experienced an increase in immigration, but the change in the way migration was treated is of greater importance. Belgium became an important country of in-migration for the first time; France became the most important importer of labor in the world. The change in the French situation from before World War I is particularly striking. Before 1914, migrants came with almost no official controls. In the 1920s, French immigration was strictly controlled by nation-to-nation agreements—for example, between Mussolini's Italy and France (Cross 1983; Reid 1993). One of the largest breaks with the nineteenth century was that during the interwar era, every economic downturn threatened to undo ties between countries. During the depression, France, and to a lesser extent Belgium, expelled immigrant workers as a way of exporting their unemployment (Cross 1983).

Initially, the victory of the democratic Allies made it appear that internationalism, especially in the sphere of labor, would actually grow after the war. The ultimate failure of labor internationalism in the 1920s and 1930s, despite some initial success, demonstrates how much internationalism is dependent on economic integration and government support. The Versailles peace treaty with Germany contained a long section on labor, Part 13, which set forth a declaration of principles, Article 427, hailed as "labor's magna carta." The ILO was incorporated into the new League of Nations (*Labor in the Treaty of Peace* 1919; Sharp 1991). These actions helped generate widespread enthusiasm and a very large body of literature advocating renewed international labor legislation (McDonnell 1920–21; Behrens 1924). The newly strengthened ILO helped secure new international agreements, including ones prohibiting the night work of young people and women in 1919, regulating the employment of sailors in 1920, 1921, and 1926, and protecting workers against lead poisoning (Wilson 1933, 95–102; Dillon 1942). Probably the most important regulation obtained by the ILO was the 1919 Washington convention establishing the eight-hour day in industrial work; in many cases, it merely codified what workers had achieved by their own strike action.

Unfortunately for the labor reformers, while they hailed the increase in international agreements in the early interwar era, the ground was shifting beneath their feet. A more critical change than the growing controls on migration was that of increasing protective and social welfare legislation *within* states. In many ways, this was the beginning of important victories for labor. Yet, from the perspective of the pre-1914 reformers, it fulfilled only half of what had been originally sought. No international agreements bound the policies of states together or pulled recalcitrant states along. Nor were state policies open to the citizens of other states. Almost every country had provisions discriminating against foreigners in this legislation. Only French citizens could vote for or be delegates on the newly created mine safety councils. This continued right down to the 1980s, even in mines where only 5 percent of the workers were French (Reid 1993). Significantly, the International Federation of Trade Unions, not the ILO, tried and failed to create an International Office on Migration (Brown 1926). The failure to have any agreement on migration meant that it was no longer a stimulus for employers, governments, and labor unions in different states to work together as it had been before 1914. Nor, in contrast to the hopes of the pre–World War I period, was there any uniformity between states. Almost all national social welfare legislation was introduced by each nation separately. The result has been a maze of differing regulations on pensions, health insurance, work safety, workers compensation, and a host of other rights. Despite all the progress for labor, social citizenship was dramatically redefined during the interwar years in ways that many labor activists and reformers before World War I would have found disappointing.

World War I itself had begun redirecting reformers and labor leaders toward national policies and away from internationalism. Between 1914 and 1918, the enormous pressures on working women, families, and labor organizations to support the war effort meant that close involvement with national policies was an absolute necessity in order to protect social welfare. After the war, reformers sought to build on this involvement in order to increase social welfare (Pedersen 1993; Alber 1981; Wall and Winter 1988; Feldman 1966; McMillan 1988). The postwar recession, the battles over reparations and the Ruhr occupation, and the effects of inflation also made it extremely difficult for reformers and labor leaders in different countries to work together. Further, the Great Depression soon preoccupied labor leaders. What little goodwill survived was nearly destroyed by the multiple conflicts over fascism and communism (Sturmthal 1943). As early as 1937, even a determined partisan of the ILO described the institution as an "unregarded revolution" at best (Gibberd 1937).

Meanwhile, even within democratic countries in the interwar era, social citizenship came to be defined in terms that were much narrower than what had seemed possible before the war. Behind this change during the 1920s and 1930s lay the power that interest groups other than labor won in both labor policy and social welfare legislation (Strikwerda 1990; Luebbert 1991; Esping-Andersen 1985). The effect of other groups desiring protection was most often to make social welfare policy nationalistic. A growing literature presents the rise of the welfare state as the most significant development in democratic societies in the early twentieth century. Yet the welfare state was only one part of what can be better understood as the protectionist state, a part that incidentally helped labor and consumers but was designed for many other purposes as well. It is striking that labor, despite the increase in its power after the war, often had less to do with the creation of national labor policy than did other interest groups—big business, the lower middle class, farmers, and the state bureaucracy.

Even before World War I, the arguments against imported goods, foreign investments, and multinational companies had attracted the support of groups, such as the lower middle classes and farmers, who suffered from the economic cycles and harsh competition in a capitalist system. Nationalist opposition to international economic integration was a convenient way for these groups to express their grievances against social and economic change under the legitimacy of patriotism (Mommsen 1981). If the benefits of economic integration were eventually to be enjoyed and, even more important, if economic justifications were not to be harnessed to the desire for war, these groups' grievances would have to be answered. While the late nineteenth century was the era of labor's mobilization, the 1920s and

1930s saw the mobilization of the lower middle class. Shopkeepers, farmers, small businessmen, self-employed artisans, and white-collar workers
successfully demanded the protection of the home market and their own
economic positions as a price for granting any protection or social welfare
for workers. Belgian, French, and German shopkeepers won special treatment under social security and labor laws and controls on competition,
which have survived in many cases down to the present (Caestecker 1993,
144–89; Baldwin 1990, 160–66). Big business was not far behind. Although big business had mobilized earlier, only in the twenties and thirties
did its close relation with the state (which has characterized much of the
European economy ever since) develop (Maier 1975). In France, Andrew
Shonfield (1965, 82) writes, "[i]t was during the period after the First
World War that the so-called 'mixed enterprise,' i.e. a partnership of private and public capital, made its début on a large scale." The close connections between business federations and governments over economic
planning, fiscal policy, and investment that have characterized the post-
1945 period all began in the interwar era (Katzenstein 1985; Shonfield
1965, 231; Hall 1986, 53–55). The decisive changes in interest-group
politics in the 1930s, furthermore, began a process that continued in the
late 1940s. As Western European states, both before and after World War
II, broke with notions of liberal economic orthodoxy, they instituted a new
kind of politics in which economic interest groups laid claim to protection
and minimum levels of social welfare (Weir and Skocpol 1985; Gourevitch
1986). In spite of market forces with their globalizing tendencies, national
states formulated the great bulk of social welfare policy with the goal, first
of all, of satisfying their constituents who were wary of the international
economy.

The European Community's Tentative Integration

In most accounts, the formation of the European Coal and Steel Community (ECSC) and the Common Market marks a decisive change. States began
to put aside their jealously held sovereignty and work toward internationalism. By comparison with the international economy of the pre-1914 era,
however, what is striking is how selective the European states actually were
in integrating their economies during the 1950s and 1960s.

   European integration, at least in its early years, represents the first triumph in institutionalizing internationalism and, at the same time, as Alan
Milward (1992) argues, the "rescue of the nation-state." The decisive
growth in national, as opposed to international, policy making in the interwar period set the stage for how European unity developed after 1945.
Rather than a return to the trend toward internationalism as in the pre–

World War I era, the Common Market created a set of state-to-state policies that left intact most of the protectionism and specifically national
policies of the 1920s and 1930s. Trade barriers between states were lowered, and subsidies were offered to certain groups across borders, but little
was done to encourage groups such as labor to see their interests as international. What we see today in the European Union is in many ways a painful
process of trying to undo the earlier decisions to preserve the national
policies of the interwar era (Coombes 1974; Freeman 1986). In this sense,
European integration, with its lowered tariffs and its agricultural subsidies
across borders, was the exception rather than the rule: a small arena where
governments agreed to give up a portion of their autonomy. The ambiguous
development of European integration makes a powerful argument for how
governments, in response to interest groups, have dictated the course of
economic change.

The European Coal and Steel Community of 1951 set a precedent in
creating an international institution but strictly limiting integration. The
ECSC did not encourage labor migration or common standards of labor
regulation, except indirectly because the industries in the member countries were selling at common prices. Proponents of European unity merely
tinkered with the system set up in the interwar period. They revived very
little of the pre-1914 era (Milward 1984, 126–67, 362–95; Gillingham
1991, 313–71). Looked at in a longer perspective, the ECSC drew more
from the interwar cartels than from the pre-1914 era. Prices and production were now strictly regulated as they had been under cartels, but national
cartels no longer had the power to struggle with each other behind the
scenes (Couthéoux 1960; Swann 1988). Raw materials and finished products were permitted to move freely, but this was done primarily in order
to make German heavy industry once again interdependent with a larger
European economy, not to create integration in all sectors. Capital and
labor, which had also moved across borders in the pre–1914 system, were
confined within states under the ECSC. The deep involvement of governments in heavy industry to protect employment also led the Common Market to prevent any re-creation or expansion of multinationals in iron and
steel (Hayward 1974).

Meanwhile, welfare state policy made European governments reluctant to
allow freer labor migration or to internationalize labor policy. Even the
United Kingdom, which had a longer tradition of liberal state policies
towards migration and was not part of European economic integration,
adopted state control over nonnationals in the labor market for the first
time (Kay and Miles 1992, 161–62). It is seldom recognized that the Common Market created economic integration in the sense of lowering tariffs,
but it, too, left intact much of the bewildering variety of national laws on
the right to work, invest, practice professions, and move capital (Swann

1988, 131–68; Milward 1992, 1–45). In its inception, the Common Market was more cautious about introducing the free movement of labor than it was about the free movement of goods. The Treaty of Rome mandated the lowering of tariffs beginning in 1959. Not until 1970 was there to be genuine free movement of labor. The actual process of legal equalization allowed the major provisions of labor movement to be put in place in 1968, a year and a half earlier than planned. The preference for nationals over foreigners from within the European Community was prohibited, and inter-Community workers no longer needed work permits. Nevertheless, workers were guaranteed residence only if they had a job; migration to seek employment was still strictly regulated. Workers could only move with complete freedom to another state if they already had a job offer (Bousearen 1969). Today, unemployed workers in the European Union still usually have only ninety days in which to look for work in another state (Hollifield 1992, 259). Furthermore, the European Union's freedom of movement applies only to a sector that has been declining as a proportion of the workforce for decades, that is, generally less-skilled industrial or service workers. Government employment, which takes up as much as one-quarter of the workforce in some countries, is still restricted to nationals.

Most critically, Articles 117 and 118 of the Treaty of Rome, which called for harmonization of social policy, have remained unfulfilled (Swann 1988). Until the 1990s, it was not even clear that workers who had worked in more than one European Community country could be certain that their pension rights in both countries were protected. In 1994, the European Court of Justice ruled that when governments deal with workers who have rights in more than one country's social security system, they must take account of the other country's regulations (*Frontier-Free Europe* 1994b, 2).

The new European institutions were possible only because the position of key interest groups and the relationship between governments and big business had changed greatly with the rise of the welfare state and social democracy. One aspect of this reorientation of European politics is that farmers and the lower middle class now have less temptation to turn to economic nationalism as a vehicle for their discontent with capitalism and industrialization. The European Community's Common Agricultural Policy and the myriad of regulations protecting small commerce have helped to ensure that a new Pan-German League or Action française would arise only with difficulty. Yet the price of winning support for integration from these groups has been high. For decades, the nationalistic and protectionistic aspects of the social welfare legislation of the interwar era have prevented social citizenship from being broadened or internationalized. The powerful voice of interest groups in national governments means that internationalizing social welfare is a much more complicated process. As Milward (1992) points out, the first breakthrough for government protection of industry, the lower middle class, and labor came after World War I, but the post–World War II era saw a large expansion of government intervention in the economy. It was during the 1940s through the 1960s that government expenditure as a percentage of the economy reached its height.

Social welfare, together with migration, has been the battleground for Europeans wrestling with their own identity. What is most striking is the very slow emergence of any larger notion of citizenship in Europe, given that some integration has been occurring for several decades (Leibfried and Pierson 1994). As Elizabeth Meehan (1993) has argued, neither the European Community, original founders nor its representative institutions have moved to create a European citizenship. Ironically, the European Court of Justice, moving in a fashion similar to the U.S. Supreme Court, has acted to force member states to consider rights as European, not simply national. It has most clearly done so, she continues, in defending and broadening the rights of immigrants. Just as before 1914, migration is today often a key to internationalizing social citizenship. In case after case, the European Court has decided that except in a few circumstances, European states may not deny benefits to, impose restrictions on, or withhold rights from foreigners who are citizens of other member states. Even immigrants from outside the European Community are protected by the European Community's charter, although they still cannot claim full legal rights.

A New View of Integration

One can draw a number of lessons from Europe's discontinuous history of integration. Despite theoretical perspectives to the contrary, economic integration has not been inevitable. Without political coalitions to allocate the benefits of integration and to ameliorate its disadvantages, integration can be derailed, regardless of the economic logic behind it. The precocious economic integration before 1914 and its curtailment by World War I point to the crucial importance of the state in shaping economic change. The European economy moved toward integration in a halting fashion dictated by politics and war; indeed, in the importance of exports in relation to GNP, the free flow of persons, and level of international direct investment, Europe is only now in our day moving towards the level of economic integration that was prevalent before 1914 (Bairoch 1989; Strikwerda 1993b).

Internationalism has a complicated relationship with economic integration. A sense of international social citizenship had some success only where the international economy created clear connections between societies and where leaders built on those connections. In many ways, international social citizenship failed to develop in the interwar period for many of the same reasons why European integration after World War II has come so slowly and in such a limited fashion. Economic integration was stunted in the interwar era, and after 1945 was encouraged only in certain selective areas. By integrating the European economy so selectively, the ECSC and Common Market helped limit the internationalism that might have grown up along with integration. The social welfare state, despite what many of its pioneers hoped, was allowed to develop strictly along national lines. Although the European Community has been an impressive institutional achievement, it has been extremely cautious about encouraging exactly those cross-border relationships between interest groups that were the essence of internationalism before 1914. Only in the late 1980s did Europe-wide organizations of employers, labor unions, and consumers become well organized and fully recognized by the European Community (Visser and Ebbinghaus 1992).

Yet the history of integration and internationalism also shows that more than one avenue to the future is possible. It may well be possible to stimulate a sense of European social citizenship if workers, consumers, women, and immigrants are included in the emerging transnational organizations of the next century. Significantly, the part of the Maastricht Treaty that concerned social policy for the new European Union had as its first mandate the creation of works councils in multinational enterprises throughout the EU by 1996. A new, broader definition of social citizenship, one that might borrow from the more complex and open definition prevalent in the late nineteenth century, is still possible, but it would require a difficult reorientation of social policy and a rethinking of the past.

Notes

1. Widely known as the "1992" plan, Delors's program, instituted as the Single European Act of 1986, was actually designed to be in effect on 1 January 1993. Delors was president of the European Commission, the governing body of commissioners over the European Community who are appointed by the member states.

2. "The 1880s ushered in an era (until 1914) of increased protectionism and reduced economic integration" (Overturf 1986, 6).

3. Numbers taken from "Mines et fonderies" 1915, 563–67; "Mines et usines" 1915, 852–54; Chambre syndicale française des mines métallurgiques 1912, 188–96. See also Hillman 1911, 89–95, 112.

4. "L'alliance provisoire franco-allemande-luxembourgeoise" 1906.

4

Citizenship and Nationality in Nineteenth-Century France

Gérard Noiriel and Michel Offerlé

Discussing with an English-speaking public the relationship between *citoyenneté* and *nationalité* in nineteenth-century France presents several difficulties. These two terms, which are encompassed by the English word "citizenship," are not easily translatable; they are not univocal in French, nor does either refer unproblematically to only one word in English. Moreover, the juridical, social, and intellectual history of these words is rooted in different constructions from those found in, for example, the United Kingdom or the United States. We will therefore be using the term "citizenship" (*citoyenneté*) in the restricted sense of civic citizenship (possession of political rights) and "nationality" (*nationalité*) in the sense of a bond uniting individuals (nationals) to a particular state.

In studying the manner in which civic citizenship and French nationality were constructed during the nineteenth century, we synthesize the research, both completed and in progress, of others and ourselves on these questions. We also note the way in which a link between these two notions—which are rarely thought about together—was established in France. Indeed, the right to nationality created a defined, delimited space in which only French nationals could take political action and benefit from the social rights that were granted to them, beginning with the Third Republic (1870–1940). Through this analysis of how the two notions became linked, we encounter once again the more general problems of the construction of the state and of state control over society (*étatisation*) through the concrete mechanisms structuring the institutionalization of citizenship and nationality. We conclude with reflections on the double meaning of the term "national": national as opposed to foreign, and national meaning unified over the whole of French territory.

The Nationalization of Civic Citizenship

In retrospect, the meaning of civic citizenship seems obvious enough. When the idea of the individual was proclaimed in the late eighteenth century, it was assumed that everything would ultimately fall into place, notwithstanding a few occasional setbacks; civic citizenship would, in the end, be accomplished: one man, one vote, one opinion. The point here is not to deny the importance, recently underscored by Pierre Rosanvallon, of the debates, discussions, and decisions that followed the establishment of universal suffrage.

> During the first half of the nineteenth century, to speak of that period only, the principle of universal suffrage was far from universally accepted. Liberal elites viewed it as a menace, for it meant the passions of the masses would enter the political arena. Conservatives were suspicious that it would lead to social disorder and change. Socialists feared that the masses brutalized by hard labor and alienated from religion had lost the capacity for independent thinking. The few republicans who believed in it did so out of the faith of the Carbonari. Over many years, then, doubts and questions about the political usefulness and philosophical validity of the extension of the right to vote to all individuals were thus central to intellectual life as well as to political debates. (Rosanvallon 1992, 12)

Hence the importance of the central question: how to handle rationally the large numbers involved in universal suffrage? In fact, then, once the "law of numbers" had been invoked, everything remained to be done.

Mechanisms had to be established to organize elections and measures taken to encourage voters to perform their electoral duty. The attempt to understand the rise of the citizen-voter raises such issues as how those who were citizens were identified and invites an analysis of the various incentives for them to vote. It was in this process of identification that the state experimented with bureaucratic technologies for classifying individuals; that the relationship between the act of voting and daily life took form; that the impact and limits of voting, in comparison with other forms of citizenship, were determined; and that the obligation to be French, the advantages of being French, and the feeling of being French were developed.

Drawing on earlier works, we emphasize three methods used to define the "people": (1) shaping an electoral body, that is, establishing lists of voters and cards that provided those who had the right to vote with the means to do so; (2) making people into voters, that is, encouraging people to vote; and (3) creating electorates, that is, establishing groups of voters whose opinions could be analyzed by commentators. Thus, we find reunited in tendency, though to differing degrees according to individuals, the three conditions resulting from the mobilization of citizen-voters: "individualiza-tion, politicization, nationalization" (Lancelot 1985).

Shaping an Electoral Body

There exists no tabula rasa in history. Indeed, the problems arising from the distribution and composition of an electoral body had already been raised during the previous political regimes. Nevertheless, it was only after the revolution of February 1848 that the government found itself urgently confronted by these problems.

Article 6 of the decree dated 5 March 1848 stipulated that "all French citizens 21 years of age or over, with at least six months residence, whose civic rights ha[d] not been suspended by a court of law, [were] considered to be voters." Although not explicitly specified, residence in a commune was implied. In order to establish electoral lists within a few weeks, it was necessary to identify voters and their places of residence, and this process had to be as universal and ethically sound as the act of voting itself.

By then, the establishment of lists—of indigents, taxpayers, and con-scripts, for example—was already common practice. While these models and the information they contained served as a basis for establishing elec-toral lists, the latter posed specific problems: Should they be regarded as a form of recruitment (a military-type enrollment) or as the granting of a claim to a right (an option left to the initiative of each eligible person)? How could the national character of the right to vote and the abstract idea of citizenship be reconciled with local registration? Were the voter's rights to be recognized by the commune and was individual reputation to serve as the basis for identification, or would such identification be verified by the presentation of identification papers, in a period when their use remained limited?

The administrative capacities of the mayors charged with the task were uneven, right up to the end of the century. These mayors, elected or ap-pointed depending on the period, were representatives of the state and, at the same time, spokespersons for their communities.[1] The familiar simpli-fied vision of a French state piloting change from the center must be re-placed by a sociological analysis of the state. Such an analysis emphasizes that even within regimes such as the Second Empire and the *ordre moral,* the state is a socially constructed social relation. Institutional analyses of the state too often obscure what ought properly to be the social historian's concern: the study of the transactions that constitute the daily work of what we call the state. To the extent that central state administrators such as prefects sought to control "their" mayors, the mayors held them hostage to the authority of the voters. And if the mayors directed the municipal councils and "their" communes, they were no less constrained by the daily tensions and power relations in which they were embedded than were the central state administrators.

To establish a list, to determine locally who qualified as a citizen and who did not therefore entailed three partially contradictory types of logic: a bureaucratic logic of legally defining the rightful claimant, a political logic ("to control these lists is to control the elections"), and a logic of communally recognizing the voter. Civic citizenship, then, was the outcome of the gradual, but never complete, rise of juridical control (juridicization) and, therefore, of the efficiency of a neutral "state" in producing rational identification techniques and standardized social identities (Noiriel 1991, 1993). This juridicization implied a restriction of the territory of the then-current "state as electoral entrepreneur," which arbitrarily eliminated its opponents by denying them registration, resorting to surreptitious invalidation, and making access to registration costly in time or money.

It also implied a simultaneous disappearance of the activist elements within a local community that might exert pressure on community authorities to increase the central state's political exclusions, reverse them, or alter their significance. What, for instance, do we really know about the exclusions and self-exclusions of those for whom local ruling forces sought to deny electoral participation—illiterates, idiots, marginals, or "individuals from elsewhere"? Conversely, how much do we know about the presence on the lists of those who were not legally entitled to be there—minors, convicts, foreigners, fictional residents? In this respect, local political personnel, elected or appointed according to the political regime and the size of the commune, had strategic importance. Indeed, the mayor and local notables stood at the juncture of the three types of logic we have mentioned: they were at the same time representatives of the central state, small political entrepreneurs tied to regional political parties and factions, and spokesmen for the local community they represented and administered.

The process of identifying with the "imagined" community of the nation was channeled through local establishments, but it simultaneously undermined them; this process of "dis-embedding," to borrow Karl Polanyi's expression, individuals from community structures was both long and ambivalent. It implied the resolution of the task of identifying, and establishing the legal residence of, the citizen-voter.

There were two ways to prove that an individual fitted within a category that entitled him to the right of civil citizenship, two ways that might complement or contradict each other. First, the mayors and the voters might use existing administrative documents to verify characteristics such as age, nationality, residence, and legal impediments to voting (for example, criminal conviction).[2] Thus, in 1848 and later, those wishing to register to vote were required to prove their eligibility by producing "papers." Those who did not have an appropriate identification card were asked to produce other documents, such as a worker's booklet (up to 1890), commuter train ticket, passport, military record, certificate of good behavior or satisfactory discharge from a job, mayor's attestation, or extract from the birth register (Noiriel 1993; Offerlé 1993a, 1993b). The historical record about these diverse practices is hard to trace.

Also difficult to ascertain is the extent to which the second method of identifying those eligible to vote and verifying their place of residence—older forms like reputation, communal recognition, or testimony by witnesses—still lingered, and how frequently it was used.

Indeed, the two methods were often mixed, as can be seen when we look at the process of verifying the domicile of the voter. For technical reasons, one had to have a domicile somewhere, otherwise, voters might move from place to place in order to influence particular elections. But how to verify this? Domicile was the cause of many controversies, not only because political and administrative authorities might intervene to challenge a voter but also because there were many other social actors—neighbors, postmen, concierges, employers, landlords, to name a few—all of whom could testify about the would-be voter's domicile in the community for the required period. This demonstrates that civil citizenship has always been local, and it is at the local level that one can trace the progressive adoption of the practices described above by potential voters and notables.

The tension about residence was apparent in the last great parliamentary debate on the municipal law of July 30 1874, in which male suffrage became the rule of the game of French democracy, one might say, despite itself. The debate was the last effort of the parliamentary Right to limit suffrage, or at least exclude from the vote those sections of the population that it most feared. It did succeed in retaining a distinction between political citizenship (eligibility to vote in national elections after six months' residence) and eligibility to vote in municipal elections (after one or two years' residence). This distinction was eliminated in laws passed in 1884 and 1886.

Thus ended the long legal debate (begun before 1848) between, on the one hand, those who would restrict access to citizenship, if not to individuals owning property, at least to individuals with a territorial or communal identification and, on the other hand, those who considered the vote a right attached to the individual person. Even among republicans, the link to national civil citizenship passed through local citizenship. The process of identifying with the "imagined" community of the nation was channeled through local institutions but simultaneously undermined them. It was at the local level that the individual's relation to politics and to public policy was constructed, the rules of citizenship were put into practice, and people were brought to recognize the advantage of being French.

Making People into Voters

How could citizens be made to become citizens, or in other words, how could they be encouraged to register and vote? For even if we consider universal suffrage to be the result of a "demand" or a popular "conquest," the fact remains that for large sectors of the population, becoming a voter was not an obvious benefit. Self-esteem, dignity, and protest would become reasons for voting only later on, once the citizen's "role" had become naturalized and fully internalized, and once the process of politicization (in the broadest sense of the word) had taken place.

Despite the peaceful images of republican historiography, the act of voting was more a mystery than a self-evident fact. To draw on the tripartite heuristic of James D. Wright (1981), the "assenters" to citizenship could probably be said to have been in the majority, compared to "dissenters" and "consenters." Léon Gambetta made this point very clearly when he declared that those who have the right to vote must be made to understand the "relationship of that act of the citizen to all the functions of the State." The citizen must learn the "importance of that piece of paper" and "how, by his choice, his vote, he influences taxes, teachers, the army, war, the system of justice, liberty, schools, and the autonomy of the municipality, or the department. Only then will all understand the great secret of democratic politics."

Indeed, to make the connection between one's daily life and a piece of paper slipped into a box is far from automatic. Nor is it easy to learn to be patient, to express one's grievances or hopes only on defined occasions, often distant in time from one another. It is as difficult to limit these claims to the choice of a ballot as it is to vote for someone who is likely to be unfamiliar. This opacity of citizenship must be neither exaggerated nor minimized; it probably varied greatly from one place to another, according to social class, and among different social agents. Politicians worried as much about protest mobilization through the ballot as about abstention; they often feared crowds or scorned them.[3] They learned only gradually to comply with the requirements of democracy, and at the same time, they helped familiarize people with the citizen's trade.

Although indoctrination in voting and calls to vote by schools, by the press, and by the church were standard practice, learning to vote was not simply a question of taking lessons; it implied repeated experience of the act of voting itself. Repetition is habit forming, and the multiplicity of electoral stakes with immediate, local significance were themselves an incentive to vote. The "domestication of the voter," however, was neither unilateral nor equal for all. Increasingly, during phases marked by the direct exercise of citizenship understood both as a right and a responsibility, professional politicians constantly sought to invent new technologies for rallying the vote. By making people into voters, through canvassing techniques or the creation of political organizations, politicians made themselves eligible, through their legitimate claim to represent others, for the electoral offices they aspired to. To produce voters was, therefore, to invent a specific political sphere, disembedded from the social sphere and yet inscribed, through a different set of rules, in the field of social relations. To produce voters was to produce agents willing to express an interest in electoral races. Thus, to borrow the expression of the republican leader Léon Gambetta, the importance of the "little square of paper"—the ballot—would be recognized once voters made the connection between politics and their own everyday lives.

It is, therefore, not surprising to note that the spreading exercise of citizenship made it necessary both to invent abstract political programs and to reappropriate traditional means of social exchange. The electoral transaction was based on what we propose to designate by the term "political goods," exchanged within the framework of elections. One type of political goods was private property (belonging to the candidate), divisible or indivisible (attributable to a particular individual or to groups of individuals). These goods might involve money, bribes, promises of private employment, favors, threats, or sanctions. Another type of political goods—the one that, according to the democratic credo, forms the legitimate manner of conquering votes—was public goods held in the exercise of a mandate, divisible (public assistance, personal favors, decorations, administrative or elective positions, or threats of discharge) or indivisible. The ideal typical opposition between private and public political goods corresponds to that between two types of political personnel, differentiated by the kinds of resources they could invest in the exchange: at one extreme were the local notables who reactivated connections with their clientele; at the other extreme, the candidates with fewer resources, who invented a connection to the voter based on the disembedding of politics, as compared to everyday political relations, and imposed a relationship of virtuous citizenship. In becoming politicians, candidates of the latter type were delegitimizing the earlier forms of transaction based on private goods, which came to be rejected as deviant and, eventually, labeled corruption.

The citizen gradually became an ideally desocialized individual, who was expected to break with his community-based loyalties in order to exercise citizenship properly. Clearly, as Alain Garrigou (1992) has argued, the rules imposed to moralize universal suffrage and the devices introduced for its proper performance (for example, the anonymous envelope and the voting booth) were not simply techniques; they were an integral part of the process that culminated in the autonomy of the citizen. As such, they should be regarded as instrumental in consolidating the new relationship between voter and representative and clearing the way for a truly political exchange within the framework of an austere ritual: a democratic bubble cut off from the world, governed by its own set of rules. The contact with the legal system (the electoral code) and with the devices present in the voting hall gave this newly created citizenship an objective dimension, undermining the enchanted world of community-based, face-to-face relationships.

Yet the transition was slow, and patronage relationships, often too simplistically associated with archaism, served on numerous occasions as a foundation for practices intended to develop voting habits among individuals. The paths of citizen construction and transactions lacked the lovely linear quality of republican mythologies. Instead, voters learned to bargain in exchange for their votes and make use of their function as the dominated group. The overly facile dichotomy between the spontaneously politicized city and the apolitical countryside should therefore be reexamined.

Creating Electorates

Historians of politics have long debated the issue of classifying votes, which has become a somewhat systematic exercise in source criticism. What they have often overlooked is that such disagreements notwithstanding, it is the very operation of classification that must be questioned. The production of national electoral statistics presupposes the resolution of a great many problems, in particular that of the equivalence of votes. Establishing such equivalence requires that each vote be extracted from its source and rationale, combined with other votes nationwide, and used to construct "electorates," that is, enduring numerical units that represent political families. Just as combining the total coal production in the north of France with that of the Cévennes in the south to arrive at a single figure presented difficulties, so counting votes, an operation that fulfilled the nationalization of the citizen and made it an objective reality, was not simple. The act of producing a global figure amounted to attributing to a myriad of varied and geographically dispersed voters a single motive for supporting interchangeable candidates subsumed under one entity, the political party; the party, in turn, could capitalize on these equally interchangeable votes. The number rendered real thus provides the evidence: the Socialist party received five million votes; thus there are five million Socialist voters, and vice versa. This form of analysis presumes a set of practices involving a group of actors, and disconnects the voters and their votes from any local context.

At the same time, it rests on the many efforts of politicians who sought to rationalize the election market by coordinating their party organization across the national territory. This coordination—which included uniform electoral propaganda (newspapers, posters, national party programs), control and distribution of candidacies, organization of elected officials in parliamentary groups, and national aggregation of votes—emerged most strongly at the end of the nineteenth century, particularly among the Social-ists. From the time of their first victories, the Socialists demanded that the equivalence of votes across the country be recognized; they constructed their party by defining and identifying their electorate (Offerlé 1988). Simi-larly, in the press and in the statistical imagination, an image was consti-tuted which either adopted models of graphic or cartographic objectification or invented new ones to classify the raw numbers. The de-bate about what the voters, grouped in electorates, always aligned on a left-to-right axis, meant by their votes thus came to involve the press, and then the first political scientists, whose investigations were often carried out in coooperation with the politicians.

The state, as well, sought to observe and homogenize public opinion. In a process parallel to that by which the parties, press, and politicians publicly demonstrated model citizenship, the state itself began to classify and explain the vote. The prefects, following instructions from the central authorities, came to use standardized reporting forms to demonstrate their expertise in divining public opinion (*esprit public*) (Phélippeau 1993).[4]

In all these efforts, voter opinion was seen as closely connected to the characteristics of the person elected (Siegfried [1913] 1979). Gradually, the analysts came to consider the voter as holding an opinion that he identi-fied with a national political party label associated with a candidate. Elector-ates came into being. From this time on, one had to make these electorates speak and act like a single individual, even though the practical knowledge of both scholars and politicians suggested that being a citizen involved mul-tiple meanings and acts. Tables, graphs, and electoral maps substantiated the new, counterintuitive ideas that although in reality French voters were diverse and spread throughout the national territory, a French citizen-voter, whose opinion could be explained, did in fact exist: "one man, one vote, one opinion."

Immigration and the Social Construction of Nationality

Broadly speaking, it can be said that by the beginning of the twentieth century, despite much variation in levels of participation and other factors, the nationalization of civic citizenship was an established fact. In other words all social groups in France had undergone a process of integration into the national polity. The precociousness of this process in France, com-pared to its development in other national states, is a key factor in explain-ing why foreign immigration took on such great importance.[5] Indeed, from the mid-nineteenth century onward, peasants represented the most numer-ically important group of voters; they were hence able to use their votes as political leverage to block those industrial transformations that potentially threatened their interests. Furthermore, most of them owned their lands, or controlled them under secure tenure, which further enhanced their ability to resist. The immediate consequence of this was that large industrial firms, faced with a shortage of available hands, turned to neighboring countries as a source of labor recruitment. Unlike in "new countries" such as the United States, Canada, and Australia, where immigration was above all a factor of settlement, in France it was the counterpart of civic citizenship. Large companies recruited workers from abroad who lacked economic or political resources to escape from proletarianization.

Further, there were two distinct stages in the process in France. First, industrial development under the Second Empire (1852–1870) resulted from the expansion of numerous industries to the countryside and their massive reliance on a labor force of worker–peasants. In mines, public works, and mechanized spinning mills, where work was particularly arduous, companies increasingly employed immigrants from neighboring countries—for the most part, agricultural laborers fleeing poverty back home—who took advantage of free trade and efficient new means of communication to seek jobs in France.

The second stage occurred when the economic crisis of the 1870s and the 1880s put a sudden end to this form of industrial development. In cities as well as in the countryside, hundreds of thousands of immigrant workers found themselves without jobs or income. Although they had originally been hired to perform tasks their French counterparts held in disdain, foreign workers were now viewed as competitors in the labor market. In this context, politicians used the electoral weapon to gain support from the popular classes who demanded labor protection measures.

Yet as Karl Polanyi (1957) has noted, the protectionist policies adopted in the final decades of the nineteenth century were not just a question of customs duties; they marked the triumph of an entirely new conception of democracy. On a monetary level, these protectionist measures led to a restructuring of central banks, the latter becoming the "impregnable bastions of a new nationalism." They reflected the appearance of national states of a different kind, which "expressed their identity through national currencies, guaranteed by a form of nationalism which was more jealous and absolute than anything we had known before." National currency, used as a barrier against foreigners, also became a powerful means of integrating the various sectors of society, for "the concerns of the businessman, the unionized worker and the housewife were defined more directly by the monetary policy of central banks than by any other isolated factor" (Polanyi 1957, 197–99). The same logic applies to the legal system. Social laws had an integrative effect among the various sectors of the labor force; yet at the same time, they established severe segregation of foreigners, who were explicitly excluded from the benefits they provided. This national protectionism was, of course, one of the consequences of the mobilization of nationalist parties from the 1880s onward, which at the parliamentary level produced a multitude of bills demanding that immigrant labor be taxed as heavily as foreign products. The idea spread that the French state must protect French workers, who had increasingly become wage earners living without any other source of income.

A new vision of the role of the state emerged as a direct result of the nationalization of civic citizenship. If the economic crisis of the 1880s had such powerful political impact, it was because citizens from every social class and every region of France could make themselves heard through the voice of their elected representatives. Finding remedies for social suffering became a vital necessity for politicians unwilling to lose their jobs. The measures adopted by the republican state were aimed not only at citizens (French adult males) but also at individuals with French nationality, including women and children. Legislation intended to protect the national labor market, such as the social laws laws passed under the Third Republic, introduced a clear discrimination, unknown before, between French nationals and foreigners.

Under the Second Empire, social legislation, such as the law of 1850 concerning mutual benefit societies, had not mentioned foreigners. The regulations establishing the conditions for receiving assistance had varied from one city to another, but the principal criterion of eligibility had most often been length of residence in the commune. In contrast, the important social legislation of the Third Republic, such as the law of 1898 on workplace accidents or that of 1910 on pensions for workers and peasants, contained clauses that explicitly excluded or penalized foreign workers. Only workers from states that had signed reciprocal agreements with France regarding the rights of the two countries' respective citizens could benefit, and then only partially. The distinction between French nationals and foreigners remained a fundamental feature of the French social formation. The triumph of the French conception of nationality was closely linked, then, to the emergence of *social* citizenship. The state made use of the same technologies that had formerly been used to construct civic citizenship. The parliament passed laws defining the categories of rightful claimants, and these laws were implemented with the support of a vast administrative campaign to identify the individuals involved.

The central category now was not the citizen but the national. For the first time, legal scholars established a clear distinction between "citizenship," understood as the right to participate in public life, and "nationality," understood as the allegiance of an individual to a particular state. The first French law on nationality was adopted, after seven years of parliamentary debate, in 1889. It explicitly defined nationality as the legal bond tying an individual to the state and established specific criteria for distinguishing between nationals and foreigners.

Henceforward, by virtue of the aforementioned bond, the state was obligated to defend its nationals against people defined as foreigners. But how were the French to be identified? In the latter part of the nineteenth century, the question of how to implement the new nationality law became one of the most crucial stakes in political debates on the issue of immigration. Indeed, until the beginning of the Third Republic, the identities of foreigners working in France were not officially registered anywhere, in any form. From the eighties onward, this situation suddenly became the object of violent criticism. When, in 1893, a law finally required foreign workers to identify themselves to the local administration, it was no coincidence that the law was officially defined as a measure to protect the labor market. Mayors and police commissioners would register only those foreigners who could provide written proof of their identity—for example, a birth certificate—and a document attesting to their employment in France.[6]

Police reports found in departmental and national archives testify to the difficulties that the public authorities encountered in applying these measures. Although, up to then, especially in the rural world, identification of individuals depended on the traditional method of intracommunity knowledge, the new legislation imposed "paper identities." It was only at this moment that many immigrants discovered the spelling of their own names. Many of them, longtime residents of France, did not consider themselves— and were not considered by their neighbors or those with whom they worked—to be "foreigners." Only with the application of the republican laws did they discover their "nationality." The registration system allowed the French state to control and channel migratory flows.

Compared with the identification techniques applied to French voters, the ones elaborated in the late nineteenth century to identify foreigners were quite complex. Identification required cooperation between the central state and local authorities. In order to register a foreigner, the mayor or police commissioner prepared two separate forms. The first was to be carried by the immigrant at all times and systematically presented to the police if asked for verification of identity. The second was sent by the mayor to the Ministry of the Interior (in Paris); there all the documents emanating from the various French communes were centralized and filed, providing the state with a crucial weapon for the struggle against illegal immigration. These bureaucratic procedures, which culminated in the invention of the national identity card during World War I, allowed the state, in times of crisis, to deny entry into the country to foreigners in search of work. In periods of economic expansion, however, these procedures could also facilitate immigration and channel the labor force toward those sectors and regions where the labor pool was insufficient. This is precisely what occurred in France from the 1890s onward, when industry entered a new phase of expansion.

In conclusion, it is important to note that innovations such as the procedures for establishing nationality and its documentation had more general consequences than those directly related to immigration. Indeed, the very fact of being considered a "national" in one's own country implies that one becomes a "foreigner" by simply crossing the border. This explains why the establishment of identification papers became standard practice throughout Europe and beyond. The example of passports is significant in this regard. Until the nineteenth century, passports were considered simply travel documents. They could be issued by a variety of different authorities—mayors, prefects, mutual aid society officials. States did not then have the exclusive prerogative to grants passports to their own nationals. In 1831, for example, during the Warsaw insurrection, the French ambassador delivered passports to Polish rebels fleeing Russian repression. But in the twentieth century, particularly following World War I, the passport became a national identification document in its own right. This revolution in identification created another problem, that of refugees who, by definition, had no passport. International organizations would have to find new ways of providing identification to those who were not identified by and with a state.

At the end of the nineteenth century, most of the developed countries took protectionist measures to resolve the contradiction between an international economic market and a political space confined within the borders of a national state. Today, many of these protectionist measures have disappeared, but not those concerning population. The latter have become one of the prime principles of modern states. The development of "social citizenship" presupposes a separation between and among individuals, a separation constructed by states and by the technologies that make it possible to safeguard the interests of the best-protected group: nationals.

Notes

1. In the years from 1831 to 1848, mayors were appointed in all communes. After 1848, they were appointed only in communes of six thousand inhabitants or more and in departmental capitals; from 1871 to 1882, only in communes of twenty thousand inhabitants or more and in the prefectures. After 1882, all mayors were elected by the municipal councils. The councils themselves were elected by limited suffrage from 1831 to 1848, and by "universal [male] suffrage" (temporarily limited in 1850 and 1874) thereafter.

2. In the early period, registration was accomplished by the mayor or through a formal complaint by the voter that he was not registered or that his name had been illegally removed from the voting list. The law of 1884 on voter registration

continued this system, but opened the possibility for voters who paid taxes in a commune to register there if they so requested.

3. See the iconography of voting during the entire period preceding 1900.

4. See also on this subject series FIC III, Archives nationales, and the literature concerning the interpretation of nonvoting and *non-représentées* votes (abstentions, spoiled ballots, and votes for defeated candidates) in the nineteenth century.

5. By the end of the nineteenth century, there were nearly a million foreign laborers in France, roughly 15 percent of the total working class.

6. Later, each immigrant worker would also be required to show an authorization to reside on French territory, granted by the Ministry of the Interior after a Labor Ministry investigation to verify that no French national claimed the job.

5

Crossing Borders and Building Barriers: Migration, Citizenship, and State Building in Germany

Christiane Lemke

The rise of nation-states in Europe is closely linked with the institution of citizenship. The concept of citizenship defines an individual's legal and political status within a nation-state. It circumscribes the role of being a member of a polity. The democratic development of modern states has gradually extended citizenship status to members of the polity regardless of class, race, or gender. Or in the words of T. H. Marshall, citizenship entails the equal participation of every individual in the resources of a civilized society. Marshall (1950; 1973) described the history of the development of citizenship as three consecutive steps that became ever more complex: (1) the endowment of individuals with civil rights in the eighteenth century; (2) the addition of political rights in the nineteenth century; and (3) the institution of social rights in the twentieth century. Citizenship thus represents the principle of universal rights and equality in modern social states. Yet the definition of citizenship resulting from the distinction between natives and newcomers in a given country and the perception of who is a "foreigner" are shaped by each country's history and political culture as much as by the legal traditions of the country. Germany's legal conception of citizenship reaches back to the process of state building in the nineteenth century. With the democratic reconstruction of the Federal Republic in the wake of the Nazi era, newly introduced criteria suggested a greatly modified idea of citizenship in the modern polity. The traditional ethnocultural concept of the German nation characterized by a common history, language, and culture of the German *Volk* was supplemented with a civil concept based on individual and equal rights of citizens and modeled on liberal enlightenment traditions. As a result, two conflicting political conceptions of citizenship coexist within the postwar consensus in Germany. Thus, the current debate in Germany about citizenship and migration is as complicated as it is volatile.

Historically, Germany's conception of citizenship has been closely linked to its particular problems of state building and to the question of what it meant to be "German." Belated state building and regional fragmentation in what became the German nation-state in 1871 put an acute strain on the legal and cultural conceptions of citizenship. The emphasis upon *ethnos,* or the *völkisch* definition of what it meant to be a German citizen, reflects the struggle to define citizenship in the German tradition. Responding to national cleavages and to changes in the international system, legal regulations in Germany employed an ethnic basis rather than follow an ideal-type liberal model as envisioned by Marshall and others.[1] Three critical junctures in German history—the Imperial Wilhelmine era, the postwar democratic reconstruction of the Federal Republic of Germany, and German unification in 1990—stand out in this development. At each of these junctures, the making of "Germanness" was a primary objective of defining citizenship. In this process, liberal conceptions of citizenship and the statist reality came in conflict with each other, as the highly contentious issue of the asylum law in Germany in 1992–1993 demonstrates. The controversy about the new law on political asylum has exacerbated historical conceptions of nationhood and citizenship. It clearly demonstrates that the German debate is closely tied to the struggle of redefining postunification German identity.

German reunification after the collapse of communism occurred at about the same time that the European Union was moving to further integrate its member states, thus posing a challenge to traditional perceptions of national states. Large flows of population in the wake of the democratic revolutions in Eastern and Central Europe have generated a controversial debate about the impact of this new migratory movement on Western—and Eastern—European countries. While east-west migration is a centuries-old pattern in Europe, current migration challenges historical conceptions of citizenship rights. Modern states identify a particular set of persons as their citizens and others as noncitizens, or aliens. Consequently, the legal debate on citizenship is closely tied to discussions of social and cultural policy, and of societal tolerance. Rogers Brubaker (1992, 23) has made the point well that citizenship is not simply a legal formula but an increasingly salient social and cultural fact, and a "powerful instrument of social closure." The mutual inclusion of citizens of member states in the European Union, with its cross-cutting cleavages and multilayered foci of self- and group-identification, has simultaneously been accompanied by the exclusion of nationals from non-EU-members.

Because of Germany's role as a key actor within the European Union, German conceptions of citizenship bear great significance for reconceptualizing citizenship in the broader context of changing parameters in Europe. The struggle to redefine citizenship after Germany's unification blocked any German contribution to European efforts to conceptualize a European citizenship as envisioned in the Maastricht Treaty. As a key to a democratic Europe, the conceptualization of citizenship within the European Union is critical to participation in the integration process as well as to building a European civil society. However, European citizenship poses a challenge to the German concept of citizenship that stresses ethnolinguistic and cultural communities. Given the multiethnic and multicultural setting of the broader European territory and the necessity to readjust solidarities and loyalties on the supranational level of the EU, the ethnoculturalist foundations of the German state building process pose an even greater challenge to reconceptualizing citizenship than that faced by countries with republican or statist traditions.

Conceptualizing National Citizenship: Critical Junctures in Germany: 1913, 1949, and 1990

In Germany, state building, nation building, and democratization occurred independently from one another. The notion of citizenship (*Staatsangehörigkeit*) predates the building of the national state as well as democracy. Originally, nation and state were distinct, posing a problem for the legal framing of citizenship. In the view of contemporary legal scholars, this distinction between state and nation still existed in the postwar Federal Republic (Grawert 1973, 216). In the eighteenth and nineteenth centuries, German national identity was framed around the notion of a common culture, language, and destiny (*Kulturnation*), but it was not quite clear which territory in Central Europe Germany encompassed as a state. It was only in 1871, with the unification of the German Reich under Prussian hegemony, that a unified German state developed. The relatively high degree of fragmentation and regional disparities—especially between the Prussian northern parts and the south of Germany—and the federalist structure of the Reich made equalizing national citizenship an arduous task and prevented Germany from implementing a national citizenship law until the eve of World War I. In the context of rapid industrialization after German unification in 1871 and the rise of imperialism, Wilhelmine Germany finally codified national citizenship in the Reichs- und Staatsangehörigkeitsgesetz of 1913.

By the time the national citizenship law came to be discussed, dissatisfaction had spread widely because citizens could lose their citizenship as a result of long-term absence from Germany, a situation in which an increasing number of Germans in the colonies found themselves. Organizations with *völkisch* nationalist orientations, such as the Pan-German League, emphasized the preservation of "Germandom" abroad and called for continued privileges for the *Auslandsdeutsche,* or Germans abroad. At the same time, these nationalistic organizations feared that the Reich was being inundated with immigrants from the east, especially Poles and Jews. Because of rapid industrialization, the number of resident foreigners in the Reich had tripled between 1890 and 1910, from 430,000 to 1,260,000 (Brubaker 1992, 118). Thousands of agricultural workers entered the eastern and southern parts of Germany, and industrial workers and miners came to the Ruhr region. Antiforeigner sentiment grew stronger at the turn of the century. The focal question in the debate before the passing of the law was whether to maintain the model that citizenship in the Reich should be based on descent (*jus sanguinis*) or whether elements of the *jus soli*—the French and U.K. basis of citizenship—should be introduced, an option favored by the Social Democrats. By facilitating the preservation of citizenship by the Germans abroad, the 1913 law severed citizenship from residence status and defined citizenry clearly as a community of descent. Section 1 of the law stated, "A German is one who has citizenship in a federal state or who possesses direct imperial citizenship."[2] Citizenship was passed by descent, at first only from father to child; in 1974, mothers received equal status in passing on citizenship, and their individual rights as citizens were confirmed.

The most important feature of this law, then, is the definition of German citizenship based on the principle of blood and descent, or *jus sanguinis,* rather than on the territorial principle. This conception became the defining basis for the modern understanding of German citizenship, a principle that has endured three political ruptures in Germany. At the critical juncture of 1913, the traditional distinction between nation and state was projected onto the plane of citizenship law, inscribing an ethnocultural definition of citizenship. That decision has shaped the German discourse until today.

The Nazi government overturned Germany's federalist structure to replace it with a centralized legal system that accorded with its ideology. It changed the Reichs- und Staatsangehörigkeitsgesetz of 1913 to declare that there "is only one German citizenship," thus enhancing the importance of the central government. Numerous decrees and other modifications then introduced the racial politics of the Nazi regime. Although the racial laws were abolished in the postwar Federal Republic, the centralizing concept of one citizenship as defined by the citizenship law remained in place, both in West and East Germany.[3] The 1913 citizenship law was reintroduced in the Federal Republic of Germany (FRG), as well as in the German Democratic Republic (GDR), after the defeat of Nazism. Later, in 1967, the GDR introduced a revised citizenship law (Staatsbürgergesetz) restricting the term "citizen" to GDR German residents. In practice, the law served to legitimize undemocratic and harsh procedures such as withdrawing citizenship from dissidents on political grounds through expatriation (*Ausbürgerung*) and forcing the adoption of their children.

The year 1949 marked another watershed for the German conception of citizenship. The 1949 constitution of the Federal Republic, the Grundgesetz, or Basic Law, responded to and reflected the postwar realities of the new international order. The dismembering of the German Reich after the defeat of Nazi Germany, the mass flight of German refugees and expellees to the West, and the division of Germany resulting from the emerging Cold War once again put the "German question" of state and nationhood on the international agenda. The framers of the Basic Law envisioned the Federal Republic as only a "provisional state" until the "entire German people" could "achieve in free self-determination the unity of freedom of Germany," as the preamble states. The constitution recognized two categories of rights: general rights (including basic human and civil rights) and rights reserved to German citizens. Given the rump status of the FRG compared geographically with the German Reich, the framers recognized a certain class of rights that inhered to the quality of being German irrespective of formal state affiliation. Article 116.1 of the Basic Law therefore granted the right of repatriation to any person who had been admitted "to the territory of the German Reich within the frontiers of December 31, 1937, as a refugee or expellee of German stock [*Volkszugehörigkeit*] or as the spouse or descendent of such person." The inclusion of ethnic Germans living outside the territory of the German state has had a troubled history. During the Nazi years, German minorities in Czechoslovakia or in the Free City of Danzig, for example, provided the excuse for Hitler's government to claim and conquer these territories to incorporate them into his Reich. The atrocities of the Nazi regime before and during World War II had terrible consequences for the Germans living in the enclaves that had formed outside of the Reich over a period of several centuries. Held collectively guilty for the Nazi crimes, Germans were brutally expelled from Eastern Europe. After 1949, the stipulation in the Basic Law (*Aussiedler*) allowed Germans expelled from the Soviet Union and Eastern Europe to settle in the Federal Republic. Of the 12.5 million Germans who had fled or been expelled by 1950, two-thirds resettled in West Germany. (See table 5.1 for resettlement figures since 1950.) Originally a transitional provision defining the legal status of refugees after the war, Article 116.1 has become a "law of entry" for ethnic Germans throughout Eastern Europe and it applies to this group only.[4]

In 1950, German immigrants constituted 16.7 percent of the Federal Republic's population, and by 1960, they had increased to 23.9 percent.

Table 5.1. Ethnic German Immigrants (*Aussiedler*) to FRG

Year	N	Poland (%)	Soviet Union (%)	Czechoslovakia (%)	Romania (%)	Yugoslavia (%)	Other (%)
				Country of origin			
1950–1959	439,714	66.4	3.1	4.6	0.8	13.4	11.6
1960–1969	221,516	49.9	3.9	25.2	7.4	9.5	4.1
1970–1979	355,381	57.0	15.9	3.5	20.1	1.7	1.7
1980–1989	984,087	64.3	17.9	1.3	15.4	0.3	0.8
1990[a]	397,075	33.7	37.3	0.4	28.0	0.2	0.4
1991[a]	221,995	18.1	66.4	0.4	14.5	0.2	0.4
1992[a]	230,565	7.7	84.8	0.2	7.0	0.1	0.2
1993[a]	218,888	2.5	94.7	0.1	2.7	0.1	0.0

Source: Datenreporten (1994), 23.
[a]Since 1 November 1990, numbers are for United Germany.

During the German "economic miracle," these refugees were quickly integrated politically and economically into FRG society. Integration was assured by the Equalization of Burdens Law of 1952, which alleviated the unequal distribution of property between new German immigrants and longtime residents. The attempt to organize the expellees in a separate political organization within the emerging party system failed, but the CDU (Christian Democratic Union) and CSU (Christian Social Union) parties successfully absorbed this bloc of voters in the 1950s (Klusmeyer 1993, 86). In addition to the ethnic Germans from Eastern Europe, about 3.5 million refugees came from the German Democratic Republic after the construction of the Berlin Wall (Übersiedler) in 1961. The integration of these German refugees and expellees is one of the great success stories of postwar political development. The number of ethnic German migrants increased again sharply after 1989, amounting to 230,000 in 1992 alone. The ethnocultural concept of citizenship laid out in the Basic Law led to a policy that remains remarkably open to ethnic German immigrants from Eastern Europe and the Soviet Union, but essentially closed to non-German immigrants.

The provisions of the new postwar order provided for easy integration of ethnic Germans, but they excluded residents who were not German. The influx of large numbers of foreign workers since the mid-1960s has posed a dilemma for FRG politics, inasmuch as most of the foreign workers (formerly called *Gastarbeiter*) hope to remain in the country. Thus, while the typical "guest worker" before the mid-1960s was a single male working and contributing to the FRG social security system, foreign workers today usually live with their families and have children who were born in Germany. How much the German economy relies on foreign labor is demonstrated by the fact that despite high unemployment and recession, the number of foreign workers working and contributing to the social security system in 1993 was 2.23 million, the record high since 1972–1973 (Meier-Braun 1995, 21). However, non-EU workers have no citizenship rights and limited political rights. Political and social integration of these immigrants, especially of the Turkish minority, has failed despite repeated political attempts by the Social Democrats (SPD), by ecologists and other left-wing groups attached to the "Greens," and by the Free Democratic Party (FDP) to introduce liberal policies for permanent legal aliens. The 1.8 million Turks are Germany's largest non-German ethnic group. Other large groups are former Yugoslavians (780,000), Italians (560,000), and Greeks (337,000). In some cities such as Berlin, non-German citizens account for about 10 percent of the population. Table 5.2 shows the increase in non-German residents since 1961.

As a result of its exclusionary citizenship regulations, the FRG has one of the lowest naturalization rates in Europe. Whereas in France assimilation

Table 5.2. Non-German Residents in FRG

Year	Number (in thousands)	% of total population
1961	686.2	1.2
1970	2600.6	4.3
1987	4145.6	6.8
1989	4845.9	7.7
1990	5342.5	8.4
1991[a]	5882.3	7.3
1992[a]	6495.8	8.0

Source: Statistisches Jahrbuch der Bundesrepublik Deutschland (1994), 72.
[a]Numbers are for United Germany

and naturalization is expected, the German government has viewed naturalization as the exception. Naturalization rates are four to five times higher in France than in Germany for workers in the larger immigrant national groups and their dependents. The gap between French and German policy is even greater for second- and third-generation immigrants (Brubaker 1992, 79–80). In 1990, a revised Aliens Law (Ausländergesetz) provided for easier naturalization of second- and third-generation foreigners. Dual citizenship (*doppelte Staatsbürgerschaft*) is now more often granted by the administration. Naturalization rates have increased, especially in cities with large ethnic minorities such as Berlin and Frankfurt, but they remain low in comparison to other European countries, and assimilation continues to face high cultural, social, and economic hurdles. The Aliens Law has been widely criticized by reformers as inadequate in respect to the integration of foreigners.

At the third critical juncture, the unification of the FRG and the GDR in 1990, choices concerning citizenship regulations were shaped again by the tradition of the ethnocultural definition of citizenship. Despite the fact that the territory of the German state was now clearly defined by international law in the so-called two-plus-four settlement concerning Germany, neither the citizenship law of 1913 nor the Basic Law provision for ethnic Germans (art. 116) was annulled or revised. Article 1 of the Final Settlement with Respect to Germany (1990) states:

> The united Germany shall comprise the territory of the Federal Republic of Germany, the German Democratic Republic and the whole Berlin. Its external borders shall be the borders of the Federal Republic of Germany and the German Democratic Republic and shall be definitive from the date on which the present treaty comes into force. The confirmation of the definitive nature

of the borders of the united Germany is an essential element of the peaceful order in Europe.[5]

It is puzzling that even when the international system provided an opportunity to redefine citizenship based on statehood and territory, the peculiar German history of conceptualizing citizenship in ethnic terms continued to shape political decisions. The federal government's decision was made for two reasons. First, openness towards ethnic Germans from Eastern Europe has become an integral feature of partisan politics in the FRG. The governing CDU/CSU coalition has long enjoyed the electoral support of former expellees. Bonds with ethnic German communities and enclaves in Eastern Europe are still strong, and pressure to maintain an inclusive policy continues. (It should be noted that the German government shifted its policy in 1992, encouraging German minorities to stay in their countries by providing assistance for them to preserve their culture and German language skills. Also, procedural changes have made immigration more difficult for ethnic Germans.)

Second, the encompassing notion of Germanness laid down in the Basic Law provided for a rather smooth legal integration of East Germans from the GDR. Legal unification arrangements were facilitated by the fact that the GDR had never been a "foreign" country by international and German law. In 1989, East Germans fled in large numbers to the Federal Republic, claiming German citizenship. This mass migration triggered the imminent collapse of the communist regime, which resulted—unexpectedly—in unification. FRG conservatives who had kept "the German question open" during the Cold War saw their position confirmed, whereas those who had wanted to adjust citizenship regulations to the realities of a divided Germany and recognize a separate GDR citizenship lost support for their arguments. At present, the emphasis on common bonds of language, culture, and history serves to ease the constraints of economic and social transition in east Germany and to buffer the "shock" waves of unification in Germany as a whole.

The changes in the international system after the collapse of communism, especially the end of the Soviet Union and the civil war in former Yugoslavia, resulted in large-scale migration to Germany, a development that challenged traditional notions of exclusion and inclusion in society. However, instead of reconceptualizing German citizenship law and migration regulations after unification, the debate focused on the issue of asylum in Germany.

The Asylum Debate in the Federal Republic of Germany: Liberal vs. Ethnoculturalist Conceptions

In the absence of an immigration law in the Federal Republic, two sets of policies regulate immigration to the country: the "laws of return" and the

"laws of entry." The former provide for the admission of people who qualify as nationals on the basis of ancestry, such as ethnic Germans coming
from Eastern Europe (*Aussiedler*). Their legal basis is Article 116 of the Basic
Law. The law of entry, based on Article 16a of the Basic Law, provides the
right to seek political asylum in Germany. Designed in 1948–1949 with
fresh memories of expulsion, wartime, and refugee status during the Nazi
period, Article 16a became the most liberal law on asylum in Europe ("Persons persecuted on political grounds shall enjoy the right to asylum"). Even
though this form of entry has been severely restricted by the new asylum
law of 1993, and even though only a small proportion of those applying for
political asylum have been granted the right to stay, about two-thirds of all
persons who have sought political asylum in the European Union came to
the Federal Republic. Although the number of asylum seekers arriving in
the FRG mushroomed from 5,388 in 1971 to 438,191 in 1992, the proportion of applicants who are granted asylum has been declining. Only 4.3
percent were granted the right to stay in 1992, as compared to 26.6 percent in 1984. After the passing of the restrictive asylum law in 1993, the
numbers of asylum seekers arriving in Germany declined. Yet the worldwide
refugee problem still causes high numbers of persons to migrate.

In addition to the legally granted rights just mentioned, bilateral agreements with other countries permit short-term residence in Germany, for
example to study or to work. At present, though, the laws of return and
the laws of entry provide the framework for national immigration policies
and legal residency in Germany. In contrast to the "classic" countries of
immigration, such as the United States, and to other major actors in the
European Union, such as France or the United Kingdom, the Federal Republic lacks a national law on immigration (*Zuwanderung*). On the contrary,
the German government has repeatedly stated that Germany is not a country of immigration (*kein Einwanderungsland*) and thus rejects any need to
pass a law of immigration. Seeking political asylum has thus become the
only gate of entry for persons who cannot claim to be ethnic German.
Especially after the opening of Europe in 1989 and the increase in east-
west migration, dissatisfaction with immigration practices grew. Popular
concerns about immigrants led to questioning of the asylum law, allowing
the government to quickly move forward to change the law.

Proponents of the new, stricter law on political asylum argued that the
postwar provisions were not designed for the large influx of foreigners that
Germany witnessed after the opening of Eastern Europe. Stressing the
limits of the country's capacity to absorb the increasing number of non-
German nationals seeking to immigrate to the Federal Republic, they argued that only a stricter asylum law could save the country from internal
turmoil and destabilization. In the months before the revised asylum law
was passed, new data showed an increasing number of persons migrating to

the FRG. These included quite different groups: ethnic Germans (approximately 230,000 in 1992), war refugees (about 300,000 from the former Yugoslavia), and persons seeking asylum (a total of about 438,000 in 1992—compared to 121,000 in 1989—and 310,000 of these coming from Eastern Europe). Faced with both the sharp rise of immigration and the growing hostility and outright violence against foreign nationals living in Germany, the German government called for quick measures to solve the problem by restricting the constitutionally guaranteed right for individuals to seek political asylum. In the fall of 1992, German Chancellor Kohl proposed far-reaching changes in the constitution.

Opposition to the new law on political asylum came from a variety of nongovernmental organizations and political parties (such as the SPD, the Greens, and Bündnis 90), intellectuals, journalists, and other representatives of public life. The Social Democratic Party in the Federal Parliament at first opposed the amendments to the constitution and proposed (1) modifying the procedure for granting asylum rights and speeding up the process; and (2) passing a law on immigration with quotas for different groups of immigrants. In the final parliamentary debate about the new asylum law in May 1993, the minister of the interior, Schäuble, referred to the proposed law as a measure to save the state from internal turmoil and to prevent a "state of emergency." A so-called asylum compromise was finally reached betwen the governing CDU/CSU and the FDP, on one side, and the SPD opposition, on the other, to secure the two-thirds majority in the Bundestag necessary to amend the Basic Law.[6] The compromise kept the liberal provision in place but severely restricted the individual right to seek asylum. Major changes to Article 16a included the provision that persons coming to Germany through a "safe" third country, such as France or Poland, would be returned to that country without considering their case. As a result, it is now impossible to enter Germany by land as a political refugee. Furthermore, the government established a list of countries in which persecution presumably does not exist; nationals from these countries may be turned away immediately. A broad and vocal opposition, expressed in mass demonstrations, public statements, and the media, continued to criticize the new law. The decision also drew the attention of international organizations such as the UN High Commissioner for Refugees. In 1996, the Federal Constitutional Court had to decide whether the new restrictions passed by the Bundestag were in accord with the constitution, since several cases of complaints challenged the law on humanitarian grounds. The authority attributed to the court in German politics and by the public made this one of the most crucial decisions in the new united Germany, since opposition to the revised asylum law was widespread. The court ruled that the tightening of the asylum process was constitutional, but it also demanded better protection of human rights for those applying for asylum.

The conflict between the proponents and the opponents of restricting the law on political asylum in Germany can be read as a conflict between two different conceptions of immigration policy (Kanstroom 1993b, 152–211). One concept holds a monocultural, ascriptive view, rooted in a "culture of ethnicity." In the postwar Federal Republic, the proponents of this conception argued for an inclusive policy towards ethnic Germans in Eastern Europe and an exclusive policy towards non-German and non-EC nationals. In the current debate, this view is often expressed and reinforced by the claim that Germany is not a country of immigration—this despite the fact that 6.2 million residents, or 8 percent of the population, are "foreigners" and that most of them work or are in school.

This "culture of ethnicity" was exacerbated by German unification. United Germany not only has adopted the ethnocultural conception of citizenship of the FRG but draws on the monocultural GDR heritage as well. During the forty years of its existence, the communist government of the German Democratic Republic used the concept of "German heritage and tradition" as a source of legitimacy; to be "German,' albeit in a peculiar reading of German history, was a key to its power. Unlike in the Federal Republic, no discourse emerged about multiculturalism, and the "socialist internationalism" proclaimed by the GDR was merely superficial. The GDR conception of statehood was monocultural. Since exchange with other countries and cultures was restricted and even punished, Germanness was the focal point of the self-conception of citizens. Ironically, once the Berlin Wall fell, the politics of nationalism fostered by the GDR government undermined its very rule, as its citizens then claimed "we are one people" and rushed towards unification (Jarausch 1994). The German situation of the 1990s is thus characterized by a paradox: in an era when deemphasizing the national cultural implications of citizenship has become important at the transnational European level, unification has pushed a reaffirmation of the connection between state building and ethnic and cultural unity in Germany.

In contrast to the ascriptive and exclusive conception just described, the second conception of immigration policy is rooted in the postwar FRG visionary ideal of a liberal, open society strongly committed to a constitution protecting human rights and the rule of law. In the "post-national era" (the term is that of Rainer Lepsius), those embracing this conception argue, it is not membership in the ethnically based nation that provides political identity but commitment to western values of democracy and liberalism, as well as to civilization. Supporters of this conception argue for the inclusion of non-German nationals living in Germany, such as the Turkish migrant workers who have settled with their families. Civil and minority rights play an important role in this approach. Supporters believe that rights for ethnic Germans should be granted on grounds of human rights, not blood and descent. The philosopher Jürgen Habermas (1993) argues, for example, that the existence of a "world society" with increasing interdependencies imposes larger responsibilities on the world community. The wealthier nations of Western Europe that profited from the large-scale migration of workers in the postwar years now have a moral and political responsibility to allow for entry on more generous terms. Rejecting the revised asylum law, Habermas also argues that minorities living in Germany should be granted full citizenship rights (p. 3). This second conception has been chiefly supported by liberal intellectuals, social and political reformers, and parts of the SPD and the FDP. The most radical approach was taken by the Greens, who opted for an open, multicultural society, unrestricted asylum rights, and nonethnic conceptions of citizenship rights. But in recent years, prominent Greens such as Daniel Cohn-Bendit have rejected the fundamentalist multiculturalism of the early Greens and have supported stricter measures controlling entry to Germany.

The predicament facing those who, before 1989, opted for a liberal, nonascriptive, "post-national" conception of citizenship is reflected in the internal split within the SPD over the asylum issue. What kinds of solidarity should the party promote and support, and with whom? Should the party support the continuation of the liberal asylum law for an unknown number of refugees in the face of the tremendous problems resulting from unification, including increasing unemployment and cuts in social welfare? Or should it prioritize German national interest, choosing to protect the interests of the unemployed over those of new immigrants? The SPD suffered an electoral defeat in postunification Germany because of its ambivalent position on unification. Then, despite earlier fierce opposition to the proposed amendments to the Basic Law, the SPD agreed to the new law in the summer of 1993. The party did not even capitalize on its strong bargaining position to push a comprehensive new law on immigration, or *Zuwanderungsgesetz,* as it had proposed earlier in the debate. Instead, government and opposition joined to restrict entry to the country on the basis of the new asylum law, with the first appealing to the national state interests, and the second claiming to defend the social welfare state.

The controversy about the asylum law and immigration reflects the struggle over the political and social consensus in postunification Germany. A recurrent theme in postwar West German politics, this is basically a struggle between civil society and the state, between a conception of statehood that is centered on constitutional rights and a vital civil society, and another emphasizing the regulatory power of the state. Where those holding the first view perceive a threat to civil society and to the political consensus centered on liberal civil rights, the others see the potential danger that immigration poses to political order. The asylum issue is but one focal point illustrating the two divergent perspectives struggling for a new consensus in postunification Germany.

European Integration and Citizenship

Two events have generated the new debate on citizenship in the context of European integration: the removal of trade barriers within the European Community/Union in 1992 and the collapse of communism in 1989. The latter has resulted in an increasing east-west migration in Europe, a fact that was not adequately taken into account in creating the internal (West) European market. In contrast to patterns in the United States, Canada, and Australia, family immigration accounts for only a small percentage of this new migration. The liberalization of laws on emigration in Eastern and East-central Europe, the reappearance of violent ethnic conflicts, and the postsocialist crisis of restructuring the region's economy are the root causes of the increasing east-west migration. The Federal Republic of Germany has been the main receiving country of migrants from this region. Between 1986 and 1990, immigration from Eastern Europe tripled, accounting for more than a third of total migration to Germany; in the same period, the proportion of those coming from countries of the European Community decreased from 20 to 16 percent of all immigrants.[7]

In sharp contrast to this new migratory movement, immigration policies in Europe have become more restrictive than in earlier postwar decades. After a phase of resettling and integrating millions of displaced and relocated persons after World War II, and after recruiting migrant workers in the phase of economic expansion in the 1960s, most West European governments have enacted stricter policies controlling entry and encouraging the return of migrants. Given the economic squeeze in most European countries—structural crises in large-scale industries, high unemployment, and growing budget deficits—the Western states are less willing to welcome new citizens than in earlier periods. This development fits a worldwide pattern, since immigration policy is currently in the "restrictive phase of the cycle," as Aristide Zolberg observes (1993, 445).

Shortly after the fall of the wall, the European Community reacted promptly to the new order emerging in Europe by agreeing to the Dublin convention (1990). This deals exclusively with the issue of asylum claims and is generally regarded as a complement to the Schengen system (1985). After the Schengen agreement, the Federal Republic of Germany, France, and the Benelux countries had been the first to agree to remove border controls; after 1990, several other EC countries joined. Anticipating a larger flow of migrants from Eastern and Southeastern Europe, the member states moved at the Dublin meeting to define immigration and asylum policies as matters of common interest (*Angelegenheiten von gemeinsamem Interesse*). The most important aspect of both the Schengen and the Dublin conventions is the agreement that states accept each others' asylum decisions. This agreement was, however, reached without defining the legal status of refugees or formally integrating asylum rights and procedures within the European Community.

Day-to-day politics and popular pressure have added to the confusion in the discourse on migration. For example, fears developed in France that the formerly more liberal German asylum law would open the doors to an unwanted (overexaggerated) number of refugees and asylum seekers. Anti-immigration forces have used the issue to stir mistrust and anti-European sentiments, hindering politicians from pursuing humanitarian goals and civil rights imperatives. In Germany, similar popular concerns and opportunistic decisions in connection with the provisions of Schengen and Dublin served as catalysts to push for constitutional changes and a revised asylum law in 1993.

Another set of regulations relating to the issue of migration in Europe was addressed at the Maastricht conference. It concerns provisions for a Europe-wide citizenship (*Europäische Staatsbürgerschaft*). Article 8b of the Treaty on European Union signed in Maastricht in 1991 grants every citizen of the EU residing in a member state of which she or he is not a national the right to vote and to stand as a candidate in municipal elections. Thus, citizenship rights have been broadened within the European Union. The German government was one of the engines of this integration, strongly supporting the European move at the Maastricht conference. In fact, it has been noted rightly that the Federal Republic anticipated the transfer of sovereign national powers to intergovernmental institutions of Europe inso-far as it is the only country in Europe with a clause in its constitution requiring the state to pursue European integration.[8] At Maastricht, the German government actively supported the concept of a European citizenship. However, this change in the legal provisions within the European Union will not solve the issue of voting rights for non-EU-citizens in Germany. Due to the peculiarities of German citizenship law, even the second- and third-generation descendants of migrant workers from the non-EU-member Turkey do not have communal voting rights, while more generous legal rights are granted to EU nationals. Provisions for a European citizenship could lay the foundations for a more flexible approach to civil and political rights of permanent aliens in European countries, but at present they complicate the German dilemma of ethnically based citizenship rights and regulations.

While the regulation of persons entering a state—a classic realm of national politics—became a matter of potentially "pooled sovereignty" at the

Dublin conference, its present status is one of dual sovereignty, national and European. Three political problems for the European integration process arise from the Schengen and Dublin regulations. First, because of their multilateral, intergovernmental quality, asylum and immigration regulations are removed from the realm of policy making in the European Parliament. Even though the EP may be consulted, it has no formal input into or control over these policies.[9] Similarly, nongovernmental organizations are excluded from the intergovernmental agreements of the European Commission and the Council. Second, as critics have noted, the "harmonization" of asylum and migration policies through multilateral agreements has again added to the complex, multilayered diversity of asylum rights and policies in Europe. This new *Unübersichtlichkeit,* or untidiness in respect to the legal rules and regulations, has fed into a third political problem, reflected in the national discourses on "harmonization." Following the Schengen and Dublin conventions, several European countries have restricted their asylum laws, including the Federal Republic of Germany, France, the Netherlands, and Austria.

So far, the European Community acted mainly as a gatekeeper, promoting stricter border controls and restricting entry to EC countries on the basis of new asylum laws. No consensus has been reached about a more general, encompassing notion of European citizenship that would enhance the notion of membership in a political community with citizenship defined along the dimensions of civil, political, and social rights. Asylum policy, as well as the integration of nonnationals, has remained subject to national jurisdiction. Therefore, a key question for future integration remains: whether it is possible that the European Union will serve as a supranational catalyst for a Europe-wide conception of citizenship that moves beyond the national state.

The difficulties within the European Union in reaching a consensus about citizenship policies indicate a fundamental problem of European integration. Even though migration is a transnational phenomenon, policies are shaped by each nation-state. (As noted in Brubaker 1992, the European countries have different, but distinctive and deeply rooted, understandings of nationhood.) Hence, policies directed at nonnationals differ sharply across Western Europe. For example, in the case of asylum policies, restrictive countries like Italy are EU members along with more open ones like Germany. In respect to naturalization policies, France has a more generous record than Germany, but a less generous one than Sweden. In the first round, the addition of an intergovernmental layer of citizenship regulation has only complicated matters.

Conclusion

The conception of citizenship in Germany shows a remarkable continuity despite the political ruptures in German history. Since its first national citizenship law in 1913, Germany has followed the model of *jus sanguinis,* or citizenship based on descent. Even when new choices were available because of changes in the international system, Germany reaffirmed the ethnocultural conception of inclusion and exclusion. The international settlement of Germany's borders in 1990 as a condition for unification is a case in point. The country chose not to change the citizenship law at the critical juncture when the settlement of the territorial question for the German state opened an opportunity to do otherwise. Instead, in an attempt to curb migration and settle the "foreigner question," it shifted the question to one of revising asylum laws.

The struggle to define what it meant to be a "German" has often had unintended consequences, such as the large-scale inclusion of ethnic Germans in the second half of the 1980s, well after World War II, and the long-term residence status of persons who were brought in to work in Germany in the 1960s. These outcomes were the result of pragmatic or opportunistic decisions rather than ideal-type constructions of citizenship. Today, however, the conception of nationhood and citizenship rooted in culture and ethnicity is far more contested, and liberal, postnational conceptions of citizenship are more widely supported (as demonstrated in the contentious debates over restricting the asylum law) than in 1913 and 1949. A possible future unintended consequence of the restrictive asylum law could be that German public opinion will move closer to the European discourse on citizenship. Recently, the German debate on citizenship has moved to include proposals to incorporate the *jus soli* principle into German citizenship law alongside the traditional *jus sanguinis.* Since migration into the Federal Republic is bound to continue, the issue of migration and the integration of newcomers will be on the agenda for years to come.

Notes

1. In the Federal Republic, research on migration is a rapidly growing field. Several conferences held after 1990 addressed the new challenges posed by east-west migration, for example. Little work has been done, however, on the concept of citizenship. Among the few exceptions is the work by the legal scholar Ulrich Preuss (1993, 117–30).

2. "Deutscher ist, wer die Staatsangehörigkeit in einem Bundesstaat oder die unmittelbare Reichsangehörigkeit besitzt." Reichs- und Staatsangehörigkeitsgesetz, 22 July 1913, RGB1. 583. For a detailed description of German citizenship law, see de Groot 1989, 54–75.

3. On citizenship in the Nazi period, which stands out as an unparalleled case of misusing the legal system for state crimes and the resulting atrocities of the Holocaust, see Kanstroom 1993b.

4. Several other countries, including Israel, the United Kingdom, Spain, and

Italy, have adopted "laws of return" providing for the admission of people who qualify as nationals on the basis of ancestry. See Zolberg 1993, 445.

5. Translation by German Information Center, New York.

6. "Zur Änderung des Asylrechts: Debattenbeiträge und Hintergründe," *Der Tagesspiegel*, 27 May 1993, 5. The amendment received the two-thirds majority in the Bundestag necessary to change the Basic Law and was passed with two states rejecting it (Lower-Saxony and Bremen) and two states abstaining (Brandenburg, Hesse). It went into effect on 1 July 1993.

7. Heiko Körner (1993) notes that projections predicting a "mass migration" from Eastern Europe have often grossly overexaggerated the trends. Data from Eastern Europe have been flawed or inadequate until recently. The OECD began only in 1992 to record migration within Eastern Europe and to the west. See OECD 1992. For an overview of international trends, see Garson 1992.

8. On 2 December 1992, the Bundestag adoopted several amendments to the Basic Law in connection with the ratification of the Maastricht Treaty. A new Article 23 was included, commonly referred to as the Article on European Union, requiring the Federal Republic to participate in the development of the European Union. To this end, the federal government may transfer sovereign powers to intergovernmental institutions by law (Kanstroom 1993, 219). In general, transfer of sovereign powers to intergovernmental institutions was already included in Article 24.2 of the pre-1990 Basic Law.

9. In Germany, several authors have addressed these problems; see, for example, Weidenfeld and Hillenbrand 1994. See also Meehan 1993, 154.

6

Foreign Workers in Western Europe: The "Cheaper Hands" in Historical Perspective

Leslie Page Moch

Speaking in Saint Louis, Missouri, in 1906, distinguished scholar and social analyst Max Weber contended that foreign Poles in eastern Germany were driving out German workers because they were, in his words, "cheaper hands." He observed that "the advance of culture toward the east during the Middle Ages, based upon the superiority of the older and high culture, ha[d] been reversed under the capitalistic principle of the 'cheaper hand' " (Weber 1958, 384). For Weber, making do with little—being the "cheaper hand"—reflected Polish inferiority. Earlier, on the occasion of his inaugural lecture at the University of Freiburg, Weber had demanded that Gemany's borders be closed against foreign in-migrants because foreigners were culturally and racially inferior. Speaking on "the physical and psychological racial differences among nationalities," he claimed that the foreign immigrant "gains ground . . . not despite but because of his inferior physical and spiritual ways of life" (Knauf 1993, 1).

Weber's statements reflect the contradictions inherent in immigrant worker systems. It is tempting to conceptualize foreign labor as the "reserve army of the labor force"—a sector of workers who can be taken advantage of and, in hard times, dismissed (Sassen-Koob 1980). But such a reified explanation fits poorly with the history of foreign workers in Western Europe. It is a poor fit because it is ahistorical and does not address the developments in immigrant communities, in receiving cultures, and in state policies that make foreign workers become "wanted, but not welcome" (Cohen 1987, 137–44; Zolberg 1987). Employers may have wanted to hire the "cheaper hands," but workers were not disembodied hands; rather, they were (and are) whole human beings who often strove to join communities, live among family members, and enjoy geographical stability.

For this reason, foreign workers have been an imperfect solution to the need for workers in Western Europe. Some foreign labor in Europe has been, as Aristide Zolberg (1987, 36–37) has pointed out, "alien in the deep sense . . . representing for the receiving society an undesirable 'otherness.' " This is not an accident. The alien character of foreign labor *makes* it profitable (and this is where the continuities lie among systems of slavery in the Western Hemisphere, the use of Asian contract laborers in the Pacific Rim and the Caribbean, and of *Gastarbeiter,* or guest workers, in Western Europe). Foreign workers have been an unstable solution precisely because they are not disembodied "cheaper hands" but, rather, visible newcomers enhancing the diversity of their host culture. Under conditions of labor competition, a search for unitary identity often emerges in the host culture and politics (Zolberg 1987, 36–37). When employers satisfy their need for labor by using foreign workers, this solution contradicts a felt need for a coherent national identity and, in turn, affects political discourse and state policy.

Foreign labor is cheap partly because workers are raised, educated, and trained in another society, which bears those costs. But foreigners become less desirable to their host society when they have their own children who must be raised, educated, and trained in the new country—and are a visible long-term presence (Noiriel 1988b). In other words, as the disembodied "cheaper hand" becomes a part of the social body, labor competition and cultural norms create negative responses to immigrant labor, often effecting political measures. Additionally, foreign workers becomes less desirable to host employers as they gain the protections and rights of native-born workers.

After a brief historical introduction, this chapter discusses the use of mass foreign labor (and of emerging reactions against immigrant workers and their families) in Western Europe during two periods: (1) between the turn of the century and World War I; and (2) during the postwar boom, 1960–1973. I focus on France, Germany, and Switzerland. In each case, a period of record use of foreign workers (against which host countries had begun to react) ended abruptly with a sort of deus ex machina—the war in the first case, the oil crisis of 1973 in the second. During the first period, markets determined migration patterns, and state intervention played a minor role, but during the postwar boom, states regulated migration comprehensively, attempting to control welfare expense and political acrimony. The concluding section briefly considers today's immigrants to European Community nations France and Germany in light of the historical experiences of Western Europe.

This chapter reflects the fundamental concerns of students of migration and the state—contrasting migration flows, regulation, and political controversy—and focuses on the periods before and after the wars and economic depression that marked the years 1914–1945. Before World War I, international labor migration went nearly unregulated in Western Europe. Workers moved as individuals, in single-sex teams, or as families, according to available employment and their own needs; few regulations existed to inhibit gang labor or family reunification. Moreover, recent research suggests that the great volume of prewar migrations affected wage levels in the Atlantic economies. The outpouring of men and women from peripheral areas such as Ireland raised wage levels at home because emigration produced a relative labor shortage. Conversely, the influx of workers into the United States, for example, produced so numerous a labor force as to reduce wage levels from a potential high. In global terms, migration effected a convergence in the wages of urban unskilled laborers, who were the majority of international migrants (Williamson 1995).

After World War II, by contrast, states of Western Europe sponsored and regulated migration in ways that shaped migration streams. Some encouraged only single-sex groups of guest workers or temporary migrants, inhibiting family reunification; after 1973, many state regulations changed to allow family reunification at the expense of worker migration. By these means, the demographics of international migration flows changed from primarily male working-age groups to female and child groups (Castles and Miller 1993). Nonetheless, the volume of international migration reached greater levels than in the period from 1945 to 1973, initiating another time of convergence in earnings between the industrial countries of North America and Western Europe, on the one hand, and peripheral areas, on the other (Williamson 1995).

International Labor Migration in Long Historical Perspective

Although foreign workers reached unprecedented numbers in the 1900–1914 period, they were by no means unknown before the late nineteenth century. In the sixteenth and seventeenth centuries, migration systems flourished that took French workers into the fields, cities, and commercial enterprises of Spain; an estimated two hundred thousand resided in the kingdom of Spain in 1655 (Poitrineau 1985, 20).

In the seventeenth and eighteenth centuries, Amsterdam and the Dutch North Sea coast attracted workers from Germany and Norway. At the peak of this migration in about 1730, at least fifteen thousand, and perhaps up to twenty-five thousand, migrant workers traveled annually to the province of Holland, most of them to cut hay; in addition, German and Norwegian sailors went to sea under the Dutch flag, and German serving girls worked in Amsterdam households (De Vries 1984, 186–90; Hart 1974, 157;

Lucassen 1987, 149–53). At the time of the Napoleonic wars, foreign migrant laborers from the far west of Ireland (and Scotland and Wales, as well) converged on London and fertile southeast England for harvest and construction work (Lucassen 1987, 108). In addition, the Paris basin, northern Italy, the Roman plain, Madrid and Castile, and the Mediterranean littoral all attracted seasonal migrant laborers numbering at least twenty thousand annually in this period. Many migrant workers in these last systems, however, did not cross national borders to reach their destinations, but rather traveled from neighboring regions, say, of France or Spain—crossing linguistic and cultural borders, perhaps, but not necessarily a political divide (Lucassen 1987, 107–11). In all, over three hundred thousand seasonal workers labored in seven distinct migration systems.

In the years between 1815 and 1880, these seven systems shifted and new migration patterns emerged with the development of new industrial cities and coal- and steel-producing regions and with the expansion of capitalist agriculture. International migration expanded rapidly after about 1880. The immigrant labor force working in Europe interlocked with two other kinds of labor migration: those international systems spanning the Atlantic Ocean, and the high mobility within nation-states on the Continent (Moch 1992, ch. 4).

The Turn of the Century

At the turn of this century, Europeans played important roles in a global labor market that encompassed Australia and New Zealand, as well as North and South America (Mörner and Sims 1985, 47; Strikwerda, ch. 3 above). Between 1860 and 1914, about 52 million Europeans left their home continent. Of this number, roughly 37 million traveled to North America, 11 million to South America, and 3.5 million to Australia and New Zealand. Escalating movement after 1880 peaked in the years before World War I, when Italians labored as seasonal harvest workers in Argentina, Poles worked for periods of years in the mines of Pennsylvania, and Britons moved to the South Pacific. Although many remained and settled at their destinations, a significant proportion of each group (usually between 20 and 57 percent) returned home after 1900, after a stint of work (Gould 1980, 56–62; Hoerder 1982). The global labor force also included hundreds of thousands of non-Europeans; most of these were Indian and Chinese workers—indentured, contract, and coolie labor in the Caribbean, Peru, and the United States (Curtin 1990; Zolberg 1987).

The number of foreign nationals working in Western Europe—almost all themselves Europeans—was rising to unprecedented heights. By 1910, there were over one million foreign workers in Germany, among them nearly 600,000 Poles and 150,000 Italians; foreigners were about 2 percent of the population. France, too, harbored over a million foreigners, over 400,000 Italians and nearly 300,000 Belgians; foreigners constituted about 3 percent of the population. Foreign immigrants were even more important in Switzerland, where nearly 15 percent of the population and 17 percent of the labor force were foreigners, with over 200,000 each of Germans and—again—Italians (Cross 1983, 21–22; Holmes 1988, 14; Lucassen 1987, 189).

Most foreign laborers were Polish, Italian, Belgian, or German, but the working reality of the immigrant labor force was more complex than that. Consider the frustrated foreman in the Ruhr valley in 1901 who could not understand any of the thirty workers under his supervision—despite the fact that he spoke five languages! Some of his workers hailed from Friesland in the northwestern Netherlands, and the rest were Poles from eastern German territories and Croatians. The foreman himself was from the southeastern Netherlands. Dutch workers were, however, a minority among immigrants in Germany (Lucassen 1987, 189).

Toward the end of the nineteenth century, systems of migration to the iron and steel regions—northern France, Luxembourg, Lorraine, and the Ruhr—developed. Other systems developed in response to demand for field labor for the large-scale production of sugar beets, grain, and potatoes in Denmark, France, and Germany. The most important node of international labor migration was the Rhine-Ruhr zone, stretching southwest into France and south into Switzerland. The international army of agricultural field laborers worked to the west and east of this central core.

Most of what Carl Strikwerda calls the "floating pool" of workers in Western Europe labored abroad temporarily—that is, for a number of years or as long as a job lasted. Unskilled laborers, as well as skilled mechanics and lathe operators who circulated through Württemberg, northern Switzerland, and eastern France, worked within the industrial heartland. Italian and Belgian workers operated the machines in the textile mills of France and Switzerland, while Poles and Italians labored in the mines of the Ruhr valley and northern France. To investigate how strands of skilled and unskilled people moved, Maurizio Gribaudi (1987, 18, 22, 50–51) has reconstituted the stories of migrants from a village outside Turin, including the Odasso brothers, who were representative of the range of skill levels of those working in Switzerland. Two sons, Guiseppe and Luigi, left for Switzerland in 1897 (the year of their eldest brother's marriage), working there as unskilled laborers and ultimately returning home to work in agriculture. The youngest, Grato, trained as an electrician in Switzerland, married there, and remained across the border all of his life. Their elder sister married a farmer in the village; their younger sister went to Turin as a domestic servant, then retired to her home village. Out of the six Odasso children who survived infancy, then, four left their native village, but three ultimately returned.

In addition to working abroad for years at a time, seasonal agricultural laborers moved to an annual rhythm—the spring vine trimming, the early strawberry and flower picking, the grain cutting, the grape harvest, the sugar beet digging, and finally, the potato digging that closed the harvest season. Teams of sugar beet workers outnumbered all other international agricultural workers; no other industrial crop needed more concentrated labor power over such extensive regions, feeding a demand for sugar, animal fodder, and alcohol. Beet fields east of the Elbe attracted about 200,000 international workers in 1900 and an estimated 433,000 in 1914, including Russian and Austrian Poles, Italians, Scandinavians, White Russians, and Ruthenians; Poles from Austrian Galicia and Russia represented the great majority. Over half the Poles were women (Chatelain 1977, 704; Rosoli 1985, 106; Perkins 1981, 106–8).

Indeed, women figured prominently among international migrant workers—more so than in earlier centuries. They were especially visible among agricultural gang workers, such as the teams of young women who left Poland to dig in the potato and sugar beet fields of the eastern German provinces and Denmark (Holmes 1988, 30, 93, 118; Lucassen 1987, plate 6; Perkins 1981, 107–8). Italian flower cutters in Provence included women. Immigrant women labored in factories as well. Italian women provided a quarter of the embroidery workers moving into the revitalized, mechanized Swiss embroidery industry of 1911; single and in their teens, Italian women were recruited and housed by their employers. A quarter of Swiss domestics were foreign women, most of them German (Holmes 1988, 30, 93, 118).

Employers and nations were willing recipients of foreign labor; indeed, the international labor force was encouraged, recruited, and sought after during this age of intense capital formation. The demand for labor, largely free of state regulation, provided the engine for mass migration. This willingness to use foreign labor was universal in prewar Europe, even in Germany, the sole state that sought to regulate closely the entry of certain workers.

The German government restricted the movement of Poles who entered the Reich from Austrian and Russian Poland; these were the Poles excoriated by Max Weber in the opening paragraph of this chapter. Of course, there was no Poland at this time, for its territory was divided among Germany, Austria, and Russia. Those whom Germans called "foreign Poles" could only work as temporary labor, and then only in the eastern provinces. They could neither bring dependent family members along nor settle; rather, foreign Poles were required to depart from German territory before 20 December of each year and were forbidden to return before 1 February

(Bade 1987, 66–67, 107–9). The position of foreign Poles in Germany before World War I forecast that of more recent foreign labor, and state regulation foreshadowed the state controls implemented during and after World War I.

It is no accident that exclusionary citizenship policies emerged during the years of mass international migrations to Germany, Switzerland, and France or that they were hotly debated. In Germany, where the number of resident foreigners tripled between 1890 and 1910 while roughly 3.5 million German emigrants lived abroad, a policy emerged making citizenship more accessible to German emigrants permanently settled outside the Reich and more difficult to acquire for foreigners who had settled in Germany. Before 1913, German law defined citizens as residents of the territorial state or as a community of blood descent; the 1913 law defined German citizenship strictly as a matter of common ethnic descent, drawing on the established legal tradition of *jus sanguinis* and closing citizenship to immigrants (Brubaker 1992, 118–19). Policies culminating in the 1913 German legislation reflect the ethnocultural, exclusionary stance of Germany toward Poles; they resricted citizenship to a community of blood descent and excluded non-German immigrants while remaining open to newcomers of German descent from Eastern Europe (those of the "older and high culture" mentioned by Max Weber) (Weber 1958, 384). Only the children of ethnic Germans became citizens at birth; naturalization was rare and anomalous (Brubaker 1992, 14, 33).

Similarly, Swiss law determined that "doors were wide open to foreigners who wanted to live or work in the country, but nearly shut to foreigners who wanted to acquire Swiss citizenship" (Holmes 1988, 33). Only the offspring of Swiss became citizens at birth. As in Germany, citizenship was assigned by blood descent, and place of birth was not recognized as a factor in naturalization, even for the second-or third-generation descendants of immigrants. However, local communities (*Gemeinde*) had the power to grant citizenship and, in some areas, granted it to prosperous immigrants despite the Swiss fear of foreign inundation. Consequently, nearly thirty-five thousand Germans became naturalized Swiss citizens (1889–1910), in contrast to some seventy-seven hundred Italians (Brubaker 1992, 33; Holmes 1984, 33).

French citizenship and naturalization laws offer a marked contrast to those of Germany and Switzerland. At first, French law was expansive and assimilationist, emphasizing the state and "the soil," the principle of *jus solis,* rather than ethnicity and blood descent. The state promoted naturalization, automatically conferring citizenship on the children of immigrants. French law thus expressed the nation's profound confidence that newcomers would assimilate (Brubaker 1992, 14–16, 33). On the other hand, during the same era, foreigners were explicitly identified and registered in

France. While legislation in 1889 automatically conferred citizenship on the children of immigrants, other laws mandated immigrant registration in 1888, a ceiling on foreign labor in public works in 1899, and possession of a work permit for foreign workers in 1912 (Singer-Kérel 1991, 282).

The details of French legislation suggest an ambivalence toward foreign labor even in a state that was relatively friendly to international workers. This ambivalence turned to hostility in border areas. Belgians were the target in the north, where a veritable collective mobilization to remove them forced some worker families to flee; literal manhunts terrorized Italians in the south, where over 20 immigrant workers were killed before World War I (Noiriel 1988b, 258–62). Both the ambiguity of French open borders and liberal citizenship policies (combined with growing regulation) and the ambivalence of Swiss and German policies welcoming foreign labor while restricting citizenship signal a widespread phenomenon: the impulse to limit the degree to which immigrant workers could join in the life of their host nation.

The movement of workers among countries ended suddenly in the summer of 1914 with the outbreak of World War I.[1] Young laborers quickly went home, where they became soldiers and war workers; labor forces became national.[2] Wartime security concerns fostered state regulation of immigration.

Thus, at the turn of the century, there was an enormous expansion of foreign immigration and foreign labor—recruited in response to an urgent need for hands in the textile, coal-mining, iron, and steel industries and in agriculture. Responses to immigrant labor show, however, that the needs of employers were not congruent with the felt needs of society, citizens, or the state. Consequently, resentment flared against foreign workers, and citizenship laws began to be formulated and tightened. The limitation of citizenship became important in the representative democracies of the late nineteenth and early twentieth centuries because citizenship granted suffrage to all (or most) adult males.

Measures to limit citizenship and control foreign labor during this period mark the beginning of our century's increasing efforts to control human mobility, which had been relatively free in the previous two hundred years. World War I saw a proliferation of state mechanisms for the exclusion of foreigners. Efforts to control immigration would be expanded on a massive scale during the postwar boom of the 1960s and early 1970s.

Foreign Labor in the 1960s and Early 1970s

Foreign nationals—numbering up to 8 million by 1973—flooded into Western Europe in the 1960s. Like the period from 1880–1914, the postwar economic boom years were a time of intense capital formation that engendered significant international migration (Sassen-Koob 1980, 7–11). Additional forces were at work as well: workers were recruited by employers and the attraction of jobs in the prolonged postwar boom but also pushed out by the decolonization that promoted movement from former colonies to Europe (Zolberg, Suhrke, and Aguayo 1989). More than before World War I, the state attempted to supervise and control the movement of immigrants in the 1960s and early 1970s. From the outset, France's National Immigration Office and the Federal Republic of Germany's Federal Labor Office sought to recruit labor for public works (Collinson 1993, 46–63). The demand for labor was such that national labor offices sought workers outside the long-standing European sources, and thousands of laborers quickly arrived from North Africa (Algeria, Tunisia, Morocco), former colonies elsewhere, Yugoslavia, and Turkey.

France's largest group of new arrivals came from Algeria (of 1.25 million North Africans living in France in the early 1970s, Algerians numbered nearly 850,000). Decolonization produced the massive migration of colonial *pied noirs* and then *harkis* (Algerians loyal to France) after Algerian independence in 1962. In addition, southern Europeans entered the country—first, from Italy (again) but, increasingly, from Spain and Portugal so that by 1971, 1.8 million southern Europeans lived in France. By then, France's population was about 6.7 percent foreign born—about 3.3 million immigrants. Half of these were workers; the others, dependents (Collinson 1993, 54; Rogers 1985a, 5–9).

The story for Germany is a bit different because Germany absorbed 8 million entries from the east from 1945 until 1961, when traffic was cut off with the construction of the Berlin Wall (Herbert 1990, 200–201). In keeping with long-standing Reich tradition, the 1913 law, and Nazi legislation, the Germans who entered became German citizens. But more labor was immediately required and negotiated in the early 1960s—especially from Yugoslavia and Turkey. By 1971, about 5 percent of residents of the Federal Republic of Germany (FRG) were foreign born. These included over a million Turks, nearly 750,000 Yugoslavs, and over 500,000 Italians. Sixty percent of the immigrants in the FRG were laborers (Collinson 1993, 54; Rogers 1985a, 5–9).

Although their numbers were much smaller, foreigners also flocked to Switzerland; they came primarily through long-standing routes from Italy (so that well over 500,000 Italians lived in Switzerland in 1971) and new migration streams from Spain, Yugoslavia, and Turkey. By the early 1970s well over 750,000 foreigners resided in Switzerland, and the foreign-born constituted at least 16 percent of the population. Sixty percent of them were workers (Collinson 1993, 54; Rogers 1985b, 5–9).

Like laborers from earlier periods, foreign workers in Western Europe in these boom years came with work teams, lived in sex-segregated housing, and made their homes in employer-provided *Heime* (dormitory housing). Immigrant workers did what they always had done—worked in construction and manufacturing at jobs eschewed by Europeans. Describing a massive project to build water and utility tunnels under Geneva that had begun in 1971, John Berger (1975) noted that Yugoslavs, Spaniards, and some southern Italians were then underground. Most workers in Geneva were immigrants, but those underground were exclusively foreign born; the two engineers and the foreman were German. The language problem resembled that in the Ruhr in 1901. Laborers worked in groups of seven or eight, but they were never all of the same nationality. Berger noted, ironically, that while Geneva specialized in international communications, the members of subterranean work gangs could share only a few words between them. On the one hand, misunderstandings bred accidents, but on the other hand, work proceeded quickly with little talk. The workers were on short-term contracts, after which they would return to their Bosnian, Andalusian, or Calabrian villages; from there, they would reapply for another year's tunneling under the metropolis. According to Swiss law (which afforded exceptional control of immigrants), these workers had residence permits with a maximum continuous stay of nine months and could not bring any of their family (Berger 1975, 157–62).

Although most labor migration began as streams of men (which is the ordinary historical pattern), this was not always true. Turkish women, for example, were recruited by the FRG Federal Labor Office to live in employers' *Heime* and work in factories packing nylon stockings, sewing blue jeans, and manufacturing automobile parts. Recruited by German firms, these Muslim women were not prepared by their culture to work outside the home or even to depart from their villages, yet their fathers and husbands urged them to go, take a job, and then apply for dependents' visas so that the men could follow. Simultaneously, in Europe, the Turkish men recruited in male groups were gradually bringing in wives. As a consequence, after 1967, about one-third of the Turks coming into the Federal Republic of Germany were women (Abadan-Unat 1977, 31; Morokvasic 1984; Yücel 1987, 127–38).

North Africans likewise sent for wives and children. The temporary laborers, or *Gastarbeiter* (guest workers), were finding ways of coming to stay. When workers arrived for gang-labor employment and lived in dormitories, they were not so visible because they were merely "hands"; at this point, workers' lack of visibility did not disturb the Swiss, French, or German sense that the native-born hosts were among people pretty much like themselves. As laborers sent for wives, husbands, sweethearts, and children, however, foreigners were not seen just on construction sites but also in schools, hospitals, and the offices of social services. This perception of increased presence explains in part the change of heart toward immigrants as the 1960s drew to a close, when over half the new arrivals were women and children coming into Western Europe not to work but for family reunification (Collinson 1993, 54; Rogers 1985a, 5–9; Tapinos 1983, 67). In attempts to curb welfare expenses, state interventions increased, but these measures made workers hesitate to visit home for fear of being unable to return. Thus, immigrant workers became even more eager to reunite their families in Western Europe.

Certain groups have borne the brunt of special hostility that originates less in an undifferentiated racism and xenophobia than in particular racisms and historical sensitivities in European culture and history. In France, where schoolchildren learn (or, at least, used to learn) that they would be reading the Koran were it not for the signal victory that turned the Moors back to the south at the battle of Tours in the year 732, North Africans were viewed the least favorably of all immigrants. Here, as elsewhere, the definition of who a people are is intimately tied with the definition of who they are not; the French historically define themselves as non-Muslims. By the late 1960s, there were attempts to increase the National Immigration Office's control over Algerian immigration. A 1974 poll by the Institut national des etudes démographiques on French attitudes toward foreigners showed that the nation was a bit unsure about Yugoslavs and Turks but had a rather good opinion of sub-Saharan Africans. The same poll showed that the French deeply distrusted North Africans, whom they identified not only with Islam but also with the revolt against French rule in Algeria and terrorist activities in the Métropole (Freeman 1979, 271–72). By the 1970s, Algerians had been murdered in southern France, and their wives denied residence permits in the north (Freeman 1979, 109; Noiriel 1988b, 262).

In the Federal Republic of Germany, hostility began to be focused on Turks, who as Muslims in the land of Luther were among the first to see the graffiti *Auslander raus* (foreigners out). (There, schoolchildren learn about the importance of the 1683 Battle of Kahlenberg, when the emperor's armies turned back the Ottoman armies outside Vienna, preventing Turkish inroads into German culture.) Polls showed that over half of all Germans in the FRG wanted to get rid of foreigners in the early 1960s; in 1964, Chancellor Erhard called on Germans to work harder to get rid of outsiders. Soon thereafter, in the mid-1960s, the Neo-Nazi Party was founded (Castles and Kosack 1973, 433–35; Castles, Booth, and Wallace 1984, 198–99; Herbert 1990, 224–28).

In the very early 1970s, then, immigration stayed high, whole families of newcomers from beyond the confines of Western Europe had settled, and hostility to foreign labor was palpable. It was in this atmosphere that the oil crisis occurred. When OPEC quadrupled the price of oil in the fall of 1973, the European dependence on cheap fuel and imported oil plunged it into a deep recession. This severe downturn made Europeans eager to rid themselves of a presence they already had come to resent (Collinson 1993, 54; Tapinos 1983, 67). Measures against foreigners multiplied quickly. In November of 1973, the Federal Republic of Germany banned labor migration from outside the European Community. Within a year, other nations of Western Europe did the same: the French banned both laborers and dependents from entry, and the Swiss made their measures against long-term stays and family reunification even more stringent (Tapinos 1983, 54–55).

Conclusion

Yet these measures did not succeed. Although many alien laborers departed Europe, the majority remained in place, and more dependent worker kin arrived. A million Turks could not disappear from Germany any more easily than 1.25 million North Africans from France or 65,000 Turks and Yugoslavs from Switzerland. By the 1980s, the English-language books on European migrants, which had borne titles like *Birds of Passage* in the 1970s, were entitled *Here for Good* and *Guests Come to Stay* (Piore 1979; Castles, Booth, and Wallace 1984; Rogers 1985b). Today, twenty years later, the legacy of alien labor testifies to its enduring role in configurations of capital deployment and social identity; migrant laborers and their descendants have become a permanent and structural part of West European society (Castles and Miller 1993). This does not mean that foreign labor has lost the capacity to inspire cultural and political conflict. On the contrary, the presence of foreign labor, state attempts at immigration regulation, and issues of inclusion framed in terms of race and ethnicity have taken center stage in policy and political discussions in the 1990s. A major focus of electoral debates, issues of foreign presence have served to translate anxieties over a host of material and social issues such as unemployment and housing (Castles and Miller 1993; Faist 1997).

In 1990, over 1 million foreign nationals resided in Switzerland (including 141,000 Yugoslavs and 64,000 Turks), 340,000 in all from outside the EU. France's 3.6 million foreigners included 2.3 million from outside the EU, of which nearly 1.5 million were North African nationals (with 805,000 Algerians) (Collinson 1993, 83). Although France has offered citizenship to those born on French soil and historically has been confident that assimilation would prevail, this country is now faced with, on the one hand, fractious immigrants, and on the other, political hostility toward immigrants. For example, many second-generation Algerians have rejected their chance for automatic citizenship at age eighteen. At the same time, the anti-immigrant governments of recent years have aimed explicitly for "zero immigration," and Muslim girls who cover their hair in school risk expulsion.[3] The election of a conservative president in May 1995 suggests that the social and political tensions surrounding the diversity of the population in France will not diminish in the near future, despite the 1997 socialist parliamentary victory.

Germany has by far the greatest number of foreigners on its soil; among its 5.2 million foreigners, 3.9 originated from outside the EU, and over 1.6 million of these are Turks. Germany currently receives more immigrants than any other EU nation (in 1991, it alone received 60 percent of all the immigrants to EU countries).[4] Once again a conduit for people leaving Eastern Europe, Germany faces the contradictions of two growing populations that Klaus Bade calls the "foreigners with German passports" and the "Germans with foreign passports" (Hoerder 1994). The "foreigners with German passports" are those of German descent who, since 1991, have come west from locations such as the Ukraine or Russia (and who often do not speak German), who are in need of housing, jobs, and aid; these immigrants are citizens according to German law. After an initial rush of immigrants from the east, these newcomers continue to number about 200,000 per year (Faist 1997). In contrast, the "Germans with foreign passports," include taxpaying skilled-worker Turks born and raised in Germany, who— even as third-generation residents of Germany—are denied citizenship and suffrage.

Perhaps the signal trend in the use of foreign labor in today's EU can be seen in Germany's current use of project-tied workers like those described by Thomas Faist in Chapter 11 of this book. These workers numbered about 73,000 in 1993. Members of Polish, Portuguese, U.K., and Hungarian male construction gangs may earn German wage-scale compensation, but they may not claim social service benefits (Collinson 1993, 135; Faist 1997; Andrews 1996). No group better illustrates the observation that capital seeks out subordinate laborers when labor as a whole is no longer subordinate (Cohen 1987, 252). Project-tied construction laborers offer a devastating example of one way workers' rights can be undermined, even after the protracted struggles for political and social rights over the past 150 years (Tilly 1995; Zolberg 1995; Sassen 1995).

It is already clear that the well-being of Western labor is undermined by the success of global capital at exporting production. Industrial and assembly tasks—from the manufacture of electronic equipment to that of garments or automobiles—are increasingly relocated in low-wage areas where workers lack European protections against exploitation and dangerous conditions. Capital has moved more quickly than labor. As the case of Germany's CEE project-tied and EU foreign construction workers demonstrates, however, in tasks, such as construction, that cannot be exported, employers are strongly motivated to employ foreign workers while denying them the benefits of denizen labor. Three aspects of this recent innovation echo historical precedents: the search for exploitable workers that leads to the hiring of alien labor, foreign workers' attempts to improve their conditions through emigration, and competing labor's ambivalence about the presence of foreigners. The "cheaper hands" working for CEE contractors (like the earlier Poles in Germany, Algerians in France, and Bosnians in Switzerland) may move to the center of a struggle among employers, competing workers, and state regulations, a struggle that will fuel public debate over identity, immigration law, and workers' rights. This recent challenge to European labor echoes the past and presages the struggles of the coming century.

Notes

1. Recent scholarship suggests that security issues of the war alone did not close borders but rather that the developing welfare state was also eager to stop foreign entries (Lucassen 1996).

2. Although this statement is generally true, it must be qualified. National labor forces lasted only for a time in Germany and France—until indigenous workers were augmented with prisoners-of-war and recruited labor. Germans used the some 200,000 Poles trapped in their country at the outbreak of war and brought in about 200,000 more during the course of the war; the French recruited about 320,000 foreign workers—voluntary Spaniards, Greeks, and Portuguese and co-erced Algerians, Chinese, and Indochinese—into war work (Cross 1983; Lequin 1988; Stovall 1993).

3. The 1889 naturalization law has recently been changed so that rather than becoming a citizen automatically at age eighteen, second-generation immigrants must apply for citizenship between the ages of sixteen and twenty-one (Wihtol de Wenden 1991, 329; Riding 1993).

4. Germany's immigration and emigration flows are the largest in Europe (Eurostat 1993, 2–4; Faist 1997 and ch. 11 below).

II

The Social Process of Developing Group Representational Institutions in Nineteenth- and Twentieth-Century European States

This part looks historically and comparatively at the importance of major conjunctural and structural changes in shaping domestic orders. In chapter 7, Michael Hanagan compares the evolution of industrial relations in France and the United Kingdom in the wake of the Industrial Revolution, in the time preceding World War I. In chapter 8, Jytte Klausen shows how the development of comprehensive state capacities in response to economic near-autarky during and immediately after World War II enabled states to assume a new role in directing economic development after 1945. In chapter 9, Martin Potůček shows how the postcommunist legacy prevents Eastern and Central Europe from appropriating the Western European postwar welfare-state model as a template for current social policies.

While the post–1945 Keynesian "revolution" rested on an intellectual breakthrough in economic thinking, it also rested on the development of a repertoire of planning "technologies"—economic forecasting, social coordination between producer interests, and a cadre of professional planners—that evolved only in the context of the civilian war economies. We have, in the meantime, become so accustomed to statist stabilization policy that earlier efforts to utilize self-regulation and carefully crafted agreements and economic organizations for similar purposes often are overlooked. In this regard, Hanagan resumes a narrative of such efforts begun by Strikwerda in chapter 3.

Hanagan compares the construction of contrasting forms of trade union legislation in France and the United Kingdom at the end of the nineteenth century and traces national diversity in trade union organization to the needs of employers and industry. Earlier patterns of labor force competition (between skilled and semiskilled workers) and the availability of labor led U.K. employers to grant training responsibility to unions, and French employers to insist on firm-specific training and, further, to provide private welfare plans to tie their workers to the firm. The degrees of state acceptance of union organizing in the two cases flowed directly from this early contrasting experience. Hanagan writes, of course, about a period when states had not yet reached the zenith of power reached by their twentieth-century counterparts. Hanagan dispels the fallacy of a liberal order based upon "pure" markets. His argument speaks directly to the (mistaken) expectation that social rigidities will melt away once exposed to the glare of an integrated European labor market. The constitutional structures of labor markets reflect the interests of industry, as well as those of labor.

Most of the literature on labor relations and economic coordination has stressed a long historical perspective; it has not assigned particular importance to the war years in shaping nationally inclusive interest-organizations capable of entering society-wide bargaining over economic objectives and means. Colin Crouch (1993) has argued that the essential patterns of neocorporatist mediation between states and economic interests were in place prior to World War I and that where they were not, state-centered social coordination was bound to fail. In his view, the British state-tradition stood in the way of a neocorporatist solution. Francis Fukuyama (1995) has also found the United Kingdom curiously lacking with respect to capacity for societal coordination.

Jytte Klausen contrasts the influence of wartime civilian economic controls in Sweden and the United Kingdom; she then contrasts both of these cases with the effect of allied reconstruction plans on postwar national economic policy in the case of the Federal Republic of Germany. Contradicting the ubiquity of British exceptionalism with respect to organizational capacities, she instead traces the demobilization of national interest-organizations to the peculiarities of British political institutions and the control exercised by the unions over the Labour Party in particular.

Once planning based on the continuation of economic controls had been ruled out, Klausen argues, coercion—or self-discipline—by organizations, and not public policy, became the foundation for stabilization policy. Social and economic coordination replaced other methods of resolving distributive conflict. In response to state initiatives, new self-governing organizations had emerged between the Great Depression and the end of the war in 1945, and these became the pillars of postwar collectivism. These worked to insert class or sectional organizations between the state and the individual, but they did not diminish state power. The state and the new organizations had expanded their activities, strengthening both (Heckscher 1946, 220–21). Politics and domestic political institutions worked to shape particular trajectories and unique compromises between divergent sectoral and class interests.

The pervasive importance of the international system in shaping domestic order is a recurrent theme in all three chapters. Hanagan locates the impetus for shaping the social organization of labor markets in the functional needs of employers in the face of rising union mobilization. In his view, the state was notably absent from the picture until industrial militancy prodded elites to consider legislation to encourage self-regulation. In the case of Klausen's study of shifts in postwar economic-planning policies, changing U.S. priorities provided an important backdrop to postwar European policy making. Martin Potůček's chapter offers a comparison between post–1945 and post–1989 welfare-state development.

The impediments to a direct shift from a communist to a "social citizenship" welfare state are many. Potůček points out that a lack of preexisting insurance programs, mutual associations, and other private organizations to sustain welfare policies—or a lack of "social capital," to use Robert Putnam's popular phrase—is part of the communist legacy. Historically, West European welfare states depended upon the ability to appropriate and consolidate earlier mutualist or private programs to help fund universal systems of social insurance. The two other chapters in this part, by Hanagan and Klausen, show how important the institutional and attitudinal legacies of large-scale historical events are in shaping subsequent policies and attitudes. They also show that in democratic societies, some measure of societal organization capable of exercising a disciplining influence on the articulation of political claims and social identities may well be a crucial variable in shaping socially inclusive stabilization policies.

Depletion of state capacities and of "social capital" is not the only impediment to a repeat of the Western European welfare-state development path in Eastern and Central Europe. On balance, an even more important structural obstacle may be the systemic incompatibility between, on the one hand, an international order emphasizing geographic and economic mobility rights ("opportunity") and, on the other, "thick" conceptions of citizenship linking citizens in an exclusive fashion to states. Hence, developments in the postcommunist countries emphatically rebut T. H. Marshall's assumptions about an evolutionary order, in which "social citizenship" represents the pinnacle.

From today's vantage point, post–1945 planning debates appear absurdly optimistic about the future. Yet near-universal agreement existed about the need for state direction of the economy. In France, Jean Monnet was appointed Commissaire Général du Plan in 1946, and that same year the first four-year plan commenced. French planners emphasized the need to "persuade" industry to concentrate its efforts and take a long view of industrial needs. In contrast, German planners (who tended to be called policy makers because of an aversion to planning but nevertheless engaged in planning just as much as did the French planners who bore the label proudly) laid heavy emphasis upon decontrolling the economy, paid lip service to the principle of nondiscrimination, and to free markets facilitated by macroeconomic stability and commodity aid.

The Dutch economist and planner Jan Tinbergen's advocacy of centralized economic planning represents the epitome of postwar hubristic planning theory. In 1964, long after coordination had replaced bureaucratic planning, Tinbergen (pp. 77–78) argued that the Soviet Union and the Western economies were converging; as the welfare state in the West worked to give "decreasing weight" to the interests of the owners of the means of production, economic planning in the East was working to equalize "the weights given to the interests of the various groups of the population." In the event, East-West convergence took place not on the basis of the ubiquitous rise to power of planners but on their demise.

The central importance that industrial relations, trade union activities, and economic coordination between business and labor had in post–1945 state building and public policy leaves us with the puzzle of having to explain their corresponding lack of importance to present-day public policy and institution building within the context of the European Union. This particular puzzle will be the subject of Bernhard Ebbinghaus and Jelle Visser's discussion in chapter 10. Meanwhile, the chapters by Hanagan and Klausen invite a reconsideration of the origins of trade union power and suggest systemic causes for the declining importance of unions in public policy making (to be distinguished from the decline of unions themselves, as measured by membership figures or wage control).

With the emergence of industry and a large, organized working-class, industrial relations, for economic and political reasons, assumed a central place in late nineteenth-century and in twentieth-century stabilization policy. Wage regulation emerged as key to the prevention of destabilizing competition between high- and low-cost producers. The events of the interwar years taught policy makers that economic and political instability were closely associated. Although unions were primarily concerned with improving the conditions of members' lives, the newfound importance of wage regulation led them to assume new roles. Maintaining uniform wage rates throughout an industry almost inevitably requires that wage movements be coordinated by political means. Hence, if wages were to be determined by means of collective bargaining, both states and industry had important reasons to favor encompassing national unions over local unions that might be vulnerable to competitive militancy and takeover by radical groups.

Confederational control gives any given employer greater certainty that union wage rates will prevail and reduces the incentives to hold out against union demands. Unable to mold union organization to the form preferred, industry and employers look instead to the state for help in shaping trade union organization. Similarly, the "weaker trades," consisting of poorly skilled and poorly organized workers, may look to the state for help in coercing employers to accept unions, provided, that is, that they can expect the state to be a "friendly" partner. As part 2 shows, even as we can identify comparable logics of trade union and industry responses to questions of wage regulation—the weaker part is more inclined to ask for assistance from the state—political and historical contingencies pay large roles in shaping industry and union strategies in relationship to the state.

The objective of full employment, a wartime concession to workers, presupposed economic planning and government responsibility for economic management. One of the ironies of the postwar welfare state was that social rights, in theory, were defined as an addendum to economic rights (Beveridge 1945). But how could meaningful planning take place without crossing over into a command economy and violating the boundaries of liberal society? The peg that fit the hole was national coordination between cohesive interest organizations, which owed their existence to the civilian war economy just as planning bureaucracies did. Liberal democracy changed as organized democracy became a supplement (occasionally even an alternative, some would say) to electoral democracy. Although the political system of the advanced welfare state formally observed the restraints of liberal democracy (by respecting private property rights for example), it also profoundly altered liberal democracy.

In place of the class struggle, the postwar Left embraced the state and a new "imagined community," an inclusive nation based on political and social community (Anderson 1991, 6). The connection between this key ideological transformation and the rise of the European Left during postwar reconstruction helps us understand some of the peculiarities of the German labor movements. Already in the early 1930s, the Swedish Social Democrats had begun to stress notions of the friendly state and the national community as a solidaristic organization, while looking for ways to mobilize electoral support for social reform. Per Albin Hansson, the party leader, routinely described the party's goals as the creation of a Swedish *Folkhemmet*; a "people's home".[1]

Claims to social rights based upon national fellowship implied a degree of Germanness and national integration that was unacceptable to German Social Democrats (SPD). The 1959 Bad Godesberg Program brought the SPD closer to the pragmatic strategies of the Swedish Social Democrats but did not embrace the communitarian perspectives so important to postwar U.K. and Swedish social democrats.[2] Instead, the SPD went further to embrace a liberal understanding of social and political justice that stressed individual responsibility and freedom. The SPD went far in the affirmation of liberal values, claiming, "man's life, his dignity and his conscience take precedence over the group."

The state-controlled trading system favored by the British Labour Party, for example, did not fit American plans for a free-trade order, and the U.K. dependency on U.S. financial assistance was one factor—albeit not the only one—in preventing its realization. The United States effectively bound the postwar Labour government to international trade liberalism by making a promise of free currency convertibility a condition for a loan agreement. Yet it was also the case that postwar arrangements allowed states a measure of insulation against an integrated international economy. As John Ruggie (1983, 215) once remarked, "The essence of embedded liberalism . . . is to devise a form of multilateralism that is compatible with the requirements of domestic stability." The fact that we today would put Ruggie's observation in the past tense is one reason that the "social citizenship" option is not available to postcommunist countries restructuring their economies to allow for a greater role for markets and restructuring their societies to allow for greater mobility.

An obvious comparison exists between Potůček's thesis regarding the depletion of state and society in postcommunist countries as an impediment to a statist, or a social democratic (as traditionally understood), welfare state today and the analysis Fred Hirsch advanced twenty years ago, regarding the "moral depletion" of capitalism in the West. Like the Great Depression and World War II, the collapse of the planned economies and "living socialism" bequeathed electorates and elites with a practical and political lesson. In the former case, it was a lesson that hurt the political Right and claimed a new role for the state in curbing volatile markets and setting standards. In the latter case, it was the vices of the state—the dead weight of large bureaucracies, the *immobilisme* of planned economies, and the injustice of a political system based upon ideological obduration— rather than the vices of capitalism that were remembered. The latter lesson stressed the importance of liberty, competition, and opportunity as powerful vehicles for social betterment for the individual and economic growth to the benefit of all. Rather than the universalist model constructed by postwar West European states, postcommunist countries have opted for multitiered welfare states combining self-insurance and government subsidies with a very modest safety net based on means testing. One exception is the Slovak Republic, where a protectionist route has been followed, ushered in with nationalist mobilization and redefinitions of who is a Slovak, who is a Czech, and who is neither. As chapter 9 shows, the exception also supports our general thesis regarding the links between state mobilization and social closure.

We have already mentioned that we see evidence, in the East European cases, for the fallacy of regarding welfare-state universalism and "social citizenship" as firm standards for future political and social development. The welfare state was, we argue, a legacy of the twentieth-century warfare state and may well cease to be an important aspect of state building in the twenty-first century.

The postcommunist paths also help us make a stronger argument for the links between international order and domestic arrangements, in part because they stress the causal importance of the *domestic* reactions to shifts in the state system. Hence, these cases contradict current theories that see the present decline of national economic controls and of the welfare state as the result of extraneous changes in the nature of economic transactions, particularly financial markets (Strange 1996). They also help us be more precise about the ways in which the international order shapes domestic social organization; that is, they help us discern that the causal chain is mediated by states.

Notes

1. Herbert Tingsten (1973, 279) cites one of the leaders in the Social Democratic youth movement as having written as early as in 1929, "'Where the concept

of class seems limited or isolated, there the concept of people opens the way to cooperation.'"

2. Willy Brandt, the mayor of Berlin, was elected party leader in 1964 and became the first postwar Social Democratic chancellor in 1969. During the war years, Brandt had escaped to Norway and worked as a courier for the socialist underground. While there, Brandt had absorbed the Scandinavian social democratic tradition, but after his return in 1945, he failed to convert the German party, which instead became dominated by the older generation of Social Democrats embittered by their experiences.

7

Markets, Industrial Relations, and the Law: The United Kingdom, 1867–1906

Michael Hanagan

How can we account for the varying institutional forms of trade union movements in the late nineteenth century, and what can we learn from that history that informs the problems facing trade unions in the modern European Union? To answer these questions, this chapter draws on two contemporary theoretical currents: the social embeddedness of markets and institutional labor economics.

The image of the boundless, all-devouring market can be traced back, beyond Adam Smith, to the Bolingbroke set of the 1730s. Herbert Spencer and Georg Simmel introduced it into sociology; Spencer viewed the prospect of the limitless market with enthusiasm, Simmel with dread. Renowned believers in the boundless market have included Joseph Schumpeter and Karl Polanyi, although they also divided on its history and meaning. Polanyi (1957) argued that through most of history, markets had been embedded in social structures and that the appearance of disembedded and autonomous markets at the beginning of the nineteenth century had provoked an inevitable reaction that took a variety of forms, from New Deal liberalism to fascism and communism.

Mark Granovetter (1985), a sociologist, follows Polanyi in stressing the "embeddedness" of markets, but has underlined the extent to which the creation and existence of all markets are conditioned by social institutions. Granovetter's usage of the term is more in line with the one employed in this chapter than is Polanyi's. Like Granovetter, and in contrast to Polanyi, this chapter shows the ways in which labor markets, at least in the nineteenth and early twentieth centuries, remained firmly embedded in social structures. Indeed, an analysis of social embeddedness is key to understanding the evolution of labor law in the United Kingdom and France between

1867 and 1906, as is attention to political process; this viewpoint is shared by some important new currents in labor economics and political science that have adopted the name of "new institutionalism," as well as by longer-established, structuralist approaches in sociology: the sociological structuralists and new institutionalists who emphasize the value of the "long view of history." In economics, William Lazonick (1991, 290) has argued for the need to study "the evolving relation between organizational coordination and market coordination in capitalist development." Lazonick maintains that economists must make cross-national historical comparisons to understand differences in economic policies and economic institutions among nations. In political science, Kathleen Thelen and Sven Steinmo (1992) declare, "Working at the level of midrange theory, institutionalists have constructed important analytical bridges . . . between state centered and society centered analyses by looking at the institutional arrangements that structure relationships between the two." And interdisciplinary structuralists such as Granovetter (1985), Tilly and Tilly (1992), and White (1981) have emphasized that all labor markets necessarily incorporate social structures. There is no single determinate relationship between markets and social structures. Granovetter, as well as Tilly and Tilly, concludes, however, that social conflicts and social solidarities, both on the shop floor and beyond it, can have profound influence on the actual structure of labor markets.

The perspective of institutionalist labor economists is particularly valuable in examining the relationship between the construction of labor markets and the development of skills. Problems of labor supply must be emphasized, as well as the role of formal and informal organizations in the formation of markets. As we shall see, the nature and quantity of labor supply strongly influence the character of institutional protection for skilled and semiskilled labor and, thus, the kinds of labor markets that can be constructed. But the more politically focused new institutionalism of the political scientists is necessary to understand the conditions in which states stepped in to regulate and to reinforce the creation of labor markets begun in the industrial arena. Finally, it is helpful to view the construction of labor markets as an outcome of conflicts. Negotiations for such outcomes are embodied in social institutions within industry and, typically, are secured and shaped by state protection. Those institutions and the laws that support them, mediating among markets, workers, and employers in strike conflicts, constitute something like what David Snyder (1975) labeled the "institutional setting" for conflict.

This discussion of trade union legislation in the United Kingdom and France between 1867 and 1906 draws on all these currents and makes four points. First of all, differing or variable problems with the supply of semi-skilled labor in these countries influenced the roles of employers and trade unionists in taking responsibility for training and protecting semiskilled workers. The relative availability of skilled and semiskilled workers in the United Kingdom led large-scale employers to allow trade unions some responsibility for training workers. In France, the scarcity of both categories of workers encouraged large-scale employers to keep this responsibility in their own hands; there, employers developed elaborate welfare schemes to tie semiskilled workers to their jobs. Second, differences in trade unionists' responsibilities for training workers for semiskilled tasks affected the formation and structure of labor markets and of labor relations. For this reason, the legitimacy of trade unions was widely accepted by employers in England, while employers in France remained hostile and suspicious. Third, the growth of trade union militancy at the end of the nineteenth century forced states to recognize the legality of trade unions, but the strength of union mobilization and the character of markets were crucial for determining which aspects of labor relations were legitimized. The English state carefully demarcated an unregulated economic terrain in which employers and trade unions could compete, free from the fear of state intervention, while the French state sought to supervise trade unions actively, thus ensuring that they would not engage in radical politics. Fourth, the strategies of employers, trade unionists, and states had important, but unanticipated, effects on the development of labor relations in the United Kingdom and France. In England, the division of labor strategies between a trade union movement committed to collective bargaining and a Labour Party committed to state intervention in the economy was inadvertently promoted by the structure of union legislation. In France, the inability of trade unions to play a recognized role in regulating the labor market, the legal prohibitions on their political action, and the legislated fostering of localism, combined with strong government supervision and intervention, encouraged the development of revolutionary syndicalism in the labor movement.

Thus, a multiplicity of coinciding and contingent variables shaped the law of 1884, also known as the law on professional organizations, in France and the British, 1906 Trade Disputes Act. Once enacted, however, this legislation endured. It exerted its own influence on national industrial relations, providing the legal foundations for the mass trade union movements that emerged after World War I. Although legal battles over unions' legal status were still to come, our analysis confirms Colin Crouch (1993) stress on the importance of the prewar period in the crystallization of state tradition in industrial relations. More important, our analysis provides a serious alternative to economistic theories that cannot explain why, in the United Kingdom, where the oversupply of labor was a constant issue, the trade unions obtained strong job control while, in France, where undersupply was a chief concern, trade unions never managed to control skill classification and the allocation of labor. Only an institutionalist perspective can help in these regards.

The Creation of Labor Markets in Heavy Industry

The years between 1867 and 1906 are important because they coincide roughly with the beginnings of what David Landes (1970, 235) called the "Second Industrial Revolution," the age of electrical power and motors; organic chemistry and synthetics; the internal combustion engine and automotive devices; precision manufacture and assembly-line production. They were also characterized according to Alfred Chandler (1990, 2), by "a new economic institution, the managerial business enterprise, and a new subspecies of economic man, the salaried manager."

Along with these innovations and this new type of manager emerged a new type of worker, the semiskilled worker. Unlike the craft worker, this worker acquired his skills on the job, learning by doing. Charles More (1980, 57) defines semiskilled work as "involving the mastery of only a limited amount of knowledge and or number of manual tasks, such as can be learnt in weeks or months, rather than years." But unlike the casual laborer of earlier times, this new worker acquired a competence that was, in the aggregate, important to employers. If worker turnover deprived the employer of an adequate supply of semiskilled workers, poorly trained replacements could slow down the pace of production or ruin expensive material (Slichter 1919).

As Oliver Williamson (1985, 243) demonstrated, "skills that are acquired in a learning-by-doing fashion and that are imperfectly transferable across employers have to be *embedded in a protective governance structure* lest productive values be sacrificed if the employment relation is unwittingly severed" (italics his). Hence, structures designed to reduce labor turnover were of considerable importance to industry, and it is significant that these structures differed considerably between Great Britain and France. In Great Britain, trade unions bore an important part of the responsibility for providing skilled workers to industry and retained some accountability as well for supplying semiskilled workers; in France, large employers assumed almost the entire burden of training semiskilled workers in heavy industry and maintaining the quality of the labor force.

Because British large-scale employers permitted apprenticeship and job training to be regulated by custom, they provided a valuable opportunity for trade unions. The distinctive role of large-scale and medium-scale U.K. employers is crucial in this regard because craft regulation of skilled work remained an important factor in small shops in both the United Kingdom and France. As the guilds weakened in the United Kingdom, rules about apprenticeship were embodied in state regulations and in the apprentice journeymen's associations that enforced them. Despite suggestions to the contrary, however, British unions were far too weak in the early nineteenth century to have been responsible for forcing apprenticeship on reluctant factory employers (Turner 1962, 295). Where it survived, apprenticeship did so because it was an important aid in obtaining skilled labor (More 1980). This is very much the thrust of Williamson's argument, and one that is entirely convincing.

However, the consequences of employers' acceptance of trade unions' apprenticeship regulation have been underestimated. By permitting trade unions to take responsibility for regulating and enforcing apprenticeships, British employers provided them with a tool that would, over time, increase their leverage. The unions' effort to regulate the character of skilled labor had an important formative influence on the character of the British trade union movement.[1]

The reluctance of large-scale employers in Great Britain to concern themselves with efforts to remold their workers to the needs of modern industry has recently attracted considerable attention. Key to this reluctance is that in Great Britain, on the eve of the Second Industrial Revolution, there already existed an abundant labor force of skilled workers, whose bargaining position was reduced by their numbers. The question becomes, as posed by Howard F. Gospel (1992), why was the predominant pattern one of minimal attachment between employers and their workers, rudimentary pay and benefit systems, and externalization? His answer: throughout most of the nineteenth century, there was an elastic labor supply in the United Kingdom, especially for unskilled but also for skilled craft labor. In a buyers' market for labor, external labor markets were sufficient; employers did not have to create internal ones.[2]

Other conditions also promoted British employers' reluctance to assume responsibility for creating structures to protect their semiskilled workers. First, British employers were slow to adopt the new technologies of the Second Industrial Revolution, precisely because England had been the progenitor of the First Industrial Revolution, and businessmen had large investments in fixed capital and skilled workers. Able to transfer skilled workers back and forth between the new machines and the old, they adopted the new technologies only slowly. Thus, the presence of skilled workers helped British capitalists who needed to keep the pace of production (what Chandler in 1990 labeled "throughput") as rapid as possible in the transition to new technologies. The exception—the only union action capable of uniting employers in their determination to curb union strength—was the effort by the Amalgamated Society of Engineers in the early 1850s to prohibit semiskilled workers from working on the same machines as skilled.

Second, British employers were also slow to adopt a routinized hierarchy of managerial employees occupying staff and line positions and hence slow to develop the administrative capacity to provide job training programs. British employers who had experienced the technological environment of the First Industrial Revolution, with its emphasis on self-education and "tinkering," remained under its sway in a new, more scientific and professional era.

Third, unlike heavy industrialists in most other countries, British industrialists were late to develop large-scale business organization run by engineers and professional administrators and taking advantage of economies of scale. Nor did they develop marketing structures for mass production that would enable them to dominate home markets and to compete more successfully in international markets (Chandler 1990).

Finally, the large-scale employers' associations that, in France and Germany, developed industry-wide schemes of industrial welfare and effectively opposed trade union initiatives at the national level came late to Britain. Efforts to combine British large-scale industry to combat the political lobbying of the Trades Union Congress (TUC) were notably unsuccessful before World War I. The National Federal of Associated Employers of Labour (NFAEL), organized in 1873, failed in its effort to block passage of the TUC-sponsored Employers' Liability Law in 1880 and disintegrated thereafter. A student of the NFAEL notes, "The prevailing ideology of individualism with its emotive terms of free enterprise and 'laissez-faire' controlled the policy and tactics of employers" (Yarmie 1984, 168). British industrialists were accustomed to competing against one another in national and international markets and reluctant to cooperate, and no single group of industrialists was strong enough to compel cooperation[3]

All these factors made British employers unwilling to assume the responsibility for training workers in specialized jobs in industry or for providing benefits that might tide these workers over periods of ill health, accident, and unemployment. As organized workers began to play a role in these areas, they relieved employers of this burden. Precisely because of the chronic oversupply of labor in British markets, employers did not necessarily feel that they were giving over vital power to trade unionists. When needed and with only modest delay, skilled workers could be found to perform newly specialized tasks. The persistence of middle-sized firms within British heavy industry and their reliance on trade unions to provide qualified workers provide the context for the triumphant observation by Sidney and Beatrice Webb in 1902 (p. xxi) that "the conditions of employment in any industry are matters for Collective bargaining."

Different conditions obtained in French heavy industry, where, for two important reasons, industrial concentration and heavy industry were less significant than in Britain: (1) sectors such as coal mining, electrical products, and metalworking played a lesser role in the French economy than in the British; and (2) industrial concentration and the development of mass-production industry were generally less extensive in France than in the United Kingdom.

Nonetheless, in some sectors of heavy industry, France had begun to overtake its U.K. rival by the end of the century, if not in the quantity of production, at least in terms of technology and concentration. Although French industrialists emulated their British rivals in seeking to conserve their old plants as long as possible, they found the continuation of traditional methods less feasible than in Britain. The introduction of new steel-making techniques, the Siemens-Martin and Thomas-Gilchrist processes, forced an overhaul of the entire French metalworking industry. Metal making moved in the direction of the Briey ore fields, forcing old centers of metalworking to turn to quality steel production or to new types of machine making. The new technologies of the Second Industrial Revolution were securely in place on the eve of World War I in France, when, according to François Caron (1979), the iron and steel industry "reached a technical level which made it rank among the highest in Europe." Along with technical innovation had come concentration, which, however, remained confined to a few sectors. In 1912, 70.5 percent of the total capital in the French iron and steel industry was controlled by ten firms (pp. 159, 169).

But the effect of the Second Industrial Revolution was not unproblematic in France. Because of their late conversion to new techniques, French employers became competitive internationally only late in the century. Also, forced to depend on their national market, they ran up against chronic problems of labor shortage. Gérard Noiriel (1988a, 28) confirms that a shortage of workers prevailed well into the 1930s; he adds that employers met this challenge with active recruitment and training programs. Unable to offer high wages as did American employers, the French depended on a labor force that was composed of substantial numbers of both temporary migrants from agriculture and women workers who would leave the labor force, at least temporarily, when they had children.

The challenge of inadequate labor supply led French employers to play a more active role in training their workers than did British employers and, more importantly, to take measures to discourage turnover. At first, of course, early skilled and semiskilled industrial workers in France were recruited directly from Great Britain, where they were promised high wages and substantial bonuses if they remained for a contracted term. At least initially, French employers generally tolerated highly skilled artisanal workers such as molders, puddlers, and glassblowers because these groups were too cohesive and possessed too many skills to challenge effectively; instead, they focused their attention on training the new semiskilled labor force that was developing in heavy industry in the 1860s and 1870s (Hanagan 1979).

Many French firms allocated space for special workshops for young apprentices.

While French employers were more willing than British to train their employees formally, they were much less willing to tolerate trade unions. Indeed, Edward Shorter and Charles Tilly (1974, 34) claim, "The one objective the employer attempted at all costs to reach in labor relations (between 1870 and 1914) was the protection of his *patronal* authority. . . . The very idea of 'collective bargaining' is inappropriate to French labor relations because the typical *patron* vastly preferred arrangements with individual employees to group bargaining" (italics theirs).

Indeed, French employers in coal mining and steel had a long history of providing extensive benefits for their employees. Such benefits were, of course, a double-edged sword for workers. In an old industrialized area such as the Stéphanois region of France, some large industries offered extensive medical care, including their own hospitals and nursing staff. By the 1880s, many of the steel companies and all the coal mines provided old-age benefits as well. The funding of these benefits came from compulsory contributions from workers' paychecks supplemented by matching grants from the company. The key provision was that benefits were offered only to workers with long years of continuous service to the company. While the benefits themselves were insufficient to provide for a worker's old age, companies sometimes made supplementary grants to particular workers or their families or provided relatively undemanding jobs for older workers who had good reputations. Thus, the companies rewarded those of their workers who stayed in industry and punished those who returned to the countryside. The privately organized and financed benefit system was clearly linked to the employers' struggle to end temporary migration into and out of industrial employment (Hanagan 1989). In this area, the difference between the United Kingdom and France is striking. Fitzgerald's survey (1988, 83) of industrial welfare in British iron and steel concludes that before 1930, U.K. factory paternalism as generally limited to "sporting and social clubs, unsystematic sick clubs in receipt of a voluntary subvention, or *ex gratia* pensions."

French industrialists found it easier than their British counterparts to organize as a distinct interest group, and this organizational strategy enabled them collectively to provide benefits to their employees by the end of this period. The four decades after the passage of the corporation law of 24 July 1867 witnessed a rapid growth in corporations (*sociétés anonymes*). French employers gained as well as trade unionists from the law of 1884 on associations that enabled them to organize together without obtaining official authorization. In 1893 and after, the personal contacts made through cooperation in the fight for the Méline tariff aided industrialists in banding together on a broader scale. In 1895, industrialists reinvigorated the moribund Comité des forges (Rust 1973, 21, 62–63). Between 1900 and 1914, no legislation affecting this group's interests was passed without its tacit approval. In 1910, the Comité des forges organized its own system of pensions for steelworkers but in so doing only formalized and centralized long-established systems of medical and insurance benefits whose origins could be traced, in some companies, back to the 1850s and 1860s.

In terms of benefits and training, then, French employers played a much more important role in constructing a labor market for semiskilled workers than did British employers. Because of their need to secure a stable labor supply, French employers used training and insurance benefits to solve their more urgent problems of labor turnover. The willingness and ability of French large-scale employers to assume such burdens made them far less willing to accommodate trade unions.

Trade Unions and Unionists, Politics, and the Law

The role played by British trade unionists in providing skilled workers and in filling the gaps in the semiskilled workforce was not based solely, or even chiefly, on their role in regulating apprenticeship. British unions also provided valuable social benefits that helped to maintain skilled workers through periods of unemployment, sickness, and injury. Employers found invaluable allies in trade unions in this regard. The unions frequently offered unemployment benefits and sometimes sickness and accident insurance, although these latter services were more commonly provided by friendly societies that were independent of trade unions. While such services aided capitalists, they also served the interest of trade unionists, providing a weapon by which trade union leaders could enforce discipline (excluded members lost the contributions that they had made to the insurance fund).

French observers were impressed by the provision of social insurance by British labor unions. In 1896, Paul de Rousiers (1896, 274) even argued that the union insurance programs were a major reason for their organizational vigor. French working-class life, as a whole, was notably deficient in such institutions before 1884. Napoleon III's government looked upon friendly societies with great suspicion. After the coup d'etat in 1851, it dissolved almost all secular friendly societies out of suspicion that they supported covert opposition to the government. The disassociation of trade unions and friendly societies was fostered by the repression of the Second Empire, but it became permanent under the Third Republic. The clandestine trade unions that grew up in the shade of illegality learned the lesson that friendly societies were the first victims of political repression. Debates raged throughout the trade union movement about whether unions should develop social insurance, or as they were called in France, "mutualist" functions. Between 1848 and 1914, trade unions often condemned friendly societies. By the end of the nineteenth century, moreover, a French "new unionism," built on the experiences of the 1870s and 1880s, had come to dominate. It assumed that collective bargaining was impossible and that direct trade union ties to political parties were undesirable. Based locally, this new unionism preached the doctrine of "anarcho-syndicalism"

While the law of 1884 on associations was critically important, legal restrictions cannot, in themselves, explain the development of anarcho-syndicalism. A trade union composed of highly skilled workers with some degree of job control—the French printers union may serve as exemplar—could obtain government authorization and provide insurance benefits for its workers.[4] But unions lacking the job control of the printers found legal restrictions an overwhelming obstacle. The failure of French trade unions to provide insurance benefits, together with their inability to retain control over job training in heavy industry, goes part of the way in explaining their grassroots orientation and their frequent refusal to follow the directions of the national trade union federation.

In the development of the British and French union movements, the political environment in which fundamental legislation regulating trade unions was initiated was as important as the structure and organization of labor markets. Long-term patterns of national politics and short-term circumstances shaped national legislation in both countries. Between 1867 and 1906, political opportunities were richer and more rewarding in Britain, and the distinctive character of trade union laws passed in Britain and France in those forty years greatly amplified the contrasting character of labor relations in the two countries. After 1884, it became increasingly clear that the French trade union movement was not simply more repressed than the British but that its repression had significantly affected the course of its development.

Trade unions attained an enduring, secure legal standing in 1884 in France and in 1906 in Britain. This difference in timing is remarkable in that attitudes toward trade unions had been about the same in both countries at the nineteenth century's dawn, when both had broken formally with old-regime patterns of regulation. The French Allarde and Le Chapelier Laws and the English Combination Acts had prohibited trade unions. Many nineteenth-century struggles had involved efforts to reduce the effect of, or to abrogate, these laws and establish a secure legal basis for unionism. These laws were the product of legislators' determination to allow markets to rule supreme. While permitting some flexibility for local officials to mediate labor quarrels, they provided that states would no longer ensure the conditions of apprenticeship or set wages; hence, these laws forbade organizations of masters and of workers, such as those that had formerly collaborated with the state in regulating labor markets. In theory, decisions about a worker's skill or the terms of his training were left to individual bargaining. In practice, however, employers sought to avoid making decisions about the quality and stability of individual workers, placing the burden for training semiskilled workers not on markets but on private training programs. In heavy industry, employers and workers took the responsibility in Britain, and employers alone in France. As a result, in Britain, although concessions made in the 1820s were grudging and incomplete, trade unions were granted much greater freedom and security than in France, where they were brutally repressed until the 1860s.

A politically moderate British trade union movement grew. Beginning in the 1850s,, the legal status of trade unions became an important political issue. Try though they might, judges found it difficult to reconcile the economic doctrine of market freedom with the existence of large organizations of workers and with strikes. Laws passed in 1859, 1871, and 1875 to legalize peaceful strikes were invalidated by court decisions declaring strikes to be breaches of contract and, so, conspiracies against employers. The *Taff Vale* case of 1901 was merely the crowning blow in a long chain of judicial rulings denying the legal status of trade unions in Britain. *Taff Vale* held that trade unions were conspiracies at civil law and, more importantly, that they were liable for their members' actions

Unsurprisingly, British trade unions mobilized to overturn this decision. Fortunately, the years after 1901 offered exceptional opportunities for trade unionists to exert influence. The extension of suffrage in 1884 to include many skilled and semiskilled male workers led both the Conservative and the Liberals to court the labor vote. In 1903 came the greatest opportunity of all, when onetime Liberal Joseph Chamberlain embraced protectionism and split British elites. He appealed to workers, on the basis that "alien legislation, sweating legislation, fair wages legislation—is absolutely contrary to Free Trade" (Chamberlain 1914, 324–25). Although many workers, particularly less-skilled workers, voted Conservative, the broad support for social welfare measures shown by organized trade unionists' championing of old-age pensions, and by their demonstrations for unemployment relief, alerted Liberals that they also had real opportunities to woo workers. Despite the Conservative effort, the Liberals won the battle for the working-class vote. The great Liberal victory of 1906 set the scene for the passage of far-reaching legislation on trade unionism.

In order to keep the new working-class voters, Liberals were prepared to deal with a judicial obstructionism that frustrated them as well. In the early years of the Liberal government (1905–1908), Prime Minister Henry Campbell-Bannerman identified labor law as an area in which Liberals like himself, suspicious of social reform, could make handsome concessions to workers. In 1906, Parliament passed a sweeping Trade Disputes Act granting trade unions immunity from actions at civil law (Brown 1982, 128). The Liberals, following the Labour members, had originally intended a more limited grant of immunity, but a series of lawsuits by employers, combined with trade unionists' growing doubts about the desirability of compulsory arbitration laws, led trade unionists to demand more extensive legislation.[5] While the 1906 law represented an unexpectedly complete victory for the trade unions, employers did not actively oppose it. By conceding that labor relations should not be regulated they felt that they had headed off the agitation for compulsory arbitration that was gaining strength within the labor movement. In this regard they were right, for trade union support for compulsory arbitration declined precipitously thereafter (Pelling 1968).

The regulation of trade unionism followed a very different path in France. Napoleon III, courting the working-class vote in the last years of his reign, modified the legal status of strikes and trade unions. In 1864, the imperial legislature removed the absolute prohibition on strikes. Then in 1868, a law on association was passed that allowed workers to assemble without special administrative authorization, so long as they did not discuss political or religious matters. This prohibition of political involvement already foreshadowed a key direction in the development of French labor law. Although the absolute prohibition of the Le Chapelier Law was repealed, the legal status of trade unions in the 1870s continued to be more doubtful than in Britain; in France, trade unions could be dissolved by local administrators' arbitrary decrees.

Basic trade union legislation in France, then, was designed and adopted at a time when trade unions had little power, when they encountered fierce opposition from employers, and when they had little opportunity to influence legislators (Rueschemeyer, Stephens, and Stephens 1992, 90). To understand political opportunities in France, the divisions over the legitimacy of the republic must be grasped. Based on both religion and politics, this issue split all classes, particularly employers and the middle classes, and undercut support for efforts to empower trade unions.

In the late 1870s, the labor movement, embittered and repressed in the aftermath of the Commune, renewed the alliances with republicans formed during the last years of the Second Empire. Working-class congresses held in 1876 and 1878 revealed the strength of the trade unionists' alliance with republican political leaders. Republicans realized that an organized trade union movement loyal to the republic was a valuable ally; they were also deeply suspicious of attacks on union movements launched by conservative large employers (Friedman 1988). As a result, republican governments frequently intervened in large-scale strikes and pressured employers to negotiate compromises with their workers.[6]

From the early 1870s on, republican leaders sought to reward their trade union supporters by providing a stable legal basis for trade unions. In France, however, no bidding war broke out, as it did in Britain between Liberals and Conservatives, that might have encouraged moderates to sacrifice their hesitations for the sake of winning working-class votes. Republican supporters of Gambetta, such as Edouard Lockroy, tried vainly in 1876 to pass a law recognizing trade unions. Lockroy argued that legalized trade unions would give workers incentives to defend their interests peacefully. Yet conservatives stoutly resisted these efforts; they feared that free labor unions would be irresponsible. In the late seventies and the early eighties, the pressure to act increased, but conservatives in the Senate resisted republican efforts to pass trade union legislation. Finally, the minister of the interior, René Waldeck Rousseau, persuaded an influential employers organization to support a law on organizations acceptable to the Senate. The law's advocates argued that it "would make trade unions easier to regulate and less likely to engage in revolutionary politics" (Barbet 1991, 7).

The law of 1884 provided the basic foundations for trade unionism and for the organization of employers during the Third and Fourth Republics and remains today the basic statute of French trade union law. It had four major provisions: (1) it required all trade union officials (and officials of other organizations) to provide their names and addresses to local government; (2) it forbade trade unions and employers organizations from dealing with religious or political questions; (3) it granted legal personality to local organizations but not to national ones (hence, local trade unions might own buildings and form mutual aid societies, but national trade union federations might not do so); and (4) it permitted individuals to join only those organizations relating to their industrial or occupational specialty.

The passage of the 1884 law failed to strengthen the connection between republicans and trade unionists, a connection that had begun to weaken after the workers' congress of 1878. Most trade unionists anticipated very little benefit from this legislation, and they feared the provision requiring trade union officials to register their names, which could easily by used in surveillance and repression.

As a part of the republican effort to win working-class support, in 1886 the first chamber of labor was established by the Parisian city council. Over the next twenty-five years, urban chambers played a pivotal role in the development of the French trade union movement. Republican politicians, disturbed by developments within the union movement, had hoped to use the chambers to orient unionists along more moderate lines. Recognizing the importance of job control to the development of moderate trade unionism, municipal politicians provided subsidies for trade unionists to provide employment bureaus within the chambers. But the most significant aspect of the chambers was that they served as the major institutional contact between elected governments and trade unions; indeed, the chambers quickly became the centers of the trade union movement.

Although they served as tools of militant trade unionism, the chambers did not perform the role in hiring and training that legislators had hoped. They supplied labor, particularly casual labor, to small concerns, but their recruits were not welcomed by large-scale employers because the chambers used their employment services to promote trade unionism. Further, they too often accepted workers' own declarations about their skills (Schöttler 1982). Instead of working together with employers to organize job markets, they were centers for union organization. They subsidized unemployed migratory workers to seek work elsewhere, rather than reducing wages in already overstocked trades, and were an invaluable means for mobilizing local support for striking workers.

These organizing activities provided the motive for the political repression of the trade union movement. When chamber activities became too militant, municipalities invariably "discovered" that many trade unions were unregistered and demanded their exclusion, or asserted that the chamber was involved in politics, and closed it down. Developing a national political strategy to respond to such repression was impossible for the chambers. Adapting to local circumstances, the chamber movement had a very heterogeneous political composition, dominated by revolutionaries in some areas, by reformists in others. Anarcho-syndicalism provided a façade of unity to a movement too deeply divided to carry out extensive and well-coordinated national actions on its own.

In 1906, the Charter of Amiens of the Confédération Générale du Travail (CGT), the overarching national organization joining union federations and chambers, reaffirmed its commitment to political independence, a stand supported by a variety of unionists, conservatives as well as anarcho-syndicalists. The Charter of Amiens only ratified the localism and autonomy that industrial organization, reinforced by the law of 1884 on worker associations, had imposed upon the trade union movement.

Markets, States, and Classes to the Present

Once legislation defining the structure and purpose of unions had been passed and a legal basis for unionism created, national labor organizations and federations of organizations began to emerge. In Great Britain, the growth of the "new model unions," which emphasized "financial solidity and central control," marked this new departure in the 1850s and 1860s (Kynaston 1976, 18). In the far more repressive climate of France, tentative movement in this direction in the late 1860s ended with the severe repression that followed the Commune. Hence, the growth period in the 1870s and 1880s marked a new beginning. In neither country did government-sanctioned unionism and the passage of fundamental trade union law meet the expectations of administrators and politicians. In both countries, trade union law played an important role in shaping the labor movement, and its unanticipated consequences were critical to further developments.

In Britain, employers continued their efforts to weaken the labor movement. The *Osborne* decision in 1908 undermined the political influence of trade unions. Trade union immunities, significantly narrowed by the Trade Disputes and Trade Unions Act of 1927, were again attacked by a series of legal decisions in the 1960s, and the Thatcher government tried, between 1980 and 1982, to abolish these immunities. Although the Conservative government modified its opposition in the late eighties, it continued to reject the "voluntarist" consensus that relied exclusively on the "peaceful exercise of collective economic sanctions in the field of industrial conflict" (Auerbach 1990, 12).

In fact, the fate of the system of industrial relations that Otto Kahn-Freund (1954) labels "collective laissez-faire" has been jeopardized by periodic political mobilization and countermobilization. Kahn-Freund argued that "the 1906 Act did not increase but greatly reduced the possibilities of state intervention."[7] However, "collective laissez-faire" is a misleading description. While the term is correct in emphasizing that routine state intervention in industrial affairs was greatly diminished by the 1906 Act, it minimizes the fact that issues of state intervention and labor law became central themes of British national politics. What prevented Conservative initiatives from reshaping the labor movement was the trade unions' pressure on the Liberal Party and, later, support for a Labour Party that would reverse antilabor legislation: the *Osborne* decision was annulled by the Trade Unions Act of 1913; the Conservative-sponsored Trade Disputes and Trade Unions Act of 1927 was repealed in 1945 by one of the earliest acts of the Labour government; between 1970 and 1974, the Labour Party, under fierce trade union pressure, sponsored legislation that limited the impact of the court decisions in the 1960s, while imposing new restrictions on the trade union movement. Trade union opposition to these restrictions contributed in part to Labour's defeat in the 1979 elections.

Regardless of its laissez-faire rhetoric, the British system of collective bargaining has been shaped by alternating political pressure by employers and trade unionists. It has been utterly dependent upon political mobilization at the highest level. Despite assertions that trade union immunities had become part of a British political consensus, only trade union power and its support for a strong Labour Party maintained the legal position of the trade union movement.

Historically, British trade unions increased their power as a result of the legal recognition of voluntarism. Within the Labour government between

1945 and 1947, some argued for direct control of the economy by public administration, and others favored market manipulation. Ultimately, the latter strategy was victorious over the former. Samuel Beer (1966, 200) explains the defeat of socialist planning within the Labour government: "The principal cause . . . was the resistance of trade unions to government control over the movement and compensation of labor." Although Beer's interpretation has been challenged, present-day analysts (e.g., Klausen, ch. 8 below) are rehabilitating his analysis. Since 1951, other Labour governments have fallen because trade unionists refused to support governmental policies involving wage controls. U.K. trade unions' stubborn commitment to collective bargaining was closely connected to their decision to enter politics and fight for legislation to ensure a favorable bargaining climate, but it has also led them to bar the route to socialism. Their failure to agree to wage regulation and compulsory arbitration not only closed the path to socialist planning but, as Klausen points out in the next chapter, also excluded the kind of cross-class interest coordination that would have promoted corporatist economic planning and successful Keynesianism.

British labor relations have not been the product of an ever-expanding labor market. Operating within the context of labor supply and taking advantage of political opportunities, conflicts between British workers and employers played a key role in *creating* the labor market for semiskilled labor. In Britain, politics and markets have been intimately intertwined. British collective bargaining developed under state auspices, and its bargaining positions continue to be refashioned by government intervention. Markets have not dominated everywhere, not even within that private arena given over to collective bargaining.

In France, also, labor legislation was of critical importance in shaping the development of labor relations. There, the effects of legislation were not those desired or sought by politicians; it is the failure of collective bargaining that needs to be explained. Asserting the importance of nonmarket forces in French labor relations is paradoxical, for the law of 1884 decreed that trade unions must operate solely in the economic realm. Both legislators and trade unionists voiced this principle; no group has ever more loudly asserted its independence from the state and politics than did the anarcho-syndicalists who dominated the French trade union movement between 1895 and 1914.[8]

In the years after the passage of the law of 1884 legalizing trade unions, the growing French trade union movement found its ties to governments and politics increasing despite its proclaimed contempt for the state. The impact of this interaction produced many of the characteristic features of French trade unionism. The inextricable links between labor markets and states can hardly be better illustrated than by the French example, in which the very laws intended to preserve an air-tight separation between state and market actually served to increase their interdependence.

At the local level, the ties between politics and unions were frequently close, for an active chamber required municipal funding, only obtainable through its close political ties to the locally dominant parties. This relationship, politically advantageous to both chamber and party, endured despite disagreements about the chamber's independence.

The character of strikes in French heavy industry also made French unionists dependent upon politicians. As we have seen, large French employers generally refused to bargain with their workers. Because negotiations were ruled out, strikes quickly became life-and-death struggles for local labor movements. Republican politicians could not view with indifference the defeat of large-scale strikes. Industrialists were often enemies of the republic while labor movements, whatever their rhetoric, were always friends of the republic. In this situation, republican politicians usually exerted pressure on industrialists to compromise. Even though the leadership of strike movements might be socialists or anarchists who were unpalatable to republic politicians, the consequences of worker defeat were often politically more damaging to republicans than compromise settlements, as Shorter and Tilly (1974) and Friedman (1988) have shown.

At the national level, the very anarcho-syndicalist leaders of the CGT and the Federation of Chambers of Labor who preached antiparliamentarianism also spent time in parliamentary maneuvering. The easiest political role for CGT leaders was always rhetorical. In many instances, it sufficed to denounce as grossly inadequate those aspects of legislation that socialists had managed to pass by compromising with Radicals and Radical Socialists. Between 1899 and 1902, for example, the CGT cheerfully denounced most of the reformist legislation sponsored by Socialist Alexandre Millerand.

Anarcho-syndicalist leaders were quick to object, however, when legislation directly affected their movement. For example, in 1895, the congress of the Federation of Chambers of Labor voted to threaten a general strike if a law prohibiting trade union membership to railway workers was passed. In 1897, it threatened the republicans that it would urge workers to abstain from voting if legislation promoting the chambers were not passed. The following year, it supported a bill to permit trade unionists to limit the number of apprentices in a trade and to organize vocational education. Similarly, the CGT hoped in 1901 to influence the legislation on the establishment of factory inspectors; on occasion, it circularized senators about its views on pieces of legislation. Nor did the CGT refrain from suing employers for infringement on the prerogatives of a labor inspector. And it also solicited select Socialist legislators to pass specific legislative proposals.

The efforts of the CGT leadership to maintain its antiparliamentarian rhetoric while attempting to influence parliamentary decision making culminated in the Chevalerie du Travail Française. This secret organization, originally modeled on the American Knights of Labor, flourished between 1893 and 1911. French trade unionists used it to reach left-wing public opinion beyond the trade union world and to propagandize broadly for syndicalist principles. This attempt, on the part of leaders committed to antiparliamentarianism, to create a political interest group reveals the emptiness of the syndicalists' denial of the relevance of the political world.

The pattern established in French industrial relations by 1914 endured into the 1950s. As the pace of French industrialization picked up and extended the factory organization of labor throughout the country, conflicts between capital and labor became widespread and bitter. Under these circumstances, the role of the state in imposing settlements in labor conflicts became all the more prominent. State intervention was underwritten by new legislation that intensified the government's power to intervene as labor laws passed in 1919, 1936, 1946, and 1950 increased the state's capacity for intervention improved greatly.

The expansion of state intervention into labor markets would have scandalized the republican legislators of the early Third Republic. The very prohibitions that they had imposed on the trade union movement reduced its ability to intervene independently in labor markets and increased its reliance on political support and government intervention. A trade union movement subject to the free-market philosophy of the Third Republic was doomed to frustration and opportunism: frustration because state restrictions imposed an impossible burden on trade unionism; opportunism because trade unions had to discover means to circumvent the legislators' intentions. Anarcho-syndicalism exemplified both these currents.

Conclusion

This study of the construction of industrial labor markets and the genesis of labor legislation in the late nineteenth century in Great Britain and France makes three chief points bearing on the major themes of this book. First, it underlines the importance of institutionalism as an explanatory framework and the inadequacy of an image of nineteenth- and early-twentieth-century markets as all-devouring and homogenizing. The work of institutional labor economists helps in understanding the significance of job-training structures in the formation of a labor force. But varieties of institutionalism developed in sociology and political science provide more help in understanding how control over training structures shaped union organization and legislation regulating trade unions, and how control over training and benefit programs, together with legal regulation, exerted influence on industrial relations. In the short run, for early nineteenth-century industrialists, it may have mattered only that job-training and benefit programs were established, but in the long run, for the character of national industrial relations, it also mattered under whose auspices they were established.

Second, the French and British cases both are exceptions to the pattern of comprehensive links between social and economic protective policies that was the hallmark of both Christian democracy and social democracy. The next chapter powerfully demonstrates that differences in union structure such as the British failure to consolidate confederal control over wage bargaining doomed any hopes for trade union cooperation in macroeconomic regulation and participation in national policy making; this chapter has explored the microfoundations of the British emphasis on individual unions and independent collective bargaining. More attention to issues such as the provision of training and benefits and the character of legal restrictions might help explain the structure of national trade union movements and, thus, their propensity for adopting a Christian democratic or social democratic path.

Third, our case studies show that, historically, units of authority other than the state have been capable of supplying job training and social insurance benefits and that distinct political power relationships are associated with *who* does supply them. If employers do it, they may try to reduce workers to a dependent constituency. If unions are the suppliers, we get a ghetto model that makes unions strong but potentially undermines their capacity to enter into national economic policy making. And if states become the suppliers, we get the "social citizenship" of the kind described by Klausen. As modern European states divest themselves of responsibility to offer social benefits, it may be important to consider the political and social consequences of private groups assuming these powers.

The examples of Britain and France reveal considerable diversity in the organization of market structures and labor relations in two closely related European countries. By themselves, neither shifts in political ideology nor exposure to Europe-wide markets will automatically change these "rules of the game." Legal foundations, trade union structures, and shop-floor training patterns, developed in the late nineteenth century, have proved surprisingly vigorous in the twentieth. They do not change easily. At the same time, the persistent differences in systems of relations continue to make it difficult for workers to cooperate across national borders. Coordinated demands are not easily generated by organizations whose institutional contexts are so dissimilar. Much attention has been paid to differences in wage levels, working conditions, trade union size and strength, and union ideology within the European Union. In the long run, variegated labor relations may pose a more serious obstacle to European labor unity than any other.

Notes

1. Indeed, More (1980) concedes that "by the end of the century unions and employers had many local agreements, often unofficial, over apprentice limitations. . . . [I]n engineering there was little formal evidence of limitation in the 1890s, but the 1915 Report found the number of apprentices was limited by custom and practice in many areas." See ch. 7 for his discussion of this issue.

2. To be sure, Gospel (1992, 30) gives this as a partial explanation and points out the need to consider capital concentration and technology to explain why some firms took on the responsibility of training their labor force.

3. Yarmie (1984) adds, "A far more effective approach would have been to develop a close association with the government in order to develop industrial policy" (p. 168).

4. For a useful catalog of social services offered by French trade unions and a discussion, see Bonnafous 1924 and Leroy 1913, 765.

5. "It is noteworthy that the blanket immunity . . . was not even limited to acts done 'in contemplation or furtherance of a trade dispute,' " as was the case in other substantive sections of the 1906 law (Orth 1991, 131).

6. Shorter and Tilly (1974, 343–45) discuss the interventionist role of the French state.

7. Cited in McCarthy 1992, 5.

8. In 1908, the syndicalist leader Emile Pouget wrote, "The trade unions pay no attention to legislative prescriptions; if they develop without preoccupying themselves with them and if they fail to carry out their required formalities, it is because they attach no importance to them. They feel themselves strong enough to be above all this" (quoted in Leroy 1913, 1:59).

8

From the Warfare State to the Welfare State: Postwar Reconstruction and National Incorporation

Jytte Klausen

The war in 1939–1945 halted international trade, throwing both belligerent and nonbelligerent countries into economic self-sufficiency. Shortages and war mobilization compelled emergency legislation and state controls on a scale hitherto unseen, followed by a comprehensive reorganization of state-society relations. The civilian war economy epitomized many of the key features of a planned economy: fixed prices and wages, state direction of capital and human resources, coordinating networks of state, industry, and labor representatives reaching from the central level to the shop floor.

This chapter argues that the war economy served as a practical and theoretical bridge to peace and the welfare state. The crisis gave birth to a new international political and economic order in 1945, but it also gave birth to a new domestic order based on national integration and enclosure. The war brought a myriad of innovations in state technologies and capacities, which later shaped the welfare state. The examples range from the obvious, like the nationalization of German properties in Austria, to the less obvious, including the forecasting tools needed for Keynesian budgetary policies and the national system of employment registration that later sustained Sweden's activist labor market policies (Chester 1951; Sweden 1952:50) Likewise, the use of minimum pricing systems to stimulate domestic agricultural production was a gift from the war years to later generations (Hedlund 1985; Self and Storing 1963). The present discussion will only touch upon two aspects of the warfare state's significance for the creation of national welfare states: (1) the shift in elite views regarding state direction of economic activity, and (2) the incorporation of voluntary associations into

147

comprehensive national interest-organizations in the context of war regulations.

The War and the Welfare State

The resemblance between the war controls and a socialist planned economy was not lost on the Left. In 1944, the British Labour Party issued a statement, *Full Employment and Financial Policy*, that reflected a dawning realization of the usefulness of the controls to socialists:

> Socialists believe in the planning of imports and exports and the present apparatus of control—foreign exchange control, import programs, allocation of scarce materials for the export trade—should remain in existence. Wartime arrangements for bulk purchase, through State agencies, of foodstuffs and of raw materials, should continue. State trading, as the war has proved, brings great benefits to the peoples. We must not let this Socialist advance be halted or turned back. (Labour Party 1944a, 7)

The reconstruction process began with the ubiquitous presence of enhanced state capacities. The machinery that had been used to mobilize society in support of war could now be put to the purpose of capitalist reform. In its 1945 electoral manifesto, the British Labour Party claimed that the party's program was a "practical expression" of the spirit of Dunkirk and the Blitz, which now should be put to the business of "winning the war of peace."

As early as 1947, the combination of consumer pressures and accommodation to the new international trade order, based upon multilateralism pushed by the United States, made the state-controlled economy of the war years impossible. The contours of its replacement would remain contested for another decade, but in place of state control emerged cross-class coordination based on the semiprivate, common mold that social scientists have described variously as "collectivism" or "neo-corporatism" (Beer 1966; Schmitter 1974). Social scientists have traced postwar structures for social coordination and incorporation to nineteenth-century political institutions, but wartime organizations were in most cases the direct progenitors and prototypes for postwar organizations (Heckscher 1946; Rothstein 1992; Crouch 1993).

Moving on from the chapters by Strikwerda and Hanagan, it is an obvious step to apply our thesis about the historical legacies of closure and national integration in the context of war to a comparative analysis, and expand the perspective to include the public provision of economic regulation. Three countries, the United Kingdom, the Federal Republic of Germany, and Sweden, present us with an ideal opportunity to test our thesis. Treated as "cases," they allow us to "test" our argument by means of an approximation to John Stuart Mill's classical method ([1843] 1949) of "agreement" and "difference." A shared organizational and doctrinal past, rooted in the 1923 Labor and Socialist International, in which the British Labour Party and the German Social Democrats assumed leadership positions, allows us to control for doctrinal differences. Another commonality is that in all three countries, the Left was strategically committed to liberal political procedures. A central difference regards the war experience: one was a neutral country, one was defeated and subjected to military occupation starting in 1945, and one was an undisputed victor. Additionally, the countries differ on a key political variable: in Sweden and the United Kingdom, the Left ascended to power, blazing a trail of social and economic reform; in Germany, it was excluded from government power, and postwar reconstruction took place under the hegemony of neoliberal principles. If we can show that the legacy of war had comparable influences in otherwise divergent cases, that is, in neoliberal Germany and in socialist Sweden and the socialist United Kingdom, our thesis is strengthened. In that case, the argument that twentieth-century closure and protectionist policies stemmed from developments in the state-system and from historically continent but converging variables gains credence.

A number of questions present themselves. If the legacy of the civilian war economy played an essential role in the development of welfare state universalism and a new economic philosophy regarding the role of the state, what role did Left-wing political mobilization play? If the opportunities for state-centered coordination were present in the United Kingdom by 1945, how do we then explain the failure of coordination in succeeding years? How durable was the wartime legacy? Did it end in 1947, when the shift from state control to indirect regulation of aggregate demand (Keynesian policies) took place, or in the early 1980s, when most states finally deregulated financial markets and lifted the few remaining currency controls?

Before we proceed to a discussion of the cases, a few remarks are required on what we mean by economic planning. We define it as state direction of the allocation of nongovernment economic resources to specific purposes. This definition is specific enough to distinguish economic planning from general economic policies (even though planning objectives may pertain to those, too) and still broad enough to leave the question of means open. That suits our purposes for two reasons: (1) it was much easier to gain a consensus around the need for planning than around the question of means; and (2) the relevance of heated discussions of means soon proved questionable, as it became apparent that different means could lead to the same general goal: a full-employment economy.

The term "welfare state" is sometimes used simply to designate state responsibility for social insurance, but the postwar welfare state was a distinct economic system, based upon a link between economic and social policies. Beveridge's promise of "freedom from want" implied the priority of economic policy over social policy and of distributive politics over redistributive politics, which was why he wrote a second report, *Full Employment in Free Society* (1945), as a follow-up to his more famous *Social Insurance and Allied Services* (1942). Economic planning was, in the view of Beveridge and his contemporaries, an indispensable element in the success of the welfare state and rested on the capacity to maintain full employment.

The United Kingdom

The mechanistic marxist thinking on capitalist reform that had shaped the Labour Party's constitution from 1918, particularly the infamous Clause 4, continued to influence the party's Reconstruction Program, in "The Old World and the New Society" from 1942 Labour declared that "[a] planned Society must replace the old competitive society." The 1945 electoral platform, "Let Us Face the Future," included a nationalization program and promised full employment, price controls, and good wages. In order to achieve these goals, economic policy should aim to cure "under-consumption" and restrict business's discretionary control over economic decisions through socialization. Keynes's conciliatory approach to cross-class collaboration and his emphasis upon distant management of the economy by means of fiscal and monetary policy did not find support in the Labor Party until the publication in 1956 of Anthony Crosland's *Future of Socialism*.

A number of explanations of the subsequent failure of the Labour Party to institute economic planning have been offered. Samuel Beer (1966, 200) argued that trade union opposition was the main cause of the failure. Andrew Shonfield (1965, 93) found the Labour Party to be naive and curiously lacking in understanding of what economic planning involved. Neomarxist scholarship placed the responsibility for the failure with the Labour Party elites. One such exponent, Leo Panitch (1976, 10), denounced Beer's explanation as "highly divorced from reality." Barnett (1986, 238, 263), in contrast, has offered a biting indictment of the "New Jerusalem" visions of the postwar Labour government that made it give priority to social reforms without concern for the capacity to pay for such. James Fulcher (1991, 325) has argued that in the absence of a national trade union confederation comparable to the Swedish Landsorganisation (LO), a stable welfare state was doomed. According to Henry Phelps Brown (1986, 131), the problem was that British business was too weakly organized to stand up to the unions.

While it is true that the "New Jerusalem" raised unrealistic expectations and that the Labour Party held to some misguided notions about the dynamics of economic progress, it is also true that the responsibility for these failings must be widely shared by political elites.[1] Panitch was probably more divorced from reality than was Beer. His imaginings were the product of a "revisionism" that took its cues from the orthodoxy that the postwar generation of labor leaders abhorred. Fulcher is right but underestimates the degree of opposition in Sweden to trade union centralization. Consequently, he also exaggerates Swedish exceptionalism (or is it British exceptionalism?).

Reconstruction and the Labour Government

In 1945, the newly elected Labour government took immediate steps to nationalize the Bank of England and a number of industries, including telecommunications, coal, electricity and gas, railways, canals, aviation, and some types of road transportation. Corporatist "working parties" were created in preparation for setting up state planning agencies for fifteen industries, continuing the work of wartime boards. Later, the iron and steel industry was nationalized.

Labour and the unions were particularly concerned about the incompatibility of free trade and domestic economic planning. Evan Durbin (1949, 52–53), a Labour Party intellectual, exemplified much of the thinking of the British Left when he called for the creation of "some kind of Central Authority with power over industry and finance" to act as a "Supreme Economic Authority." A state-controlled trading system did not fit American plans for a tree-trade order, nor did it resolve the problem that Britain consumed more imports than it could make up for in exports. When the United States bound the postwar Labour government to a promise of free currency convertibility in exchange for a loan agreement, the state trading system was effectively made impossible.[2] (That is not to say that the United States was exclusively responsible for the failure of economic planning in Britain. There were other causes, too.)

During the war, Labour members of the wartime coalition government favored the corporatist model of FDR's National Recovery Administration. Stafford Cripps, who would be one of the key economic policy makers in the postwar Labour government, claimed to have been inspired by the Tennessee Valley Authority when making plans for government's role in postwar economic development (Barnett 1986, 256). During the war, the Trades Union Congress's General Council had obtained a monopoly upon the official representation of trade union interests to the coalition government. Since wartime controls involved direct governmental oversight of wage setting, the unions—represented by the national confederation, the Trades Union Congress (TUC)—became more engaged in wage policy than they had been or would subsequently become.

One of the first acts of the Labour government was to repeal the Trade Disputes and Trade Unions Act of 1927. The act had been passed in response to the 1926 General Strike, a nine-day strike called by the TUC in support of striking miners. On several occasions, it had been debated if the Labour Party should seek to amend the act rather than aim for its repeal Most of the TUC's anger was focused upon the clauses prohibiting civil service union affiliation and regulating the collection of political contributions, and the debate centered on whether to retain the provisions against political strikes. The TUC Legal Advisory Bureau had, for example, recommended in 1929 that the General Council accept an amendment defining an area of legality for striking. This recommendation had been brought up again in 1941. During World War II, the TUC had repeatedly petitioned the coalition government for changes in the 1927 act. By the 1945 election campaign, some cautioned that a demand for repeal would provide the Conservative Party with an opportunity to accuse Labour of supporting political strikes. In the end, a compromise was forged that committed the Labour Party leadership to a complete repeal, while the TUC officially asked only for an amendment (TUC 1945, 244; Allen 1960, 261–64). The new Labour cabinet promptly lived up to its promise and repealed the 1927 act. However, the compromise included an agreement to keep other wartime regulations curbing trade union immunity on the books.

Trade union immunity was also at issue in connection with a wartime regulation (Order 1305) that had made it illegal to strike and had created a National Arbitration Tribunal with the power to impose binding agreements upon trade unions and employers. The antistriking provisions had been used sparingly d ring the war, as evidenced by the continuation of work stoppages during the war (Brown 1986). Until 1951, the TUC General Council and the cabinet repeatedly agreed to extend the order. Although some unions attacked the order at successive annual TUC congresses, the TUC General Council defended it while steering a narrow course of compromise.[3] On the one hand, the General Council acknowledged that the order constituted an infringement of the voluntarist principle because it "cut both ways," meaning that it could be applied against unions as well as employers. It was argued that the order was worth keeping, despite this problem, because it gave the unions a weapon against recalcitrant employers. (If a union provided notification of intent to strike, the employer was obliged to initiate contract negotiations.) Support for the order came especially from unions representing poorly organized industries, often with many small employers.

We can speculate that the General Council gambled that under a Labour government, the benefits from the provisions compelling employers to submit to binding arbitration outweighed the political risk of the order's application against strikers. Sine the arbitration system rested on temporary extensions which the TUC had to accept, the unions were protected against the possibility that arbitration would be used by a Conservative government. The 1945 Wage Councils Act contained replacement language designed to kick in once the order was discontinued, but the replacement provisions called only for voluntary and nonbinding arbitration, to be activated if both employers and unions agreed. Those provisions later proved to be wholly ineffectual in containing union militancy.

In 1951, the tenuous compromise over the use of the arbitration system broke down when a strike by 1,700 gas maintenance workers against a contract signed by their union interrupted the supply of gas. The Labour government applied the order against the strikers, ten of whom were given prison sentences (Allen 1960, 268–70). In a second incident, seven members of the transport workers union (TGWU) were arrested for inciting dock workers to strike. The General Council demanded that the order be discontinued, and the government complied (TUC 1951, 233).

The repeal restored the immunities conferred upon unions by the 1906 Trades Disputes Act. The 1906 act had been intended to protect unions against hostile courts. It had been passed by a Liberal government as part of efforts to encourage self-regulation and the development of a voluntary framework for cooperation between employers and trade unions. This never happened, and with the order's repeal, the unions enjoyed a protected status above the law, *super legem*. Although the 1906 act stated simply that a trade union could not be sued for "any tortious act alleged to have been committed by or on behalf of the trade union," in due course a doctrine of trade union "voluntarism," which prohibited any regulation of union activities, sprang up based on the act. The doctrine was finally revoked by a series of Employment Acts passed after the election of Margaret Thatcher in 1979.

The discontinuance of the order's arbitration system had been opposed by some unions. At the 1950 TUC annual congress, a motion calling for immediate revocation of the order had been defeated overwhelmingly, indicating broad support for the order. But a year later, a motion by the smaller unions to reinstate compulsory arbitration was rejected, and the majority followed the lead of the General Council in defending voluntarism. The so-called weaker trades were embittered. One speaker accused the large trade unions of "soap-box oratory" in the matter and called the constant demands of the large trade unions for "freedom of action" disturbing (TUC 1951, 232, 508, 512). Several speakers pointed out that the arbitration provisions of the order had been used overwhelmingly by unions against employers, not vice versa. If a union declared its intent to strike, it triggered the process of compulsory arbitration and forced employers to the bargaining table.

It was evident that the TUC was in a dilemma. On the one hand, the relationship between the unions and the government had become strained; on the other, the TUC was losing control over the unions. In the General Council's report to the 1951 annual congress, it condemned "unofficial" striking, but in the absence of rules protecting existing contracts, no legal foundation existed for distinguishing "unofficial" from "official" striking (TUC 1951, 233). The disadvantage of arbitration and conciliation procedures is that unions are prevented from using the strike weapon to force employers to concede. The advantage is that they enhance trade union wage control by obligating employers in weakly organized industries to negotiate and to comply with contracts. In addition, they also facilitate union centralization by preventing dissatisfied union groups from exiting from a concluded agreement. The primary beneficiaries of regulated industrial relations are the so-called weaker trades and governments and industry wishing for predictable wages.

Trade Union Autonomy and the Failure of Planning

Disagreements over arbitration were linked to the larger issue of a "national wage policy." The "weaker trades" tended to favor a strong role for both government and the national confederation in wage determination, particularly in connection with issues like minimum wages and the extension of union contracts to unorganized areas. In 1945, they wanted to keep most of the wartime machinery for wage regulation. At the 1945 TUC congress, the Furnishing Trades' Association for the second time proposed measures that would create TUC oversight of collective bargaining (TUC 1944, 237–39; TUC 1945, 246). The resolution was actually carried, but it was opposed by the TUC and had no effect on policy. The stronger unions defended "voluntarism" and "unfettered unionism."

The following year, full-blown conflict erupted between proponents and opponents of a national wage policy. A proposal calling for minimum wage legislation and an equitable wage policy that would reduce occupational pay differentials was narrowly defeated in a card vote, with only 57 percent opposed. Had it passed, the General Council would have been obligated to prepare a report on "the means whereby a more satisfactory lasting and equitable wage standard [could] be achieved." One speaker called the existing wage system "out of date" and dared the delegates "to tell [him] that the labourer's child eats less food than the skilled man's child." Some speakers proposed a general norm linking wage setting to productivity improvements. Bevin's successor, Arthur Deakin from the large TGWU, rejected the resolution because the consequence would be that the wages of the better-paid workers would be dragged down, as the pay of the lowest and poorest industries would set the standard. He found the proposal "water on the Tories' mill" and an unfair criticism of the TUC. Hallsworth from the General Council called the proposal "naive" (TUC 1946, 418, 422, 424).

Conflicts between government economic policy makers and the unions had been anticipated already in 1944, when Beveridge, in connection with his work on his report on full employment, took the initiative and proposed a meeting with the TUC. He was concerned that full employment would not be possible unless mechanisms to prevent wage inflation were found.[4] He asked the TUC to outline what its responses would be if wage inflation occurred. The General Council refused discussion and issued a statement to the effect that the TUC would give "suitable guarantees about wage settlements and reasonable assurances that such guarantees would be generally observed" (TUC 1944, 420).[5] Restraints on unions and their ability to pursue maximum wage gains would violate the principles of a "free society" and cause the unions to "cease to be Trade Unions."[6]

In the face of currency crises and escalating foreign trade deficits, the government began to attack inflationary wages. A 1948 white paper, *Statement on Personal Incomes, Costs, and Prices*, reflected the change in government policy by endorsing wage restraint and explicitly tying wage increases to productivity increases. The paper had not been through the normal joint consultation process with the unions, but impressed with the gravity of the economic problems, the General Council nevertheless accepted the paper and its recommendations. At a special March 1948 TUC conference, 1500 trade unionists condoned the white paper and its call for a voluntary wage freeze. This agreement would not last.

In response to some of the conditions for Marshall Plan aid, the government worked out a four-year plan. In October 1948, another white paper on postwar international collaboration, titled *European Cooperation*, also tied British economic recovery to currency convertibility, multilateral trade, and balance of payment stabilization. In three years, the Labour Party had moved from state trading to multilateralism. National priorities were being brought into step with the international economic principles guiding the Recovery Program and the new international economic order under construction. Subsequently, the government's main planning document, the 1949 *Economic Survey*, reiterated the same stabilization goals.

In September 1949, the government once again appealed to the unions for wage restraint in the face of the looming payments crisis, and the TUC once again supported the government. Six months later, in January 1950, the government imposed strict limits on wage increases by tying increases to the price index. But in the absence of a legal framework for monitoring wage settlements and enforcing the government norm, compliance hinged on union self-discipline. At the 1950 TUC congress, the unions rebelled. A resolution demanding that steps be taken to control profits instead of wages and that all wage restraint policies be abandoned was narrowly defeated, but the General Council's annual report was voted down in protest against the government's economic policies. The TUC, in effect, went into opposition against its own government (TUC 1950, 467–73). Conflict subsided when the government backtracked, and in 1951 the economy began to improve. That year, election campaigning put a lid on further discussion of wage policy. Later in the year, a Conservative government was elected. For the next thirteen years, the Conservatives held power.

What about the argument of Phelps Brown (1986) that employer organizations were too weak to enter into a social partnership relationship with labor? There were significant divisions within industry over how to deal with labor. The large companies, as a rule, preferred to deal directly with the unions on issues related to wages. In the 1970s, industrial relations reform failed in part because of lack of cooperation from industry. In 1945, the situation was quite different, and still malleable. The chambers of commerce, the National Union of Manufacturers, the British Employers' Confederation (BEC), and the Federation of British Industries (FBI) all assumed new political roles in the context of the war and in the representation of business interests to the Labour government after 1945. Samuel Beer (1966, 333) estimated that by the 1950s, the BEC represented 270 affiliates who negotiated wages with 70 percent of the employed population. In the interwar years, the FBI had repeatedly encouraged industry rationalization and self-regulation. In 1942, a group of 129 industrialists had produced their own platform, "A National Policy for Industry," which had called for the creation of an Industrial Tribunal to weed out inefficient firms and "rationalize" industries. A 1944 report by the Organization of Industry Committee of the FBI had argued that closer collaboration between government and industry was needed in order to fulfill the dual goals of maintaining full employment and fixing trade imbalance. Samuel Courtauld (1949), a large industrialist with many public interests, was an exponent of Christian commercialism, much like Stafford Cripps was of Christian socialism. Courtauld was a forthright exponent of the "social partners" approach to economic regulation that came to dominate on the European continent. In 1945, business groups were as divided as labor was over the benefits and disadvantages of a national wage policy. The government was the missing actor.

While the conflict between free wages and an otherwise controlled economy was apparent, there were still some within the Labour Party who favored direct controls and a "planned economy" approach to economic policy (Dow 1970, 34). As late as 1950, Cripps insisted that the press was wrong that the government had abandoned economic planning. He did admit that it was not possible to use "the violent compulsions . . . appropriate to totalitarian planning" (quoted in Cairncross 1985, 332). Cripps's successor, Gaitskell, had written a memorandum in 1949 arguing for the necessity of keeping exchange controls and import controls as permanent measures and as "a distinguishing feature of British socialist planning" (quoted in Cairncross 1985, 329–30). But once the possibility of fixing wages in correspondence with other economic priorities had been foreclosed, it was logical that the Labour Party would begin moving towards the distant management embodied in Keynesian macroeconomic management theory and Anthony Crosland's revisionism (Minkin 1991, 92–93). The conflict between, on the one side, trade union autonomy and the unions' short-term objections and, on the other, long-term social and economic reform had pitted the unions against the party of reform, the Labour Party. The tools for a national wage policy—mandatory arbitration and conciliation procedures, confederational authority, and embryonic national organizations of business and labor—were present.

Sweden

Swedish trade unions have historically had a close relationship with the Social Democratic Party (SDP). As early as 1909, however, the Social Democrats decided that too close an association between the two could be a hindrance to organization, and eliminated collective trade union membership in the party. Hence, local unions could affiliate with the local party organization only after a vote by their membership, and the unions had no formal say over the party. An unintended consequence was to shift the relative balance of power between the unions and the party within the combined labor movement in favor of the latter. This has been particularly evident when conflicts have arisen between trade union groups and Social Democratic governments. Union interests have generally been made subservient to the political interests of the government.

A milepost in the relationship between trade unions and the party occurred when a strike among construction workers in 1933–1934 threatened to cause a parliamentary crisis for the minority Social Democratic government. The strike was brought to an end when the national trade union confederation, the LO, imposed a contract upon the striking construction workers after the strikers' third rejection of a contract proposal.[7] The threat of statutory regulation of industrial action—regulation of strikes as well as lockouts—brought employers and the trade unions into talks regarding a voluntary framework for collective bargaining and industrial action. They resulted in the 1938 Basic Agreement between employers and the LO, which established a framework for self-regulation and cross-class negotiations. However, neither the LO nor the national employers confederation, Svenska Arbetsgivareföreningen (SAF)—was yet equipped to carry out the degree of self-regulation presumed by the agreement. Both were fraught with sectional strike, and affiliates commonly denied the national confederations the authority to represent them on issues of importance.

SAF was organizationally weak compared to labor. In 1935, more than one million workers belonged to unions affiliated with the LO. In contrast, the employers association had only about twenty-five hundred members employing three hundred thousand organized workers, less than one-third of the LO's membership. The large companies, the "families" that controlled the key Swedish export industries—paper and paper pulp, iron, and metal—were reluctant to tether themselves to organizations encompassing a large number of smaller employers. They worked through their own special-interest organization, Direktörsklubben, or "The Big Five," which was active from 1933 to 1953.[8]

War Controls

The Finno-Russian Winter War in 1939 gave Sweden an early exposure to the difficulties associated with being a neighbor to war. With the German occupation of Norway and Denmark, Sweden was cut off from trade with most of the world. National service, price and wage controls, public-private collaboration, rationing and shortages, and rigid import controls dominated civil and economic life from 1939 to 1945. In June 1939, the government passed emergency legislation that aimed to put the country in a state of war "preparedness." Six months later, a national government encompassing all the major parties was formed. A national planning department, *folkhushåll-ningsdepartementet*, as well as a range of regulatory boards—including one each for food, industry, fuels, trade, transportation, and price controls—and a war reparations board that primarily benefited the Swedish shipping industry were established.[9] The planning department was closed down in 1950, but the general emergency legislation was subsequently extended until 1952.

The institutional legacies of the war administration endured beyond the suspension of emergency legislation. New agencies were created, and old ones were given greater resources and enhanced responsibilities. One example was the Institute for Economic Research, originally established in 1937, which began publishing regular economic surveys and economic analyses in the last years of the war. After 1945, the institute became a key player in economic policy. Another example was the 1940 reorganization of national unemployment and relief work programs into a national system of employment boards. After 1945, these employment boards became central to the administration of active labor market policies aiming to maintain full employment (Rothstein 1996).

The war economy relied extensively on administrative controls based on public-private collaboration and self-regulation. The consensual character of the war controls belied the coercive backdrop. Collaboration was accomplished under the penalty of law, including legislation permitting the government to proceed to involuntary cartelization when self-organization failed. The wartime machinery for administration of controls furthered the integration and organization of national business organizations. The head of the Industrial Commission was Gustaf Söderlund, who was also director of the employers association. In 1942, Söderlund presented a memorandum on economic policy that formed the basis of the national government's consensual approach to wartime regulation, an approach that relied on currency subvention, tight price controls, wage controls, and tight monetary policies. Through Söderlund's involvement, business became the sponsor of economic planning and of public control of private activity.

The warfare state anticipated not only the administrative and institutional aspects of the postwar welfare state but also postwar stabilization policy, including incomes policy. Wages were set by contracts negotiated by employers and unions, backed by legislation that stipulated that all workers were to be paid contractual wages. Technically, the government did not interfere with wage setting, but from 1941 onwards, existing contracts were extended and wage increases tied to the price index.[10] (Although price indices had been used earlier to measure inflation, the technological capacity to do so was now greatly improved.) The wartime wage agreements were the first examples of a national wage contract. Participation in the war controls radically changed both SAF and the LO. Because SAF's climb to the position of principal arbitrator of a business's interests was littered with conflict, it required the stimuli of government and wartime coercion. The LO similarly benefited from war regulations, assuming an undisputed position as the representative of labor.

Postwar Stabilization Policy and Free Unions

Unions and employers agreed that free bargaining had to be reestablished as quickly as possible in 1945. Both opposed the continued fixing of wages through so-called indexation agreements, which tied them to the price index. While the unions saw immediate economic advantages to decontrol, SAF wanted to escape from the restraints of the war economy mostly for strategic, as opposed to economic, reasons (de Geer 1986, 108). Nonetheless, almost as soon as collective bargaining had been decontrolled, SAF began to ask for the LO's cooperation in conducting centralized contract negotiations. In 1945–1948, wage setting was returned to free contract negotiations between unions and employers. In 1949, when a currency devaluation precipitated by the U.K. exchange rate adjustment caused the LO to fear a return of the kind of hyperinflation that had taken place in 1920–1921, it recommended an extension of existing contracts.

Like the British Labour Party, the Swedish Social Democrats had become increasingly suspicious of foreign-trade liberalism in the 1930s. In the 1944 revision of the party program, one of the changes regarded foreign economic policy. A new paragraph calling for "government control of foreign trade" replaced one that instead simply called for "free trade" (SAP 1944, 268).[11] There were other parallels. A prolonged strike among metalworkers in 1945, in which communists played an important role, put the social democratic unions on notice that wage controls and incomes policy were in conflict with trade union mobilization. The strike was ended after the strikers voted down the contract reached by means of a conciliation procedure and the government, together with the LO, intervened to impose the contract. Outside the metal industries, the intervention did not arouse critics. No resolutions challenging cross-class collaboration had been proposed at the 1944 SAP congress nor at the 1946 LO congress (Johansson 1989, 234.) The LO nevertheless responded by reasserting the principles of trade union autonomy and passed a resolution to that effect.[12]

The unions were deeply divided on questions of "planned wages" and confederational authority. Wage policy remained a contentious issue for two decades. The debate unfolded in union newspapers and journals and at congress meetings. At the 1946 LO congress, August Lindberg, the general secretary of the confederation, sharply attacked the idea that the LO should conduct a planned wage policy. That would involve a transfer of authority (from the affiliated union to the LO) that lacked constitutional and practical foundation, he argued. Solidaristic wage policy was a matter of "moral support" from the LO to the weaker trades. Anything more than that he considered a highfalutin principle that perhaps would be right for the future but not now. Lindberg was subsequently forced to swallow his words when a resolution in favor of "a planned wage policy" and greater LO authority in wage determination passed on a 186 to 185 hand vote (LO 1946, 167, 190, 192). Yet no apparent change in policy followed.

The 1949–1950 wage freeze put the LO back in the position of negotiating directly with SAF, the employers association. In 1951, a report written by two LO economists, Gösta Rehn and Rudolf Meidner, *Fackföreningrörelsen och den fulla sysselsättningen* was published. It presented a comprehensive economic theory for how to make full employment compatible with economic stabilization and real growth by means of a planned wage policy. In 1951, relations between the unions and the Social Democratic government reached a low point. The government tried to persuade the LO to take responsibility for wage bargaining and to curb wage inflation. The finance minister, Per Edvin Sköld, concluded that the LO was not capable of living up to the task. In meetings with the LO and SAF, Sköld made it clear that if the upcoming agreement proved to be overly generous, the government would step in afterwards with restrictive measures.[13] A real possibility existed then that Swedish economic policy, like that of the U.K. would be marred by the inability to control collective bargaining and that governments would be put in a position of habitual conflict with the unions when they tried to control inflation.

The 1952 contract ended up combining a centrally negotiated frame agreement with local agreements determining industry-specific details. In the succeeding years, contracts were concluded either under threats of lockouts or strike threats. A crucial shift took place in 1955–1956, when employers decided to force the LO to engage in a centrally negotiated process. For 1956, the LO agreed to a centrally negotiated contract, which also for the first time involved separate but coordinated contract negotiations with the white-collar confederation (TCO). After negotiations broke down, a contract was finally reached by means of arbitration. As late as the initial stages of the 1957 contract negotiations, Arne Geijer, the general secretary of the LO, repeated the view that the national confederation did not have the authority to coordinate wage negotiations. However, negotiations were resumed between the LO and SAF in February 1957, and the resulting contract provided for a fixed wage-increase for all trades to be determined with a prognosis of future economic trends in view. A far cry from the high expectations with respect to the role of the state in economic planning that had dominated debates at the war's end perhaps, this was nevertheless a viable example of democratic economic planning based upon societal collaboration.

Sweden and Britain Compared

Swedish union and employer federations shared with their British counterparts a strong distaste for compulsory arbitration. In the place of statutory regulation, they agreed to self-regulation (Lewis 1967). However, despite the fact that Swedish regulation of industrial relations has been based primarily upon private agreements, confederational control over affiliated unions, extensive regulation of pay-bargaining routines, and coordination between the trade unions and a succession of Social Democratic governments (1945–1976) have all served to infuse wage policy with concerns for public priorities.

Despite the subsequent different trajectories of Swedish and British wage policy, the war years present us with instances of basic commonalities of significant theoretical importance. In both countries, the unions and the Left embraced the war controls as models for postwar capitalist reform. But wartime wage controls had also made the unions weary of too close an association with the state, and in both countries the unions exploited their powerful position in 1945 to evade wage controls. The consequence was that the fundamental imbalance between unbridled trade unionism and full-employment policies predicted by William Beveridge in 1944 became a reality. The difference was that in Sweden a resolution was eventually found, but none materialized in the U.K.

The issue of confederational authority had temporarily been resolved in the war years by the need for labor representation in the regulatory machinery, but after the war, sectional conflicts reemerged and disabled the confederations. The parallels between Swedish and British trade union policies on these issues have often been neglected because there has been a tendency to regard the war years as a temporary interregnum and of little consequence for the postwar welfare state. The causes of trade union centralization have often been seen as a "bottom up" phenomenon, reflecting the predominance of the natural interests of different industries, but in fact the war controls were essential in producing centralization of economic interests by both industrial workers and employers. When the unions agreed to incomes policy, it was also wartime wage agreements that provided the model.

The contested history of trade union centralization and the national contract after 1945 points also to the importance of national institutional frameworks in compelling different policy responses to analogous problems. The willingness of the Social Democrats and the LO leadership to confront rebellious trade unions stands in sharp contrast to the response of the TUC leadership to "unauthorized" industrial action in 1950–1951. Surely, the balance between union opponents and proponents of confederational oversight varied in the two countries, but in the end it was the predominance of long-term political interests articulated by the Social Democratic Party leadership over the short-term economic interests of trade union elites that compelled the unions to a collaborative framework.

Germany

The German Social Democratic Party (the SPD) was reconstructed in 1945 by members who had survived since the National Socialists banned the party in 1933. Kurt Schumacher, the party leader, survived twelve years of imprisonment. Schumacher represented an orthodox socialism that dated back to the days of the 1923 Labor and Socialist International. He blamed capitalism for Nazism and regarded the elimination of capitalism as the only cure for the evil of totalitarianism. In a public speech given in October 1945, a decisive period for the Allied forces' creation of a German transition authority, Schumacher announced that "the crucial point on the agenda [was] the abolition of capitalist exploitation and the transfer of the means of production" (Scholz and Oschilewski 1953, 36–50). Like the British Labour Party, the SPD in 1945 called for immediate socialization of the means of production, although by that the SPD implied merely some form of worker ownership, not necessarily nationalization. The SPD called as well for the "implementation of the Socialist ideal in the economic sphere" (Miller 1986, 155).

Some economists argued then, as did Friedrich von Hayek, in his *Road to Serfdom* (1944), that all planning was incompatible with liberty. But the most influential contemporary critic of planning was a junior minister in the Federal Republic, Ludwig Erhard, from the Christian Democratic Party (the CDU), who became the principal architect of postwar German economic policy.[14] In place of a romantic reverence for economic "freedom," Erhard and the German neoliberal economists that inspired him stressed the importance of a commitment to a "competitive order," a contradiction in terms that nevertheless perfectly described their program.[15] They included what was known as the "Freiburg school," represented chiefly by the economist Walter Eucken, who died in 1950.

Erhard, in the course of 1948 and the 1949 election campaign, articulated a vision of the Social Market Economy, Soziale Marktwirtschaft, as the German road to prosperity and social welfare (Erhard 1958, 1992). The program stressed the positive social implications of economic growth and the liberty issues associated with the exercise of state controls. As head of the bizonal (the combined British- and U.S.-occupied zones) economic administration, he decontrolled the economy as early as 18 June 1948. Two days later, a comprehensive currency reform in all three Western zones followed. Both measures laid the ground for a largely deregulated bizonal market economy as early as the second half of 1948. Decontrol came slightly later in the French zone.

Christian Democratic Hegemony

Erhard owed his power to the Allied forces, who had picked him as head of the bizonal government, but key aspects of Allied ideas about countervailing forces and social reform did not fit his ideas about the Social Market Economy. Referring to discussions in the British zone over the summer of 1948, Erhard later (1958, 1) wrote, "I outlined my attitude to the ideas which were then in the air about the distribution of incomes. I explained my refusal to allow them to take hold again, for I considered them false." The British, in particular, disapproved of Erhard's currency reform.

It was a matter of great strategic importance who assumed control of the government in the first postwar elections. Early elections in 1946–1947 in the occupied zones of what would become the Federal Republic favored the CDU, but the SPD got more votes than the CDU in Berlin, Bremen, Hessen, and Hamburg. In the first bizonal representative organs, set up in 1948, Social Democrats and Christian Democrats were evenly balanced.

There was hardly a popular groundswell in favor of the Soziale Marktwirt-schaft espoused by the CDU. In 1953, some 56 percent of respondents in a survey still answered that they did not know what it was (Eschenburg 1983, 440). But in the early postwar years the SPD became increasingly isolated from power (except in West Berlin). It did not begin to pose an electoral challenge to the postwar Christian Democratic governments—made up of the combined alliance of the CDU and the Bavarian Christian Social Union, the CSU (supported by the small Liberal Party), and the Free Democratic Party, the FDP—until after 1959, when its program underwent significant revision (Miller 1986). The Christian Democrats reached their peak of power in 1957, when they received 50.2 percent of the vote.

Erhard's neoliberalism was not left unchallenged. It shipwrecked in part on the institutional checks on power put in place by the Allied forces and in part on the interests of small business and industries, interests that came to dominate in the party's later embrace of protective policies for the middle class, what became known as its *Mittelstandspolitik*. A 1952 proposal of a restrictive practices law that would have prohibited cartels and price fixing, and made various types of horizontal and vertical agreements between companies illegal, was met with opposition; it passed only in 1957 in a modified version.

Labor

The foundations for postwar labor relations were laid early, and without heed to CDU interests. At the Potsdam conference of 5 June to 2 August 1945, when the Allies shaped the occupational government, it was also decided to impose Allied control over the economy. With Allied assistance, the German trade unions were swiftly rebuilt between 1945 and 1949, when the German trade union confederation, the DGB, was founded with approximately 5 million members. To the chagrin of the Christian Democrats, Allied actions ensured that there would be only one national trade union confederation, an effectively socialist-dominated one. In the interwar years, a Catholic and a liberal or nationalist, trade union confederation had been created to challenge the socialist trade union movements.[16] The trade unions reappeared at the end of the war in spontaneously created works councils set up for the purpose of denazification. In 1946–1948, the unions were rebuilt, and in 1949, the DGB was formally founded as a nationwide and nonpartisan trade union confederation. In 1946, the Allied forces encouraged trade union representation in the administration of the occupied territories and in company management as a matter of official policy—part of the denazification process. Transition legislation protected the unions as a "social partner" and encouraged organization.[17] The military government also recognized the creation of works councils in the iron and steel industries. The trade unions were represented on the economic councils set up by Allied forces as part of the governing process of "Bizonia."

The new constitution, the 1949 Basic Law, both bolstered the neoliberal project and secured a statutory role for trade unions. It prohibited compulsory membership in any organization and, hence, the concept of the closed shop. Political trade unionism was also prohibited, constraining the unions not to assume a constitutional role in the running of the SPD. (the Basic Law also prohibited political striking or general strikes. (See art. 9, sec. 3.) In practice, however, the unions continued to have close ties with the SPD. Through the actions of the federal courts (labor court, constitutional court, and civil court), a body of industrial relations law has developed regarding the legality of striking and the rights of employers and employees. The emphasis on legal regulation, or *Verrechtlichung*, of industrial relations stands in contrast to the pre-Thatcherite system of trade union immunities in the United Kingdom and the emphasis on self-regulation in Sweden. The right to organize was also sustained by the new constitution. In some respects, new legislation enhanced the role of the unions. The autonomy of collective bargaining, *Tariffautonomie*, was protected by the 1949 Collective Agreements Act, which also included a crucial provision making it possible to extend collective agreements to unorganized employers and employees by means of a declaration of "general binding."[18]

On 12 November 1948, the trade unions called for a one-day general strike in protest against inflation, raising fears that the unions would become an unmanageable partner in the reconstruction process. The biggest conflict turned out to regard not wages but industrial democracy centering on the right to codetermination (a statutory right for unions to be involved in workplace management) and the status of the works councils. After prolonged conflict, the Works Constitution Act, requiring any industry with at least five employees to form a works council, was passed in 1952. The councils facilitated consultation and conciliation between management and employees; they extended from the plant level to the boardroom. They did not handle contract disputes and negotiations; the unions did. Nor were the councils regarded as instruments for economic planning or industrial policy; rather, they were a forum for industrial democracy.

Farmers and Business

Initially, Allied policies aimed to liquidate Germany's industrial strength, particularly big industry, through a breakup of the cartels that had sustained the military machine. U.K. and U.S. economic policy objectives were often at odds, for example on questions of planning and the future of the German economy. The British government wanted to nationalize the Ruhr industries and to promote socialization. In the United States, the Morgenthau Plan proposed wholesale dismantling of German industry. It regarded the rea-grariarization of German society as the only means of curbing German belligerence. In 1947–1948, containment of the Soviet Union became a primary strategic objective, and priorities changed to require instead the rebuilding of the German economy. On 5 June 1947, George C. Marshall announced the Marshall Plan, which made the Federal Republic a primary beneficiary, in a commencement speech at Harvard University.

The role of German industrialists and big industry in supporting Hitler made decartelization and denazification an objective upon which the Allies could agree. To that end, the National Socialists' economic organizations were dissolved and business organizations suspended. New organizations were permitted as long as they served "nonpolitical" purposes, but the formation of national organizations was deterred. One exception was the system of chambers of commerce, which encompassed not just retail but also craft associations such as *Handels* and *Handtwerkskammern*. Because of widespread economic shortages, the Allies saw some utility in keeping the craft chamber system. The National Socialists had formally dissolved and reorganized the associations in 1943. Heirs to the old guild system, the craft chambers were nineteenth-century organizations, para-public cartels with compulsory membership (Bührer 1989, 141). Like the unions, the craft associations had been driven out by the National Socialists but were revived by the occupation government. In compliance with denazification policies, tainted associates were replaced, but soon the chambers gained influence as representatives of small business, sources of expertise, and partners on parity boards with trade unions. In the course of the summer of 1945, the chambers were essentially reconstituted as branch-specific organizations: in the French and British zones, on the basis of pre-1933 laws, but in the American zone, only as private, voluntary trade associations. (The new constitution subsequently forbade compulsory membership.)

The Allies not only relied on organizations that had suffered under the Nazis. They also reconstituted employer organizations through the participation of representatives of employer interests on parity boards set up by the occupational government. The central ideological and economic importance of the farmer to the National Socialists' program had caused farm organizations to become deeply implicated with the Nazi system. Despite the tainted origins of the Reichnährstand, which was a national, compulsory organization of all producers, manufacturers, and distributors of agricultural products, it remained in place after the Allied invasion and continued to be responsible for the distribution of agricultural products, albeit sliced up along zonal boundaries. Its regulatory competencies were transferred to the Ministry of Agriculture. In 1946, a precursor to what became the German Farmers Union, the Deutsche Bauernverband, was formed as a national peak organization for the local and regional farm organizations. It organized as much as 90 percent of all farmers (Katzenstein 1987, 28).

In all major respects, the postwar German system of interest representation and coordination was created by the occupation government prior to the creation of the Federal Republic in 1949. Unlike in Sweden and the United Kingdom, postwar organizations were the product not of the war economy but of the occupation economy. The Allied powers sought to create a civil society of countervailing interests and used a number of different prototypes for its organizational system. Like a bride, the Federal Republic was sent off with something borrowed, something old, and something new. The format for industrial relations was inspired in large part by American trade unionism; old business and farm organizations were reformed to fit new needs; and the new constitution ensured that the unions would play both a larger role in economic regulation than the CDU wanted and a lesser role than the SPD wanted.

The German case is exceptional because neoliberal perspectives of reconstruction dominated, but in other respects it conforms to the general thesis that the postwar welfare state was shaped by the international crisis created by the war—literally by an occupation government. In other ways as well, the interests of the war settlement overrode domestic politics. The neoliberal agenda was tempered by the need to include labor and other classes in social and economic stabilization. Erhard, like other reformers at the time, relied heavily on the special powers to compel social and economic change that were vested in government by the crisis. Reconstruction provided a boost for neoliberalism by limiting the reach of government in key respects and creating, in Peter Katzenstein's words (1987), a semisovereign state. That cannot however obscure the fact that reconstruction took place under the tutelage of states, represented first by the occupational government and then by elected governments.

Conclusion

By midcentury, the competing blueprints for societal reconstruction after 1945 drew heavily upon nineteenth-century political theories, pitting socialism against liberalism. But neither worked out as adherents had hoped. In the case of socialism, concessions had to be made to competition. In the case of neoliberalism, concessions were made to interests demanding protective policies reining in competition. The need for societal collaboration, and the analogous interests of the "two sides of industry" in protecting against the diluting effects of competition were moderating influences. They were also a source of cross-national convergence in countries with somewhat similar class systems. Although beyond the boundaries of this chapter, the role played by constitutional designs—particularly the divergent dynamics of proportional representation (with its tendency to render majority government impossible) and the party governments associated with the plurality method of assigning seats to parties—cannot be neglected.

Traditional historiography on the postwar welfare state has ascribed state expansion to the rise and political mobilization of the Left (Korpi 1983; Esping-Andersen 1985; Fulcher 1991). The argument presented here suggests that it was the Left that adjusted to the postwar state, rather than the other way around. In international relations theory, standard wisdom has held that one of the singular achievements of the new international economic order created on the dual pillars of dollar hegemony and trade multilateralism was that it produced what John Ruggie (1983, 215) called "embedded liberalism." This in turn permitted nation-states to reap both the benefits of international trade and a measure of protectionism needed to regulate the domestic economy. There was widespread support—among business, farmers, and labor—for protective measures and insulation against foreign competition from business and agricultural interests. But with the exception of farmers, whose contribution to state building generally is overlooked, fears of hostile state-action and of the usurpation of organizational prerogatives by the state also compelled national interest-groups to protect their autonomy and resist planning. There were liberal as well as antiliberal forces at play in the domestic context.

It has been common to see the liberal agenda as one imposed upon the Western European countries by the United States, motivated by self-interest in opening up European economies to American businesses. This view ignores the significant pressures for liberalization that emerged from consumers demanding the ability to purchase desirable goods, be they Argentinean beef for British workers or specialized products needed by industry. It also ignores the macroeconomic effects of trade union opposition to rigid controls on incomes and on consumption.

The warfare state was the progenitor of the welfare state but sometimes in counterintuitive ways. The central contribution of the war rested partly on the expansion of state powers precipitated by war mobilization and by international shortages, and partly on the associated mobilization of cohesive national associations of economic interests capable of entering into collaboration with the state. After 1945, labor-inclusive policies became vested not in the nationalized industries and the planning institutions envisioned by reconstruction programs but in the protective institutions of the welfare state and in economic policies based upon cross-class conciliation.

Notes

1. The Federation of British Industries (FBI) in paragraph 20 of its 1942 platform, "Reconstruction," argued for maintaining wartime controls on foreign

trade for "some considerable period." At the same time, it insisted that it was of paramount importance that the government impress upon the Americans the need to preserve "the Empire" as a protected trading system.

2. On 21 August 1945, five days into the tenure of the newly elected Labour government, the United States abruptly canceled the Lend-Lease Agreement that had sustained the United Kingdom during the war. In December, Keynes commenced negotiations about a loan agreement. The agreement was ratified, with some difficulty, by the U.S. Congress in July 1946. On 15 July 1947, sterling was made fully convertible with dollars; on 20 August, convertibility was withdrawn. Limited convertibility was not reinstated until 1958–1959.

3. Among the large unions, only the National Union of General and Municipal Workers supported the arbitration procedure as a means for disciplining employers (TUC 1946, 369).

4. The exchange between Beveridge and the TUC has been poorly researched, but Lewis Minkin (1991, 59) asserts that the conflict not only caused a split in the Labour Party–TUC leadership but also made Bevin go into prolonged self-imposed exile from the Labour Party.

5. Panitch (1976, 16) uses this statement to justify his view that the unions were willing to accept a national wage policy, as long as the Labour Party kept its part of the bargain. I find Panitch's interpretation unconvincing.

6. One concession that the TUC feared was that the unions might have to relinquish some control over job specifications and assignment (TUC 1944, 421).

7. Divergent accounts exist of the roles of the LO and the government in bringing the strike to an end (Kupferberg 1972; Stephens 1986; Swenson 1991; Klausen 1995a).

8. It was constituted by the chief executive officers of five large companies, Asea, Electrolux, LME, SKF, and Separator. Later, a sixth joined. For a history see Söderpalm 1976.

9. This account is based on Sweden 1952. A comprehensive list of rationing measures and price controls is contained in the national planning department's annual report. See, for example, Sweden 1944.

10. Agricultural wages were permitted to rise ahead of the price index because the government wanted to prevent agricultural workers from taking advantage of tight labor markets to shift into better-paid occupations.

11. There was no absence of controversy. The SAP congress debated the different aspects of foreign policy at length, often contentiously. See SAP 1944, 200–232.

12. The resolution asserted that the unions' opposition to state intervention in wage determination was "equally justified with regard to the inevitable consequences for both individual and organizations of the replacement of freedom of negotiation by State control" (translation taken from LO 1953, 16).

13. Per Edvin Sköld was finance minister from 1949 to 1955. His notes are found in Jonasson 1976, 192.

14. Erhard was minister of trade in 1949–1963 and then chancellor until 1966.

15. For a description of German planning theory and practice, see Maclennan, Forsyth, and Denton 1968, 2.

16. In 1920, the social democratic DGB represented about 75 percent of all trade union members; the Christian confederation, only 10 percent (Visser 1990, 147).

17. The 1946 Allied Control Act established a framework for conciliating disputes. It involved a mandatory schedule for conciliation but granted both employers and unions veto rights against contracts reached by means of the procedure.

18. Either side could ask for general binding, but it could not take place before a vote in a parity committee consisting of representatives from employers and trade unions. That meant that either side could block its application.

9

Markets, States, and Social Citizenship in Central and Eastern Europe

Martin Potůček

This chapter examines recent developments in social policy-making in the Czech Republic, the Slovak Republic, Hungary, and Poland, considering variations in each nation's historical background and the changing roles of market and state as embodied in postcommunist economic and social policies. I focus on the importance of the administrative and fiscal capacities of the state, as well as changes in political ideology and in the processes of social policy-formation and implementation in each of the national states under discussion. I am speaking here of contingent, open-ended processes, and it is still difficult to discern fundamental elements from more conjunctural ones. Yet distinctive patterns emerge in cross-national perspective. I will provide an overview of social policy regimes in the region, tracing the growth of directed social doctrines from their inception and summarizing developments during the seven-year period since the demise in 1989 of the regime of communism. Both drawbacks and opportunities will be identified. The broader context of European integration will be considered, too.

Social policies have been proposed in Central and Eastern European countries to ensure relatively broadly defined social rights for citizens and to facilitate the means for introducing the kind of "social citizenship" envisioned by T. H. Marshall (1950). In light of recent developments in national social policies, I question the feasibility of social citizenship in the region. The formation and implementation of social policy during these societies' transition from socialism to free-market democracy are a process of conflict resolution. In such a transitional period, state social policy is determined not only by public stereotypes and the inertia of old legislative and institutional structures but by expectations of a "miraculous transition" and demands arising from rapidly changing legal, political, and economic conditions.

Since 1989, postcommunist countries have undergone a series of profound, rapid institutional and behavioral changes in economic, political, and civic life. Some of these changes have been the product of steps taken by policy makers, with both desired and unintentional outcomes; others emerged as a result of spontaneous destructions and creative efforts of awakened civil society. In seeking to explain the social dynamics of the process of postcommunist transition, some authors emphasize the importance of political ideologies. Zsuza Ferge (1994, 2) suggests that social policy in the region "successfully got rid of the former ideology. Yet . . . it continues to be heavily influenced by new ideological trends." This offers only a partial explanation. Economic and institutional factors cannot be ignored. Directly or indirectly, they influence all aspects of social policy formation and implementation. Most importantly, social policy is shaped by the economic and institutional capacities of the state.

Analytical Framework

In the transition from communism to capitalism, certain structural variables stand out and assume primacy over elite ideologies. Key economic variables include both economic growth rates and patterns of income distribution. Institutional capacity is determined both by the organizational efficiency and the administrative capabilities of the state apparatus, as well as by the quality and resolve of political elites. In the postcommunist countries, social policy-formation and implementation take place in an open-ended, contingent process with a number of variables interacting. Particularly important in this response are (1) the speed and complexity of political democratization, which are associated with the political culture; (2) the stability of the government and the extent of its decentralization; (3) the speed and complexity of introducing market institutions and raising the economic awareness of citizens; and (4) the scope and strength of civic-sector institutions, including nonprofit associations, nongovernmental organizations, trade unions, and communal self-governing bodies. In addition, historical legacies shape individual, collective, and institutional memories as well as values, expectations, identities, and patterns of behavior.

Market liberalization and political democratization are among the region's most notable reforms. Claus Offe (1991a) has drawn attention to the potential negative-feedback effect caused by the opposition to privatization and marketization by those who feel their privileges threatened by democratic political institutions. This results in the inability of economic institutions to create wealth. Low growth creates public discontent, which endangers democratic political institutions. Few academics and politicians would dispute that the ultimate triumph of political and economic reforms will involve finding a new balance between political and civic rights, a free-market economy capable of creating new wealth, and a social welfare system with the means to ensure at least minimum requirements for a decent standard of living for all. This balance has been difficult to achieve and maintain even in the relatively stabilized and affluent capitalist countries (Dahrendorf 1985). It has been even more difficult to attain in the rapidly changing, politically volatile, and economically unstable environment of the postcommunist countries.

Communist Legacies: A Four-Country Survey

The collapse of communism coincided with the struggle to reestablish civic values characteristic of an open society. In Czechoslovakia, for example, the Civic Forum led the movement against the old regime and emerged victorious in the parliamentary and municipal elections of 1990. The introduction of a free market quickly became the priority in many postcommunist countries. A new government replaced the old, but the economy remained unchanged—or more precisely, its insolvency and internal paralysis was exposed, no longer masked by a facade. The inheritance of a totalitarian political system and a centrally planned economy left an urgent need for fundamental societal reforms. Nevertheless, to transform authoritarian, politically coercive social-policy institutions of the past into democratic, integrated welfare-state institutions was a task that seriously interfered with the simultaneous process of economic liberalization and marketization. That is why postcommunist states found themselves in a substantially different historical situation from that of welfare states as they emerged in Western and Northern Europe after World War II (Klausen and Tilly, Ch. 1 above).

Before the political big bang of 1989, totalitarian political systems and centrally controlled social policies were common features of all the Central and Eastern European countries, with the exception of the former Yugoslavia. Following the collapse of communist regimes in the region, there began a combination of partly spontaneous, partly controlled processes of rapid political, economic, and social change. Thus, it is difficult to identify to what extent these processes have been influenced by conscious, organized collective actions and/or deliberate decisions of the state authorities and to what extent these actions, when taken, were as effective as anticipated.

In the following sections, I analyze the development of social policy in the Czech and Slovak Republics, Hungary, and Poland. The historical background of each country and alternative paths of social and economic development taken after 1989 are detailed. My concluding remarks evaluate whether the evolution of "social citizenship" welfare regimes is likely or even possible in the Central and Eastern European region.

The Czech Republic

The process of industrialization in the area that is now the Czech Republic began in the early nineteenth century. During the era of the Austro-Hungarian Empire, the Czech lands belonged to the Austrian part, which translated, from 1867 onwards, to a rather liberal political system, a highly efficient state administration and local self-administration, and an extensive national network or schools, hospitals, and voluntary associations. When Bismarckian reforms—including compulsory social insurance schemes—were introduced in Prussia in the 1880s, Austria-Hungary followed suit.

The relatively affluent Czech lands became part of Czechoslovakia at the end of World War I. In the interwar period, it was an island of relative, though limited, political freedom, as authoritarian regimes were common in neighboring countries. Modernization of the social security system was realized by the 1920s. The Czechs were an industrially developed and politically aware people when they—partly through conscious decision, partly through coercion—joined the communist camp in 1948. The enduring importance of economic development at this time is clear when we consider that, by 1990, Czechoslovakia was the wealthiest of the countries analyzed here.

The communists had no reason to weaken the existing state administration; in their hands the state was an important instrument of power. The state took responsibility for nearly all social policies, which in the former Czechoslovakia were quite similar to those of other Central and Eastern European countries. Social policy was based on the principle of compulsory full employment, and in practice, that indeed meant virtually full employment. Given their relative affluence and an inherited modern welfare system, Czech citizens enjoyed a moderately comprehensive package of benefits and services. Employment was key to the establishment of social status. From the beginning of the 1960s, universalistic schemes ensuring selected social rights of citizens became more important. Especially during the 1970s and 1980s, specific social services for employees flourished in various branches of material production. At the same time, further deterioration in the capacity to provide social services occurred, particularly in the areas of technical equipment and the education and motivation of staff.

Not only was Czechoslovakia the wealthiest of the countries studied here, but it also achieved greater income equality. Prior to November 1989, Czechoslovak governmental policy accomplished something quite unprecedented: the equalization of incomes. This was a remarkable feat unmatched anywhere else in Central and Eastern Europe. Czechoslovakia enjoyed a reasonable standard of living for almost everyone, with a relatively small proportion of the very rich and the very poor, and the rest somewhere in between.

This was manageable only through massive regulation of prices and wages and fiscal redistribution within a centrally planned economy. It can be attributed mainly to the hard-line position of Communist Party leaders and a technically efficient state apparatus However, by the 1980s, the limitations of such a cumbersome, unmotivated, and economically inefficient system had became even more apparent.

After 1989, what is now the Czech Republic inherited a civil service with little corruption and a relatively disciplined state apparatus that provided fairly productive and effective in the crucial area of macroeconomic management. It also inherited a balanced state budget with a comparatively

Table 9.1. Visegrad Countries and Russia: Selected Socioeconomic Indicators, 1985–1992

Indicators	Czechoslovakia	Hungary	Poland	Russia (RSFSR)
Population (in millions)[a]	15.7	10.6	37.8	148.0
Purchasing power parity (% of US)[a]	35	30	25	31
Hard currency debt per capita (US $)[b]	480	1858	1058	170
Distribution of earnings (Gini coefficient)[c]	.197	.221	.242	.275
Distribution of household per capita income (Gini coefficient)[d]	.199	.209	.253	.278
Population below poverty line (%)[e]	5	18	20	≅50
Decline in GDP (%)[f]	15	16	19	—

Sources: Atkinson and Micklewright (1992); Barr (1994); Deacon (1993a); Miller et. al. (1993); Možný (1993); Woleková (1994); unpublished data and internal reports available from author.
[a]1990.
[b]1989.
[c]Full-time workers. For Czechoslovakia, Hungary, and Russia, numbers are based on 1986–1987; for Poland, 1989.
[d]For Czechoslovakia and Poland, based on 1985; for Hungary, 1982; for Russia, 1989.
[e]For Czechoslovakia, number is as of end of 1992; for Hungary, Poland, and Russia, as of 1992.
[f]1988–1992.

Table 9.2. Visegrad Countries and Russia: Selected Socioeconomic Indicators, 1993

Indicators	Czech Republic	Czechoslovakia	Hungary	Poland	Russia (RSFSR)
Per capita GDP (US $)	3029	2420	3755	1885	2100
Average wages (% of average in Czech Republic)	100	—	140	110	—
State Budget Deficit	no	yes	yes	yes	yes
Unemployment (%)[a]	3.5	14.4	13.5	16.4	—
Population in favor of individual responsibility (%)	54	43	40	15	—
Population in favor of more government spending (%)[b]	74	72	55	56	—

Sources: Atkinson and Micklewright (1992); Barr (1994); Deacon (1993a); Miller et. al. (1993); Možný (1993); Wolleková (1994); unpublished data and internal reports available from author.
[a]Percentage of economically active population, as of end of 1993.
[b]Favor more spending on education, health, and pensions through higher taxation.

small balance-of-payments deficit; an institutional tradition of a work-related social security, enhanced by universalistic state social support; the long tradition of compulsory health and social insurance forcefully interrupted during the communist period; and a population that was relatively performance-oriented and supportive of liberal democratic political values.

The first years of social-policy reform in post–1989 Czechoslovakia have been studied elsewhere (*Czech Sociological Review* 1993, 1995; Potůček 1993, 1994). It is worth noting here the important shift in government ideology after 1992, when the Czechoslovakian federation split into two separate states, the Czech and Slovak Republics. Until 1992, Czech government doctrines were partly social liberal and partly social democratic. Many important social-policy reforms were conceptualized and implemented during the pre–1992 period, including compulsory health and social insurance and a state-guaranteed minimum subsistence benefit for every citizen. Most new social-policy institutions were established at this time as well, including the tripartite Council for Economic and Social Agreement and a network of regional labor offices responsible for both passive and active employment policies.

In June 1992, a new, neoliberal (libertarian) Czech government came into power, under the leadership of Prime Minister Vaclav Klaus. This government benefited from the legacies of both the communist and the social democratic liberal regimes: the accumulated potential of wealth among the Czech population, little poverty, a fully operational state apparatus, an active employment policy, and the newly established institutions of compulsory health and social insurance. All these factors helped to prevent poverty on a massive scale, which contributed to continued popular support for the liberal government. Klaus's ultimate priority was, however, economic reform based on the rapid introduction of a free market. Essential reforms in areas of apparently lower governmental priority—including housing, education, and social support and assistance—were deferred. Neglected health services reform fell into a serious fiscal crisis followed by the radicalization of the health profession. In 1995, important social policy innovations inspired by the liberal government's ideological position were introduced. Means-tested family and other social benefits replaced universal citizen-type benefits. The level of old-age pensions relative to the average wage would be reduced substantially after 2010, as the new Old-Age Pensions Law prescribed. Trade unions opposed these proposals ardently and organized protests, including strikes.

In addition, President Havel argued that together with regional governments and self-governing public bodies, the civic sector and its nonprofit, nongovernmental organizations, professional associations, and foundations constituted a vital link between the central government and the individual. But Prime Minister Klaus showed little interest in establishing a legal framework for this link, preferring instead an unrestrained market economy. Klaus opposed the idea of separating the Social Insurance Fund (with its steadily increasing surplus) from the state budget to establish it as an independent, self-governing public body. He also sought to weaken the role of the government in the tripartite Council for Economic and Social Agreement, intending, evidently, the ultimate withdrawal of all government involvement in that institution. Thus, general agreements among the central state, regional governments, professional associations, and business groups for 1995 and 1996 were not signed (Orenstein 1995).

What type of social-policy regime is now emerging in the Czech Republic? Some years ago, I suggested that Czech social policy should be described as a neoliberal regime (Potůček 1993, 224). I now believe that I overestimated the importance of the government's liberal ideology. Instead, Czech social policy integrates elements of the social democratic welfare state with some liberal elements. The result is a mix of public and private efforts that confound Marshall's expectations of the universalist welfare state as destiny.

The Slovak Republic

Although Slovakia was also part of the Austro-Hungarian Empire until 1918, and of Czechoslovakia until the end of 1992 (excluding the Nazi period, 1939–1945), its history and contemporary situation differ from these of the Czech Republic in many respects. After World War I, Slovakia was still a mostly rural region. Moreover, during the imperial period, it had belonged to the Hungarian part of the empire, which meant that local administration was far more authoritarian. Due to continuous pressure from the Hungarian authorities to limit the use of the Slovakian language in education, the Slovaks had almost no national intelligentsia. Between the two world wars, the liberal capitalist Czechoslovak state expanded educational and cultural opportunities, but economic development was much less successful. Not until the communist takeover after World War II did Slovakia experience a period of substantial and relatively rapid industrialization and urbanization. A centrally planned economy allowed the communists to employ powerful instruments of redistribution to balance the level of social and economic development in the two regions. By the end of the 1980s, there was no substantial difference between Czechs and Slovaks as expressed by the main social and economic indicators.

Nonetheless, there was one paramount difference in the collective recollection of the Slovak and Czech people: Slovaks had few reasons to complain about state socialism in economic terms. In Slovakia, the communist regime was responsible for a relative affluence that had never before been experienced there. In contrast, Czechs had many reasons to regard the communist era as a time of a relative deceleration, or even deterioration, of their national development. This was one of the reasons why general elections held in 1992 led to the final breakup of Czechoslovakia. Most Czechs opted for right-wing parties stressing a return to a market economy, while most Slovaks preferred centrist, leftist, or nationalist parties stressing protectionist policies. The Slovak Republic began its first years as an independent state with an inexperienced political elite and state bureaucracy and an unstable government that lacked a clear idea of economic and social-policy reform. Woleková (1994) describes the situation as stagnation of the reform progress, due to the inability of social groups to soften the effects of economic liberalization. In 1993 and 1994, three consecutive governments were formed, the third as a result of the extraordinary general elections of September 1994. Moreover, the proportion of political appointees installed in the civil service after each change of government far exceeded "normal" European standards.

Nearly all Slovak social-policy institutions and provisions resembled their Czech counterparts—including the tripartite Council for Economic and Social Agreement—given that the previous legal system had been accepted.

There were, of course, differences, especially in the systems of education, health insurance, and social security. While the Czechs opted for separate health and social insurance funds, the Slovaks chose in January 1993 to establish a single body, the National Insurance Fund, financed independently of the national budget. The government also adopted a measure that allowed all contributions collected by the National Insurance Fund to be transferred to the national budget in 1993, in effect using the fund to subsidize the general government. The main reason for this was financial. Right from the start, the newly created Slovak state faced serious budgetary problems. Funding for education, health care, employment policy, and the like had to be cut. As of 1994, the National Insurance Fund once again became independent of the state budget. Combining the health and social insurance fund proved to be inefficient and cumbersome, so at the beginning of 1995, the National Insurance Fund was split into two independent bodies, the Health Insurance Fund and the Social Insurance Fund.

Unemployment was the Slovak Republic's most serious problem. At the end of 1992, the unemployment rate was 10.3 percent. This rose to 14.4 percent in January 1994, and the high rate of unemployment was expected to continue. Long-term unemployment was also on the rise, contributing to increasing impoverishment (Woleková 1994). Diminishing employment opportunities led many workers to seek either early retirement or a disability pension. As a result, the number of pensioners increased substantially between 1991–1993, producing an additional financial burden on the state budget, which financed the pension system. Moreover, a "culture of dependency" had developed such that Slovak citizens were accustomed to relying upon the state as the exclusive provider of jobs and social services. At the same time, however, the fiscal resources necessary to create an active employment policy were steadily dwindling.

Restrictions on services were a necessary consequence. Paradoxically, the center-left Slovak government implemented several draconian fiscal measures, cutting various social welfare provisions that even in 1993–1994, the neoliberal Czech government did not. Like the governments in Poland and Hungary (to be discussed later) the Slovak state was faced with a budget deficit in 1993, whereas the Czech Republic was blessed with a balanced budget and was thus not forced to make such drastic cuts. In Slovakia, health services were allocated less funding in 1993 relative to 1992, and the budget allocation for 1994 was even lower. Family benefits were redefined from universal to means-tested ones. And beginning in 1994, employers were entitled to receive state funding to build new workplaces, but only in the form of a loan. In the past, such grants did not have to be repaid.

What type of social-policy regime is emerging in the Slovak Republic? We may think of the new regime as a form of postcommunist conservative corporatism that obliterates boundaries between public and private sectors, in a system of responsibilities shared among the major societal actors (Heidenheimer, Heclo, and Adams 1990). The self-governing bodies of the health and social insurance funds and the activities of the Council for Economic and Social Agreement are prime examples. These are surprising developments considering the "statist," even authoritarian, response of the Slovak central government to many other political issues. The lack of both political will and administrative capacity impedes implementation of state responsibility. The ongoing fiscal crisis has drained disposable financial resources for existing social security schemes as well as for the innovations required to meet the changing needs of clients. As a result, from 1993 onward, we have witnessed in the Slovak Republic a somewhat inconsistent muddling-through, with a gradually disintegrating state paternalism that has been replaced by embryonic corporatist institutions, unable to face up to the challenges of a market economy.

Hungary

Hungary, like Slovakia, was still a predominantly rural country at the end of World War II. It shared with Slovakia not only a common political history within the Austro-Hungarian Empire but also the experience of relatively rapid industrial development during the communist period. In contrast to the regime maintained by Czechoslovak hard-liners, the Hungarian communists gradually liberalized political life and attempted—albeit unsuccessfully—to revitalize the economy with a series of cautious and limited economic reforms. The 1980s saw not only a weakening of the Communist Party but also the retreat of the state from important areas of economic and social life. Civil society was given a greater chance to develop institutions and patterns of individual behavior than it was in Czechoslovakia. Gradually, civil society assumed part of the space that was de jure still in the charge of the charge of the state. Most notably, shadow and black economies began to flourish and fill in the holes of the official system of production and distribution of goods and services. The weakened state was unable to control its own budget, and the state deficit increased.

Economic and political reforms attracted much of the attention of politicians after the political upheaval of 1989. The first steps towards introduction of a free market and political democratization did not coincide with a consistent reform strategy of social policy. What occurred instead was a gradual, incremental process of dismantling, and sometimes replacing, some of the old social-policy institutions. This included the establishment of the self-governing Social Insurance Fund. In 1992, a voluntary health insurance scheme replaced the previous national health scheme; as a consequence, part of the population, especially many unemployed and self-employed people, was left without health insurance. Also, the number of child care institutions, including nurseries, kindergartens, and primary-school day care centers, decreased. Means-tested poverty relief was introduced, with the threshold of eligibility set well below the official poverty line. Despite the provision of limited poverty-relief and unemployment benefits to tackle the threat of poverty and rapidly rising unemployment, the share of the population living in poverty is increasing (Ferge 1994, 13).

Meanwhile, wage inequality increased, and a widening gap developed between the average level of earnings and the average level of benefits paid to supplement low incomes. In the middle of 1992, official salaries in the upper echelons of the state bureaucracy were ten to fifteen times higher than the minimum wage, and salaries of managers in the private sector were twenty to thirty times higher (Ferge 1992a, 4).

We see in Hungary a curtailing of universalism, either by switching to the

Table 9.3. Visegrad Countries: Dynamics of Economic Performance Indicators

Indicators	Czech Republic	Czechoslovakia	Hungary	Poland
Percentage change in GDP (1988–92)	−15	−15	−16	−19
Percentage change in GDP (1992–93)	−0.9	−3.7	−0.6	3.8
Percentage change in GDP (1993–94)	2.6	4.9	2.9	5.2
Percentage change in GDP (1994–95)	4.8	7.4	1.6	7.0
GDP per capita in purchasing power parity (US $) (1994)	8808	5670	6085	4901
GDP per capita in purchasing power parity (US $) (1995)	10530	6700	6550	5750
Unemployment (%) (1993)	3.5	14.4	12.6	16.4
Unemployment (%) (1994)	3.2	14.8	10.9	15.5
Unemployment (%) (1995)	2.9	13.1	10.9	14.9
Average monthly salary (US $) (1993)	198.7	174.2	294.4	218.2
Average monthly salary (US $) (1994)	242.7	198.2	314.8	237.5
Average monthly salary (US $) (1995)	311.6	245.1	300.7	301.5

Sources: Barr 1994, 55, 142, 233; unpublished data and internal reports available from author.

insurance principle—as in health care—or by transforming hitherto universal or insurance-based benefits into selective, means-tested ones. The growing pubic dissatisfaction with the social consequences of political and economic reforms became manifest in the 1994 general elections, when the Socialist Party emerged victorious over the liberal parties. However, it would be wrong to assume that a change in government ideology can bring about a substantial adjustment in social-policy reform. Quite the opposite: the new government replaced universal family allowances with means-tested ones as early as the fall of 1994. Clearly, the general pattern of development in Hungarian social policy has not moved towards a Marshallian social citizenship.

Poland

After World War II, Poland needed to recover from the enormous cost to the nation in material damage and human casualties. And following recovery, industrial modernization and urbanization were hindered by an inefficient economy. A corrupt and irresponsible party-state apparatus under the leadership of Edward Gierek had, by the beginning of the 1980s, provoked discontented groups of civilians to mobilize the Solidarity movement in open opposition to the Communist Party. The imposition of martial law and subsequent political developments led to further political deadlock, economic deterioration, increasing foreign debt, and a continued weakening of party-state power. Poland achieved less "success" in the areas of earnings equality and income redistribution than did Hungary and, of course, Czechoslovakia, as shown in table 9.1. As a result, poverty increased steadily after the early 1980s (Ksiezopolski 1993, 179).

The situation after the political "big bang" of 1989 was favorable for Balczerowicz's well-known shock therapy. The withdrawal of state responsibility for social policy was initiated by sharply cutting state expenditures in several areas of social welfare policy, including employment, housing, health, education, and culture, and by cutting back on the social functions of state enterprises and privatizing some social-policy services. Clearly, these changes originated in neoliberal economic policies, but were there any clear-cut conceptions of a social-policy transformation? Perhaps not. The situation has been well-documented by Ksiezopolski (1993, 174), who argues that "neither the main protagonists on the political scene in Poland nor the academics are sufficiently prepared to redefine the goals of social policy within the context of economic transition." The situation is frequently described as a crisis, of social policy as well as institutions. As an inefficient system of public services teeters on the verge of bankruptcy, the gradual withdrawal of government commitment to social welfare has not been matched by a takeover of these responsibilities by private organizations. The elimination of a social minimum has been accompanied by a simultaneous fall or stagnation in individual income from work.

One of the changes figuring most prominently in the process of Polish social-policy making after 1989 was a transfer in the responsibility for providing some aspects of social welfare from the central government to the municipalities, which had very modest economic resources, or the private sector. As in Slovakia, the number of old-age and disability pensions increased. All pensions continued to be paid from the state budget. The state-run and state-financed health services remained practically unchanged, except after 1991, when new opportunities for the involvement of the private sector opened up in the development of a two-tiered health services system. But financial resources shrank, decreasing the number and quality of public health services. The same applied to education, particularly higher education, which saw a concomitant increase in market-based services. Some institutional reforms were considered—including the introduction of a mandatory private pension insurance scheme, health insurance, and copayments for health care—but these were not implemented. In addition, although unemployment benefits have begun to relieve some economic deprivation, unemployment has continued rising unrestrainedly. Poverty has increased during the 1990s, raising fears that Poland might be headed towards poverty on a massive scale (Ksiezopolski 1993; see also table 9.2).

In sum, the post–1989 Polish governments have been unable to take an active stand in shaping social-policy matters. This is true for a number of reasons, but the chief problems are the inability to pay and the escalation of need that threatened to bankrupt the system. During the period of economic transformation, a lack of consistent state action accompanied the state's withdrawal from many important social-policy spheres. Few changes were made regarding institutionalized patterns of negotiation between employers, workers, and the state. Thus, most people seemed to be on the losing end, and the result was increasing polarization and impoverishment of the Polish people, at least in the short run. An indicator of how different Poland is in this respect is a public opinion survey showing that only 15 percent of the Polish population were in favor of individuals taking responsibility for themselves. In comparison, that proportion was between 40 and 54 percent in the other countries studied here (see table 9.2). Unlike the Czech and Slovak Republics, Poland lacked a consensual social-policy making culture. As a consequence, social tensions flared. Solidarity, which had historically guided the opposition to the communist party-state, again led strikes. The outcome was similar to that in Hungary: in 1993, leftist and agrarian political parties took power.

Not everything that has occurred since 1989 was due to the failure of government policy. From the outset, Poland was plagued by an acute economic crisis, an enormous foreign debt, an impotent state bureaucracy, and

an increasingly unequal distribution of wealth. A politically and economically underdeveloped agricultural sector provided a living for about one-
third of the electorate. This inhibited the capacity of Polish society—
particularly its most vulnerable members—to absorb the impact of rapid
marketization. I do not see any signs of corporatism emerging in Poland, as
an alternative to state-centered social schemes. In my view, two paths seem
more likely. Either Polish social-policy makers will persevere in recon-
structing principal areas of the welfare mix and relieving mass poverty, or
they will continue to be hamstrung by a "do nothing" government as the
nation's human capital deteriorates.

Is Social Citizenship in Central and
Eastern Europe a Possibility?

My conclusions are threefold. First, the countries under discussion are neither prepared nor willing to transform rapidly the state paternalistic social-
policy regime that existed under communism into a social welfare regime
based on the notion of "social citizenship." Second, the central governments
of all of these countries are seeking to limit financial expenditures for social
welfare by shifting their former financial responsibilities either to local governments or to families and individuals. The impact of budgetary constraints is stronger than the influence of a political ideology. Third, both
the market and civil sectors are still too weak to assume obligations from
the paternalistic system. As a result, many legitimate social demands are
not met at all.

It is a mistake to believe that the postcommunist countries can move
directly from state paternalism to a social citizenship state and, in effect,
jump the developmental hurdles to the generous welfare state that Western
European countries were able to achieve in the decades after World War II.
It is worth remembering that in the Western European countries, governmental responsibility for a social minimum was typically an extension of
preexisting private insurance schemes, often set up by trade unions or civic
organizations, that had helped ensure both the financial security and the
normative legitimacy of social citizenship. Moreover, social citizenship was
crucially dependent upon a concomitant commitment by governments to a
full-employment guarantee. Presently, the postcommunist countries lack
both the financial and organizational capacity and the civic and economic
microfoundations for welfare state expansion that is reflective of a social
citizenship norm.

None of the Central and Eastern European countries analyzed in this
chapter are seriously considering adopting social policies that embody social
citizenship standards at this time. Indeed, the empirical evidence shows

clearly that these states, intentionally or unintentionally, have followed the opposite path. All, irrespective of the ideological persuasions of their governments, have attempted to reduce social welfare expenditures and replace many universal benefits with means-tested ones. This seems to me an understandable process: socialist paternalism was able to produce a very special system of social rights that, together with the inefficiency of the political and economic system, contributed to discrediting communism. In the absence of the preexisting gift of the well-developed, generous, and democratically run welfare state (as emerged in many Western and Northern European states after World War II), Central and Eastern European states are neither prepared nor willing to move directly from state paternalism to social citizenship; their policies hence assume decidedly liberal or fragmented forms.

Will social policy create a significant obstacle to the four Visegrad countries' existing association agreements with, and anticipated full membership in, the European Union? It is worth nothing that the West European welfare state also has undergone considerable change and hardly conforms to the "social citizenship" mold. Hence, social policy is unlikely by itself to present an obstacle, but touch economic criteria for the acceptance of new members and the necessity to harmonize national legal systems with the EU legislation are, and will remain, more serious barriers to successful and rapid integration. In political terms, we can expect the Visegrad countries to have both warm admiration for the "social dimension" of the European Union and an open reluctance to embrace this dimension, as expressed many times by the Czech prime minister, Vaclav Klaus. The modes of integration can be expected to emerge more clearly after the EU Inter-Governmental Conference, which is expected to end in 1997. This conference seeks to adapt EU structures to the needs of the future, including EU expansion to the east.

III

Citizenship and Group Representation at the Transnational Level

Transnational political organization and cross-border mobility are key emblems of open societies. In our case, both also serve as lenses for studying current changes in social order deriving from the creation of new European political institutions. The creation of a "social dimension" to European integration has increasingly become a practical and political test case for how far integration will go, and for the prospect of the creation of a European polity. While analyzing the successes and the failures of integration in this respect, we also treat transnational social mobilization as a theoretical problem. In chapter 2, Gary Marks discussed European institution building as a conscious process of political creativity. This approach is again applied in chapter 10, by Bernhard Ebbinghaus and Jelle Visser, to the activities of trade unions and in chapter 11, by Thomas Faist, to immigration policy. In both cases, the authors conclude that national institutions and national interests continue to exercise powerful restraints on transnational political creativity. In chapter 12, Chiara Saraceno discusses one of the areas in which such creativity has been somewhat successful, namely, the creation of feminist networks and a "women's interest" in European institution building.

The presence of significant variation across policy areas illustrates the importance of preexisting national institutions in shaping future policies. It also illustrates, at a more general level, how difficult it is to engineer political change by means of conscious elite-driven strategies. In this respect, Eric Hobsbawm's argument, in the final chapter, that there is no singular European identity assumes importance. Democratic national political institutions were created in response to nineteenth-century swells of national movements and twentieth-century wars. The European Union is, in comparison, a weak organization, based on self-interests (rather than power) and dependent upon consensus building among the member states (rather than competitive citizen politics) for progress toward projected goals.

Yet, as Strikwerda, Marks, and Moch have described in previous chapters, there is also an older European legacy of a liberal European regime, consisting of collaborating interdependent states and integrated societies. (Hobsbawm takes the fact that this older legacy has stumbled, on war and nationalist mobilization, as evidence that the European dream is impossible. Marks and Strikwerda take that stumble as evidence that there is an alternative to the twentieth-century statist regime.) Article 13 of the 1986 Single European Act (SEA) refers to the free movement of persons as one of the fundamental principles of the European Community (now Union). As a result of EU treaties and rule making, the powers of the fifteen member states to enforce citizenship have been restricted, but the result is hardly a return to an unregulated "state of nature." The mobility rights and associated protective rights anchored by EU rule making can be claimed only by citizens of the EU member states. In the EU countries, net migration rose in 1992 to approximately 1.2 million people. As much as 75 percent of all European immigration goes to Germany, which received over 1 million foreigners in 1992, but only 15 percent of entrants to Germany have, in recent years, come from other EU countries (Eurostat 1993). After 1992, stricter immigration control caused a reduction in immigration.

Frontiers are like doors. You can go through an open door from either side, but locking it from one side stops all traffic. In recent years, the EU has tried to lock its doors to the outside world, but with mixed results. Aiming to reduce the stream of immigrants, new rules have, in part, simply driven it undergrouond.

A long history of internal European migration exists, as demonstrated by Leslie Moch in chapter 6. With open borders, signs of a common European culture appeared. (There is some disagreement among the contributors to this book about the significance of a common culture. In the last chapter, Eric Hobsbawm paints a bleak picture of the likelihood that such culture will continue to develop.) In the nineteenth century, Europe was like an open door. Italian Jacobins, for example, raised the issue of a national Italian state after deriving their conception of a state from the French revolution (Lyttelton 1993). The First and Second Internationals were international political organizations that joined national socialist movements on a common ideological ground. They foundered first on sectarian battles over dogma and then on national divisions, when the national parties belonging to the International sided with their states in the mobilization in preparation for World War I (Eley 1992). The reformed Labor and Socialist International (1923) was destroyed by World War II. Is it unthinkable to imagine another international political and cultural revival? Strong states pose many impediments to transborder activity; weak states, fewer. In the contemporary situation, European interconnectedness reemerges as a significant fact of European life in response to the reduced importance of the nation-state.

Citizenship is part of a basic historic transformation linked to the definitions of state, rights, and representation. It is, in complex fashion, also linked to collective mobilization and institution building. At the same time, it has provided a means by which states could strengthen territorial control and individuals could make claims against the state. In a historical comparative perspective that reaches beyond the twentieth century, the equation of citizenship with the nation-state appears less essential. We have models for nonnational conceptions of citizenship. Elizabeth Meehan (1993, 4–8) has compared the development of European citizenship to the Greek city-state, to the Roman republic and the Greater Roman Empire, and to the ideal of the cosmopolis. In her view, the addition of European citizenship rights to rights enforced by states produces a system of rights that may bear some resemblance to that under the Holy Roman Empire. Other claims to precedence can be made, as well. Discussing how we may conceptualize territoriality in an international system consisting of a mix of states and nonstate units (e.g., offshore markets), John Ruggie (1993, 149) has brought up the Ottoman Empire and the Mongol tribes as comparative examples. The Hapsburg Empire illustrates yet another link between nationhood and civic obligation. There, authority remained divided (between the emperor, the Catholic and Protestant hierarchies, and the princely-states), while citizenship was confined to the city; citizenship was local in practical administration but culturally and normatively tied to a broader conception of a pan-Germanic identity.

In highly mobile societies, citizenship cannot remain tied to parochial and "national" criteria, except when applied as a tool of exclusion. When acquired as a birthright, citizenship defines entitlement and obligations that seamlessly blend in with the sociology of growing up. But as Michael Walzer (1970) points out, birthright is a deceptively simple criterion. There is, at any time, an "oddly assorted" group of people who are partial members of the state-community. It is the misfits that remind us of the constraints of citizenship.

The chapters in this part address different aspects of the clash between national policy and budding transnational initiatives in the social area, ranging from national immigration policy to labor market regulation and the attempts of postcommunist countries to catch up with the Western European welfare states. Despite different points of departure, the next four chapters all conclude that the model for postwar welfare-state expansion that T. H. Marshall described with his concept of "social citizenship" is insufficient both as a descriptive and as a prescriptive model. As a criterion for redistributive justice, it fails because it disregards the crucial importance that work and access to the labor markets in the rich countries play for people living in poorer countries. Confronted with immigrants, citizenship becomes an exclusionary category. Social citizenship fails, also, as the national polities relinquish—by design or by accident—competencies to new, emergent authorities organized on different foundations.

Bernhard Ebbinghaus and Jelle Visser compare the foundations for strong trade unionism in the postwar welfare states to the conditions provided by transnational institutions. The obstacles to transnational solidarity range from employer hostility to conflicts over goals and means between national confederations and a weak trade union elite. Paradoxically, the strength of national trade unionism becomes a cause of the weakness of trade union internationalism.

Thomas Faist contrasts divergent political and economic interests in German immigration law. The German case is particularly important in a broader European context because Germany has high stakes in EU immigration policy with respect to the outside world. Western and Northern European immigration was stable for a decade between 1975 and 1987, when all types of immigration increased rapidly.

Chiara Saraceno writes about the ambiguous responses of women to EU technocrats' invitations for women's organizations in the member states to participate in the new networks of interest representation. European integration has picked up due, in no small measure, to the active encouragement of a new European elite anchored in EU institutions. But the strategic ambitions of EU policy makers are not alone in pushing European integration; the willingness of national elites to participate is of crucial importance for the success of transnational institution building.

Stretching our imagination (including some quick rethinking of what the key defining characteristics of a state may be), we may decide that the European Union is a new state, or at least statelike. But it is difficult to imagine the EU rigged up as a new democratic "imagined community" (to borrow a term from Benedict Anderson) similar to those that fueled nineteenth-century national movements for democratic self-determination. The political-ideological pillars for EU representative systems based upon popular mobilization are also very difficult to imagine.

What will tie people together in cohesive political organizations? Interests, rather than identity. A partial, rather than an encompassing, basis for making popular appeals, this helps explain why there is significant support for economic integration, but none for political integration. A mismatch between economic and political boundaries might ultimately be more detrimental to business interests than to popular interests. Because the self-protective instincts of society remain attached to national rather than international institutions, a mismatch would keep alive latent protectionist instincts. An immediate concern is that a mismatch would put business at a disadvantage because the current levels of economic integration indicate a comprehensive need for supportive state-action. Hence, the impulse to political internationalization is, in the long run, more likely to come from business than from the popular classes. Yet a certain skepticism is impossible to avoid. The EU remains vulnerable to the very same impulses that ended the last international liberal order, that of the late nineteenth and early twentieth century, as described by Strikwerda.

We can speculate about many different scenarios that might either promote or retard European integration. Based upon our thesis regarding the origins of protective rights and autonomy guarantees, there is one scenario that predicts a concentration of power in the European Union associated with significant guarantees to citizens, but is one that we will not wish for: the evolution of the EU as a military actor. A fragmented and deconcentrated international order, associated with both a declining willingness on the part of the United States to provide a security umbrella for Europe and the possible deterioration and collapse of Russia and the adjoining straggler states, may create new threats to the current and prospective boundaries of the EU. Historically, this is the stuff that states and citizenship are made of. Of course, this prediction rests on certain assumptions about military technology. We need to know the answer to some important quetions about military strategy. Is this still the age of "total war" or are we, *pace* Brian Downing, in the midst of yet another military revolution, this time toward the use of professional armies in place of conscription? New military technologies enabling what has become known as "distant welfare" may exempt elites from the onerous task of conducting war by means of *levée en masse* and, hence, also from the need to provide appropriate recompense to citizens.

10

European Labor and Transnational Solidarity: Challenges, Pathways, and Barriers

Bernhard Ebbinghaus and Jelle Visser

Workers of the world unite! A century and a half have passed since *The Communist Manifesto* called workers to international solidarity. Beginning in Europe and North America, workers organized worldwide, in *national* unions. International solidarity has been, and is, an elusive, idealistic goal. Today, global economic interdependence and European political integration challenge the existence and effectiveness of national labor unions. While capital and political power go international, labor seems to fall behind. For organized labor in Europe, transnational class action has become crucial. The "social dimension" of the European Union (EU) depends on whether labor unions succeed in mounting solidaristic action in defense of Europe-wide labor standards and social policies. Without a strategy of internationalization, national labor unions may be caught in a downward spiral of desperately defending their declining domestic power base, and they are in danger of falling for the sirens of protectionism in defense against trends beyond their control.

In this chapter, we will survey the challenges, pathways, and barriers to European labor solidarity. We will look at the pathways that European labor unions have used thus far to counter the double challenges of economic and political integration. We argue that organized labor's transnational endeavor is so difficult precisely because European political integration in the social and labor domain lags behind economic integration. But we will also identify barriers to European labor unity that are internal to Europe's labor movements. We argue that organized labor is embedded in national labor relations and that its organizational rights and strategies are tied to the national polity and economy. Transnational labor solidarity is difficult, given a century of labor's integration into national welfare states. The main bases of solidarity between workers are still grounded within domestic borders. "In the process of growing from small sectarian groups into large mass organizations, the labor movements were inevitably 'nationalized'. They took on the characteristics and, with them, the diversities of the nations in which they developed" (Sturmthal 1953, 16). Labor's very success in mobilizing for modern mass democracy and the welfare state stands in the way of its international reorientation. Transnational solidarity presupposes that workers transcend the collective identities, social ties, and solidarity conceived within the "concentric circles" of their own nations, and calls for them to develop "cross-cutting," international class ties and multiple identities as *European* workers and citizens (Simmel [1908] 1983).

With regard to international class action, there may be different "logics" of collective action at work: internationalization appears to be a greater challenge for labor than for capital, which is more mobile, and a greater challenge for labor unions than for the less institutionalized social movements (Offe and Wiesenthal 1980). Despite the cultural obstacles to cross-national management, capital is nevertheless capable of creating "transnationally centralized decision systems, staffed by cosmopolitan 'technocrats' responding to criteria of economic rationality in their choices of industry, employment or earning." Transnational corporations (TNCs) are the "private sector incarnations of the old functional dream, tying the world together along global lines of economic rationality" (Nye 1972, 52). Why are there no truly international unions that follow the example of TNCs and operate beyond national borders? We also witness the development of new social movements across Europe such as the environmentalist and the feminist movements. Why would European labor not organize for promoting the social rights of its constituents as worker–citizens as feminist organizations have pressed for equal rights of women as EU citizens (Saraceno, ch. 12 below).

We begin this chapter with a brief exposé of the challenges that compel labor unions to seek transnational rather than national solutions. In principle, there are three pathways to meet these challenges and to advance transnational labor solidarity across Europe. Using Powell's typology (1990), we call these the "market," the "hierarchy" and the "network" options. The market option is based upon the expectation that unions and employers will eventually decide to bargain internationally. It assumes that transnational union action will result from mutual benefits across borders and will develop in a voluntaristic framework of international industrial relations in which states and supranational authorities play a secondary role, if any. According to the hierarchy option, national unions are capable of centralizing decisions and resources supranationally. This pathway presupposes a political dynamic not unlike the upward, centralizing spiral from local unions to national union movements. By contrast, the network option relies on cross-border contacts without pooling resources in, or transferring authority to, higher-level organizations. Such cross-border networks of unionists and works council members allow the exchange of information and the coordination of activities in a relatively ad hoc and flexible, albeit fragmented, form of cooperation.

European labor has moved along all three pathways, though only at a slow pace. Organized labor at the European level lacks the unity, centralization, resources, and power that most national union movements have enjoyed. We argue that there are three kinds of barriers to transnational labor solidarity. The first kind is internal and must be understood in the context of labor's own history and organization. Nationally entrenched union diversity and country-specific patterns of industrial relations across Europe stand in the way of transnational coordination and interest intermediation. Not only is it difficult to combine the goals and interests of so many and such different actors, but different repertoires of action are institutionalized in distinct national ways. There are also two kinds of external barriers that derive from the limits of European interest-intermediation: the first having to do with mediation between unions and the state; the second, between unions and employers. We argue that the weak "stateness" of the European Union and the "empty seat" politics of European employers act as brakes on the Europeanization of organized labor.

The study of the impact of European integration on organized labor calls for a comparative and historical analysis of the social processes of transnationalization (Klausen and Tilly, ch. 1 above). We will combine insights from cross-national comparative analysis with European integration theory, as both perspectives are needed in order to understand the full complexity of Europeanization. A top-down analysis, focusing exclusively on EU policy processes and institutions in Brussels, cannot tell the whole story. Because comparative analysis helps to identify the conflicts of interests that result from European diversity, our analysis combines a cross-national comparison of the diversity of labor organization and a multilevel analysis of the interaction between national interest-intermediation and supranational coordination. Europeanization is a multiple social process at several levels. It calls for a comparative historical view that can highlight the barriers to transnational solidarity and a multilevel perspective that looks at the challenges and opportunities for European organized labor.

The Challenge of Internationalization

Since the 1980s, the intensity of global economic competition, persistent high unemployment, the ascendancy of neoliberalism, and new steps toward European integration have tended to undermine the effectiveness of organized labor at the national level. From a European perspective, globalization refers to three interrelated processes: (1) the rise of transnational corporations as the dominant producers of goods and services, combined with important changes in international finance, research, and marketing; (2) the partial loss of economic and political autonomy and of the sovereignty of national states; and (3) the global shift in economic power from Europe and North America to Pacific Asia and low-wage economies in general (Barnet and Cavanagh 1994).

The rise of the transnational corporation and the globalization of the economy have changed the balance of power between firms, states, and unions. With the possibility of shifting production from country to country and pursuing a strategy of locational arbitrage, the TNCs' power has increased. The capacity of national governments to control the movement of international capital is limited. Since today's firms are increasingly dependent upon access to international sources of finance, markets, research, and technology, governments can no longer rely on and protect national industrial champions (Hayward 1995). National states are under pressure to transform into attractive locations for investment by offering them the best possible mix of infrastrucutre, communication facilities, educational and research institutions, skilled labor, low wage costs, and favorable taxation policies, as well as "good" industrial relations.

Early analysts of European integration have suggested that the increased power of transnational corporations could be subordinated to the political will of a European "would-be" polity (Lindberg and Scheingold 1970). The hope that closer political integration might reconcile a century-old European tradition of social citizenship with economic globalization was expressed once again during the negotiations of the Maastricht Treaty, but was soon disappointed. The "1992" project of the European Community (EC), initiated in 1985, and the reform of the EC political structure in 1991 were first and foremost concerned with advancing economic integration. The twelve EC member states hoped to create a single European market by reducing or eliminating national barriers to cross-border flows of goods, services, capital, and labor. The promise of recapturing political control through a new system of supranational governance and an added social dimension was never realized (Streeck 1993, 88).

Internationalization highlights the conditional viability of social institutions like national states and labor unions. J. R. Commons (1909) argued that any labor union seeking to influence market outcomes must have an organizational domain that is coextensive with the particular area of market competition (cf. Reder and Ulman 1993). In union history, this meant that once product markets expanded, unions had to centralize their resources and decisions nationwide in order to take wages out of competition between employers. Otherwise, unions that controlled only part of their labor market segment would have been subject to cost competition from market participants beyond their reach. Thus, when product and labor markets become truly international, organized labor must follow.

Yet the challenge of internationalization entails a dilemma for labor unions. If political integration lags behind market integration and if national states are still central in policy making on social and labor issues, national labor unions have good reasons to remain locked into national institutions and domestic strategies. This may hold particularly where labor unions have a position to lose in the national arena and when uncertainty about the payoffs of an international strategy is high. Union leaders may believe, even experience, that national alliances with employers or with the state cushion the hard facts of international competition. Political pressure at home may pay off more, at least in the short run, than international cooperation. The French public-sector strikes in December 1995, or those in road haulage in November 1996, are cases in point.

Moreover, there are substantial differences in the prosperity of Europe's national economies. Labor's interests and objectives may, therefore, vary considerably across Europe. Poorer countries tend to perceive Europe-wide labor standards as devices to protect the richer countries against the transfer of investments and jobs towards the weaker economies. High labor standards thus draw only half-hearted support and are often undermined, especially when common social minimal standards are not backed up by a redistributive policy of the richer countries paying in order to enhance the productivity of the weaker economies and poorer regions.

The main economic rationale of European integration has always been to enhance factor mobility and efficiency rather than to promote redistribution and equity. Initially, it was assumed that increased economic interdependence should, or would, produce the convergence of economic factors. Yet, when no such tendency was observable, European politicians abandoned the harmonization target in favor of the principles of "mutual recognition" of national producer standards, a qualified majority on EU deregulation measures, and subsidiarity in matters of social-policy regulation. Despite the EU cohesion measures assisting the weaker economic regions, the EU is not a redistributive welfare state guaranteeing social rights against the vagaries of markets (Leibfried and Pierson 1995; Marks et al. 1996). Labor market institutions and social security arrangements in Europe still have a high national content, in spite of today's deregulated market forces and thirty years of European integration. The influence of unions over social and economic policies is typically confined within, and dependent upon, the national welfare states and, hence, different from one country to the next.

In general, there are different responses of organized labor to the growing global and European interdependence. One is to retreat into a mercantilist stance and call for the state to protect national interests. Such an antagonistic nationalist repsonse was initially chosen by the communist unions that supported the protection of French industry (Rose 1987).

Most union movements in Europe have instead adopted what might be called an international strategy, which welcomes greater international cooperation on the condition that it serve national interests. Already in the early period, the leaders of the socialist and Christian unions from the original six Common Market countries were torn between their ideal of a united Europe and their need to bring back advantages to their domestic union membership (Haas 1958). A more recent example was provided when the British union movement changed—almost overnight—from an anti- to a pro-European strategy upon their discovery that "to be pro-EC was virtually synonymous with being anti-Thatcher" (Teague and Grahl 1992, 208).

A solidaristic, supranational response is the more inclusive strategy, but it remains utopian. Were it a reality, truly transnational unions would organize solidaristic action across domestic borders and beyond the national state, favoring functional interests (class) over territorial allegiance (nation). Instead of relying on national states to guarantee social rights, organized labor would invent new international support structures and global coalitions (Tilly 1995). We will now examine the three pathways to transnational collective action taken by labor unions in Europe, beginning with the market option.

The Pathway to Transnational "Bargaining": The Market Option

If market forces were uppermost, one would expect transnational collective bargaining to occur in those labor and producer markets that have become truly international. Thus, the same process would be repeated on a transnational level that happened in many industrialized countries—the transition to national collective bargaining following the expansion from local to national markets. However, the transnational bargaining solution, driven by markets, requires particular conditions. Lloyd Ulman (1975) specified three major market processes that force unions to switch from lower-level to higher-level bargaining: (1) downward pressures on wages through increased market integration; (2) an increase in factor mobility of capital and labor; and (3) the use of whipsaw tactics by employers. These phenomena do occur in Europe: real wages came to a standstill in many countries and for large sections of the (less-skilled workforce in the 1980s; the factor mobility of capital, and to a lesser degree of labor, has increased; and with the rise of TNCs, employers have gained locational arbitrage, playing off workers in different plants against each other. The Europeanization of producer markets has led to a rise in cross-border trade, and in some sectors it has added to growing world-market competition.[1] Whether the single-market project and further deregulation of financial, producer, and labor markets will in fact promote, on a substantial scale, a reallocation of investments away from high-wage areas remains contested.

Why was transnational collective bargaining never successful? An overview of the literature yields a harvest of arguments: (1) national differences in labor law, union organization, power of labor, bargaining methods, and concertation practices; (2) resistance by national unions, due to ideological differences, reluctance to give up authority, and competition for investment relocation; (3) management opposition in principle and, more recently, the decentralization into divisional, rather than regional, subsidiaries; (4) indifference by employees, due to lack of knowledge, cross-border conflicts of interest, and chauvinism; (5) lack of support from national governments and major political parties, which seek to retain control over major industries and companies (national champions) as well as over (allied) trade unions; and (6) weak support by international agencies (EU, OECD, ILO) for international codes of conduct, recognition rules, and bargaining rights, not to speak of the legal hurdles to international sympathy strikes and the doubtful legal status and efficacy of transnational collective bargaining outcomes (Flanagan and Weber 1974).

Moreover, only the two thousand or so TNCs with significant employment in two or more countries would be the target of transnational bargaining, while about 95 percent of all firms and 80 percent of the labor market would not be affected in any direct way. Transnational collective bargaining would, therefore, create severe intra- and interunion tensions, especially in countries and sectors whose unions negotiate sectoral multiemployer agreements that cover employees in both large and small firms. The facts that many TNCs operate on a global, rather than a European, scale and that even within the EU, wages and productivity levels vary widely are further obstacles to Europe-wide collective bargaining. Moreover, a common perception of mutual benefit is not easily established. Organized labor representing workers in both northern and southern Europe would have to engage in extensive rounds of interunion settlements on how far the common norm should favor advanced labor standards and how much subsidy should go to the weaker members of the alliance (cf. Reder and Ulman 1993). Transnational bargaining would also entail the delicate question to what degree the alliance should turn a blind eye to lax application of the norm by members who stand to lose the most in the short term.

Nevertheless, some transnational collective bargaining has occurred in Europe. Without exception, however, this has taken place on a voluntary basis following the new Social Protocol procedures of the Maastricht Treaty and as a last resort for employers to prevent or soften pending EU legislation. As a voluntary process, entirely based on a perception of mutual gains by employers and unions, and as the best way to meet the pressure of the combined labor market power of unions, international collective bargaining has so far proved to be a nonstarter. In view of their dependency on government support and public regulation, and of the need to balance the wide differences in power and interests across Europe, labor unions have turned to the hierarchy option as a remedy.

The Pathway to Transnational Coordination: The Hierarchy Option

By relying on the hierarchy option, labor unions have tried to repeat, on an international scale, the national success stories of union centralization. Over the past century, unions evolved from locally fragmented worker coalitions into nationwide organizations. In this process, local or regional union federations lost most of their powers and functions; they were subordinated to national union bureaucracies with control over administration and finances. Furthermore, sectoral and occupational labor organizations, rather than regional and local unions, became the basis for interest aggregation, especially in northern Europe. This union centralization was also promoted through political conflicts and alliances. National unions in Europe predated universal suffrage and were among the main societal forces that advanced the political rights for workers. In these struggles, they forged close alliances with socialist parties (and, in some cases, communist parties or Christian democracy), which in turn reinforced the tendency to centralize. As a consequence, national union confederations emerged in all countries and became the centers of national labor movements, though their power and prestige varied widely (Windmuller 1975; Visser 1990). Similar efforts begun by the Second International as early as the turn of the century proved less successful. The International soon faced the problem of political schism and the crisis of internationalism that led to reorganizations in the aftermath of both world wars.

In order to evaluate the hierarchy option for European labor today, it is important to recall that the timing, speed, and synchronization of economic and political development have been extremely important in the case of national union movements. Where political and economic struggles coincided in a relatively brief period of time, the centralizing influence on unions and labor relations was strong, but where they arrived at different times, or with a low intensity, earlier organizational solutions became settled and could not easily be displaced (Ebbinghaus 1995). There seems to have been a feedback process between the organization of labor and capital: the more that labor became a credible centralizing force, the more that capital (qua employer) was compelled to organize in response. The upward centralization spiral created a pattern of industrial relations typical of national welfare states, "a figuration in which opponents compel[led] one another to evolve to higher levels of integration" (de Swaan 1988, 175).

A comparable centralizing dynamic, however, seems to be absent in to-day's European industrial relations. Even in countries and sectors where sectorwide bargaining structures are maintained, we witness a shift towards the company as the major arena and actor in industrial relations (van Ruy-seveldt and Visser 1996). The underlying processes are decentralization of production, outsourcing and leaner management, a search for flexible employment, and the withdrawal of the state from industrial relations whenever possible. The prospect of a European "would-be" state recouping the terrain abandoned by national states is extremely dim. Moreover, unlike in the development of welfare states in most European countries, there is no compelling dynamic of a European socialist party that seeks to unite labor and, in alliance with it, fights for more power of the European Parliament and for Europe-wide social rights. Nevertheless, organized labor in Europe has found ways to cooperate across borders and to centralize some of its scarce resources. Some tripartite consultation and Europe-wide bargaining has taken place. Mostly, this has led only to noncommittal joint opinions or declarations of good will. However, the joint statement of unions and employers of November 1991 has been the basis, almost word for word, of the Social Protocol that was added to the Maastricht Treaty and binds all EU member states but the United Kingdom. In December 1995, European labor unions and employers signed their first collective agreement on parental leave for workers.

The European Trade Union Confederation (ETUC) is the central player on the side of labor in Brussels. By the end of 1995, forty-nine national confederations from twenty-eight countries with a combined membership of 46 million had joined this Europe-wide peak organization. ETUC's affiliates have organized about 30 percent of all workers in the EU, but ETUC also includes organizations from non-EU countries, in particular, EFTA member states and, more recently, countries of Central and Eastern Europe (Visser and Ebbinghaus 1992). While Western Europe's total union density is higher than in Japan (24 percent) or the United States (14 percent), the trend is downward (from 40 percent in 1980 to 34 percent a decade later). Variations in levels and trends are large across Western Europe. The highest density levels are found in Scandinavia (Sweden with over 80 percent); the lowest, in southern Europe (France with less than 10 percent). The largest decline (from 53 to 33 percent in sixteen years) was observed in the United Kingdom (Visser 1991; OECD (1994a).

Indisputably, ETUC is Europe's main union organization; with over 90 percent of all unionized workers, its associational monopoly is assured. Until the foundation of ETUC in 1973, European labor organizations were divided by politics and ideology (socialist, Christian, and communist) and by territory (Common Market vs. EFTA). ETUC was more encompassing than the worldwide union movements in admitting organizations that did not belong to the International Confederation of Free Trade Unions (ICFTU) or predecessor (and ICFTU's European regional organization), EFTUC). ETUC does not see itself as a substitute or as a regional suborganization of worldwide union organizations such as ICFTU. It restricts itself to Europe, with a particular, though not exclusive, emphasis on influencing the policies of the European Union. ETUC statutes describe the organization's objectives as "the common representation and promotion of social, economic and cultural interests of workers at the European level and, in particular, in the European institutions." In 1974, the larger Christian unions joined; as a result, ETUC enhanced its position, particularly in the Benelux countries and in Switzerland.[2] Under the impact of a strong tendency towards reunification at home, the two Italian founding members of ETUC secured the membership of the largest Euro-Communist confederation in the same year. This was the wedge through which other (ex)communist unions, from Spain (1990) and Portugal (1995), later entered. Today, the only major confederation outside ETUC is the French CGT, which has retained its communist orientation and has seen its earlier dominance and membership decline in the 1980s and 1990s.[3]

From its start, ETUC embraced the white-collar organizations of Scandinavia; around 1990, its organizational domain was once again widened by admitting organizations that had similar status in other countries. Although there are two small rival Europe-wide peak federations, one of managerial staff and the other primarily of senior civil servants, ETUC leads in all sectors and occupations.[4] By including union federations from non-EU countries (in particular from the remaining EFTA member states after Britain, Ireland, and Denmark left EFTA to join the European Community in 1973), from southern Europe at the time of suppression of political rights, and in recent years, from Central and Eastern Europe after the fall of communism, organized labor was, and is, ahead of the European political unification process, at least in its territorial scope.[5]

The price for ETUC's astonishing inclusiveness is organizational frailty, lack of effective supranational authority, and low direct membership involvement. In response to the challenge of the single European market and the revision of the EU treaty in 1991, ETUC strengthened its executive committee and introduced qualified majority voting (two-thirds). The move towards supranational decision making and stronger central institutions in 1991 was a modest one. It did not solve the problem that ETUC and the European sectoral unions are understaffed and depend upon the European Commission and other public sources for financial support. Still only a small fraction (2 percent or less) of union income in Europe goes to international union organizations. With the help of funds from the European

Commission, labor's organizational resources were improved by auxiliary institutions: the European Trade Union College, the European Trade Union Technical Bureau of Health and Safety, and jointly with employers, the Center for European Industrial Relations. The European Trade Union Institute (ETUI), the Brussels-based research institute, also received more funds.

Even with majority voting, ETUC tends to seek unanimous decisions, since it cannot afford to antagonize its larger member organizations. Given the diversity of its affiliates in terms of strength, interests, culture, politics, and ideology, the adoption of a rather symbolic lowest-common-denominator policy is often unavoidable. Furthermore, ETUC suffers from the fact that its two largest affiliates, the German DGB and the British TUC, have no bargaining mandate. (Affiliated unions are responsible for collective bargaining. See Klausen, ch. 8, for a discussion of the historical roots of the TUC's weakness.) The two are, moreover, opposites in union structure, organization, and resources, as well as in their traditions and modes of interest-intermediation and industrial relations. Until recently, the DGB and TUC were deeply divided over European integration and held different views regarding ETUC's role in Europe. In addition, a Franco-German alliance, similar to the Bonn-Paris axis in European politics, was never possible, given the political division and the related weakness of French unions.

As a supranational peak association of national union confederations (and now also of European sector committees), ETUC is an organizational animal of far greater complexity than any of its national affiliates. Quite similar to the Euro-technocracy, ETUC remains by and large the affair of national union leaders meeting sporadically, and of some officials serving permanently in Brussels. In particular, the Nordic unions have criticized the democratic deficit of ETUC, since union leaders make decisions in Brussels that they need not defend at home. On the other hand, there is a decision deficit, since national union leaders and delegates are constrained by various complex and time-consuming decision-making procedures, which any reluctant member organization can invoke whenever expedient. ETUC thus resembles its weaker affiliates more than its stronger ones.[6]

In short, indirect membership relations, a restricted and twice-filtered mandate, organizational diversity, scarce and unequal resources, and decentralization in the national arena, as well as the absence of a state interlocutor and a mobilizing political dynamic, are among the factors that restrict the hierarchy path for the European union movement. Of these, the lack of a clear bargaining mandate and power basis is probably the most important impediment to ETUC's capacity to negotiate social pacts with European employers and the European Union. At the national level, collective bargaining is usually conducted by the affiliated unions and not by the national confederations, but only the latter can be direct members of ETUC. Only in some countries do union confederations actually negotiate agreements or have a strong coordinating role with regard to collective bargaining of their affiliates.

Yet how sectoral or occupational unions cooperate across national borders has received relatively little attention. Historically, these unions' international cooperation in international trade secretariats (ITSs) has preceded the efforts of national union confederations, but sectoral unions were subject to the same ideological schisms as national ones.[7] Two sets of European sector organizations have developed over the past decades: (1) Brussels-based pressure groups, specializing in technical expertise and advice in highly integrated sectors, in particular in coal, steel, agriculture, and food; and (2) European offsprings of the ITS, which initially suffered from ideological fragmentation at the international level. Consequently, the existing European sector organizations differ widely in structure, membership, representation, resources, and strategy. Their importance varies across sectors; in some sectors (for instance, sea transport), they have acquired a strong monitoring role, but almost nowhere do they have a significant influence on national collective bargaining or on coordinating or financing transnational strike action.

With the recent advancements following the Social Protocol, sectoral union cooperation across borders has been boosted, but resources are only a fraction of what is needed. Before ETUC's foundation, the development of European sector organizations was not coordinated with, and it sometimes even hindered, attempts to build a political alliance between national union centers. After its foundation, ETUC started to recognize some sector organizations as European industrial committees (EICs), though it took considerable time before the EICs fell in line with the ETUC policy of encompassing not only socialist but also Christian and (ex)communist unions. Currently, ETUC recognizes fifteen EICs of very different size, scope, and composition; in addition, it includes also a European organization of retired-worker unions (see table 10.1).

Since the ETUC reform in 1991, EICs send one-third of the delegates to the ETUC congress and have voting rights, except on financial and statute matters. National representatives of EICs are nominated as delegates at the ETUC congress, while EIC officials have a consultative role only in the ETUC executive committee. Although the reform acknowledged the need to integrate functional interests directly rather than through the national circuit, the problem of hierarchical ordering in a transnational peak association, in particular the dominance of the political (territorial) pillar over the functional (sectoral) pillar, remains. The resulting dual structure of representation contrasts with the organizational development of national union confederations in most European countries, where territorial inter-

Table 10.1. European Industry Committees Affiliated with ETUC

Abbrev.	European Industry Committee (EIC)	Founded	Reorganized	Entered ETUC	N of unions	Members[a]
EPSC	European Public Services Committee	1974	1981	1979	100	7,000
EMF	European Metalworkers' Federation	1963	1971	1973[b]	43	6,000
EURO-FIET	International Federation of Commercial, Clerical, Professional, and Technical Employees—European Regional Organization	1964	1973	1973[b]	129	6,000
EFBWW	European Federation of Building and Woodworkers	1958	1974	1984	51	3,100
ETUCE	European Trade Union Committee for Education	1956	1975	1981	67	2,800
CSTCE	Committee of Transport Workers' Unions in the European Community	1958	1979	1979	89	2,500
EMCEF	European Mine, Chemical, and Energy Workers' Federation	1958	1988	1988	51	2,000
EFA	European Federation of Agricultural Workers' Unions	1958	1971	1973[b]	26	2,000
PTTI-EU	Postal, Telegraph, and Telephone International European Committee	1967	1973	1973[b]	67	1,900
ECF-IUF	European Committee of Food, Catering, and Allied Workers' Union within the IUF	1958	1975	1978	70	1,400
ETUC-TCL	European Trade Union Committee for Textiles, Clothing, and Leather	1964	1975	1988	43	1,300
EGF	European Graphical Federation	1973	1985	1987	44	700
EGJ	European Group of Journalists	1988		1989	45	180
EURO-MEI	Media and Entertainment International	1973		1973[b]	24	100

Source: Visser and Ebbinghaus (1992), table 7.6, p. 226; updates: information from ETUC and Martin and Ross (1995).

[a]Most recent membership figure, in thousands.

[b]Unions recognized at foundation of ETUC in 1973.

ests became, over time, subordinated to functional interests. Within ETUC, the national channel of representation will probably remain dominant as long as national governments are central in EU politics and labor solidarity is nationally bound.

The Pathway to Transnational Links: The Network Option

The network strategy may be the default option on the road toward international labor solidarity. Here the focus is on building horizontal links among workers and unionists from different countries in order to exchange information, coordinate action, and enhance solidarity. These cross-border links might be established at different levels, and with different degrees of formality and involvement. In contrast to the hierarchy option, the emphasis here does not lie on a peak or sector organization to which resources and competencies would be transferred. Instead, the idea is to build "flat" transnational networks of unionists, local unions, and works councils. The building of such networks is a first step in countering the information advantages and whipsaw tactics of employers. Furthermore, these networks enhance common understandings and possibilities for joint action. Given the legacies of national traditions and the diversity of cultures, not to speak of the language problems, cross-border cooperation between workers is a difficult task, but there is no way around it. These networks may gradually form closer ties and foster trust, a precondition for effective transnational collective bargaining.

The promotion of a solidaristic logic of collective action between workers from different countries is essential for the achievement of transnational solidarity. Given that the company and regional level are crucial in this context, it will be necessary to go beyond a top-down analysis of European interest groups and look at what unionists actually do in cross-border regions and in transnational companies. For organized labor, building rank-and-file support is an important stepping-stone on the road to international solidarity. Starting in the region or company, coordination may take place territorially (in interregional union networks as a response to cross-border regional integration) or functionally (in Europe-wide works councils in response to the rise of TNCs in Europe).

In a number of regions with considerable cross-border movement of labor and economic integration, interregional trade union councils (ITUCs) of regional or local union bodies have been formed. The first ITUC was founded in 1976 and included the border region of the Saar (Germany), Lorraine (France), and Luxembourg. The second followed two years later between Belgian, Dutch, and German unions for the Maas-Rhine area. The growing importance of these transnational bodies is mirrored by their increased number, from eleven in 1990 to thirty in 1995; since 1993, they have spread beyond the EU's eastern border.[8]

Originally, labor unions were rather reluctant about cross-border regional cooperation because they did not know how to integrate these activities within existing national union structures. In 1991, ETUC gave the ITUCs an observer status and acknowledged their status as official representatives in border areas; ETUC's official policy is now to promote these networks. However, the ITUCs often run up against language problems, a lack of resources, and weak lobbies in Brussels, in the national capitals, and in the regions. In the years ahead, regional coordination will probably gain in importance to the extent that EU cohesion measures and regional policies become more momentous. The ITUCs may be elevated in status as a result of EU attempts to devolve power to the regions under subsidiarity arrangements—in particular, as a result of the augmented EU regional funds and the new consultative European regional committees.

A network that holds greater promise, and receives more attention due to EU regulative efforts, is the cross-border contacts between works council members and unionists within Europe-wide transnational companies. The European Works Councils (EWC) Directive, passed in September 1994 under the Social Protocol (thus excluding the United Kingdom), applies to some fifteen hundred to two thousand TNCs. This directive, which became effective after a decade-long stalemate and a considerable watering down of initial ambitions, has been presented as a prime example of the EU's post-Maastricht policy innovations. Characteristically, implementation occurs through labor–management negotiations, and TNCs that have already established their own voluntary structures are exempted from EU regulation. If negotiations do not start or if they fail to produce acceptable procedures for consultation and information, a set of fixed, secondary provisions specified in the EWC Directive will be imposed, probably by 1999. However, the directive stipulates that the provisions are not intended as a compulsory reference model for voluntary agreements made pursuant to it.

The EWC Directive is extremely modest in its ambitions and hardly compares with attempts begun in the 1970s to create worker participation rights in transnational companies. The directive obliges member states in the European Economic Area (with the exception of the U.K.) to regulate nationally in such a way that TNCs which engage in significant employment in other European countries will be encouraged to negotiate with a body representing their entire European workforce in order to establish a Europe-wide consultation-and-information framework. In terms of rights and resources, these European works councils (EWCs) cannot be compared with works councils or codetermination rights as they exist in, for example Germany, the Netherlands, Austria, Sweden, Italy, Spain, or even France.

Yet the negotiation process around the EWCs has revived the EICs, both directly by creating a need for their negotiation teams and indirectly by awakening their interest, and that of the European Commission, in the sectoral social dialogue. By the implementation deadline of 22 September 1996, some 250 voluntary company agreements had been negotiated, including ones for U.K., U.S., and Japanese firms operating in the European Economic Area (these agreements often include, on a voluntary basis, workers in U.K. subsidiaries). Full implementation will eventually lead to between forty thousand and sixty thousand people serving as grassroots representatives (on average there are thirty members in a EWC) in TNC-based networks. EWCs are best characterized as clearinghouses for information between employee representatives, union officials, and other works councils within TNCs; they meet at least once a year. Although they might have some influence on collective bargaining through personal links to union representatives in national structures, it is still a long way before the EWCs become a structure for transnational collective bargaining. For the present, these thousands of small networks of employee and union representatives might add a valuable dimension of learning and "best practice" to the emergent transnational labor relations in Europe.

Barriers to Transnational Union Cooperation

Why has progress on each of the three pathways been so slow? Before discussing the external barriers that stand in the way of transnational union cooperation in Europe, we will first consider the internal barriers deriving from the limits to labor organization set by national conditions. Comparative studies have shown, time and again, that Europe is a continent of peoples with different histories and languages. European industrial relations are also characterized by persistent national diversity (Crouch 1993; Rhodes 1995). Hence "making the most of diversity" is the challenge for European organized labor. European labor unity poses the same problem as political union: how to encompass and manage national diversity?

The sources of union diversity are rooted in the national histories of labor movements in Europe. The social and political conflicts emerging from rapid industrialization and the pressures for democratization by the working class shaped the labor-capital cleavage in all European countries (Lipset and Rokkan 1967). However, the particular form of party-union relations within the labor movements varied widely across countries (Ebbinghaus 1995). Although labor movements emerged everywhere, political and religious cleavages gave rise in some countries to deep schisms in working-class organization, which split into socialist, communist, and Christian labor movements. Conflicts in the labor market and social differentiation engendered further class fragmentation and led to competing principles of organization within and between union movements: craft or industry, exclusion or integration of nonmanual employees, and private versus public sector.[10] The fragmentation of interest aggregation across and within national union movements in Europe became institutionalized. Enduring conflicts in the national arena have left their marks not only on how unions define and organize the collective interests of workers but also on how they represent and defend interests in confrontation with employers and in the public domain (Crouch 1993).

This "nationalization" of organized labor has deep and lasting roots far beyond natoinal intersts, values, and symbols. Since nationally distinct patterns of representation and collective action are strongly institutionalized, these are obstacles to transnational solidarity. How can labor unity be organized from such disparate fragments across Europe? How can it be achieved at the European level, if it was, and is, not realized within each society? Union movements of a particular political orientation or organizational type find themselves confronted with rival organizations abroad to which they are antagonistic at home. Functional cleavages add to these difficulties, especially since almost no sector or occupation is organized in the same way when we move from one country to another. The lack of "fit" in membership domains poses problems for transnational bargaining. In addition, the problem of transnational action is complicated by differences in size and unionization levels (see table 10.2). Indicators of membership, resources, and collective action reveal a deep and enduring cross-national diversity in mobilization patterns across Europe (Shalev 1992; Visser 1992). In some countries, unions are dependent upon public support, whereas in others they have relied on voluntary action. Such differences have inevitable consequences for the role of unions in each society.

Union diversity creates a number of problems for transnational union action: exploitation of the strong by the weak, overlapping or fragmented membership domains, and different conceptions of what unions "ought to do" and "how to do it." The current downward trend in unionization, the financial crisis, and unions' dependence on state or party support do not make the problem any easier. As national labor unions come under pressure to spend their meager resources on visible membership services, European activities are hardly likely to receive priority. Even the staff and budgets of national confederations have been reduced in many countries, partly in response to the current decentralization of collective bargaining. Expenditure on international commitments is under severe scrutiny in many unions and confederations, since it is the farthest removed from rank-and-file concerns. Hence, transnational union organizations are commonly hampered by lack of resources (Visser and Ebbinghaus 1992).

Even if problems of diversity and unequal strength were resolved, the pronounced cross-national variations in interest representation would cre-

Table 10.2. National Union Movements and ETUC Affiliates

Country	Density	National Movements		ETUC Affiliates		
		N of confederation	N of unions	N of confederations	N of unions	Share in membership
Sweden	82.5	4	71	2	43	91.7
Finland	72.0	4	99	2	39	75.6
Denmark	75.2	4	115[a]	2	76	85.3
Norway	56.0	3	156	1	29	59.8
Ireland	50.8	1	81	1	58	90.9
Belgium	50.1	3	37[a]	2	36	91.1
Austria	46.2	1	15	1	15	100.0
UK	39.1	1	287	1	74	82.4
Italy	38.8	3	72[a]	3	72	100.0
Greece	34.1	2	—	2	—	100.0
Portugal	31.8	2	—	2	—	90.0
Germany	32.9	5	140[a]	2	17	82.9
Netherlands	25.5	4	232	3	116	89.0
Spain	16.1	5	—	3	—	90.0
France	10.8	5	—	3	—	44.3

Source: Ebbinghaus and Visser (forthcoming).
Note: Union density and affiliation to ETUC as of 1992.
[a]Number understated.

ate a third, partly exogenous barrier to transnational union action. Across Europe, union movements maintain different linkages to the political system. In the past, union movements have drawn strength from their partisan linkages, especially when the allied party was holding government office. On the other hand, this partisan involvement has caused deep divisions within, and large variations across, European countries. Moreover, union movements in some countries or sectors are deeply embedded in established practices of bi- or tripartite concertation; others have rejected such practices. There is considerable variation in the impact of interest-group politics on national policy making in Western Europe (Mazey and Richardson 1993). Expectations of convergence and cross-fertilization of interest-group systems have proved unwarranted. If anything, interest representation and political class alliances have been further fragmented, reducing the primacy of the comprehensive peak associations of capital and labor in national and EU lobbying.

Cross-national diversity in industrial relations has been described in numerous studies in the arenas of employer associations, collective bargaining, state regulation, and institutionalized forms of worker participation (Ferner and Hyman 1992; Rogers and Streeck 1995). Despite the expectations of convergence theory, political, legal, and cultural contexts bear heavily on industrial relations in each country (Poole 1986). There is no universal dynamic that transforms industrial relations from a national into an international game. Moreover, the Brussels power play does not appeal equally to each national union movement; its appeal depends largely on national contingencies. Some union movements have reason to fear the loss of "quasi-public" status at home (for a definition of the term, see Offe 1981); others hold so little status in the domestic public arena that they can only gain from going to Brussels. One often has the impression that the unions that would benefit most from cooperation are least able to achieve domestic endorsement and to pursue a transnational strategy, whereas those unions that would be capable of putting pressure on Brussels are reluctant to share power or fear losing their home advantage.

Unions in Germany and Scandinavia, for instance, appear to be skeptical toward European collective bargaining and to prefer to take the legislative route. They believe that political regulations from Brussels are needed as a shield against "social dumping," and they distrust the feeble democratic base and efficacy of collective agreements in countries with weak union representation. Unions in France, Spain, Portugal, or Greece, on the other hand, expect more of the self-regulation route opened under the Social Protocol of the Maastricht Treaty, partly because of national traditions of "bargaining in the shadow of the law," partly because they distrust their national states (Groux, Morinaux, and Pernot 1993). But how strong is the "would-be" European state in matters of social policy regulation?

Barriers to European Social-Policy Regulation

Even if unions were pushed enough by economic and political developments and overcame the many internal barriers on the road to transnational
solidarity, they would still meet formidable exogenous barriers residing in
the nature of the supranational EU regime. Our main argument here is that
the European Union is far removed from the "stateness" of the national
welfare states that hold strong regulatory powers in the social-policy and
labor domain (Kapteyn 1995; Leibfried and Pierson 1996). The pull factors
that have promoted nationwide coordination and centralization in the domestic industrial relations arena appear to be lacking at the European level.
As an intergovernmental institution, the European Union lacks many of the
competencies and means of even the weakest of its member states.

From the very beginning of the Common Market, the social- and labor-
policy domain was of secondary concern. The Common Market's social
provisions mainly dealt with measures to improve labor mobility and avoid
the distortions that different national health and safety standards might
cause in product-market competition. With the exception of equal rights
and some employment protection measures, the debate on European social
policy remained dormant until the new initiatives on the "social dimension" led to the signing of the nonbinding Social Charter (from which the
United Kingdom abstained) in 1989 and to the related EC action programs
(Teague and Grahl 1992). With few significant exceptions, EU social and
labor policies remain subject to unanimity and thus intergovernmental bargaining, with ample space for the threat and use of the national veto. Moreover, the European Union must rely on the apparatus and instruments of
the member states for legal enactment and implementation, which may give
rise not only to implementation failures but also to institutional regime
competition (Streeck 1996). The fuzzy principle of subsidiarity that was
introduced in the Maastricht Treaty is readily invoked to set further limits
on supranational competencies and EU regulatory internvention.

When organized labor engages in EU lobbying, it encounters a complex
set of supranational and intergovernmental institutions with restricted regulatory competencies, underdeveloped executive powers, and a multiplicity
of dispersed and often elusive actors. Many of the most important industrial
relations issues are explicitly excluded by the EU treaty from supranational
policy making, including the main rules of the game for collective bargaining, strike action, and worker representation. European supranational institutions, however, constitute a number of points of access for lobbying: in
particular, the European Commission, the European Parliament (EP), the
Economic and Social Committee (ECOSOC), and since Maastricht, also
the regional committees. Yet the powerful but remote governmental committees (the European Council, the Council of Ministers, and COREPER),

composed of representatives from EU member states, elude labor unions and can be reached, if at all, only through the national circuits.

Crucial for interest representation at the European level are whether a proposed policy measure is within the authority transferred to the EU by member states, whether decisions can be taken by a qualified majority vote, and particularly, whether cooperation of the EP is required. If these conditions are fulfilled, the pull for transnational union cooperation is greater. However, given the EU's intergovernmental nature in the social and labor domain, national governments can easily adopt a reactive strategy. Employers can hide behind governments ready to use their veto powers, and count on the competitive deregulatory agenda of mutual adjustment that indirectly pervades the social- and labor-policy domain. Unions have more to fear from the gap between the EU's inability to re-regulate and the member states' desire (and the EU treaty's objectives) to deregulate. Unlike employers, unions cannot expect to gain from negative integration policies, while positive integration policies are often beyond their reach, since one or a few governments may suffice to block such policies.

Of the supranational EU institutions, the European Commission, with its right to draft legislation and take policy intiatives, remains the prime target for proactive pressures from labor unions. The commission has its own vested interest in entertaining good and stable relations with organized interests, for reasons of enhancing its own legitimacy, expertise, and power. It has, in fact, promoted a relatively open and unstructured pluralist system for pressure-group politics (Streeck and Schmitter 1991). After failed attempts in the 1970s, the commission under Delors relaunched an informal tripartite "social dialogue" to balance the deregulatory thrust of the 1992 project, yet without significant advancements until lately.

For many years, employers did not want to go further than to sign non-binding joint options. Yet in December 1995, they surprised friend and foe by signing an agreement with ETUC over parental leave. They may have calculated that this agreement was more flexible than pending EU regulation, but on the other hand, ETUC was criticized because the agreement was particularly weak on wage compensation during leave of absence. The previous attempt to hammer out an agreement on EWCs failed due to the opposition of British employers; in this case too, the calculus of European employers was to water down, or even prevent, EU legislation. Nevertheless, the first serious top-level negotiations after the ratification in late 1993 of the Maastricht Treaty, with its new qualified majority and colegislation procedures, which changed the rules of the game for the employers, have taken place. Currently, the commission has shifted its attention to the social dialogue for particular sectors (e.g., retail and textile), although this poses even greater problems given the weak organization of European employers at the decentralized level.

Since Maastricht, the commission prefers to deal with transnational and comprehensive, rather than national and sectional, interest groups, but these attempts at reorganizing its outside contacts are still weak and inconsistent. The commission has spent considerable resources to subsidize the international research, training, and coordination activities of organized labor, especially in preparation of the firm-level negotiations of EWCs. This sponsoring role has certainly helped organized labor to be present at the European level and has overcome some of labor's transaction and organizing costs (Martin and Ross 1995). (The budget line funding the implementation of the EWCs is temporary.) Yet the commission is unable to bestow a measure of quasi-public status on major transnational organizations of labor or capital, as governments can in the national arena. Thus, it is the national governments, not the commission, that nominate labor representatives to EU advisory committees such as ECOSOC.

The compartmentalization of the commission into over twenty Directorate Generals and a proliferating network of supporting working groups, committees, and consultants furthermore operates to the disadvantage of organized labor. Union access is mainly confined to EU institutions dealing with the social and labor domain, while labor issues are kept out of the many nonpolitical technical, advisory, or regulatory committees. This compartmentalization reinforces the decoupling of the economic "single European Market" and European Monetary Union projects from the "social dimension" and relegates labor issues to a secondary, often politically blocked, policy debate.

Other supranational points of access are even less promising. The Economic and Social Committee, founded under the Rome treaty (1957), may be seen as a step towards "Euro-corporatism" from afar, but it is generally acknowledged that ECOSOC plays only a minor role in EU decision making (Visser and Ebbinghaus 1992). The potential for bi- or tripartite interest intermediation is impaired by ECOSOC's mixed composition (one-third labor, one-third employer representatives, and one-third mixed interests). The new Committee of the Regions, modeled after ECOSOC, will be of even less importance to labor interest representation. The rulings of the European Court of Justice, though remote from union pressures, have tended to expand the scope of initially restricted social regulations under the EU treaty. Under the revised treaty, the role of the European Parliament has increased; this body will now influence about half of EU legislative projects, but its powers are still very limited by comparison to national parliaments. The Social Protocol requires the cooperation of the EP in several new labor- and social-policy areas, but in these domains, the position of the Council of Ministers, and hence national governments, remains strong.[11]

The impact of the EU's "variable geometry"—the coexistence of several different regulatory regimes varying in space and scope—is uncertain (Streeck 1993).[12] We may add the uncertainties surrounding the membership of the European Monetary Union and its future impact on European political unity, on national labor markets, and on EU social policy. The extension of qualified majority voting and the signing of the Social Protocol have nevertheless changed the rules of the game for many governments and national interest-groups. Since the 1997 elections of a Labour government, neither of these can any longer hide behind the inevitable U.K. veto and will now have to show their real preferences (Lange 1992). Even under the qualified majority rule of the Social Protocol, a coalition of Spain, Portugal, Italy, and Greece against the other seven could still block legislation that increased costs and impaired these countries' competitiveness. With the entry of Austria, Finland, and Sweden in 1995, these four are a few votes short, which seems to worry Spain in particular.

The Maastricht Treaty's Social Protocol includes a self-regulatory path, in accordance with the principle of subsidiarity and with the joint proposal that organized labor and capital signed in 1991. This *fuite en avant,* however, depends on the organizational incentives and political support for a social partnership, as well as the internal compliance of organized labor and capital. On the eve of the Maastricht negotiations, when European employers and unions agreed on the content of the Social Protocol, and in the case of the agreement on parental leave, this extralegal route has brought some success. Yet the self-regulation path will be limited, owing to the unwillingness to cooperate in such tactics of European employer associations, as we will show in our discussion of the last barrier.

Barriers to European Collective Bargaining

The organization of European business interests is as diverse as that of labor. Supranational interest-organization above the level of transnational corporations is no sinecure. At the national level, business interest-associations are often divided among producer interests (trade associations), labor market interests (employer associations), and regional-business-community interests (chambers of commerce).[13] In most countries, small firms, the handicraft trades, agriculture, finance, commerce, and private services, as well as the public sector, are organized, if at all, in separate employer associations. The organization density of employer associations, measured by the number of firms who belong or the number of people those firms employ, varies from very low in the United Kingdom to very high in Germany, Austria, Switzerland, Scandinavia, and the Benelux countries. However, discipline, not size or density, is probably the Achilles' heel of employer organization. We must bear in mind that the members of business associations are not individuals, as in the case of labor union membership, but corporate organizations that vary in size and resources. Large firms often have a greater voting power than small ones, and a viable exit option. The centrifugal tendencies and large differences in employer organizations across Europe have important consequences for these organizations' transnational relations with organized labor.

At the European level, we find a large number of Europe-wide employer organizations, national pressure groups, and company lobbyists, but strong employer associations at the sector level are missing (Lanzalaco and Schmitter 1992, 203). In 1958, with the start of the Common Market, the Union of Industrial and Employer Confederations of Europe (UNICE) was founded. Initially, UNICE was mainly a presure group for industry in the European Community, with some advisory functions. In the 1970s, mainly in response to the establishment of the Standing Committee on Employment and other forms of social dialogue, UNICE assumed the additional role of coordinating the national employer associations. Today, UNICE incorporates the dual representation of both producer and labor-market interests and thus encompasses business and employer associations across Europe. Like that of ETUC, UNICE's territorial scope reaches beyond the EU, though UNICE assigns associate-member status to affiliates from non-EU countries. By 1994, thirty-three national employer and trade associations from twenty-five countries (including the six members of EFTA, plus Turkey, Cyprus, Malta, and San Marino, and three CEE countries—Poland, the Czech Republic, and Slovakia), had affiliated with UNICE. UNICE is quite happy to spare itself the quandry of an additional layer of Europe-wide sub-national associations, but this may change under the current pressures toward social dialogue at the sector level.

UNICE shares the fate of ETUC insofar as its resources and competencies are also quite limited. It publicly admits to being understaffed (with a full-time staff of thirty-four in 1994) and complains of being underfinanced compared to the "subsidized" ETUC (Tyszkiewicz 1991). The turnover of staff, often provided from national affiliates, appears to be large. As in ETUC, UNICE's national affiliates differ strongly with regard to resources and competencies, particularly in their authority to bind members and conduct centralized collective bargaining. Moreover, UNICE's associational authority is undermined by the direct representation in Brussels of national employer associations, independent branch organizations, and TNCs and by independent lobbyists in Brussels as well as by the informal, but influential, consultation groups of large companies, in particular the European Round Table. There is a separate European employer association in the public sector (CEEP), which has shown greater readiness to cooperate with ETUC, in particular, since the U.K. public sector is not a member of CEEP.

Wolfgang Streeck (1996) has persuasively argued that in contrast to the weakness of ETUC, that of UNICE serves its members well, for it furnishes an excuse for a hands-off strategy toward EU social and labor-market regulation. The unions reproach UNICE for presenting itself as a letterbox, just passing on demands to its national members. It is probably fair to say that UNICE is not just unwilling but also incapable of transnational collective bargaining, that is, serious coordination of bargaining targets or outcomes across borders, due to the limited authority given by its member organizations, though this also holds to a large extent for ETUC.

UNICE's dual functions, the large differences in organization and bargaining practice across countries, the competition between different countries for investments, the divergences in producer interests, its own limited resources, and the exit threat of TNCs—all would make anything beyond a loosely organized pressure group an organizational miracle. No such pressure group is likely to happen without considerable pressures from an interventionist European "would-be" state and a successfully mobilized European union movement. From national labor histories, we can learn that once party-union ties and electoral power helped labor to obtain citizenship rights and invite state intervention on its behalf, employers were compelled to combine in central organizations in order to counter these efforts (Klausen, ch. 8 above). Neither an EU welfare state nor a strong European Parliament, eager to integrate worker-citizens into a "social Europe," is yet on the horizon. Therefore, employers have not had much incentive to pursue the self-regulatory path.

Conclusion

We have argued that national labor unions, faced with a domestic crisis and an erosion of national power, do not necessarily seek to ally themselves internationally with other union movements or to pool resources. If they do, they find many obstacles on their road, some of their own making, some built and reinforced by others. Analyzing the challenges that compel unions to transnational collective action, we find it useful to distinguish between push and pull factors. On the one hand, there are pressures from below that force labor unions on a path of transnational cooperation; on the other, there are incentives from above that make such a path more promising. We have shown that neither push nor pull factors have been strong enough to make transnational action the unequivocal and dominant strategic choice of union movements in Europe. There are a number of endogenous and exogenous barriers to transnational solidarity. Even if European unions were well organized and overcame their differences, without some minimal cooperation of the European "would-be" state and of European employers, it would be very difficult to conceive of any transnational dynamic. Theoretically, one could construct a scenario, comparable to the development of national industrial relations and welfare states, that entailed a mutually reinforcing spiral of centralization of interest representation in Europe. However, given the present configuration—the weak power of European unions, the weak organization of European employers, and the weak "stateness" of the European Union—such a dynamic is relatively unlikely.

Notes

1. Over 70 percent of EU trade is still between EU member states and thus contained within the internal market (Hirst and Thompson 1992, 376–78).

2. A dispute between French unions delayed the affiliation of the Catholic CFTC until 1991. The German DGB kept the tiny CGB out; the small Christian-Democratic union confederation in Spain, a very small Protestant union center in Denmark, and a Vatican workers association have also remained outside ETUC.

3. The CGT's affiliation has been blocked by rivalry between French unions, and by the CGT's continued allegiance to Communist Party doctrine. CGT's membership has dwindled, from more than 2 million in the mid-1970s to less than five hundred thousand; this decline is reflected in the decline of votes at works council elections (Visser 1989).

4. The European Confederation of Independent Unions combines fourteen minority confederations from eleven countries; an independent European union of train drivers; and the European Federation of Senior Civil Servants, which itself has twelve members in eight EU member states. The European Confederations of Managerial and Professional Organizations has eleven members.

5. Since 1996, ETUC has admitted nine national union confederations from Central and Eastern Europe (Poland, the Czech Republic, Slovakia, Hungary, Bulgaria, and Romania) and awarded observer status to four associations from Hungary and Romania (Seideneck 1996).

6. ETUC has only a small staff of thirty-two, as well as seven paid officials in Brussels.

7. Beginning in 1873, numerous international trade secretariats (ITSs) were founded, mainly on the European continent. Later, especially after 1945, they expanded worldwide; between the wars they were already caught in the ideological and political conflicts that plagued all international unionism (Windmuller 1980).

8. In 1993, the first ITUC at the EU's eastern border was set up in the Elbe-Neisse area, among unions from Saxony (Germany), Bohemia (the Czech Republic), and Poland.

9. Directive 94/45/EC provides for "the establishment of a European Works Council or a procedure in Community-wide undertakings and Community-scale groups for the purpose of informing and consulting employees." To be covered by the directive, a TNC must have more than 1,000 employees in all and must have subsidiaries in at least two countries, with at least 150 employees in each subsidiary.

10. Craft unionism has left a lasting mark on British, Danish, and Irish union structure. White-collar federations are typical in Scandinavia, Germany, the Netherlands, and Switzerland, and special white-collar unions are found within the main federations in Austria, Belgium, Britain, and Ireland. Separate peak associations of public servants exist in Scandinavia, France, Germany, Greece, and the Netherlands. Regional splits are found most notably in Spain.

11. The Maastricht Treaty introduces a codecision procedure (art. 189b) and a cooperation procedure (art. 189c) in some policy domains. Yet in the social- and labor-policy domain, the latter procedure applies in the case of health and safety only (art. 118a2). Article 2 of the Social Protocol extends the cooperation procedure to directives setting minimum standards for working conditions, employee information-and-consultation rights, equal opportunities, and reintegration into the labor market.

12. In the field of social policy, several regimes exist: the provisions of the Rome treaty binding all EU member states, the binding Social Charter of 1989 from which the United Kingdom opted out, and the Social Protocol of the Maastricht Treaty, by which all EU member states except the United Kingdom can regulate some social policies, partly by qualified majority.

13. In Denmark, Germany, Finland, Norway, Sweden, and Switzerland, producer and employer interests are represented in different organizations. While chambers of commerce exist in most countries, they vary in their functions and mandate. Note that only in Austria is the chamger of commerce entitled by law to engage in collective bargaining (Lanzalaco and Schmitter 1992).

11

Migration in Contemporary Europe: European Integration, Economic Liberalization, and Protection

Thomas Faist

In recent years, the dynamics of European integration have proceeded as a twofold transnational process. First, national states in Western and Southern Europe have cooperated more closely in the European Union (EU). Increasing cooperation of European governments about the freedom of movement of EU citizens, rules for labor market access, and social policy coordination on benefits accrued from working in other member countries has been a political by-product of the common market. Yet this economic liberalization and partial regulation has also been characterized by conflicts over the implications of the freedom that companies have to post contract workers from one member state to another. For example, should construction workers sent from Portuguese companies to Germany be entitled to the wage levels and working conditions prevailing in the receiving country or only to the lower standards in the sending country?

Second, the "great transformation" of the Central and Eastern European states (CEE countries) has raised anew the question of how to deal with migration from Europe's peripheries. This has been a long-standing issue with respect to German–Turkish and French–Maghreb relations. The new freedom of companies in member states and selected associated states (e.g., Poland) to provide services abroad by sending workers there has also raised fears, among actors in the more affluent member states, concerning the loss of jobs, wage depression, and a deterioration of working conditions. Similar perceptions, even more pronounced, have been expressed over continuing cross-border movements from third countries, labor migration and refugee movements alike. For example, European states have restricted the access of asylum seekers and have implemented regulations that make it harder to be recognized as a refugee.

Third, to add to this already complex situation, new immigration from third countries is taking place at a time when the future of resident immigrant populations from non-EU states, a legacy of guest worker recruitment in the 1960s and early 1970s, is unclear. The future of these former guest workers' integration into labor markets and other spheres of social, political, and cultural participation in the countries of settlement is uncertain. For example, the unemployment rate among former guest workers in Germany has been consistently more than twice as high as among native workers since the mid-1970s.

The important question underlying all three areas is whether and how international migration may dilute the protective rights of domestic workers and the status of the migrant workers. Two questions emerge. The first relates to the dynamics of European integration and migration and the interests of the main actors involved: how have relevant political actors on the domestic, foreign policy, and supranational level—governments inside and outside the EC, unions and employer organizations, EU institutions such as the EC Commission, the European Court of Justice, the European Parliament, and the Council of Ministers—responded to the increased transnationalization of labor markets in the EU, to the continuing labor migration from third countries, and to the future of permanently residing immigrants from third countries?

The second question concerns the internal political dynamics of migration regulation and the strategies of the actors involved. The freedom of worker mobility and service provision, the abolition of internal borders, and continuing immigration from third countries have contributed to a politics of competition towards immigrants. Moreover, the possible consequences of immigrant employment have not remained confined to those such as wage depression, job substitution, changes in the industrial relations between unions and employers in the countries of destination, and welfare-state expenditures. Important political actors at all levels of policy making have found it convenient to tie immigration to such diverse political issues as housing shortages, ethnic and national identity, and increased crime and drugs. The issues involved in labor migration in particular and immigration in general have thus experienced an elevation from a relatively minor policy area in the 1960s to a central issue in politics during the 1980s and 1990s.

This analysis focuses on Germany and its role in the process of European integration and migration. Therefore, east-west migration (e.g., from Poland to Germany) takes a more prominent role than south-north labor flows (e.g., from Maghreb countries to France). Nevertheless, the analysis of Germany, a central destination for immigrants from Southeastern and

Eastern Europe and an influential actor in EU policy making, offers a glimpse of the general issues involved.

Migration and European Integration: A Sketch

The free movement of workers within the European Community has been an integral part of "an area without internal frontiers in which the free movement of goods, persons, services and capital is ensured" (Single European Act 1986, art. 8A). Thus, freedom of movement is part of an ambitious program of market integration and liberalization. Every citizen of the EU has the individual right "to move and reside freely within the territory of the member states." This right is based on the principle of nondiscrimination among citizens of the member states regarding employment, remuneration, and other working conditions. EC institutions have argued that this right is a basis for increasing economic efficiency. All member states will profit from the freedom of services, goods, capital, and persons. One would think that some governments have an incentive to find a common solution on this issue because the effects of wage differentials and unemployment could lead to movements of workers from less-advantaged regions to richer economies, eventually underbidding workers in the more prosperous countries. However, it is worth noting that no large-scale movements from southern European countries to northern welfare states in the EU have occurred since the 1970s. Income differentials of one-to-four between countries such as Portugal and Germany have not led to significant labor movements (Stalker 1994, 155–56).[1]

These arguments would require common border-control towards third countries and, internally, a common understanding about the working conditions, pay levels, and so on of workers posted in other member states. The debates address questions such as the freedom of mobility of citizens from non-EC states (*extracommunitari*) who have acquired legal permanent resident status in an EC country. There were some 9.3 million of these in 1990. In addition, there were about 5 million EC citizens residing in other member countries. In total, the foreign population in the member states amounted to about 14 million out of a total population of 320 million. And out of 140 million persons employed in the EC, 5 million were *extracommunitari* and about two million were EC citizens working in another member state (OECD 1994b).

Undeniably, the debates over labor migration have been exacerbated by external pressures brought about by increasingly high levels of refugees and other immigrants since the 1980s. One of the dominant crisis scenarios concerns the transformation in CEE countries. The perception has been that the migratory threat to the EU (east-west migration) has increased very rapidly. In fact, net migration to Europe has increased every year since 1985, with substantial increases from 1989 on (table 11.1). In absolute figures, Germany was the European country with the highest immigration and emigration flows in 1992: more than 1.5 million immigrants and 720,000 emigrants. Nevertheless, immigration also rose in Greece, Spain, France, and Ireland. As to countries of destination, more than 65 percent of all immigrants went to Germany, 9 percent to the United Kingdom, 8 percent to the member states of the Benelux, 5 percent to Italy, and 5 percent to France.

Most *extracommunitari* in the EU countries come from associated countries such as Turkey and the Maghreb states, a legacy of postwar labor migrations and continuing family reunions. Again, Germany has the highest absolute number and proportion. The total foreign population in Germany constituted 8.5 percent in 1993—as compared to 8.6 percent for Austria, 9.1 percent for Belgium, 5.1 percent for the Netherlands, 6.3 percent for France, 1.7 percent for Italy, 1.1 percent for Spain, and 3.5 percent for the United Kingdom. Among EU member states, Germany has the highest share of non-EU foreigners and the third highest share of foreign workers, 8.8 percent (1993 figures). First comes Luxembourg with 38.6 percent and, second, Austria with 9.6 percent (OECD 1995, 27).[2] A look at table 11.3 gives a sense of the different rights immigrant groups are able to claim. It is necessary to consider the specific claims each group can make because this information is used in arguments over the effects of immigration on the receiving countries.

Table 11.1. Annual Migration into EU (in thousands)

Year	Regular immigration of foreigners	Asylum seekers	Ex-nationals having a constitutional reight to immigrate	Illegal entrants	Total
1985	700,000	170,000	100,000	50,000	1,020,000
1986	750,000	200,000	100,000	50,000	1,100,000
1987	800,000	180,000	150,000	50,000	1,180,000
1988	950,000	220,000	300,000	100,000	1,570,000
1989	1,150,000	310,000	800,000	100,000	2,360,000
1990	1,200,000	430,000	450,000	200,000	2,280,000
1991	1,300,000	550,000	300,000	300,000	2,450,000
1992	1,300,000	1,040,000[a]	300,000	400,000	3,040,000

Source: Brochmann (1995), 38.

[a]Includes 350,000 ex-Yugoslavs offered temporary status

Table 11.2. Foreign Population and Labor Force in EU Countries

Country	Foreign population N (in thousands) 1983	1993	% of total population 1983	1993	Foreign labor force N (in thousands) 1993	% of total labor force 1993
Austria	297	690	3.9	8.6	305	9.6
Belgium	891	921	9.0	9.1	340	8.3
Denmark	104	189	2.0	3.6	54	1.9
Finland	16	56	0.3	1.1	—	—
France	3,714	3,597	6.8	6.3	1,544	6.2
Germany	4,535	6,878	7.4	8.5	3,432	8.8
Ireland	83	94	2.4	2.7	40	3.0
Italy	381	987	0.7	1.7	—	—
Luxembourg	96	125	26.3	31.1	65	38.6
Netherlands	552	780	3.8	5.1	278	3.9
Spain	210	430	0.5	1.1	82	0.5
UK	1,601	2,001	2.8	3.5	1,026	3.6

Source: OECD (1995), 27.

Table 11.3. Access of Immigrants to Protective (Social) Rights in Germany

Immigrant category	Citizenship acquisition	Unemployment insurance	Social assistance	Housing	Children's education
Privileged groups:					
Ethnic Germans	Upon arrival	Yes[a]	Yes	Yes	Yes
Recognized refugees	After five years	Yes[a]	Yes	Yes	Yes
Temporary workers					
Settled guest workers	After 10 years[b]	Yes[a]	Yes[c]	Yes	Yes
Rotating Workers[d]	No	No	No	No	No
Refugees					
Asylum seekers	No	Yes[e]	No	Yes	No
Defacto refugees	No	Yes[e]	No	Yes	No[f]
Unauthorized migrants[g] (Illegal and clandestine)***	No	No	No	No	No

Source: Faist and Haeussermann (1996), 88.

[a]Based upon employment (same as for German citizens).
[b]Legal claim after 15 years.
[c]Drawing social assistance may cause a denial of the residence permit for those who do not yet have an unlimited residence permit.
[d]E.g., seasonal and project-tied workers.
[e]Based upon employment.
[f]Based upon programs modeled after social assistance.
[g]Includes clandestine migrants (those who enter without any official document or authorization) and illegal immigrants (those who enter legally, for example with a tourist visa, or even a work authorization, that they fail to renew).

Policy on Multiple Levels: Domestic, Foreign, and Supranational

Three levels of migration policy must be considered simultaneously: (1) domestic policy within nation-states (hiring of immigrant labor, acceptance of refugees, and the consequences for domestic labor markets); (2) foreign policy (relations between migrant-sending and migrant-receiving states); and (3) supranational (and international) dimensions of policy (the efforts of nation-states to cooperate in common institutions). These three levels are intrinsically interconnected because governments and collective actors within nation-states have joined in the establishment and further development of a single market, emphasizing economic liberalization. As one domestic consequence, unions in affected sectors experience and perceive a threat to their position and the jobs and wages of their members. For example, they fear that workers from other member states and from third countries will undercut their wages and take their jobs. Deregulation through the freedom of service provision and worker mobility has engendered calls for re-regulation on either a supranational or, alternatively, the national level.

The Domestic Policy Level

Is there a need for immigrant labor and if so, what are the consequences of immigration for labor markets? There are two possible reasons for the current demand for foreign (i.e., immigrant) workers in member states of the EU—structural factors and demographic developments. First, it has been argued that even under conditions of comparatively high unemployment by post–World War II standards, employers in certain sectors demand low-cost and flexible labor, whether foreign or domestic (*billige und willige Arbeitskräfte*). Regarding foreign labor, there is a structural demand that is relatively decoupled from the business cycle. Certain jobs have become very unattractive to domestic workers—for example, those in agriculture, construction, and certain services. In essence, this argument is that native-born workers find dirty, dangerous, and physically demanding jobs unacceptable. Even in periods of high unemployment, they are not forced to take the jobs at the bottom of the ladder that are considered to be socially undesirable. Moreover, once immigrants have entered a field, these jobs are even less attractive to native-born workers, as they become tainted with the label "immigrant jobs."

Second, demographic projections suggest that over the next thirty years, the EU countries will see a natural increase of only 2 million people while the North African countries on the south coast of the Mediterranean will increase by 165 million. The EU countries foresee aging populations and will experience a corresponding fall in the working population. Immigration can be perceived as one way of overcoming future labor shortages. However, unlike the first argument, this second proposition does not explain the current employment of labor migrants.

In corporatist systems in particular, immigrant labor is sometimes seen as a threat to domestic labor because of possible (1) substitution and wage depression ("social dumping"); (2) endangerment of consensual industrial relations and decline in union strength; and (3) increased burdens upon welfare-state expenditures. The main thrust of this perception of danger has always focused on less-skilled labor. First, the danger of substitution for domestic labor is that low-cost foreign workers constitute a flexible reserve army. However, empirical evidence on labor market divisions in the main areas of employment of immigrant labor hired in the 1960s and 1970s (manufacturing) suggests that this is not the case (see, e.g., Grüner 1992). Moreover, in European countries with developed welfare states, immigrant labor has usually been employed under the same conditions as domestic labor, at least until the late 1980s. In the present period of deregulating labor markets and abolishing internal borders in the European Community, however, the threat of substitution, as well as wage depression, has again been raised. Nevertheless, the empirical evidence is mixed. Instead of depresing wages, outcomes may even work the other way in labor markets segmented or split along ethnic divides. For example, there is some evidence that the employment of foreign workers has provided indigenous workers with opportunities for upward occupational mobility and thus higher wages in the 1960s and 1970s (Böhning 1984).

Second, the employment of immigrant labor endangers industrial relations. Since employment relationships in highly regulated welfare states are covered by regulations that do not allow cutthroat price competition (e.g., adherence to wage bargaining agreements), the threat to indigenous labor is more indirect than the flexible-reserve-army hypothesis suggests. High levels of immigration lead to a situation in which many more persons are willing to enter nonstandard forms of employment. First-generation labor migrants are particularly prone to enter them because of their readiness to accept wages and working conditions unattractive to native workers. This development reinforces a further weakening of the standard employment relationship. For example, it is easier for employers in certain industries to find persons willing to accept fixed-term contracts, thus increasing the flexibility of employees' status, or to find workers who accept long working hours and work on Sundays. A massive influx of immigrant workers has the effect that a lower proportion of the workforce is unionized, thus decreasing the bargaining strength of unions. The potential political consequences seriously undermine the "social partnership" of unions and employer associations in the joint regulation of wage bargaining and working conditions.

And because organized labor and labor parties are less powerful politically, there are repercussions for legislation and adjudication around these issues.

Third, asylum seekers, who are usually not allowed to work, have access to minimal assistance provided by local communities. In times of mounting numbers of refugees, together with welfare-state retrenchment, these costs are subject to debate. In short, open borders threaten welfare-state regulation of labor markets and thus endanger the relative advantages that workers in rich countries enjoy over workers in poor countries. On the individual level, this means that an abundance of cheaper-priced labor in the context of open borders increases labor market competition, leading to higher unemployment among indigenous workers.

In order to observe in which sectors immigrants are employed and in which areas conflicts could occur, we need to go beyond the hypothetical considerations just presented and delve into an analysis of foreign and domestic worker employment across the primary countries of immigrant worker employment. In Germany, Belgium, and the Netherlands, the proportion of foreign workers employed in extraction (e.g., coal mining) is much higher than that of domestic workers, probably due to the dangerous and unpleasant working conditions. In Germany, a declining industry such as coal mining has become a typical "immigrant job" for the former guest workers and their sons. Further, the proportion of foreign workers in manufacturing is much higher than average in these three countries but especially in Germany. In the United Kingdom and Luxembourg, by contrast, the area in which the proportion of foreign workers is much higher than average services (other than banking, insurance, etc.). These differences reflect the general structure of labor markets in the individual countries. Interestingly—and of great importance for the more recent political conflicts on labor migration within and among the EU member states—foreign workers are highly overrepresented in construction in Belgium, France, the Netherlands, and Germany (OECD 1994b, 36; 1995, 41–42). The construction industry constitutes a sector of high employment density. In 1988, about 7 percent of all persons employed in the EU were active in construction (Knechtel 1992, 74).

In sum, the empirical evidence supporting the job substitution and wage depression, breakdown of industrial relations, and welfare arguments is mixed at best. What is important, however, is that these arguments offer plausible scenarios of dangers for domestic workers if the level of immigration is "too high" or if foreign workers are employed at conditions below those of domestic workers.

The Foreign Policy Level

An argument, at once alternative to and complementing the structural-demand hypothesis, is that on the part of (some) receiving countries, the admission of new labor migrants was not primarily motivated by the need to compensate for shortages in the labor market in order to rebuild postwar economies with low-cost and docile foreign labor. Rather, in countries such as Germany, foreign policy considerations could have provided an overriding rationale.

How foreign policy considerations shape labor migration policies and politics is most visible in the conflicts over new temporary labor migrants from third countries. Of course, there must be social and political linkages between two regions for labor migration to occur—for example, former colonial ties (the France–Maghreb states and the British Commonwealth), explicit recruitment of labor migrants (Germany–Turkey), or the revival of older labor migration patterns dating back as far as the nineteenth century (Germany–Poland). The dissolution of the communist Eastern bloc has presented a changed situation regarding labor migration. There is now a dual process of European integration and economic liberalization: (1) further integration within the European Union; and (2) the association of the Central and Eastern European (CEE) countries in response to their demands for integration. Still in the future, albeit with much less likelihood of early success is the admission of Turkey and the Maghreb states.

In the early 1990s, the EC signed association agreements with the "Visegrad Four"—Poland, Hungary, the Czech Republic, and Slovankia—and, more recently, with Bulgaria and Romania. Association agreements envision the free mobility of labor at a future date. Since there is no supranational regulation of labor migration, governments of nation-states are the main actors. Labor migration agreements can be interpreted as a first, albeit tenuous, step toward future free labor-mobility. The CEE sending countries argue that temporary labor migration offers a way of gaining much-needed hard currency.

The Supranational Policy Level

Both EU institutions and national governments have interests in cooperating about immigration from third countries. It is plausible to assume that each member state is affected by the policies of the other participants. Therefore, one would think that this interdependence makes immigration a prime candidate for coordination. Following this line of thought, one member state's liberal or restrictive admission policies affect the others. For example, if there were no common border controls toward the territory outside the EU, this could have negative effects upon labor market control of all member states. If someone entered the EU territory anywhere and by any means, he or she could move freely throughout the EU, possibly heading for the more prosperous economies and generous welfare states. The possible consequences of the entry and employment of illegal and clandestine immigrants could be wage depression, job substitution, and a deterioration of industrial relations and welfare-state regulation. Fear of illegal immigration has been voiced in public opinion and by some Western European politicians. Such speculations gain added plausibility in the political discourse of European integration in a period in which transformation of the welfare state is proceeding, accompanied by increased blaming of groups believed responsible for these developments (Faist 1995b).

There has been no transfer of authority to regulate labor migration to the supranational level. Intergovernmentalism continues to be the dominant mode of coordination, as member states have remained the major players in this game (Collinson 1994). Nevertheless, supranational institutions have made some efforts at a common policy, which can be perceived as an important beginning for agenda-setting.

The European Community measures regarding immigration are included in each of the three "pillars" of the Maastricht Treaty (1991). The first pillar, the treaty provisions concerning Community matters, include a new article (100c) stating that the Council of Ministers "shall determine the third countries whose nationals must be in possession of a visa when crossing the external borders of the member states." The second pillar (foreign and security issues) touches, albeit indirectly, upon migration questions because security issues are related to the movement of persons. The third pillar (intergovernmental cooperation in justice and home affairs) lists the areas that "member states shall regard . . . as matters of common interest." These matters include asylum policy; rules governing the crossing of external borders; immigration policy; policy regarding nationals of third countries, more specifically conditions of entry and movement, residence, family reunion, and access to employment; and unauthorized immigration. The development of a common migration policy in Europe concentrates on three main policy lines: (1) action on the causes of migration pressure; (2) action on controlling immigration flows; and (3) action to strengthen the integration policies for legal immigrants (EC Communication 1994, 1b–1c). Overall, then, policy makers on the nation-state level have accepted the free movement of labor and services under the umbrella of enhanced economic liberalism and have eased the barriers to migration by EU citizen–workers. However, nation-states have not lost their sovereignty concerning the conditions of admission and employment of third-country workers.

Intra-EU Flows: Freedom of Movement and Services

In the postwar period, labor migrants within Europe have been employed, above all, as manual workers and in less-skilled positions. At the managerial and administrative level, mobility has been very limited. If we differentiate three segments of the labor market—unqualified, qualified/occupational, and high-tech—the creation of a single market has most likely been advanced in only two segments, the unqualified and the high-tech. As European business undergoes further transnationalization and as many companies launch Europe-wide operations, highly skilled and managerial employees are becoming increasingly mobile (Salt 1992). Yet despite efforts to recognize diplomas mutually, these employees' mobility is likely to remain very limited because entry barriers are still considerable. The highly skilled and managerial is the segment most highly regulated and protected at the national level in all member states (Marsden 1992). Hence, political conflicts between and within member states have focused on the unqualified segment.

The mobility of unqualified workers in Europe has been diminishing over the past decades, and (according to informed opinion) capital mobility has substituted significantly for labor migration (Straubhaar 1988, 127). Hence, it is not surprising that greater occupational mobility for the former has not resumed with the completion of the common market. Nevertheless, the considerable sectoral differences that exist with regard to unemployment rates have persisted. Temporary labor mobility seems to be attractive to both employers and workers in industries such as construction. In countries such as France and Germany, the construction industry has employed a particularly high proportion of immigrant workers; manufacturing, an immediate proportion; and services, a lower one.

Political conflicts at the supranational and domestic levels have not centered on the freedom of movement of EU citizens legally employed by an employer in another member state. As long ago as the Treaty of Rome (1957), the representatives of national governments declared efforts to reduce restrictions on labor mobility as desirable social policy in the EC. Since then, the European Union has acquired legal authority to guarantee equal treatment for migrating EU citizens, to regulate their internal movement by protecting their rights to mobility, working conditions, and settlement, and to oversee transfers of social insurance claims from one country to another (Meehan 1991, 139). In Germany, EU citizens have preference over *extracommunitari* in obtaining working permits in the labor market. Indeed, the EC has directly intervened in the coordination of social rights of EC citizens through regulations defining how periods of employment and contributions to social insurance in various member states qualify as claims to social benefits and whether these claims may be exported to other EU states (Regulations 1612/68 EC, 1408/71EC, 574/72 EC).

Yet conflicts have arisen over the provision of services, defined as the posting abroad of workers who are still employed in the sending country (Single European Act 19, art. 7A).

Fears have been expressed that the provision of services may result in "social dumping."[3] Originally, this term referred to the danger that production would shift to employers using substandard employment practices— for example, through moving production to countries with low costs. Lower costs of production would be based, at least partially, on lower social wages including employer expenses (Falkner 1994). Project-tied work, guaranteed by the freedom to provide services, implies a relocation not of capital but of labor in transnationalizing EU labor markets. It is a characteristic feature of the construction industry that buildings generally have to be assembled at the work site. In the case of project-tied work in the construction industry, then, the notion of social dumping refers to the problems of wage depression, job substitution, and dangers to industrial relations.

The issues become clear when looking at the Portuguese–German interaction. In 1991, between 30,000 to 40,000 of the more than 270,000 Portuguese construction workers were at one time or another posted to Germany. Between 10 and 15 percent of the total Portuguese labor force in this sector worked in Germany during that year. Unemployment in Portugal has been high and rising. The issue gained renewed urgency after 1993, when the media reported increasing numbers of cases of abuse by "firms of convenience" that were exploiting cheap labor in the framework of the provision of services. Reportedly, these firms were established in member states where wages were rather low and/or in regions greatly affected by unemployment, like Portugal, and recruited workers in order to send them to another member state (Germany, the Netherlands, Belgium, and France) where wages and social security contributions were much higher (MNS 1995, 2). Workers from the United Kingdom were also reported to be entering German labor markets as officially self-employed, while they actually were employed by United Kingdom construction companies. Such workers accepted much lower wage rates than German workers because the companies hiring them did not need to pay social wages for them. Reports of alleged misuse of contract workers made headlines in the postreunification building boom of Berlin. Portugal and Germany tried to remedy some of the problems by a bilateral agreement. The agreement explicitly focuses on two linkages made in public debate: (1) immigration and integration (the deployment of Portuguese workers in Germany and the training of Portuguese youth in both countries; and (2) avoidance of irregular employment by means of stricter border controls and workplace inspections.

Construction in the Federal Republic has depended on immigrant labor since the 1950s. After supplies from the rural countryside were exhausted and migration from East Germany interrupted by the building of the Berlin Wall in 1961, immigrant construction workers first came from Italy, later from Yugoslavia and Turkey. Since 1989, they have come from Eastern

Europe, Portugal, and the United Kingdom. This industry has been plagued by an inability to recruit enough school-leavers to enter apprenticeships and train to be skilled workers (Streeck et al. 1987). One option for remedying the problem has been to subcontract with companies, especially those from abroad, to furnish workers. Indeed, labor markets in the construction industry have long been characterized by a core of native-born skilled workers, supplemented by a fringe of subcontracted workers.

Although the commission in 1991 proposed a directive on the provision-of-services problem, it took the Council of Ministers until 1996 to agree on the general terms. The formula advanced in the agreement is simply "equal pay for equal work at the same place." Those member states—the United Kingdom and Portugal—whose citizens are frequently posted to other member states tried to block this agreement; France, Germany, the Netherlands, and Belgium (receiving states) supported it. Among the contentious issues were those relating to the minimum rates of pay and minimum paid holidays. Nonetheless, even with the Council of Ministers' agreement, the individual member states have a wide latitude to specify the precise terms under which EU workers from other states should be employed within their borders.

Even before the EU member states agreed on a guideline for detached workers, most of whom are tied to projects, France and Belgium had their own national legislation that guaranteed to posted workers working conditions similar to those of national workers. In corporatist Germany, there has been a continuous debate, before and after the European agreement, on protecting national construction companies and workers from foreign competitors. An issue contested between the general employer association, on the one hand, and labor unions and small construction companies (competitors of foreign subcontractors), on the other hand, has been a fixed minimum wage for construction workers. The former group has called for economic liberalization and low minimum wages, while the latter has continued to demand temporary protection by legal means.

To sum up, overall migratory movements within the EU have decreased rather than increased since the 1970s. Intra-EU migratory movement, such as that to Germany from Portugal pursuant to the freedom to provide services, is only a small fraction of the immigration to Portugal herself from third countries; indeed, Portugal has become one of the magnets for immigration from North Africa. Receiving-country conflicts over wage, job, and market competition have been addressed by the EU agreement and by national protective regulation, such as a minimum wage for all workers employed in construction, irrespective of origin and specific work status.

"New" Migration from Associated and Other Third Countries

Germany can certainly be considered to be a "large actor" with respect to migration from third countries; it has played a leading role among the external actors concerned with transformation policies in the CEE countries. Domestically, conflicts about labor migration in Germany have centered on the new labor immigrants from Eastern Europe, even though ethnic Germans (*Aussiedler*) have constituted the bulk of immigrants in the late 1980s and early 1990s (tables 11.4 and 11.5).

In contrast to the unified guest worker program of the 1960s, Germany has had several distinct programs through which approximately three hundred thousand non-EU workers on average have been employed annually in the early 1990s. This is much fewer than the guest worker program, which at its height in 1973 provided 10 percent of the Federal Republic's total labor force. First, there is a seasonal-worker program that permits the employment of foreign workers up to three months a year. Second, there exist several project-tied (e.g., subcontract) programs, or *Werkvertrags-arbeitnehmer-Vereinbarungen,* that Germany has entered into with CEE countries, most notably Poland and Hungary. In these, a German company subcontracts to a company from a CEE country for part of a construction program. The foreign company sends its workers and machinery to Germany to complete the work. Third, there are much smaller programs under which border commuters (*Grenzgänger*), trainees (*Gastarbeitnehmer*), and nurses are permitted to work temporarily in Germany (table 11.6).

Unlike the 1960s guest worker program, these new policies are best seen as responses to two distinct impulses, with the foreign policy impulse clearly overriding the domestic concerns. First, domestically, employers in very few sectors have been interested in foreign-worker programs. Only in sectors such as agriculture have employers requested additional labor.

Table 11.4. Immigration to FRG, 1950–1989: Average Annual Inflow (in thousands)

Immigrant Category	1950–59	1960–69	1970–79	1980–89
East Germans	220.3	61.8	14.9	58.5
Other ethnic Germans	44.0	22.1	35.5	100.4
Asylum seekers	—	—	15.6	77.6
Other non-Germans	—	—	—	3.3

Sources: Statistisches Bundesamt (1992), 91 and (1977), 21; MNS, various issues

Table 11.5. Annual Immigration to FRG, 1984–1995

Year	Asylum seekers N (in thousands)	Recognition rate[a]	Ethnic Germans N (in thousands)
1980	107,818	12.0	—
1981	49,391	7.7	—
1982	37,423	6.8	—
1983	19,737	13.7	—
1984	35,278	26.6	—
1985	73,832	29.2	38,968
1986	99,650	15.9	42,788
1987	57,379	9.4	78,523
1988	103,076	8.6	202,673
1989	121,318	5.0	377,055
1990	193,063	4.4	397,075
1991	256,112	6.9	221,995
1992	438,191	4.3	218,765
1993	322,599	—	218,900
1994	127,210	—	222,600
1995	127,937	9.0	

Sources: Statistisches Bundesamt (1992), 91; (1977), 21; *MNS.*
[a]Recognition rate in the first instance.

Employers in the construction sector have been much less vocal in demanding foreign labor even though some evidence suggests that reducing costs by employing high numbers of low-cost and docile labor is a standard practice. Second, and more important, foreign policy considerations have led the German government to enter into agreements with CEE countries who seek foreign currency and new markets for services and products in Western Europe. There are at least two differences between the guest worker programs of the 1960s and the new temporary-worker programs of the 1990s.

The genesis of the agreements on project-tied work, seasonal work, and guest workers indicates that foreign policy considerations in a restructuring Europe have played a crucial role in establishing and continuing foreign-worker arrangements. After all, while Germany has been among the member states holding up the accession of Turkey to the European Union, it has recently been the main advocate of a widening of the EU to include CEE countries such as Poland, Hungary, and the Czech and Slovak Republics.

Table 11.6. Temporary Workers in Germany, 1991–1994

Country of origin	Year	Project-tied workers[a]	Seasonal workers	Guest workers
Poland	1991	41,945	—	—
	1992	45,903	—	—
	1993	31,710	143,861	943
	1994	12,698	136,659	1,002
Hungary	1991	11,348	—	—
	1992	13,190	—	—
	1993	13,220	5,346	1,370
	1994	8,333	2,458	1,450
Former CSFR	1991	7,826	—	—
	1992	11,464	—	—
	1993	7,660	12,027	1,557
	1994	1,570	3,465	1,209
Other	1991	15,474	—	—
	1992	39,808	—	—
	1993	27,100	19,803	1,901
	1994	13,507	12,645	1,168
Total	1991	76,593	—	—
	1992	100,365	—	—
	1993	79,690	181,037	5,771
	1994	36,108	155,217	5,529

Source: Bundesanstalt für Arbeit; own calculations.
[a]Figures for 1993 represent maximum number authorized; for 1994, actual number utilized.

The inclusion of these CEE countries would be limited to a common foreign and security policy, based on the argument that economic and social inclusion would be far too costly for the member states at this time.

Underlying the German government's position is an articulated interest that by cooperating with CEE countries, Germany can enlist their support in limiting immigration from farther east. About 85 percent of German subcontract work has gone to Poland, Hungary, and the Czech Republic, the countries that are closest to Germany geographically. In a manner similar to the role they play in the "safe country" rule in the new 1993 regulations on asylum, these countries provide a migratory *cordon sanitaire* for the Federal Republic of Germany and, hence, have a lever for influencing German government decisions on labor migration. For example, Poland and the Czech Republic have been willing to cooperate with Germany to reduce the movement of unauthorized aliens through their countries and into Germany.[4]

This foreign policy dimension is most obvious in the case of Poland. Polish workers were employed in the former German Democratic Republic (GDR), especially in the construction industry. After reunification, the German government sought a way to accommodate Polish demands for further employment of Polish workers. After all, according to the Unification Treaty between the GDR and the FRG, the successor federal government assumed responsibility to fulfill previously contracted agreements. Indeed, almost half of all contract workers in recent years have come from Poland.

For countries such as Poland, these agreements wtih Germany (and, on a smaller scale, with France and Belgium) hold great significance, given the need for hard currency. Almost two-thirds of Poland's close to 300,000 workers legally living abroad work in Germany. In addition to those 300,000, an estimated 100,000 Poles work in countries with which no agreements are in place (Golinowska 1994, 172). Poland's share of the remittances and profits from its expatriate workers is believed to have amounted to about 640 percent of its direct investment in 1992 (IDW 1993, 27).

The new labor immigration programs, especially the ones on project-tied work, are politically much more contentious in Germany than were the former guest worker programs. This is so despite the fact that new foreign workers now make up a much smaller proportion of the total workforce. However, their proportion of the total construction workforce is high. For example, in 1996 about 350,000 Germans and 200,000 foreigners (from both the EU and third countries) worked in project-tied construction jobs. Two vexing questions have arisen: (1) are these new foreign workers substitutes for domestic construction workers, do they depress wages, and do they ultimately endanger the relatively consensual industrial relations in this sector; and (2) do these new programs contribute to an increase of illegal practices in construction (and other) industry work sites in Germany?

One of the most important characteristics of project-tied employment is that although workers must be paid wages according to German bargaining agreements, their participation in the German social insurance system is not required. Unlike seasonal workers and guest workers, these contract laborers acquire no claim to future pension or other social insurance benefits in Germany that can be transferred to their country of origin. By paying the lower social security contributions for CEE countries, foreign subcontractors (and, indirectly, German companies) thus save considerable wage costs. Small- and medium-sized construction companies have opposed project-tied workers because they fear for their existence, due to the lower labor costs of foreign companies.

The use of subcontracted project-tied workers who occupy an extraterritorial position regarding employment law has also been intimately tied to the ongoing debate over illegal immigration and irregular employment. In 1990, there were about 2.5 million workers employed in the German construction industry (Knechtel 1992, 75). Employment in that sector may well have risen even higher in the construction boom following unification. In 1996, according to union estimates, there were about 500,000 unauthorized workers. This certainly would be a high number when compared to the total construction workforce. Whether or not the number of clandestine and illegal workers has actually risen over the past years is open for debate. What is important is that the legal conditions of subcontract arrangements are very difficult to enforce; there are plausible arguments suggesting the misuse of these arrangements (Reim and Sandbrink 1996).

When claims of misuse of project-tied workers from Eastern Europe mounted, the German government re-regulated this area by, for example, enforcing stricter control of contracts and work sites and limiting the number of crews allotted to individual countries. However, this policy change coincided with the introduction of unrestricted freedom to provide services within the EU. Therefore, Portuguese and U.K. workers swiftly replaced their Polish colleagues, not least because they could be paid wages even lower than the latter. The former, at least for some years, were more cost-effective than Polish workers. The implementation of minimum wage laws may again change preferences in foreign subcontractors, and thus foreign workers.

The role of asylum seekers in the irregular labor market is even harder to determine. Their numbers have risen significantly in all EC member states, but most dramatically in Germany. Almost two-thirds of all asylum seekers seeking refuge in Europe during the 1980s and early 1990s went to Germany (see tables 11.4 and 11.5). It may be that the refugee policy of the most restrictive member state will become the policy guide for others; that is, if those states with more liberal policies receive the largest share, a policy alignment at the lowest common denominator may result. Perceptions during the German debate on asylum in the early 1990s reflected these fears.

The applications of most asylum seekers have been rejected, but those who do not return home add to the reservoir for both regular and irregular employment. Insofar as asylum seekers are labor force participants, the action of other member states is even more decisive than in the case of labor migrant recruitment because much higher numbers are involved than in legal labor migration. What connects the discussions concerning all migrants, labor immigrants and refugees alike, is the growing fear that both new immigrants and refugees might participate in irregular activities. Moreover, it is easy to argue that asylum seekers constitute an immediate drain upon welfare-state resources because they can claim assistance upon arrival (See table 11.1).

"Old" Immigration: The Control/Integration Thesis

Not only new immigration but also the legacies of earlier labor recruitment raise the question of long-term immigrant integration. As we have seen, some of the newer attempts to regulate transnational labor markets strictly enforce the rotation principle. Also, border control has gained new prominence because of freedom of mobility and the removal of internal borders. Going one step further, one justification for stricter border controls has emerged in the debate over resident *extracommunitari* in the EC. This policy proposition—forcefully argued by the EC Commission and the European Parliament—is that strict oversight of new immigration is necessary in order to advance and secure the integration of (foreign) immigrant populations and avoid the formation of ethnic ghettos. In short, it is claimed that a successful immigrant integration policy depends on strict entry control. Integration can be most easily defined in terms of labor market integration, using statistical indicators such as unemployment rates, income, and labor force participation. Integration, then, would be said to have occurred if immigrants were to have rates of labor force participation, unemployment levels, and average incomes close to those of natives. According to these indicators, however, it appears that immigrant populations in the EU are disadvantaged, with significant cross-country variations and differences between various immigrant groups (Werner 1994).

Supranational actors play a decisive role, mostly in setting the immigration policy agenda but partly also in urging national governments to adhere it. Two issues have emerged in this policy arena, the first concerning the free mobility of resident third-country citizens, the second relating to the long-term consequences of the settlement of some former labor migrants. With regard to the first issue, the EC Commission has proposed that some of the rights currently afforded to European Union workers be extended to *extracommunitari*. It has advanced two arguments. One points to problems arising in the provision of services across member states, as in the construction sectors already discussed. The second is a job match argument: a third-country worker who becomes unemployed in, say, the Netherlands could fill a vacancy in Germany, provided EU citizens or *extracommunitari* residing in Germany cannot be found. This proposal addresses the demand that resident third-country workers be entitled to some of the same rights as European Union workers. It corresponds to the common-market logic in favor of establishing transnational labor markets in the Community.

A second concern has been the integration of resident immigrants from third countries. The EC Commission has sought to integrate permanently residing *extracommunitari*. Its first action came in the 1970s with the adoption of a European Community Action Programme for Migrant Workers and Their Families (1974), which (1) encouraged intergovernmental consultation on policies to deal with workers from non-EC countries and to develop common standards for their treatment; and (2) connected integration to stricter immigration controls, calling for common efforts to avoid illegal migration and irregular employment. This document was a noteworthy attempt to set a common agenda, but it had no short-term practical consequences in aligning the policies of national governments. Later, an EC Directive (1977) that urged member states to undertake concerted efforts to improve educational opportunities foreign workers' children was greeted with contention by member-state representatives over its inclusion of third-country citizens in the integration process. Ultimately, the directive's application was limited to member-state citizens. The EC Commission also argued for a limited local-level suffrage by 1980 for third-country immigrants meeting certain residency requirements: "Excluding them from the exercise of civic and political rights seems to contradict the very principle of the free movement of people and the political objectives of the Community as concerns European union" (Ireland 1995).

The most active and effective institution advancing the integration of *extracommunitari* has been the European Court of Justice (Garth 1986). Although there is no general EU competence over third-country nationals, the EU does have power to enter into agreements wtih third countries, and the ECJ may make decisions binding on national states. The status of many *extracommunitari* working and residing in EC states, then, is regulated not only by a mix of national law and EU regulations but also by agreements between their home countries and the EU, in particular the EU/association agreement with Turkey (1964). The purpose of this agreement is to facilitate Turkey's entry into the EU. This has not been achieved, nor has freedom of movement for Turkish workers in the Community, as required by Article 36 (P) of the Turkish association agreement and by council decisions, which prescribed that such mobility was to be gradually implemented between 1976 and 1986.

The ECJ ruled that when a right under an association agreement is directly enforceable, it becomes part of the *acquis Communautaire* and must be applied by the Community's national courts. According to European Court precedents relating to the Turkey association agreement, workers from Turkey have directly enforceable rights to employment and/or social security benefits. For example, Article 6 of Decision 1/80 of the Association Council stipulates that those Turkish citizens who have already been employed in an EC country for one year have a claim to renew their work permits with the same employer. They also are permitted, after three years,

244   *Thomas Faist*

to respond to another offer of employment for the same occupation and, after four years, to take up any employment of choice. Adult family members, as well as children, of these workers also enjoy eased access to labor markets after some years of residence in a member state (Guild 1992). In the latter case, Turkish workers (including family members if they are workers) in Germany have the same rights as EU citizens.

The German government resisted implementation of these and other decisions, and the German national courts upheld this resistance. The primary interest of the German government, in particular of the Federal Ministry of the Interior (*Bundesministerium des Inneren*), was to prevent further growth of the Turkish immigrant population in Germany. The highest administrative court (*Bundesverwaltungsgericht*) and the highest social court (*Bundessozialgericht*) upheld the opinion that Decision 1/80 did not constitute law that could be claimed by Turkish citizens. Nevertheless, they finally were obliged to accept the more inclusive jurisprudence of the ECJ.

The European Parliament has been clearly the most outspoken advocate of the rights of resident *extracommunitari*. In a recent report, the status of it considered non-EU citizens residing legally in the member states and declared that the Council of Ministers should define "the notion of resident of the union" (European Parliament 1994, 9). The council should also make the necessary legal arrangements for non-EC citizens residing in EU member states to receive the same political and economic rights as EU citizens to exercise their occupational activities throughout the whole territory of the EU.

In sum, then, EU institutions such as the commission and the EP have set the agenda regarding the relationship between the integration of older immigrants and the control of new immigration. However, nation-states have not heeded their calls to advance the rights-status of settled *extracommunitari* to a sort of permanent residence status in the EU. The European Court of Justice has pushed national governments to heed the important provisions regarding mobility and access to social rights spelled out in the association agreements the EU has entered into with Turkey, the Maghreb states, and the CEE countries. In advocating freedom of mobility for privileged *extracommunitari,* the jurisprudence of the court has pursued the goal of economic liberalism. However, this goal, and an improved rights-status for *extracommunitari* on the EU level, conflicts directly with the potential interests of organized groups such as labor unions.

There is an even more immediate problem of consistency because EU institutions have advocated contradictory policies. They have argued for extended socioeconomic integration of, and even local voting rights for, permanently residing *extracommunitari*. At the same time, however, European institutions such as the EC commission have called for the development of a "European consciousness." Ultimately—and this is so even if the latter position is mainly symbolic politics—it has real consequences for the political discourse shaping the debate on immigration and integration of *extracommunitari*. An appeal to European consciousness mainly serves to underline the differences between EU citizens and *extracommunitari*.

Conclusion: Migration as a European Meta-Issue

The politicization of immigration and integration at the supranational level has added to the long-standing problem at the national level. The two dynamics of European integration process and the transformation of Eastern and Central Europe have reinforced the salience that migration now has in political discourse because of the opening of internal borders and the transformations in Eastern Europe. Immigration has become a meta-issue. As we have seen, interested parties such as governments, unions, political parties, and EU institutions have made plausible the linkage of immigration and integration to broader questions about (1) unemployment, housing, crime, and drugs (the domestic realm); (2) development aid and cooperation in controlling the movement of asylum seekers and unauthorized migrants (the foreign policy field); and (3) social solidarity and the evolution of European "citizenship" (the supranational sphere).

Metapolitics regarding immigration can be found in all West European countries. Since the late 1970s, political discourse in Western welfare states has been replete with references to immigrants being unwilling to assimilate culturally and being economic competitors. The gradual restrictions placed upon immigration and political asylum have not been peculiar to German policy. Indeed, restrictive policies have emerged in all West European and North American national states since the early 1970s. Nor has increased xenophobia been a singularly German phenomenon. Immigration has been more and more discussed in connection with structural problems such as economic contraction or sluggish growth, stubbornly high unemployment rates, and the resulting "absorption capacity" of receiving countries. By the 1990s, governments of European receiving countries, under pressure from an increasingly hostile public opinion and using it instrumentally, have turned with rising frequency to often symbolic efforts to deter new immigration: implementing stricter border controls, making it harder for asylum seekers to enter, discouraging permanent settlement, and rolling back social rights and entitlements formerly enjoyed by immigrants and would-be refugees. One reason for the surge of metapolitics is that immigrants are both easy to blame and highly visible in some sectors of the economy. Hence, by implication, immigration raises issues not only of interest but also of identity, belonging, and citizenship. However, such an explanation is simplistic, for it does not explain the process by which immigration becomes a contentious political meta-issue.

The rise both of conflicts around labor migration and of meta-issue politics regarding migration in Europe has been accompanied by two noteworthy developments.

First, once immigration has begun, it is close to impossible for governments in liberal democratic states to control the chain-migration process. *A fortiori,* in cases where immigration is supported by active recruitment policies by the receiving states, the process is even more difficult to control. Immigration occurs in waves, not only because of labor recruitment but sometimes also because of movements of refugees in response to temporally bounded events such as social revolutions, ethnic conflicts, and state implosion. Earlier movements of labor migrants and refugees have established, via migrant networks, bridgeheads through which newcomers enter. The fact that almost half of all asylum seekers in Germany in the 1990s came from the former Yugoslavia and from Turkey is not simply due to presumably liberal asylum policies. Rather, earlier labor recruitment of guest workers from these countries set the stage for later refugee flows. For international movement to be sustained over longer periods of time, communities in both countries of origin and countries of destination are a necessary condition. Once communities are established in the receiving countries, immigration streams are difficult to block. European welfare states are fundamentally different from other wealthy states that import labor, such as Saudi Arabia, Nigeria, or Singapore, for the former are liberal democratic systems that guarantee certain basic civil rights, such as family reunification. This guarantee is by itself able to sustain population flows over long periods, becoming at least partially independent of the economic conditions in the receiving countries and their explicit migration policies.

All West European governments stopped recruiting immigrant labor after 1973, only to be faced with continued flows characterized as family reunification and refugee flight. The latter temporarily decreased due to stricter administrative controls in the early 1980s but resumed on an even larger scale in the late 1980s. In short, ending labor recruitment and instituting stricter asylum regulations had only temporary effects, for immigration, both authorized and unauthorized, later resumed. Through international and national control mechanisms, European governments have been able to control transnational flows in the short run only. What appears to be a loss of control of sovereign national states over their borders is less the outcome of a diminishing capacity to guard their territory in the face of a transnationalizing flow of capital, goods, services, and people, and more the long-term consequence of earlier recruitment policies promoted by governments and employers in the receiving countries themselves. This unanticipated consequence is a major factor contributing to the unease, even obsession, that characterizes political discourse about regaining control of borders.

The second development that has facilitated the emergence of a metapolitics is exogenous to immigration flows. It lies in the close connection between, on the one hand, freedom of movement within the European Union and high levels of immigration from third countries and, on the other, labor market and social policies. Starting with the latter, we note the weakening of the postwar political consensus around welfare universalism, in which principles such as equality and security have been characteristic—to be sure, with important cross-national variation in institutions and policy outcomes. We cannot understand the saliency immigration has gained for the discourse on social citizenship if we limit our discussion to the structural deficiencies of certain labor market segments characterized by a high representation of immigrant workers, and to certain social services in which we find a high proportion of immigrants. Instead, the broader question is how issues of material interest—wage depression, job substitution, industrial relations, but also dependency of immigrants on social services— have fueled debates over ethnic and national identity, multiculturalism, and a host of related issues (Faist 1996). Debates over identities and norms are generally much harder to resolve than conflicts over interests.

EU institutions have begun to enter this stronghold of nation-state sovereignty in the course of economic liberalization. The efforts of institutions such as the ECJ to extend the rights of resident *extracommunitari,* such as freedom of movement and labor market access, have met with strong opposition within nation-states and, where pressure has been high, also from national governments. The feeble attempts by the EC Commission and the European Parliament to advance a more inclusive agenda for the integration of third-country citizens on the EU level, and the call for a closer cooperation with Turkey and with the sending countries in North Africa in order to fight the "root causes" of migration, are above all agenda-setting exercises. In principle, the policies proposed by the EU institutions are not modest at all. Freedom of movement for settled *extracommunitari* within the EU is an integral part of the common-market liberalization program. But the demand to extend social rights to these migrants on an EU level clearly presupposes some sort of welfare "state" structure to be in effect. Alternatively, the institutionalization of rights for *extracommunitari* could be seen as an effort that contributes to European state building. However, welfare-state building, immigration control, and protective rights for both residents and migrants require a degree of cooperation between member-state governments that is hard to imagine. Up until now, the governments of national welfare states have used the EU platform only selectively to regain nation-state sovereignty over borders and domestic control over immigrants.

22248248248 *Thomas Faist*

Notes

1. Factors other than expected income and employment differentials between sending and receiving country have to be taken into account, such as prospects for economic improvement and potential migrants' sociocultural and political ties to the home country (Faist 1997).

2. These statistics have to be interpreted with care. First, they exclude the illegal and clandestine immigrants who have figured very prominently in public debates. The number of such immigrants is notoriously hard to estimate (for careful estimates, see Baldwin-Edwards and Schain 1994, 5). Second, and even more important, these figures cannot take account of the fact that immigrants in some countries have easier access to citizenship than in others and, therefore, are more likely to be counted as citizens rather than as foreigners. In determining citizenship, Germany, Portugal, Ireland, Belgium, and Denmark assign prime importance to parentage and descent (*jus sanguinis*) while in other member states, notably France, the birthplace has more or less determined citizenship (*jus soli*). Moreover, citizenship laws have ranged from liberal (for the Netherlands: five years' residence, minimal knowledge of Dutch, and no criminal offenses) to Germany's more restrictive laws (ten years' residence, strict requirements regarding language proficiency, employment and residence history, and acceptance of German culture; since 1992, a residence of fifteen years in Germany authorizes a claim to naturalization). In countries with *jus soli* principles and more liberal "naturalization" procedures (e.g., France and the Netherlands), we therefore would expect to see a lower percentage of foreigners, while in those with *jus sanguinis* principles and stricter citizenship acquisition rules (e.g., Belgium and Germany), a higher percentage.

3. The use of the term "social dumping" by political actors in this context is incorrect because it would only be dumping in strict economic terms if foreign workers were paid less abroad than in their sending country.

4. Another aspect of growing Europeanization is the development of an infrastructure to deal with immigration. As did the southern European countries during the 1980s, CEE countries such as Poland are changing from countries of emigration into ones of immigration. In the early 1990s, Poland enacted and amended laws facilitating the employment of foreigners, as well as a new foreigners law. There are an estimated 55,000 Russian and Ukranian citizens working in Poland, but only about 10,000 have a work permit (OECD 1995). Most of them come from those parts of the former Soviet Union in which many Poles still live.

12

Gender and Europe: National Differences, Resources, and Impediments to the Construction of a Common Interest by European Women

Chiara Saraceno

In recent years, the conception and fabric of the European Union (EU) have become a target of critiques from Western feminists. These critiques had been developed earlier, directed against both liberal notions of citizenship and the gender-asymmetrical foundations of national welfare states. Similar critiques have undergirded the resistance to the EU by feminist groups based in countries—at first Denmark, and now possibly Sweden or Norway—in which welfare states offer greater support to gender equality and women have a fairer share in political decision-making bodies than in other Western states.

At the same time, however, the existence of a European political and symbolic space is increasingly being used both to develop and to lobby for a European policy that is more attentive to gender equality and more supportive of women's rights, one that might influence, or supersede, less favorable national policies. Such a European space has also encouraged the building of transnational women's networks and lobbies, which use national differences as resources to develop common outlooks and goals. The focus is increasingly on strengthening women's presence in the European governing and decision-making bodies. Women's political participation, therefore, is becoming one of the crucial issues not only in the section of the EU agenda specifically devoted to equal opportunities for women and men but also with regard to the meaning and practice of European citizenship itself. In preparation for the elections of the European Parliament (EP) in June

Chiara Saraceno

1994, the EU's Women in Decision-Making Network launched a campaign to support a larger presence of women among both the candidates and those elected, particularly in those countries—Greece, France, the United Kingdom, Portugal, Italy, and Belgium—where women held 10 percent or fewer of the seats in the national parliament, and often even fewer in the European one. The campaign was not very successful, however.

Women's policies and mobilization within the EU have developed on the uneasy ground marked, on the one hand, by the inconsistency of their different stakes in the EU due to the specific policies of their home states and, on the other, by their common interest in having a less gender-blind and gender-asymmetrical European Union. The result is mobilization amid contradictions and misgivings, as well as amid alliances and mutual learning. Parallels, but also differences, might be drawn with the situation of trade unions: the stronger the women's movement and the position of women at the national level, the less useful and even the more risky, at least in the short term, appear mobilization and cooperation at the European level, while weak national women's movements hope to gain from involvement at that level.

The very loose definition of women's common interest even at the national level—hence the looseness of the structure of women's organizations (even where they have long existed)—leaves more flexibility for feminist groups than for trade unions to organize across nations and to use the European level as a political resource. The identities and strategies of unions are more rooted not only in locally based interests and experiences but also in long-established institutional cultures and practices. One might even wonder if the relative ease with which women coming from different national political and organizational cultures have integrated into the complex EU-created web of networks, lobbies, and groups is a function of their relative organizational weakness at the national level—even of their lack of national representativeness.

The main difference from trade unions, of course, and possibly the greatest weakness of any women's lobby or organized interest group, is that in the case of women, the very concept of representation and representativeness is misplaced, for women are not a homogeneous, self-identified, and organized group. Women's interests are not self-evident and given; rather, they are intentionally constructed by all interested parties and may have quite different contents and meanings. As Borchorst (1994) observes, within the feminist discussion of interest theory there are two basic questions: (1) whether women have interests basically different from men's; and (2) whether one may distinguish between subjective and objective interests. The degree to which the construction of such interests should be given space and voice within the European Community, through explicit and implicit EU policies, is part of the debate within and among women's groups and intellectuals at the national and European level. It is fair to say that the content of this debate varies in meaning from country to country, not only according to the overall status of the European question in the national political discourse but also according to the strength and organization of women's groups and their ability to define women's interests and to shape the national political agenda.

Gender Gaps within the European Community: Labor Force Participation and Earnings

In all EU countries, women's labor-force participation rate has increased substantially since the late seventies, and women's share of employment has grown more rapidly than men's. This is largely due to a decline of men's employment in traditional manufacturing industries, to a shortening of men's working lives, and conversely, to an increase in service sector employment, where most women are employed. Along with a feminization of employment, however, an even greater feminization of unemployment has taken place. In 1986, women were 46 percent of the unemployed in the EC; this figure rose to 52 percent in 1989. Women also account for the larger share of the underemployed, the "casually employed" and those employed part-time.[1] Therefore, they are clearly more exposed than men to the market vagaries and to economic dependence, both within their families and vis-à-vis the state. At the same time, they are often excluded from the most secure and legitimized social security and social rights attached to working status.

Since most citizenship rights, both at the national and at the EU level, are linked to worker status, this weakness of women as workers results in relatively greater insecurity of women's status as citizens. In addition, equal opportunity initiatives at the level of the EU have been the result not of women's political mobilization but of negotiation between national political authorities and EU officials acting within the EU regulatory framework. (As noted in Marks, ch. 2 above, and Majone 1994, the EU is a regulatory regime, depending upon formal legal regulation and the implementation process, in contrast to political mobilization and the legislative process, for bringing about political change.) For example, equal opportunity legislation in Italy came about through the implementation of an EU directive. How such directives are negotiated depends as well on power relations and the general political climate within countries. In Italy, Spain, and Portugal, national governments were eager to enter the European Union, so they accepted the implementation of equal opportunity laws without much opposition. The Danes, who already had such laws, did not have to discuss the EU directive at all. According to a report of the EP's Social Affairs

Committee, the "existing forms of segregation, discrimination and unequal opportunities for women in the labor market make women particularly vulnerable to adverse effects in the completion of the internal market, for example job losses, increase in types of work without social protection, and an increasing demand for flexible and excessively long working days in certain regions, thereby increasing the number of women living in poverty" (European Parliament 1990, 6–7).

The relative presence of women in the different sectors of the labor force varies from country to country. For instance, the more prosperous countries, excepting Germany, have a larger service sector than the poorer ones. In Denmark and the Netherlands, service sector employment is around 70 percent female, compared to 44 percent in Portugal and 48 percent in Greece. This accounts partly for differential rates of women's employment, although in the poorer countries, women are heavily employed in agriculture. Further, the greater the extent of welfare provisions in each country, the greater the participation of women as workers in welfare services and administration.

In all countries, both within manufacturing and within services, women remain segregated from men and concentrated in a smaller number of jobs. They are also likely to work in jobs that are less skilled than men's. According to the EC Commission's *Employment in Europe* report, women make up between 30 to 45 percent of employees in half of the forty sectors of industrial employment that are most sensitive to restructuring and hence to job losses. In sensitive sectors in which women constitute a smaller portion of employees, they are clustered in those manual and assembly-line jobs that are similarly vulnerable to restructuring (Pillinger 1992; Commission of the EC 1989, 1990a, 1990b).

Although trends in other indicators and in gender inequality are broadly similar, the specifics of women's position and gender balances differ widely within the European Community. See tables 12.1 and 12.2 for data concerning labor market participation and incidence of part-time work and table 12.3 for the ratio of women's earnings to men's earnings. However, the picture is far from clear cut, nor does it delineate a neat continuum. For example, countries low in female labor-force participation, such as Italy, not only have a higher percentage of women working full-time but also report a smaller gender gap in earnings than countries such as Denmark, where female labor-force participation is almost double that in Italy.

Moreover, the proportion of the female labor force employed in industries sensitive to restructuring or plant closing is much higher in the poorer southern countries, and in parts of Italy and the United Kingdom (but not in Ireland), than in the more prosperous central and northern countries; hence another gender-specific exposure to unemployment. At the same time, the availability of a cheap labor force, "accustomed" to little or no

Table 12.1. Labor Force Participation Rates in EC Countries, by Gender

Country	Men (%)	Women (%)
Belgium	72.5	51.4
Denmark	90.3	78.3
France	75.4	55.7
West Germany	82.9	54.4
Greece	75.6	43.4
Ireland	83.9	37.6
Italy	77.8	44.0
Luxembourg	88.2	47.6
Netherlands	81.1	52.0
Portugal	85.1	59.7
Spain	77.4	39.9
UK	86.8	65.2

Source: OECD (1990), 200, table 2.
Note: Rates based on population 14 to 64 years of age. Rates for Belgium, Denmark, France, Western Germany (former FRG territory), Greece and Luxembourg refer to 1988; those for Italy, Netherlands, Portugal, Spain, and UK, to 1989.

Table 12.2. Part-time Workers as Proportion of All Employees in EC Countries, by Gender

Country	Men (%)	Women (%)
Belgium	2.0	23.4
Denmark	8.9	41.5
France	3.4	23.8
FRG	2.1	30.6
Greece	2.9	10.3
Ireland	3.7	17.0
Italy	3.2	10.4
Luxembourg	1.9	15.0
Netherlands	14.5	57.7
Portugal	3.6	10.5
Spain	2.1	13.0
UK	5.5	44.2
EC as a whole	3.9	28.1

Source: Eurostat (1991), tables 5 and 7.

Table 12.3. Women's Gross Hourly Earnings (in All Industries) as a Proportion of Men's, 1987–1988

Country	% of male earnings
Belgium	75.3
Denmark	75.3
France	80.8
FRG	73.4
Greece	78.7
Ireland	67.1
Italy	82.7
Luxembourg	66.9
Netherlands	74.2
UK	68.9

Source: Pillinger (1992), tables 2 and 3; and Eurostat (1987–88).

social protection, could result in its utilization as a vehicle for social dumping in internal market competition; alternatively, it could be used as an excuse for reducing social security and social-policy standards in better-off countries. Both men and women are implicated in this dual threat and in intercommunity and intragender conflicts. Women, however, are in a weaker position, not only because of the relatively higher share of the less skilled and/or the less protected who are female but also because of women's position in the division of labor within the family, and the whole range of social policies affecting that sphere.

Gender Gaps within the European Community: Welfare Regimes

National differences in women's and men's relative earnings, rates of labor force participation, and vulnerability to economic and social change are partly accounted for by differences in national labor markets and economies but partly also by the gender models incorporated in social arrangements and in national welfare regimes—one might say by national concepts and embodiments of social citizenship.

Gender relations have long been totally neglected in analyses of welfare policies and models. The concept of social rights, which has been seen to some degree as the key to the development of welfare states, was formulated largely within the labor and social democratic tradition (with variable outcomes across European states). Thus, policies have focused much more on enabling men, as (full-time, stable) workers, to exercise civil and political rights than on overcoming the socially constructed weaknesses and disabilities that derive from the gender division of labor. Even social policies that address women specifically, such as maternity leave and child care services, do so after having construed a woman's ability to give birth as a weakness with regard to the ideal worker and her exclusive responsibility for the care of her children as a "natural" given. Not only welfare regimes but also welfare-state analysts take gender relations and gender structures for granted, as Langan and Ostner, Orloff, and others persuasively argue (Langan and Ostner 1991; Orloff 1993).

Given the largely marginal presence of fathers in caring for children, child care is one of the areas that most affect women's decisions about work. Therefore, the availability of child care may bear heavy responsibility for the differences among, as well as within, countries in men's and women's access to stable employment with benefits. Indeed, the unequal division of labor in the household is the central reason why family and parental status exercises such great influence on the differential rights of men and women as workers and as citizens. In all EC countries, with the exception of Denmark, fathers of children less than four years old take almost no part in child care, irrespective of the mothers' employment status. Only in Denmark was considerable joint responsibility for children's care reported. In the words of Phillips and Moss (1988, 4), "the single biggest childcare problem in the Common Market is simply the lack of it. Most European working parents cannot choose to go out to work in the secure knowledge that their children will be well cared for."

Indeed, the word "mothers" should be substituted for "parents," as fathers are rarely hampered from entering the labor market because of a lack of child care services. Conversely, mothers who work may be accused not only of "abandoning" their children to child care services but also of shifting their duties and their costs to the collectivity. Mothers' social rights, from this point of view, are less institutionalized and legitimate than the long-acknowledged workers' rights to sick pay or health care.

There is a particular shortage of child care for children under three (although in countries such as the United Kingdom or Portugal, services for older preschool children are also scarce). In Italy, for instance, more than 80 percent of children three and older are in kindergarten, while fewer than 10 percent of those under three are in day care although there are wide local variations (Saraceno 1993a). Moreover, while in Denmark, France, and Italy most child care services are publicly funded, in the United Kingdom and Portugal they are not.

Policies about maternity and parental leave also differ widely within the European Community, as do the amounts of, and criteria for, compensation for lost wages. The Netherlands, the United Kingdom, and Portugal have the shortest antenatal and postnatal leaves; Italy has the longest, followed by France, Spain, and Luxembourg (Commission of the EC 1989). In the United Kingdom, which has the lowest level of leave entitlement, compensation is linked to job tenure with the same employer for at least two years full-time or five years part-time. Many part-time workers, who make up a large proportion of the working women in this country, therefore, have no entitlement whatsoever. In Italy, which seems very generous, not only do many working mothers lack any leave entitlement, either because they work in the informal labor market or because they are self-employed, but even some formally employed workers such as housekeepers and servants are entitled only to short leaves and to very reduced compensation.

Some kind of parental leave, which entitles either women only or both women and men to take time out to care for a newborn baby, a sick child, or a disabled or sick relative, exists now in thirteen out of fifteen EU countries, although with different degrees of legitimization and entitlement. In Ireland and the United Kingdom, however, there is no provision whatsoever that takes account of workers' parental duties and family responsibilities beyond that of giving birth. Sine this is combined with a lack of child care provisions, mothers in these two countries are particularly hard put to continue employment when their children are young. These two countries, together with the Netherlands, are those in which single mothers, unlike elsewhere, are more likely than mothers in dual-parent families to be either working part-time or out of the labor force altogether. Sixty-three percent of single mothers in Luxembourg, 50 percent in Denmark, 49 percent in Italy, 46 percent in Belgium, and 44 percent in France work full-time; only 5 percent do so in the Netherlands, compared to 74 percent who are out of the labor force; in the United Kingdom, only 7 percent, compared to 69 percent out of the labor force. This means that these single mothers and their children are more dependent on state-funded, means-tested benefits, which in turn may have not only short-term but long-term effects on their well-being, insofar as long periods out of the labor force render reentry more difficult and greatly reduce old-age security and benefits (Pillinger 1992; Eurostat 1985; Joshi 1989).

According to the EU Women in Employment Network, women's labor-force participation is influenced less by the number of children they have or the availability of child care than by strategies for coping with family obligations. From this point of view, the European countries fall into four categories: (1) those in which having children does not influence mothers' labor-force participation (this category includes Denmark only); (2) those in which having children has a minimal impact on the female activity rates, as in both France, where the percentage of mothers who work does not fall noticeably until the third chid, and Italy, although there the overall labor-force participation of women is lower than in France; (3) those in which the difficulties of combining family life and career lead to part-time work, as in the former GDR and the United Kingdom; and (4) those in which women's labor-force participation drops with the birth of the first child, as in the Netherlands and in Ireland (*Women of Europe* 1992).

The degree to which social security systems are linked not only to status in the labor force but also to family status may influence women's economic autonomy and their strategies vis-à-vis the labor market. In countries such as Belgium, the Netherlands, Italy and the United Kingdom, different statutory pensionable ages for men and women are based upon assumptions about marriage and the "normal" age difference between husband and wife. In the United Kingdom, a widowed woman entitled to an employment-related pension must decide which pension to take: her own or that deriving from her husband's contributions and work record. This means that many working women pay contributions from which they will not benefit. Further, more women than men are employed in the informal labor force and, hence, are not entitled to any work-related pension. Since in most EU countries (except Denmark), there is no universal flat-rate state pension, in old age many women must rely only on either a social assistance pension, which is usually very low (as in Italy), or a survivor's pension. Given the increasing instability of marriages, the latter can no longer be viewed as a viable solution.

In many countries, income supplements are paid on a family basis and to a family head; that is, there is no individual entitlement to income support, not even one measured on the basis of a family income. Consequently, women often do not have access to an individual income even when entitled to social assistance. At the same time, however, they are discouraged from seeking an income-producing job, since this will be taken into account when testing the family's entitlement to support. In Stuart Holland's words (1993, 163), "The institution of the family payment—one payment for the entire family, comprising a payment for the main claimant and his (in a few cases her) dependents—is probably the single greatest testament to the state's unwillingness to provide an independent income to women when they are married."

Equal Opportunities and Gender Equality in EU Policy

Elizabeth Meehan (1993) writes that in the eighties, "sex equality had pride of place in the Community social policy." (Nevertheless, the EU itself has not been above criticism as an equal opportunity employer.) Indeed, gender equality in the EU, given its focus on citizen-as-worker, means first and foremost equal opportunity at work. Particularly in the late seventies and early eighties, and then again most recently, the scope of the European

Commission's interventions (and its goals) has been widening. It has even been suggested that the commission has in the past used gender equality as a means to develop a European social policy, evading the restrictions imposed on it by the principle of subsidiarity, and that it might do so now as well.

Equal pay for the same or equal work is prescribed in Article 119 of the Treaty of Rome. Drawing on their powers to promote related EC objectives, the commission and the Council of Ministers have extended the application of equal treatment to other areas. For example, a 1975 EEC directive requires equal pay for work of equal value. Another directive (1976) stipulates equal treatment in other conditions of employment, such as recruitment, promotion, and training and forbids discrimination based on marital and family status (with exceptions possible in order to protect pregnant women and mothers). This latter directive has been cited at the national level to promote positive actions (see, for instance, the Italian law 125/91). Other directives deal with people working in family businesses, especially family farms; and statutory maternity leave. Social security has also been a target of equal opportunity and equality policies of the EC, particularly in view of the general aim of harmonization in this field. Hence, there is a directive aimed specifically at removing any direct discrimination against married women in unemployment and pension benefits (Directives 75/117, 76/207, 79/7, 86/378, 86/613, 92/85 EEC; Meehan 1993; Curti-Gialdino 1993; Ballestrero 1993).

In cases concerning the meaning of Article 119 and subsequent directives, the European Court of Justice has further strengthened the principles that "the elimination of discrimination based on sex forms part of those fundamental rights" that lie at the roots of the European Union itself and that the unity of EU law imposes a duty on all institutions, including national courts, to enforce such rights. The European Court has been instrumental also in ensuring that part-time workers have rights and in dealing with inequality between women and men arising from occupational segregation. As a consequence of these decisions, national legislation (e.g., in the United Kingdom and in Denmark) has been amended. In 1986, the court extended the scope of the social security directive to enable married women in the United Kingdom to claim an invalid care allowance (Meehan 1993, 111; Pillinger 1992).

In making use of this legislation and in seeking recourse before the European Court of Justice individual women and women's organizations or trade unions have been more active in some countries than in others. These differences depend on several interacting factors: specific national juridical cultures, the extent to which women's movements are organized as such and perceive themselves as institutional subjects, national traditions and cultures concerning gender equality, and even different feminist approaches. (On the relevance of this last factor, see Meehan 1993.) In the United Kingdom and Ireland, individual women as well as women's organizations, including equal opportunity commissions, have looked to the European Court of Justice both to redress individual wrongs and to modify national legislation. In Italy, notwithstanding the existence of two national equal opportunity commissions (at the Prime Minister's Office and at the Ministry of Labor) and a number of statutory commissions at the regional and municipal level, recourse to the court is very rare. It is also true that countries such as the United Kingdom and Ireland have a number of overtly discriminatory regulations and laws that other countries, including Italy, have long since abrogated and that implicit discrimination, although unlawful according to EU legislation (now incorporated also in many national laws), is much more difficult to prove in court.

The directives pursuant to Article 119, and the ECJ rulings based on them, are not intended to address gender equality in general but are aimed only at the situation of men and women as workers. Moreover, since the costs of enforcing equal rights at work increasingly fall upon national governments, it has become increasingly difficult to persuade the latter to carry out such directives.

According to Meehan, "in general there has been a move towards equal treatment in matters where men and women have been treated differently because of conventional assumptions about their domestic roles; that is, where jobs are different or done under different hourly conditions, or apart from place of employment." Less clear are the consequences of the EU provisions that allow special treatment for the protection of mothers and make exceptions for cases where sex is a genuine occupational qualification. Again in Meehan's words, "for example, the Court's rulings on motherhood could be construed as reflecting traditional male attitudes, inhibiting more flexible boundaries between the public and private realms and discouraging choice for both sexes about inhabiting either or both of them; alternatively, they may be seen as maintaining the significance of motherhood, argued by some feminists to be the only valued status that society grants to women." She cites a number of controversial court decisions as examples. The ECJ rejected the European Commission's claim that Italy was contravening an EEC directive by not allowing parental leave to adoptive fathers as well as adoptive mothers. And it upheld a German decision that an unmarried father who looked after his child was not entitled to the leave and allowance granted to unmarried mothers. Conversely, however, it has strongly supported the rights of pregnant women in the United Kingdom in cases in which the English courts held that since a man cannot become pregnant, a pregnant woman has no point of comparison unless analogous treatment of a sick male can be brought in (Meehan 1993, 113).

In any event, neither the EU directives nor the ECJ rulings have touched the conditions that make it difficult for women to be "equal workers" in the first place: the gendered division of labor and gender-asymmetrical power relations within the family, together with a conception of "worker" and an organization of work that are oriented to the experience of men having wives (or mothers) on which care they may depend. This is made clear by the fact that equal opportunity policies remain ad hoc policies, which act side by side with but do not interfere with, much less change, "general policies"—that is, those very policies affecting the conditions of women's experience and gender relations (Vogel-Polsky 1993).

From the late seventies to the mid-eighties, a tension developed between the Commission and the European Parliament, on one side, and the Council of Ministers, on the other, over the issue of equal opportunity policies. Under pressure from increasingly vocal women and feminist lobbies, the EP (and particularly its socialist members) became increasingly committed to develop policies that went beyond the EC directives and, indeed, criticized their implementation. The Council of Ministers resisted this widening of the scope of EC intervention, either blocking new policies or watering down their implementation at the national level. Such resistance occurred with the four-year Action Programme 1982–85, followed by the Second Action Programme 1986–90 and the Third Action Programme. These action programmes' chief results have been research; debates; encouragement of networking among women within, as well as across countries; and the development of a women's lobby alongside the numerous lobbies that are an integral part of European policy making. Only the Third Action Programme focuses explicitly on questions of child care and the reconciliation of work and family, both for men and women (the same issues are mentioned in the Social Charter and repeated in the white paper issued by the European Commission (1993b), as well as on the role of women in EU decision-making bodies (the EU's Women in Decision-Making Network is a result of this initiative).[3]

Recent developments in European policy concerning women seek to address as well those dimensions of gender inequality and of full citizenship that are not linked to the labor market or to working status. Particularly, the Council of Ministers' recommendation on childcare attempts to go beyond the restrictions of simple labor policy. Indeed, it sees both men and women as parents with child care responsibilities and stresses the need for fathers to be involved in these responsibilities through the cooperation of governments, social partners, and private organizations. The recommendation's stated objective is to reconcile employment with the "upbringing responsibilities arising from the care of children." That is, children, and their needs for care are considered to be as important as labor market needs. Children, therefore, have begun to be conceived of as citizens themselves; the services addressed to them must first and foremost respond to their needs. Therefore, employers must make the workplace responsive to the needs of both workers and children (Moss 1993).

The implications of this recommendation are in principle far-reaching; they reverse the priority traditionally given to worker status and to labor market needs. A whole range of issues—such as the length of paid and unpaid leaves; the quantity, quality, and affordability of child care services; their availability to children of nonworking as well as working parents; the work schedule; the length and profile of the work-life-course; and so forth—are at stake here. Nevertheless, the European Union cannot properly address them, because of its limited competence with respect not only to children (and other European citizens not in the labor force) but to almost everything that is not linked to labor force participation or other economic dimensions.

These limitations appear all the more glaring if one considers that during the same time period (the second half of the eighties) when the European Council issued its recommendation, even measures that were specifically focused on the labor market and labor force abandoned their concern with gender disparities. For instance, the European Social Fund stopped identifying women as a special category for vocational training and retraining, although the Ad Hoc Committee on Women's Rights had reported in 1984 that even taking into account that women on average had lower skills and needed more additional training than men, the situation of women in Europe had deteriorated and the European Social Fund had failed to benefit girls and women. The success of the New Opportunities for Women program, launched in 1990, in addressing this problem has been, as evaluated by the Network of Information about Women's Training, at best controversial. (For somewhat different views on these matters, see Meehan 1993 and Pillinger 1992, ch. 7).

A Full European Citizenship for Women? Shortcomings, Ambivalences, and Strategies for Women's Mobilization

The debate over a "citizenship deficit" for women in the European Union intersects and sometimes overlaps with two other debates: that concerning the "democratic deficit" within the EU and that concerning the future of "social Europe." These latter two debates usually tackle only marginally the question posed by the former, at best listing the "women's question" as one item in a long list of problems to be solved (together with social exclusion, immigrants, the handicapped, and so forth). In EU debates over the principle of subsidiarity in the area of social policy, there is, at present, little or no acknowledgement of the differential relevance that this area has for women's citizenship. Hence, the disproportionate attention the EU de facto gives to men's citizenship conditions in allocating responsibilities at the EU level or at the national level.

No wonder, then, that women living in countries, such as Denmark, Sweden, and Norway, where their citizenship rights are superior to those of women in other countries, are wary of entering or remaining in the European Union, or of enlarging the EU's scope, as long as the subsidiarity principle and the democratic deficit remain (Liebert 1996). Particularly so, in view of the fact that their representation in their national parliaments, compared with that of women in the European Parliament, enables them to have a say in national policies and politics to a degree far beyond that attained at the European level. If, as Leibfried and Pierson (1992) maintain, welfare-state development historically has been a crucial component of the process of building national states, and therefore national identities and national models of citizenship, it is particularly crucial for women, since their access to citizenship is linked to specific constellations of social rights much more than is men's.

Another position, held by both men and women in the northern countries of the European Union in order to protect themselves from a diminution of their welfare systems and from the risks of intra-EU social dumping, is that there ought to be some European "social snake," which would define the basic social rights that should be granted in each member country. This outcome, however, seems unlikely under the principle of subsidiarity that regulates social matters and policies in the European Union. And certainly the poorer countries, and the United Kingdom as well, are likely to object strongly to such an onerous measure.

In any case, what constitutes national or European social citizenship, what might be perceived as negotiable or dispensable, and so on is far from being gender neutral. The only binding (excepting the United Kingdom) agreement is the Social Charter, which speaks exclusively of (gender-neutral?) workers. All those social rights that are relevant for women's citizenship, such as social caring services, minimum universal pension rights, and minimum income guarantees, are included, at best, as recommendations.

Only if women succeed in placing the gender issue at the center of the debates on democracy and on the "social dimension" of European citizenship will they be able to build firmer foundations for their access to citizenship than that afforded by the principles of equal opportunity, equality of treatment, or equality under the law. All these latter approaches, in fact, have demonstrated their weakness with respect to equality of outcomes because they have more or less explicitly assumed "man the worker" to be the yardstick of equality.

Eliane Vogel-Polsky (1993) expert of the Parity Democracy Group at the Council of Europe and member of the EU's Women in Decision-Making

Network, formulates this position quite forcefully: "No authentic democracy is possible in Europe, if the question of equality between men and women is not posed as foundational, having to do with the constitutive principles, exactly as are universal suffrage and the separation of powers." On the basis of the long, if controversial, history of feminist critique of the concept and history of citizenship, she argues that policies developed so far, both at the EU level and at the national level, have failed to grant women full citizenship, exactly because they treated women as a special category, with particular shortcomings to be overcome. Insofar as being women is treated as a weakness, or as a difference that must be overcome, thereby accepting the male standard as it has developed in the social relations between genders as given, women will remain shortchanged and their citizenship imperfect. The male standard thus accepted as the norm of universality is based on the historical gendered division of labor. Vogel-Polsky is more radical than this formulation suggests; indeed, she clearly speaks of women's domination by men.

On the basis of this analysis, a few Euro-feminists, including Vogel-Polsky herself, have come to the conclusion that only if women are included as political subjects on parity with men in the decision-making processes and in the decision-making bodies will both democracy and equality between men and women come close to realization. They use the concept of "parity democracy" (*démocratie paritaire*), first introduced in the Council of Europe, and now also in the EU by the Women in Decision-Making Network. The goal of parity democracy is highly ambitious and far reaching: "It is practically necessary to re-write all major legal texts: treaties, constitutions, laws. And this is not possible until we have criticized and reformulated the basic concepts of democratic theory—the rights of man, the subject of rights, citizens, social contract, general interest, social solidarity and so forth" (Vogel-Polsky 1993, 65). A group at the European Parliament has begun this work of rewriting and reformulating the relevant texts.

Leaving aside the controversial issue of what it means concretely, in legal and constitutional terms, to treat sexual dimorphism not as a handicap (for women) but as the condition without which human existence is not possible, the most immediate result of the parity democracy movement, but also of the Third Action Programme, is the focus on the critical importance of political representation. This is, at least in part, an outcome, in turn, of those very equal opportunity measures that have correctly been denounced as limited and shortsighted. First, the very fact that gender equality, albeit in conventional terms, has become a European issue and policy has contributed to the organization of women's interests (networks, lobbies, research groups). We might say that EU intervention in support of equality between men and women has contributed in a fashion similar to how national-states intervene to help women to define their own interests and policy needs.

Second, the EU has contributed to the creation of a public space for debate and for testing feminist theories and critiques that otherwise would have remained confined within academic circles. Feminist critiques of historical theories and practices of both citizenship and welfare regimes have played a role in developing goals and policies. In formulating such critiques, feminists also have become (self-)critical of much feminist theory and practice on the basis that it underestimates the importance of political, not simply social, inequality. (On the state as employer and provider of services, see Siim 1991 and Phillips 1991.)

It is interesting, from this point of view, that the tension between an equal opportunity approach, under which women continue to be treated as a "special," underprivileged category, and a broader approach, which addresses the question of gender-asymmetrical power relations both within the family and within the national and European decision-making bodies, is present even within two recent documents of the European Commission—the white paper titled *Growth, Competition, Employment* (1993b) and the green paper titled *European Social Policy* (1993a).

The latter in particular, although it continues to focus on access to citizenship mainly through labor market participation, testifies to the degree to which feminist analyses and critiques have influenced European policy thinking:

> Social and labour market structures continue to operate on the assumption that women are primarily responsible for home and child care while men are responsible for the family's economic and financial well being. . . . The gender-based division of family and employment responsibilities not only constrains women's lives but also deprives men of the emotional rewards resulting from the care and development of children. . . . The strategic objective should be to go from equal rights to equal treatment in the labour market through equality of opportunity in society, thereby making better use of women's experience and skills, for the benefit of society as a whole, including increased participation in the decision-making process. . . . In view of their first hand experience of the extent to which labour market structures have failed to keep pace with changing technological, economic, social and political realities, women have a vital interest in participating directly in the process of change. The importance of promoting such participation in all sectors of society, including key decision-making processes, cannot be underestimated. (European Commission 1993a)

Among the questions that governments have been called upon to answer, one renders explicit the linkage between a gender-asymmetrical concept of the family and women's risk of being socially excluded: "In the field of taxation and social security, how can we offer appropriate incentives for the social and economic participation of women, again through the individualization of rights or through the removal of the 'two-adult/sole breadwinner' concept of family from taxation and social security policies?" (European Commission 1993a, 44).

These affirmations and perspectives, however, risk remaining purely abstract principles in a process of integration that is based exclusively on market criteria and processes, unmindful of its consequences in terms of social exclusion and growing gender inequality, as well as other types of socio-economic inequality among women and among men. Concern over this is increasingly shared by different groups and has been authoritatively voiced by the Comité des Sages, appointed by the commission itself in 1995 to prepare a report on the issue of European citizenship (European Commission of 1996).

Thus, while the consequences of European integration appear to be an increasing differentiation of women and of women's interests from those of men, the former interests have not yet found a voice in the policy-making process, given the dual democratic deficit: institutional imbalance and gender imbalance. Certainly, if more women were present in the decision-making bodies and processes, conflicts among women of different nationalities, political affiliations, and interest groups would develop. The emergence of divergent public positions among women, however, is not a scandal, nor is it dangerous. If more women of various experiences and outlooks were elected, women would be obliged to negotiate among themselves, as well as with men, about their common and varying interests. No longer would such interests be defined solely by men. Therefore, no longer would they be defined either on the basis of men's own interests, perceptions, differences, and conflicts or on the basis of men's often conflicting views concerning women's proper position and women's needs and rights.

Notes

1. See Pillinger 1992, 17, for a cross-country comparison of women's unemployment. Additional figures are available in Commission of the EC 1990a and *Women of Europe* 1992.

2. A first attempt at comparing European welfare regimes from the point of view of women's experience may be found in Lewis 1993.

3. See the opinion of Gaiotti de Biase, Italian MEP, in European Parliament 1984.

13

An Afterword: European Union at the End of the Century

E. J. Hobsbawm

Throughout most of its history, "Europe," insofar as the word has not been a merely geographical description, has referred to a plurality of separate states lacking any common institutional coordination specifically designed for this continent. When "Europe" was envisaged as some sort of a unity, it was usually by a European state that had conquered or subordinated its neighbors and hoped to establish a permanent hegemony or domination over the continent. For example, in the case of both France under Napoleon and Germany under Adolf Hitler, "Europe" was a wartime slogan, directed against the conqueror's adversaries or against states beyond his power—usually the Great Britain and Russia—and it disappeared from sight after their defeat.

On the other hand, the movement that has actually produced the existing European Union is based on the exact opposite: weakness, not potential or actual conquering strength. In two wars, all but one of the European-based states ceased to be "great powers" in global terms and were reduced, at best, to regional powers. After World War II, the need to avoid suicidal wars of mutual destruction also became evident, at least to (West) German and French governments, and coordination between these two states formed, and still forms, the cornerstone of Brussels politics. Weakened as single states, former "great powers" could now count only as part of a coordinated Europe. Great Britain, which even after 1945 hoped to maintain itself as a world power and global empire, only abandoned this hope after the collapse of Suez, although France's veto kept it out of the EEC until after the retirement of General de Gaulle.

Four problems derive from this origin of the European Community and complicate the task of European integration. First, this pragmatic development of the community would probably not have taken place but for the cold war, that is, the combination of fear of one superpower and strong pressures from the other—notably the pressure to integrate western Germany into the anti-Soviet front. The European Economic Community (European Union) grew up as part of the American anti-Soviet bloc, though formally outside the military system (NATO) and not necessarily in the form that Washington would have preferred. With the end of the cold war and the collapse of the Soviet Union, it lost the stability of bipolar confrontation that had kept its member states united, and found itself faced with problems for which it could not have prepared itself as part of the American alliance. The two most obvious were (1) how and how far to extend the European Community to formerly communist parts of the Continent, which raised enormous and hitherto unconsidered complications; and (2) how to acquire a common foreign and military policy for Europe, after emerging from under the common umbrella of U.S. cold war policy? The difficulties faced by the European Union over the successor states of communist Yugoslavia (Croatia, Slovenia, Bosnia) have dramatized this predicament.

A second problem arises out of the nature of the construction of the European project, as it developed from the European Coal and Steel Community of 1951 through the six-country Rome treaty of 1957 and its extension (by 1997) to fifteen states, to the Single European Act (SEA) of 1985 and the Maastricht Treaty of 1992. Considering that electoral democracy was an essential qualification for membership, its absence from in the institutions of the European Community is striking. The EC was constructed from the top down, and outside the scope of the democratic politics of its member states. The machinery of the EC made no real provision for an all-European democratic element, although it took over from the European Coal and Steel Community a consultative assembly (renamed the European Parliament in 1958) composed of legislators in the member states' parliaments, delegated to the European assembly by those legislative bodies. Some slow and reluctant concessions to the public rhetoric of democracy and the pressure of the European Parliament have been made, notably since 1979, when the members of the European Parliament came to be directly elected. However, even in the later 1990s, the relation between the EU's effective authorities and its parliament resembled those in British imperial colonies between governors and their legislative councils rather than those between national governments and the parliaments to which they are accountable.

Hence, it is misleading to speak of the "democratic deficit" of the European Union. The EU was explicitly constructed on a nondemocratic (i.e., nonelectoral) basis, and few will seriously argue that it would have got where it is otherwise. It may be transformed into a directly elected democratic entity, but if it is, its character will be profoundly changed. However, one must add that for its first decades, the EU benefited enormously from the fact that neither voters nor candidates in the member states took much interest in its affairs, knew much about them, or—except for special-interest groups like businessmen and farmers—saw them as of more than marginal importance for themselves. The eyes of newspaper readers, television watchers, and radio listeners tended to glaze over when "Europe" was reported on or debated. Generally speaking, the citizens of member states regarded the Community as concerned with technical matters like tariffs and as broadly beneficial, with relatively minor and manageable drawbacks. Since the SEA of 1986, this has changed. "Europe" has become a major issue in the national politics of all its member states and has sharply divided their politicians and electorates. Moreover, as the European Union has moved closer to political integration since the mid-1980s, the feebleness of its democratic component has become increasingly evident and ideologically embarrassing.

The third problem arises out of the divergence between the objectives, strategies, and tactics of the decision-making groups that actually constructed and now operate the European Union. The EU was built by a marriage between, on the one hand, national governments that for one reason or another, thought of union as helpful to the interests of their nation-states and, on the other, a pressure group of ideological missionaries who believed in and worked toward the building of a single federal, or at least confederal, Europe. Up to a point, there was no incompatibility between what General de Gaulle called "*L'Europe des patries*" (Europe of nation-states) and those for whom the "ever-closer union among the peoples of Europe" (preamble to the Rome treaty of 1957) meant a political authority, based on a "European identity," superior to these states. Beyond that point, clearly reached with the SEA, the conflict between the two conceptions of "Europe" became evident. On some issues, the SEA substituted majority voting for unanimity; by depriving member states of their automatic veto on unacceptable Community decisions, this highlighted the conflict. It was essentially a conflict between the member states and the European Union as, in effect, a European government superior to the nation-states, whose territorial sovereignty it inevitably reduced or replaced. Thus, the official commitment (1985) by all members to abolish all border controls between states within the EU has so far proved impossible to implement.[1] Henceforward, debate about "Europe" became sharply politicized even among decision makers and, for the first time, became prominent in democratic politics.

Moreover, after the end of the golden age of the Western economy, it became clear that the European Economic Community could no longer rely on the socioeconomic consensus that had underpinned it: the combination of market and welfare, the partnership of state, capital, and organized labor, whether in the form of the "social market economy" of Christian democratic inspiration or in the form of secular social democracy. The rise of free-market extremism undermined the Community's cohesion as much as had the collapse of communism. In ultraliberal theory, even a large trading bloc like "Europe" arming itself against rival economic-political blocs (the United States, Japan) was an unacceptable interference with free enterprise in the global economy. Politically, the Community was now under attack from two sides: from those who disliked its encroachment on the national state and from the champions of a single, free-trading world economy against trading blocs. Oddly, some politicians (for instance, in the United Kingdom and the United States) had no difficulty in combining both these views.

In any case, the ideologists' project of building Europe based on a "European identity" had never had a real political constituency in the member states, although it enjoyed a considerable vested interest in the project in the powerful community institutions in Brussels. This throws light on the fourth problem of integration: the heterogeneity of the Continent, which is perhaps its principal historic characteristic. The "European project" tried to minimize this problem by making common political and economic institutions a condition of membership and by avoiding too great a disparity between the economic and social levels of its components. (For both these reasons, the application of Turkey to join the community has so far been rejected). After the 1970s, the accession of notably poorer and more backward economies (Greece, Portugal) to the EC underlined the scale of the problem. Though the Treaty of Rome had not considered problems of economic and social inequalities within the EC, increasingly the effort to diminish them by transferring income from richer to poorer areas, mainly through the three main "structural funds" of the Community, and now (the European Agricultural Guidance and Guarantee Fund, the European Social Fund, and since 1975, the European Regional Development Fund), has become a central function of the Union. In 1995, expenditures in these fields constituted roughly one-third of the EU's total budget and were second only to the Common Agricultural Policy, which swallows half of it. The applications of even poorer and differently structured ex-communist countries to join the European Union naturally raises the problems of Europe's internal heterogeneity even more dramatically.

However, even if we suppose that the economies, political systems, and living standards of Europe's countries and regions converge more rapidly than seems likely at present and that cultural differences (including religious ones) are attenuated, Europe remains heterogeneous, not least in one crucial respect: language. The European Union in 1997 gives official recognition to eleven separate languages for its fifteen member states, plus a diplomatic nod to a twelfth, Irish Gaelic. Almost one-quarter of the administrative staff of the European Union consists of translators and interpreters, making it into the world's largest linguistic service. Any further extension of the EU, any recognition by Brussels of the languages with some official regional status (e.g., Welsh, Catalan, Basque) would raise the height of this tower of Babel. Though the European Union exists to facilitate freedom of movement within its borders, the surprisingly low rate of population shifts within it (compared, say, to intercensal shifts of the population of U.S. states) indicates the reality of these cultural barriers (Faist, ch. 11 above).

In fact, for most Europeans, the recognition that European national economies are too weak to stand alone today does not amount to a positive "European identity." Insofar as it exists, "European identity" is negative, that it, directed against third parties, whether competing regional economies, immigrants seeking to breach the defenses of "Fortress Europe," or attempts to extend U.S. national law outside the U.S. borders, as by the Helms-Burton Act. For states and for most of their citizens, "Europe" is not an alternative to their narrower collective identities but something valued only insofar as membership in the European Union offers advantages, or non-membership has disadvantages. Thus, the Norwegian electorate rejected EU membership not because it felt less European than the Danes but because membership was seen, rightly or wrongly, as a threat to their superior welfare state. Conversely, Scottish and Catalan nationalists are enthusiastic Europeans not because they feel an affinity with Belgians or Portuguese but because the European Union offers them a way of bypassing the central governments of their (British and Spanish) nation-states and thus, hopefully, acquiring separate international status. At best, "Europe" symbolizes something desirable on nongeographical grounds—for example, in post-Franco Spain, modernity and recognition as a democratic country; in post-1989 Central and Eastern Europe, breaking the bridges to communism and Russia.

From 1951 to the late 1980s, the evolution of the European Community, safely ensconced in the framework of the cold war and substantially out of sight of mass public opinion and media attention, proceeded in the way described in Gary Marks's chapter: an odd combination of general objectives and ad hoc decisions. It was not seriously retarded by national politics, for even in Britain, where joining the EC was a hotly debated issue, 67.2 percent voted in favor of membership in 1975. (Similar referenda in various countries in the early 1990s showed national opinion far more evenly divided.) Essentially, the considerable advances in European integration made in this period rested on two pillars: (1) the powers of the European Commission, only incompletely controlled by the governments of the member states; and (2) those of the European Court of Justice as the de facto judicial branch under a European constitution. This period of comparatively unproblematic advance is now at an end.

The powers of the commission with its body of Brussels officials, acting as the EU's government, rested on the fact that it initiated, as well as executed a policy, that was all-European by definition, and was constitutionally protected against any demand to favor the interest of any single member state, and operated out of the sight of electoral politics. (By their oath, the commissioners engage "neither to seek nor to take instructions from any government or body.") While, technically, the commission was subordinate to bodies representing the member states (the Council of Ministers and, since 1974, the European Council of heads of governments, which is today officially the supreme political authority), in practice those bodies did not *make* policy but, rather, reacted to commission initiatives. In short, while member governments, or until 1987 any one government, could from time to time veto commission proposals, they were not in a position to be the real makers or directing agents of policy. They were not even a continuous presence in Brussels, except in the form of a less high-powered body of ambassadors, the "Permanent Representatives," but met only a few times a year.

The increasing politicization of "Europe" (not to mention the sheer increase in the number of member states) has dramatically reduced the commission's ability to pursue its objectives untroubled by member governments' politics, but no other effective initiator of policies has appeared. The nominally supreme political authority in the European Union, the European Council ("summit"), is chiefly effective in demonstrating the lack of unanimity of its members. Insofar as there is effective pressure to continue the process of integration, the joint decision of France and Germany (now de facto the hegemonic power within the European Union) has become critical to any effort to pursue further integration.

However, there is still room for the old Brussels-initiated process of "Europe-building" to continue in those areas that have not yet been politicized—at least until they are. For instance, as we have seen, the European Union's redistributive function, especially its regional policy, has grown rapidly, no doubt because a majority of the countries that were member states in 1980 benefited by this redistribution. Even in countries that paid more into the EU budget than they received back, poor and backward regions benefited from EU subsidies. Yet this development, which has introduced a recognition of regions and a direct link between them and Brussels, bypassing their national governments, has political implications. These have already been recognized by separatist movements in countries like Spain and Great Britain, and by the novel and even more controversial phenomenon of the Italian Northern League's separatism for an artifact called "Padania," which is now forcing member states and the European

Union itself to define their hitherto unspecific positions on what constitutes or does not constitute a "region" and its rights.

The power of the European Court of Justice rests on the facts that member states have given EU law precedence over their national law and that there is no appeal to any superior court. To this extent, the European Court's judgments, which inevitably affect the constitutional law of the member states, imply a significant diminution of their sovereignty. The European Court was originally set up to settle problems of the interpretation of the treaties establishing (and later extending and modifying) the European Economic Community, but with the extension of its scope and functions, its importance has grown substantially. Most of its decisions take the form of a preliminary ruling on a case referred to it by a national court when a point of European law is at issue, with its ruling then being applied by the national court. Only the belief that the European Economic Community was primarily concerned with technical rather than political matters, and the massive lack of public interest in its affairs, can explain why so major an abdication of national sovereignty was allowed to pass into the member states' legislation so easily and with so little fuss.[2] Yet once accepted, the supremacy of European law cannot be ended, except by leaving or ending the European Union, which no member government can afford to do. So at present, and for the foreseeable future, the standardization of national laws through the decisions of the European Court of Justice constitutes the most powerful and permanent element in European integration.

Yet, even here, the curious interweaving of institutions, politics, and the economic and social change that occurs independently of either, inevitably push as European legal integration into unintended and unpredicted directions. The judgments of the European Court both shape, reflect, and set the balance between European and national law, that is, the nature of the principle of subsidiarity determines which activities should be left within the scope of the nation-states, and which should be undertaken by the European Union. Again, changes in the world economy since 1951 may require reinterpretations of the "four freedoms," that were the basic principles of the European Community (freedom of movement for goods, persons, services, and capital), since the European Union's function today is increasingly that of strengthening and protecting the global economic competitiveness of a regional bloc against rivals, as well as preventing the freedom of movement of persons (i.e., mass immigration) into Fortress Europe. Europe's "Supreme Court," like its member states, also faces the unexpected problem of defining the relation of its own institutions and jurisprudence to the new informal institutions and conventions developed by the transnational economy, which have been perceptively discussed by Sassen (1996) and others.

Where, in conclusion, do the states and inhabitants of Europe stand with regard to the European Union at the end of the century? First, the economic integration of the region is patchy. While intra-European trade in goods and services has, unlike EC trade with the rest of the world, risen quite sharply since the start of the EEC, from 7 percent of the region's social product in 1960 to 24 percent in 1990 (when there were twelve member states), intra-European movements of labor have stagnated at a low level—between 1 and 2 percent of the labor force—and always remained lower than extra-European immigration. Curiously enough, there is little sign of the integration of European capital. Since the end of the 1960s, a stagnant share of not more than 1 percent of the available capital in the member states has been invested in other member states—distinctly less than European direct investment outside Europe and direct foreign investment into Europe. Even the latter two streams of extra-European investment, though rising substantially, have remained modest up to the time of writing (Molle 1990, 232, 472). In short, Europe has functioned best as a common market for its own goods and services.

Second, while the European Union has become an accepted part of life for most inhabitants of the member states, there is still no positive "European consciousness." Nor is one likely to develop. Politically, the nation-state remains the basic reference-unit, even for movements that want to break it up. In terms of private consumption, buyers hardly distinguish on "European" grounds between, say, cars made in Europe by European firms like Renault or BMW, those made in Europe by non-Europeans like Ford or Nissan, or those imported directly from Korea or Japan. The horizons of both elite and mass culture remain national or are today global, even if it is true that historically Europe has been the main source of the elite culture (at any rate through the period between the world wars) and the United States, of the latter.

Third, it is now evident that the original hope of the ideologists, namely, that economic integration would automatically lead to political integration, has been, and can be realized only to a very modest extent, at least in democratic societies. Conversely, the attempt to push forward both economic and political integration essentially by political means, as in the later 1980s and early 1990s, has run up against—indeed has created—enormous obstacles, as witness the problems of the European Monetary Union and its new currency, the Euro. In short, we can now see that "a process of integration driven by technocrats and elites provides an insufficient foundation for successful long-term integration" (Ambrosius 1996, 207). On the other hand, no other effective driving force is in sight, although the process of integration is by no means at an end and, in any case, seems irreversible. Europe will remain "a Europe of nations," possibly including some regions classifying themselves as nations.

Fourth, "Europe" will remain incomplete. Of the twenty-four geographically European countries not at present in the European Union, it is certain that several—mainly in the east and in the Balkans—will not become members in the foreseeable future, though probably all or most would want to. Moreover, it is increasingly likely that even the European Union will not be a homogeneous region but will be one in which regional or national differences and inequalities, though hopefully contained within the common framework, persist.

Lastly, within the foreseeable future, Europe will not become anything like the Maastrict Treaty's vision of a single political entity with an independent, common foreign and defense policy, if only because this is likely to be strongly opposed by the United States. Nevertheless, it may move some way in this direction as part of the construction of the border controls with which Fortress Europe, still the largest accumulation of the world's rich, prepares to surround itself against the world's poor.

Notes

1. The abolition of border controls within the EU had, in practice, to be provided for by a separate agreement between member states (the Schengen agreements, 1985, modified 1990), which by the mid-1990s had not been signed by all EU members. Some signed but added provisions to maintain or reimpose controls over their own borders. Schengen is specifically not part of the EU arrangements.

2. Thus, the accession to the European Community in 1972, the SEA in 1986, the Maastricht Treaty in 1993, though all containing far-reaching constitutional implications for the United Kingdom, ratified by simple majorities of the U.K. Parliament under governments whose politicians were later to denounce the predictable consequences of these votes.

Bibliography

Abadan-Unat, Nermin. 1977. "Implications of Migration on Emancipation and Pseudo-Emancipation of Turkish Women." *International Migration Review* 11: 31–57.

Addison, John T., and W. Stanley Siebert. 1991. "The Social Charter of the European Community: Evolution and Controversies." *Industrial and Labor Relations Review* 44 (4): 597–625.

Alber, Jens. 1981. "Government Responses to the Challenge of Unemployment: The Development of Unemployment Insurance in Western Europe." In *The Development of Welfare States in Europe and America*, edited by Peter Flora and Arnold Heidenheimer. New Brunswick, N.J.: Transaction Books.

Aldcroft, Derek. 1968. "The Mercantile Marine." In *The Development of British Industry and Foreign Competition*, 1875–1914, edited by Derek Aldcroft. Toronto: University of Toronto Press.

Allen, Victor L. 1960. *Trade Unions and the Government*. London: Longmans, Green.

Ambrosius, Gerold. 1996. *Witschaftsraum Europa: Vom Ende der Nationalökonomien*. Frankfurtam Main: Campus.

Anderson, Benedict. 1991. *Imagined Communities: Reflections on the Origin and Spread of Nationalism*. London: Verso.

Anderson, Jeffrey J. 1995. "The State of the (European) Union: From the Single Market to Maastricht, from Singular Events to General Theories." *World Politics* 47: 441–65.

Anderson, M. S. 1993. *The Rise of Modern Diplomacy*, 1450–1919. London: Longman.

Andrews, Edmund. 1996. "The Upper Tier of Migrant Labor: German Builders Cut Costs Importing Eager Europeans." *New York Times*, 11 December.

Arter, David. 1993. *The Politics of European Integration in the Twentieth Century*. Aldershot, England: Dartmouth.

Ashworth, W. 1974. "Industrialization and the Economic Integration of Nineteenth-Century Europe." *European Studies Review* 4:291–314.

Atkinson, A.B., and J. Micklewright. 1992. *Economic Transformation in Eastern Europe and the Distribution of Income*. Cambridge: Cambridge University Press.

Auerbach, Simon. 1990. *Legislating for Conflict*. Oxford: Oxford University Press.

277

Averyt, William 1975. "Eurogroups, Clientela, and the European Community." *International Organization* 29: 949–72.

Bade, Klaus. 1987. "Labour, Migration, and the State: Germany from the Late Nineteenth Century to the Onset of the Great Depression." In *Population, Labour, and Migration in Nineteenth- and Twentieth-Century Germany*, edited by Klaus Bade. New York: Berg.

Baglioni, Guido, and Colin Crouch, eds. 1990. *European Industrial Relations: The Challenge of Flexibility*. London: Sage.

Bairoch, Paul. 1989. "European Trade Policy, 1815–1914." In *Cambridge Economic History*, edited by Peter Mathias and Sidney Pollard. Vol. 8. Cambridge: Cambridge University Press.

————. 1993. *Economics and World History: Myths and Paradoxes*. Chicago: University of Chicago Pres.

Baldwin, Peter. 1990. *The Politics of Social Solidarity: Class Bases of the European Welfare State, 1875–1975*. Cambridge: Cambridge University Press.

Baldwin-Edwards, Martin, and Martin A. Schain. eds. 1994. *The Politics of Immigration in Western Europe*. London: Frank Cass.

Ballestrero, Maria Vittoria. 1993. "Pari opportunità e azioni positive: Il diritto comunitario e la sua applicazione nell'ordinamento giuridico italiano." *Pari e Dispari Annuario* 4:49–63.

Bamyeh, Mohammed A. 1993. "Transnationalism." *Current Sociology/La Sociologie Contemporaine* 41(3): (entire issue).

Bance, Pierre. 1978. *Les fondateurs de la C.G.T. à l'épreuve du droit*. Claix: La pensée sauvage.

Barbet, Denis. 1991. "La production des frontières du syndical et du politique: Retour sur la loi de 1884." *Genèses* 3:5–30.

Barbezat, Daniel. 1989. "Cooperation and Rivalry in the International Steel Cartel, 1926–1933." *Journal of Economic History* 49:435–47.

Bariéty, Jacques. 1977. *Les relations franco-allemandes après la Première-Guerre mondiale*. Paris: Editions Pedrone.

Barnet, Richard J., and J. Cavanagh. 1994. *Global Dreams: Imperial Corporations and the New World Order*. New York: Simon and Schuster.

Barnett, Correlli. 1986. *The Audit of War: The Illusion and Reality of Britain as a Great Nation*. London: Macmillan.

————. 1995. *The Lost Victory: British Dreams, British Realities, 1945–1950*. London: Macmillan.

Barr, N., ed. 1994. *Labour Markets and Social Policy in Central and Eastern Europe*. Oxford: Oxford University Pres.

Bartlett, Christopher A., and Sumantra Ghoshal. 1989. *Managing across Borders: The Transnational Solution*. Boston: Harvard Business School Press.

Bean, Richard. 1973. "War and the Birth of the Nation-State." *Journal of Economic History* 33:203–21.

Beer, Samuel H. 1966. *British Politics in the Collectivist Age*. New York: Alfred A. Knopf.

Behrens, E. Beddington. 1924. *The International Labour Office*. With a foreword by Harold Laski. London: L. Parsons.

Bendiner, Burton. 1987. *International Labour Affairs: The World Trade Unions and the Multinational Companies.* Oxford: Clarendon.

Bendix, Reinhard. 1977. *Nation-Building and Citizenship.* Rev. ed. Berkeley: University of California Press.

Bercusson, Brian. 1992. "Maastricht: A Fundamental Change in European Labour Law." *Industrial Relations Journal* 22: 177–90.

Berger, John. 1975. *A Seventh Man: Migrant Workers in Europe.* New York: Viking.

Beveridge, William H. 1942. See United Kingdom.

————. 1945. *Full Employment in a Free Society.* New York: W. W. Norton.

Bevin, Ernest. 1941. *The Balance Sheet of the Future.* New York: Robert M. McBride.

Bliss, W. D. P. 1910. "What is Being Done for the Unemployed in European Countries?" *Bulletin of Bureau of Labor Statistics* 76:741–829.

Blumenberg-Lampe, Christine. 1989. "Wirtschaftordnung aus dem Widerstand." In *Soziale Marktwirtschaft: Bilanza und Perspective.* Bonn: Bundeszentrale für Politische Bildung.

Boezee, Frank. 1991. "Militancy and Pragmatism: An International Perspective on Maritime Labour, 1870–1914." *International Review of Social History* 36:165–200.

Böhning, W. R. 1984. *Studies in International Labour Migration.* London: Macmillan; New York: St. Martin's.

Böhning, W. R., and Jacques Werquin. 1990. *Some Economic, Social, and Human Rights Considerations concerning the Future Status of Third-Country Nationals in the Single European Market.* Geneva: International Migration for Employment Office, ILO.

Bonnafous, Louis. 1924. *Les oeuvres d'amélioration sociale réalisées par les syndicats ouvriers en France.* Paris: Editions Rhéa.

Bonnet, Serge. 1962. "Les Italiens dans l'arrondissement de Briey avant 1914." *Annales de l'Est*, 5th ser., 13:3–92.

Borchorst, Anette. 1991. "The Scandinavian Welfare States: Patriarchal, Gender Neutral or Woman-Friendly?" Unpublished paper, Institute of Political Science, University of Arhus, Denmark.

————. 1994. "Welfare State Regimes, Women's Interests, and the EC." In *Gendering Welfare States*, edited by Diane Sainsbury. London: Sage.

Bouscaren, Anthony Trawick. 1969. *European Economic Community Migrations.* The Hague: Martinus Nijhoff.

Boyer, George R. 1988. "What Did Unions Do in Nineteenth-Century Britain?" *Journal of Economic History* 48:319–32.

Brochmann, Grete. 1995. *European Integration and Immigration from Third Countries.* Report no. 95 (3). Oslo: Institute for Social Research.

Brody, David. 1960. *Steelworkers in America: The Nonunion Era.* Cambridge: Harvard University Press.

Brown, Henry Phelps. 1986. *The Origins of Trade Union Power.* Oxford: Oxford University Press.

Brown, John W. 1926. *World Migration and Labour.* Amsterdam: International Federation of Trade Unions.

Brown, Kenneth D. 1982. "Trade Unions and the Law." In *A History of British*

Industrial Relations, 1875–1914, edited by Chris Wrigley. Amherst: University of Massachusetts Press.

Brubaker, Rogers. 1992. *Citizenship and Nationhood in France and Germany*. Cambridge: Harvard University Press.

Bührer, Werner. 1989. "Unternehmerverbände." In *Die Geschichte der Bundesrepublik Deutschland. Wirtschaft*, edited by Wolfgang Benz. Frankfurt am Main: Fischer.

Bussière, Eric. 1984. "La sidérurgie belge durant l'entre deux-guerres: Le cas d'Ougrée-Marihaye (1919–1939)." *Revue Belge d'Histoire Contemporaine* 15: 303–80.

Caestecker, Frank. 1984. "Het Vreemdelingenbeleid in de Tussenoorlogse Period, 1922–1939 in Belgie." *Belgisch Tijdschrift voor Nieuwste Geschiedenis* 15:461–86.

———. 1993. *Ongewenste Gasten*. Brussels: Vrije Universiteit Pers.

———. 1994. "Alien Policy in Belgium, 1830–1940: The Creation of Guest Workers, Refugees, and Illegal Immigrants." Doctoral dissertation, European University Institute, Florence.

Cairncross, Alec. 1985. *Years of Recovery: British Economic Policy, 1945–51*. London and New York: Methuen.

Calavita, Kitty. 1994. "Italy and the New Immigration." In *Controlling Immigration: A Global Perspective*, edited by Wayne A. Cornelius, Philip L. Martin, and James F. Hollifield. Stanford: Stanford University Press.

Cambon, V. 1914. *Les derniers progrès de l'Allemagne*. Paris: P. Roger.

Caporaso, James A. 1996. "The European Union and Forms of State: Westphalian, Regulative, or Post-modern?" *Journal of Common Market Studies* 34:29–51.

Cappelletti, Mauro, Monica Seccombe, and Joseph Weiler, eds. 1986. *Integration through law: Europe and the American Federal Experience*. Vols. 1–2. Berlin and New York: Walter de Gruyter.

Caron, François. 1979. *An Economic History of Modern France*. New York: Columbia University.

Castles, Francis G. 1978. *The Social Democratic Image of Society*. London: Routledge and Kegan Paul.

Castles, Stephen, Heather Booth, and Tina Wallace. 1984. *Here for Good: Western Europe's New Ethnic Minorities*. London: Pluto.

Castles, Stephen, and Godula Kosack. 1973. *Immigrant Workers and Class Structure in Western Europe*. London: Oxford University Press.

Castles, Stephen, and Mark Miller. 1993. *The Age of Migration: International Population Movements in the Modern World*. New York: Guilford.

Centrale des métalluristes de Belegique. 1913. *Rapport du comité exécutif au congrés de 2me semestre 1913*. Liège: Centrale des métallurgistes de Belgique.

Chamberlain, Joseph. 1914. In "Trade Unionism and Tariff Reform, London, 17 May 1905." In *Mr. Chamberlain's Speeches*, edited by Charles W. Boyd. London: Constable.

Chambre syndicale française des mines métallurgiques. 1912. *Annuaire, 1912–1913*. Paris: Chambre syndicale française.

Chandler, Alfred D., Jr. 1990. *Scale and Scope: The Dynamics of Industrial Capitalism*. Cambridge: Harvard University Press, Belknap.

Chatelain, Abel. 1977. *Les migrants temporaires en France de 1800 à 1914*. Vol. 2. Lille: Publications de l'Univesité de Lille III.

Chesnais, J. 1993. "Globalization, World Oligopoly, and Some of Their Implications." In *The Impact of Globalization on Europe's Firms and Industries*, edited by M. Hubert. London: Pinter.

Chester, D. N., ed. 1951. *Lessons of the British War Economy*. Westport, Conn.: Greenwood.

Cohen, Robin. 1987. *The New Helots: Migrants in the International Division of Labour*. Aldershot, England: Avebury.

Collinson, Sarah. 1993. *Europe and International Migration*. London: Pinter.

———. 1994. "Towards Further Harmonization?" *Studi Emigrazione* 31: 210–37.

Commission of the European Communities. 1989. 1990a. *Employment in Europe*. Luxembourg.

———. 1990b. Equal Opportunities Unit. "The Impact of the Completion of the Internal Market on Women in the European Community." Working paper prepared by Pauline Conroy-Jackson. Brussels.

———. 1993a. *European Social Policy: Options for the Union*. Green Paper. Luxembourg.

———. 1993b. *Growth, Competition, Employment*. White Paper. Luxembourg.

———. 1994. *See* EC Communication.

———. 1996. Comité des sages. *Pour une Europe des droits civiques et sociaux.* Brussels.

Commission of the European Communities. 1988. *See* European Childcare Network. Phillips, Angela, and Peter Moss.

Commission of the European Communities. *Eurobarometer*, November, 1991. Luxembourg: European Union.

Commons, John R. 1909. "American Shoemakers, 1648–1895: A Sketch of Industrial Revolution." *Quarterly Journal of Economics* 19:1–32.

Conroy-Jackson, Pauline. *See* Commission of the EC.

Coombes, David. 1974. "Concertation in the Nation-State and in the European Community." In *Between Sovereignty and Integration*, edited by Ghita Ionescu. London: Croom Helm.

Corwin, Edward S. 1947. *Total War and the Constitution*. New York: Alfred A. Knopf.

Cotteeau, Alain. 1986. "The Distinctiveness of Working-Class Cultures in France, 1848–1900." In *Working-Class Formation: Nineteenth-Century Patterns in Western Europe and the United States*, edited by Ira Katznelson and Aristide R. Zolberg. Princeton: Princeton University Press.

Courtauld, Samuel. 1949. *Ideals and Industry: War-Time Papers*. Cambridge: Cambridge University Press.

Couthéoux, Jean-Paul. 1960. "Les pouvoirs économiques et sociaux dans un secteur industriel: La sidérurgie." *Revue d'Histoire Economique et Sociale* 38:339–67.

Cox, Robert W. 1972. "Basic Trends Affecting the Location of Decision-Making Power in Industrial Relations." In *Transnational Industrial Relations: The Impact of Multi-National Corporations and Economic Regionalism on Industrial Relations*, edited by H. Günther. London and Basingstoke: Macmillan.

Craig, Lee, and Douglas Fisher. 1991. "Integration of the European Business Cycle, 1870–1910." Working Paper no. 163, Department of Economics and Business, North Carolina State University.

Crosland, C. A. R. 1956. *The Future of Socialism*. London: Jonathan Cape.

Cross, Gary. 1983. *Immigrant Workers in Industrial France: The Making of a New Laboring Class*. Philadelphia: Temple University Press.

Crouch, Colin. 1993. *Industrial Relations and European State Traditions*. Oxford: Clarendon.

Curti-Gialdino, C. 1993. "Recenti sviluppi della giurisprudenza comunitaria in tema di parità uomo-donna." *Pari e Dispari Annuario* 4:22–48.

Curtin, Philip. 1990. "Migration in the Tropical World." In *Immigration Reconsidered*, edited by Virginia Yans-McLaughlin. New York: Oxford University Press.

Czech Sociological Review. 1993. Yale 2, Special issue on social policy.

Czech Sociological Review. 1995. Vol. 3 (Fall), special issue on Social Policy.

Dahrendorf, Ralf. 1985. *Law and Order*. London: Stevens.

Daudet, Léon. 1909. *L'avant-guerre: Etudes sur l'espionnage juif-allemande en France depuis l'affaire Dreyfus*. Paris: Nouvelle Librarie Nationale.

De Vries, Jan. 1984. *European Urbanization, 1500–1800*. Cambridge: Harvard University Press.

Deacon, B. 1993a. "Developments in East European Social Policy." In *New Perspectives on the Welfare State in Europe*, edited by C. Jones. London and New York: Routledge.

———. 1993b. "*Global Social Policy: A Conceptual Framework and the East European Case Study*." Paper presented at the International Sociological Association's Research Committee 19 conference, "Comparative Research on Welfare States in Transition," Oxford.

Deken, J. J. de. 1991. *Each according to His Ability or Each according to His Needs*. Florence: European University Institute.

Del Fabrio, René 1989. "Italienische Industriearbeiter im wilhelminischen Deutschland (1890–1914)." *Vierteljahrschrift für Sozial- und Wirtschaftsgeschichte* 76:202–28.

Déloye, Yves, and Oliver Ihl, eds. 1993a. *Politix* 22, special issue ("Des votes pas comme les autres").

———, 1993b. *Revue Française de Science Politique* 1, special issue ("L'acte due vote").

Dietz, Mary. 1992. "Context Is All: Feminism and Theories of Citizenship." In *Dimensions of Radical Democracy: Pluralism, Citizenship, Community*, edited by Chantal Mouffe London: Verso.

Dillon, Conley Hall. 1942. *International Labor Conventions: Their Interpretation and Revision*. Chapel Hill: University of North Carolina Press.

Dinan, Desmond. 1994. *Ever Closer Union? An Introduction to the European Community*. Boulder, Colo.: Lynne Rienner.

Dolvik, Jon Erik. 1992. "The Nordic Trade Unions and the Dilemmas of European Integration." Revised paper, originally presented at conference on "European Integration in a Nordic Perspective," Stockholm, 1–2 June.

Dommanget, Maurice. 1967. *La chevalerie due travail française, 1893–1911*. Lausane: Editions Rencontres.

Dow, Jr. C. R. 1970. *The Management of the British Economy, 1945–60*. Cambridge: Cambridge University Press.

Downing, Brian M. 1992. *The Military Revolution and Political Change: Origins of Democracy and Autocracy in Early Modern Europe*. Princeton: Princeton University Press.

Drachkovitch, Milorad M. 1953. *Les socialismes français et allemand et le problème de la guerre 1870–1914*. Geneva: E. Droz.

Dunning, John H. 1983. "Changes in the Level and Structure of International Production: The Las One Hundred Years." In *The Growth of International business*, edited by Mark Casson. London: Allen and Unwin.

Durbin, E. F. M. 1949. *Problems of Economic Planning: Papers on Planning and Economics*. London: Routledge and Kegan Paul.

Durbin, Elizabeth. 1985. *New Jerusalems: The Labour Party and the Economics of Democratic Socialism*. London: Routledge and Kegan Paul.

Dürmeier, Silvia. 1996. "The Increasing Importance of the Interregional Trade Union Councils." In *European Trade Union Yearbook, 1995*, edited by E. Gabaglio and R. Hoffman. Brussels: ETUI.

Dziewiecka-Bokun, L. 1993. "Social Policy at a Cross-Roads: A Post-communist Experience." Paper presented at the 19 conference, "Comparative Research on Welfare States in Transition," Oxford.

Ebbinghaus, Bernhard. 1995. "The Siamese Twins: Citizenship Rights, Cleavage Formation, and Party-Union Relations in Western Europe. In *Citizenship, Identity and Social History*, edited by Charles Tilly. *International Review of Social History Supplement 3*. Cambridge: Cambridge University Press, 1996.

———, 1996. "Spiegelwelten: Vergleich und Mehrebenenanalyse in der Europaforschung." In *Das Europäische Mehrebenensystem*, edited by T. König, E. Rieger, and H. Schmitt. Frankfurt am Main: Campus.

Ebbinghaus, Bernhard, and Jelle Visser. Forthcoming. *The Development of Trade Unions in Western Europe 1945–95*. Frankfurt am Main: Campus.

EC Communication. 1994. *Communication from the Commission of the E.C. to the Council and the European Parliament on Immigration and Asylum Policies*, COM 94/33 final, 23 February.

Edwards, P. K. 1979. "The 'Social' Determination of Strike Activity: An Explication and Critique." *Journal of Industrial Relations* 21:198–216.

Eichengreen, Barry. *Elusive Stability: Essays in the History of International Finance, 1919–1939*. Cambridge: 1990.

Eichengreen, Barry J., and Timothy J. Hatton, eds. 1988. *Interwar Unemployment in International Perspective*. Boston: Kluwer.

El-Agraa, Ali, ed. 1982. *International Economic Integration*. London: Macmillan.

Eley, Geoff. 1992. "Reviewing the Socialist Tradition." In *The Crisis of Socialism in Europe*, edited by Christiane Lemke and Gary Marks. Durham, N.C.: Duke University Press.

Enderwick, Peter. 1987. "Trends in the Internationalization of Production and the Trade Union Response." In *Trade Unions in a Changing Europe*, edited by G. Spyropoulos. Maastricht: PIE.

Engels, Gerd. 1972. *Die Entwicklung des französischen Rechts der Koalitionen*. Berlin: Walter de Gruyter.

Erhard, Ludwig. 1958. *Prosperity through Competition*. London: Thames and Hudson.

———. 1992. *Deutsche Wirtschaftpolitik: Der Weg der Sozialen Marktwirtschaft*. Düsseldorf: Econ-Verlag.

Ertman, Thomas. 1994. "Rethinking Political Development in Medieval and Early Modern Europe." Paper presented at the American Political Science Association meeting, New York.

Eschenburg, Theodor, ed. 1983. *Geschichte der Bundesrepublik Deutschland: Jahre der Besatzung, 1945–1949*. Stuttgart: Deutsche Verlags-Anstalt.

Esping-Andersen, Gøsta. 1985. *Politics against Markets: The Social Democratic Road to Power*. Princeton: Princeton University Press.

———. 1990. *The Three Worlds of Welfare Capitalism*. Princeton: Princeton University Press.

European Parliament. 1984. *Debates in the European Parliament*, nos. 1–308. Luxembourg.

———. 1990. Committee of Social Affairs, Employment, and the Working Environment. *On the Communication from the Commission on Its Action Programme Relating to the Implementation of the Community Charter of Fundamental Social Rights for Workers: Priorities for the Period 1991–2*. Brussels, 4 July.

———. 1994. Commission des libertés publiques et des affaires intérieures. *Deuxième rapport sur un projet de Charte de droits et des devoirs des ressortissants des pays tiers résident dans l'Union Européenne*. Doc. PE 208.166/déf., Brussels, 16 March.

Eurostat (Statistical Office of the EC). 1985, 1991. *Labour Force Survey*. Luxembourg.

———. 1987–88. *Earnings in Industry and Services*. Luxembourg, 1990.

———. 1993. "Population and Social Conditions." *Rapid Reports*, # 12.

Faist, Thomas. 1994. "How to Define a Foreigner? The Symbolic Politics of Immigration in German Partisan Discourse, 1978–1992." *West European Politics* 17 (1): 50–71.

———. 1995a. "Ethnicization and Racialization of Welfare-State Politics in Germany and the USA." *Ethnic and Racial Studies* 18: 219–50.

———. 1995b. "A Preliminary Analysis of Political-Institutional Aspects of International Migration: Internationalization, Transnationalization, and Internal Globalization." ZeS-Arbeitspapier no. 10/95, Zentrum für Sozialpolitik, Universität Bremen.

———. 1995c. "Transnationale Arbeitsmärkte und soziale Rechte in Europa." *Zeitschrift für Sozialreform* 34 (1): 36–47 and 34 (2): 108–22.

———. 1996. "Immigration, Integration, and the Welfare State." In *The Challenge of Diversity: Integration and Pluralism in Societies of Immigration*, edited by Rainer Bauböck, Agnes Heller, and Aristide R. Zolberg. Aldershot, England: Avebury.

———. 1997. "Migration und der Transfer sozialen Kapitals." *Soziale Welt* 48, special issue ("Internationale Migration"): 31–64.

Faist, Thomas, and Hartmut Haeussermann. 1996. "Social Citizenship, Immigration, and Housing in Germany. *International Journal of Urban and Regional Research* 20 (1): 83–98.

Falkner, Gerda. 1994. *Supranationalität trotz Einstimmigkeit. Entscheidungsmuster der EU am Beispiel der Sozialpolitik.* Bonn: Europa Union Verlag.

Featherstone, Kevin. 1988. *Socialist Parties and European Integration: A Comparative History.* Manchester, England: Manchester University Press.

Feldman, Gerald. 1966. *Army, Industry, and Labor in Germany, 1914–1918.* Princeton: Princeton University Press.

Ferge, Zsuza. 1992a. "Human Resource Mobilization and Social Integration: In Search of New Balances in the Great Transformation." Paper prepared for the International Expert meeting, "Towards a Competitive Society in Central and Eastern Europe," Kellokoski, Hungary.

—————. 1992b. "Social Change in Eastern Europe: Social Citizenship in the New Democracies." Paper presented at the First European Conference of Sociology, Vienna.

—————. 1994. "The Reform of Social Policy in the Post-Totalitarian Countries: Comments on the Various Reform Strategies." Paper presented at the Third Central European Forum, "Labour Market Changes in Central Europe: Lessons for Social Policy," Vienna.

Ferner, Anthony, and Richard Hyman, eds. 1992. *Industrial Relations in the New Europe.* Oxford: Blackwell.

Finer, Samuel E. 1975. "State and Nation-Building in Europe: The Role of the Military." In *The Formation of National States in Western Europe*, edited by Charles Tilly. Princeton: Princeton University Press.

—————. 1990. "Problems of the Liberal-Democratic State: An Historical Overview." *Government and Opposition* 25:334–58.

Fitzgerald, Robert. 1988. *British Labour Management and Industrial Welfare.* London: Croom Helm.

Flanagan, Robert J., and Andrew R. Weber, eds. 1974. *Bargaining without Boundaries: The Multinational Corporation and International Labor Relations.* Chicago: University of Chicago Press.

Forberg, Martin. 1987. "Gewerkschaftsbewegung und Arbeitsimmigranten: Agitationsstrategien und Organisierungsversuche der Freien Gewerkschaften in Deutschland, 1890–1914." In *Internationale Tagung der Historiker der Arbeiterbewegung: 22nd Linz Conference, 1986*, edited by Gabriella Hauch. Vienna: Europa verlag.

Francke, Ernest. 1909. "International Labour Treaties." *Economic Journal* 19:212–23.

Freedman, Charles E. 1993. *The Triumph of Corporate Capitalism in France, 1867-1914.* Rochester, N.Y.: University of Rochester Press.

Freeman, Gary. 1979. *Immigrant Labor and Racial Conflict in Industrial Societies: The French and British Experience, 1945–1975.* Princeton: Princeton University Press.

—————. 1986. "Migration and the Political Economy of the Welfare State." *Annals of the American Academy of Political and Social Science* 485:53–61.

Fridenson, Patrick. 1992. "Introduction: A New View of France at War." In *The French Home Front, 1914–1918*, edited by Patrick Fridenson. Providence: Berg.

Friedman, Gerald. 1988. "The State and the Making of the Working Class: France and the United States, 1880s–1914." *Theory and Society* 17:403–30.

Frontier Free Europe. 1994a. No. 9, special issue ("At Last: European Works Councils!").

———. 1994b. No. 8, special issue ("Free Movement of Foreign Workers").

———. 1994c. No. 9, special issue ("Social Security and Neighboring States").

Fukuyama, Francis. 1995. *Trust: The Social Virtues and the Creation of Prosperity*. New York: Free Press.

Fulcher, James. 1991. *Labour Movements, Employers, and the State: Conflict and Co-operation in Britain and Sweden*. New York: Oxford University Press.

Gallarotti, Giulio. 1995. *The Anatomy of an International Monetary Regime: The Classical Gold Standard, 1880–1914*. New York: Oxford, 1995.

Garrigou, Alain. 1992. *Le vote et la vertu*. Paris: Presses FNSP.

Garson, Jean-Pierre. 1992. "International Migration: Facts, Figures, Policies." *OECD-Observer* 176:18–24.

Garth, Bryant G. 1986. "Migrant Workers and the Rights of Mobility in the European Community and the United States" In *Force and Potential for a European Identity*. Vol. 1, bk. 3 of *Integration through Law: Europe and the American Federal Experience*, edited by Mauro Cappelletti, Monica Seccombe, and Joseph Weiler. Berlin and New York: Walter de Gruyter.

Geer, Hans de. 1986. *SAF i Förhandlingar*. Stockholm: SAFs Förlag.

Germany. 1908. Bundesarchiv. *Consular Report, Paris to Berlin*, 13 July 1908. R 85/64, Abteilung II, Auswärtiges Amt. Koblenz.

———.1910. Bundesarchiv. *Consular Report, Paris to Berlin*, 14 April 1910. R 85/65, Abteilung II, Auswärtiges Amt. Koblenz.

Germany. 1994. IDW (Institut der deutschen Wirtschaft). *Die wirtschatlichen Implikationen der Werkvertragsabkommen für die Bundesrepublik Deutschland und die Reformstaaten Mittel-und Osteuropas*. Sozialforschung, no. 233. Bonn: Bundesministerium für Arbeit und Sozialordnung.

Gibberd, Kathleen. 1937. *I.L.O.: The Unregarded Revolution*. London: J. M. Dent.

Gillingham, John. 1991. *Coal, Steel, and the Rebirth of Europe*. Cambridge: Cambridge University Press.

Goldsmith, Mike. 1993. "The Europeanisation of Local Government." *Urban Studies* 30:683–99.

Golinowska, Stanislawa. 1994. "Polen: Schnittstelle der Ost-West-Wanderung", In *Migration: Eine weltweite Herausforderung für soziale Sicherheit* edited by Internationale Vereinigung für soziale Sicherheit. Studien und Forschungen, no. 35. Geneva: IVSS.

Gospel, Howard F. 1992. *Markets, Firms, and the Management of Labour in Modern Britain*. Cambridge: Cambridge University Press.

Gould, J. D. 1980. "European Inter-continental Emigration: The Road Home, Return Migration from the U.S.A." *Journal of European Economic History* 9:41–112.

Gourevitch, Peter. 1977. "International Trade, Domestic Coalitions, and Liberty: Comparative Responses to the Crisis of 1873–1896." *Journal of Interdisciplinary History* 8:281–92.

———. 1986. *Politics in Hard Times: Comparative Responses to International Economic Crises*. Ithaca: Cornell University Press.

Granovetter, Mark. 1985. "Economic Action and Social Structure: The Problem of Embeddedness." *American Journal of Sociology* 91:481–510.

Grawert, Rolf. 1973. *Staat und Staatsangehörigkeit Verfassungsgeschichtliche Untersuchung zur Entstehung der Staatsangehörigkeit.* Berlin: Duncker und Humblot.

Great Britain. 1942. Interdepartmental Committee on Social Insurance and Allied Services. *Social Insurance and Allied Services: Report by Sir William H. Beveridge.* New York: Macmillan.

Gribaudi, Maurizio. 1987. *Itinéraires ouvriers: Espaces et groupes sociaux à Turin au début du XXe siècle.* Paris: Editions de l'Ecole des Hautes Etudes en Sciences Sociales.

Groot, Gerard-René de. 1989. *Staatsangehörigkeitsrecht im Wandel.* Cologne: Carl Heymanns Verlag.

Grote, Jürgen. 1987. "Tripartism and European Integration: Mutual Transfers, Osmotic Exchanges, or Frictions between the 'National' and the 'Transnational.'" In *Trade Unions in a Changing Europe*, edited by G. Spyropoulos. Maastricht: PIE.

Groux, G., R. Mourimaux, and M. Pernot. 1993. "L'européanisation du mouvement syndical: La Confédération Européenne des Syndicats." *Le Mouvement Social* 162:41–68.

Grüner, Hans. 1992. *Mobilität und Diskriminierung: Deutsche und ausländische Arbeiter in einem betrieblichen Arbeitsmarkt.* Frankfurt am Main and New York: Campus.

Guild, Elspeth. 1992. "Protecting Migrants' Rights: Application of EC Agreements with Third Countries." CCME Briefing Paper no. 10. Churches' Committee for Migrants in Europe, Brussels.

Günther, H., ed. 1972. *Transnational Industrial Relations: The Impact of Multi-National Corporations and Economic Regionalism on Industrial Relations.* London and Basingstoke: Macmillan.

Gutehoffnungschütte, Historische Archiv, *Ubersetzung einer der Briefe des Herrn Le Chatelier vom 29 Okt 1913.* 300193006/5. Oberhausen.

Haas, Ernest B. 1958. *The Uniting of Europe: Political, Social, and Economic Forces, 1950–1957.* London: Stevens.

———. 1961. "International Integration: The European and the Universal Process." *International Organization* 15:366–392.

———. 1971. "The Study of Regional Integration: Reflections on the Joy and Anguish of Pretheorizing." In *Regional Integration*, edited by Leon N. Lindberg and Stuart A. Scheingold. Cambridge: Harvard University Press.

———. 1975. "Is There a Hole in the Whole?" *International Organizations* 30 (2) : 173–212.

Haber, E. 1958. *The Chemical Industry in the Nineteenth Century.* Oxford: Oxford University Press.

Habermas, Jürgen. 1993. "Die Festung Europa und das neue Deutschland." *Die Zeit*, 28 May, 3.

Hall, Mark. 1995. *European Works Councils: Planning for the Directive.* London: Eclipse.

Hall, Peter. 1986. *Governing the Economy: The Politics of State Intervention in Britain and France.* New York and Oxford: Oxford University Press.

Hall, W. E. 1895. *International Law*. 4th ed. Oxford: Oxford University Press.

Hamer, D. A. 1972. *Liberal Politics in the Age of Gladstone and Roseberry: A Study in Leadership and Policy*. Oxford: Clarendon.

Hanagan, Michael. 1979. *The Logic of Solidarity: Artisans and Industrial Workers in Three French Towns, 1871–1914*. Urbana: University of Illinois Press.

————. 1989. *Nascent Proletarians: Class Formation in Post-Revolutionary France*. Oxford: Blackwell, 1989.

Harbison, R. 1992. "Human Resources and the Transition Process." Paper presented at the Regional Senior Policy Seminar, "Economic Restructuring and the Social Safety Net for Central and Eastern Europe." Budapest, Hungary.

Harrison, Martin. 1960. *Trade Unions and the Labour Party since 1945*. London: Allen and Unwin.

Hart, Simon. 1974. "Gens de mer à Amsterdam au XVIIe siècle." *Annales de Démographie Historique 1974*: 145–63.

Hartl Jr. 1994. *Politické souvislosti měnících se sociálních jistot* (Political context of changing social security). Prague: Nadacepro vyzkum sociálni transformace.

Hatton, Timothy J., and Jeffrey G. Williamson. 1991. "International Migration, 1850–1939: An Economic Survey." In *Migration and the International Labor Market, 1850–1939*, edited by Timothy J. Hatton and Jeffrey G. Williamson. London: Routledge.

————. 1992. "International Migration and World Development: A Historical Perspective." Working Paper Series on Historical Factors in Long Run Growth, no. 41, National Bureau of Economic Research, Cambridge, Mass.

————, eds. 1994. *Migration and the International Labor Market, 1850–1939*. London: Routledge.

Haupt, Georges. 1972. *Socialism and the Great War*. Oxford: Oxford University Press.

Hayek, F. A. 1944. *The Road to Serfdom*. London: Routledge.

Hayward, J. E. S. 1974. "Steel." In *Big Business and the State: Changing Relations in Western Europe*, edited by Raymond Vernon. Cambridge: Harvard University Press.

Hayward, Jack. 1995. "Europe's Endangered Industrial Champions." In *Industrial Enterprise and European Integration*, edited by Jack Heyward. Oxford: Oxford University Press.

Heater, Derek. 1992. *The Idea of European Unity*. New York: St. Martin's.

Heckscher, Gunnar. 1946. *Staten och Organisationerna*. Stockholm: KFs Bokförlag.

Hedlund, Stefan, and Mats Lundahl. 1985. *Beredskap Eller Protektionism? En Studie av Beredskapsmålet i Svensk Jordbrukspolitik*. Malmö: Liber.

Heidenheimer, A. J., Hugo Heclo, and C. T. Adams. 1990. *Comparative Public Policy*. New York: St. Martin's Press.

Herbert, Ulrich. 1984. "Zwangsarbeit als Lernprozess: Zur Beschäftigung ausländischer Arbeiter in der westdeutschen Industrie in Ersten Weltkrieg." *Archiv für Sozialgeschichte* 24:285–304.

————. 1990. *A History of Foreign Labor in Germany, 1880–1980*. Ann Arbor: University of Michigan Press.

Hernes, Helga Maria 1987. *Welfare State and Woman Power: Essays in State Feminism*. Oslo: Norwegian University Press.

Hetherington, H. J. W. 1920. *International Labour Legislation*. London: Methuen.

Hillman, Walter. 1911. *Die wirtschaftliche Entwicklung der deutschen Zinkindustrie*. Leipzig: Buchdruckerei von Robert Noske.

Hills, John, John Ditch, and Howard Glennerster, eds. 1994. *Beveridge and Social Security*. Oxford: Clarendon.

Hirsch, Fred. 1976. *Social Limits to Growth*. Cambridge: Harvard University Press.

Hirschman, Albert O. 1986. "Rival Views of Market Society." In *Rival Views of Market Society and Other Recent Essays*. Cambridge: Harvard University Press.

Hirst, Paul, and Grahame Thompson. 1992. "The Problem of 'Globalization': International Economic Relations, National Economic Management, and the Formation of Trading Blocs." *Economy and Society* 21 (4): 357–96.

Hix, Simon. 1994. "The Study of the European Community: The Challenge of Comparative Politics." *West European Politics* 17: 1–30.

Hobsbawm, E. J. 1987. *The Age of Empire, 1870–1914*. London: Weidenfeld and Nicolson.

———. 1990. *Nations and Nationalism since 1780: Program, Myth, Reality*. Cambridge: Cambridge University Press.

———. 1992. *Nations and Nationalism since 1780: Programme, Myth, Reality*. Cambridge: Cambridge University Press.

———. 1994. *The Age of Extremes: A History of the World, 1914–1991*. New York: Pantheon Books.

Hoerder, Dirk. 1982. "Immigration and the Working Class: The Remigration Factor." *International Labor and Working-Class History* 21:28–41.

———. 1994. "Foreign Workers in Germany: A Historian's Perspective." Public address, University of Michigan at Flint. October. Copy available from Leslie Moch.

Hoffmann, Stanley. 1966. "Obstinate or Obsolete? The Fate of the Nation-State and the Case of Western Europe." *Daedalus* 95:862–914.

Hohenburg, Paul. 1966. *Chemicals in Western Europe*. Baltimore: Johns Hopkins University Press.

Holland, Stuart. 1993. *The European Imperative: Economic and Social Cohesion in the 1990s*. Nottingham, England: Spokesman Bertrand Russell House.

Hollifield, James. 1992. *Immigrants, Markets, and States: The Political Economy of Postwar Europe*. Cambridge: Harvard University Press.

Holmes, Colin. 1988. *John Bull's Island: Immigration and British Society, 1871–1971*. London: Macmillan.

Holmes, Madelyn. 1984. *Forgotten Migrants: Foreign Workers in Switzerland before World War I*. Rutherford, N.J.: Farleigh Dickinson University Press.

Holmes, Stephen. 1995. *Passions and Constraints: On the Theory of Liberal Democracy*. Chicago and London: Chicago University Press.

Holthoon, Frits van, and Marcel van der Linden, eds. 1988. *Internationalism in the Labour Movement, 1830–1940*. 2 vols. Leiden: Brill.

Humphrey, Thomas, ed. 1992. *Citizenship and Social Class*. London: Pluto.

Huntington, Samuel P. 1964. *The Soldier and the State: The Theory and Politics of Civil-Military Relations*. New York: Vintage Books.

(IALL) International Association for Labour Legislation. 1901. *Compte rendu de l'Assemblée générale du Comité*. Paris: IALL.

ILO (International Labour Office). 1922. *Emigration and Immigration: Legislation and Treaties*. Geneva: ILO.

————. 1994. *See* Stalker, Peter.

ILO (International Labour Organization). *See* Böhning, W. R., and Jacques Werquin.

Ireland, Patrick. 1995. "Migration, Free Movement, and Immigrant Integration in the EU: Bifurcated Policy Response." In *European Social Policy: Between Fragmentation and Integration*, edited by Stephan Leibfried and Paul Pierson. Washington, D.C.: Brookings.

IVSS (Internationale Vereinigung für soziale Sicherheit), ed. 1994. *Migration: Eine weltweite Herausforderung für soziale Sicherheit*. Studien und Forschungen, no. 35. Geneva: IVSS.

Jarausch, Konrad. 1994. *The Rush to German Unity*. New York and Oxford: Oxford University Press.

Johansson, Anders L. 1989. *Tilväxt och Klassamarbete: En Studie av den svenska modellens uppkomst*. Stockholm: Tidens Förlag.

Joll, James. 1974. *The Second International, 1889–1914*. New York: Harper and Row.

Jonasdottir, Ana. 1988. "On the Concept of Interest, Women's Interests and the Limitations of Interest Theory." In *The Political Interests of Gender*, edited by Kathleen Jones and Ana G. Jonasdottir. London: Sage.

Jonasson, Gustaf. 1976. *Per Edvin Sköld, 1946–1951*. Stockholm: Almquist och Wiksell.

Joshi, Heather. 1989. "The Cash Opportunity Costs of Childbearing: An Approach to Estimation Using British Data." *Population Studies 6.*

Jurriens, R. 1981. "The Miners' General Strike in the Dutch Province of Limburg, 21 June– 2 July 1917." *Low Countries History Yearbook* 14:137–39.

Kahn-Freund, Otto. 1954. "The Legal Framework." In *The System of Industrial Relations in Great Britain: Its History, Law, and Institutions*, edited by Allan Flanders and H. A. Clegg. Oxford: Basil Blackwell.

Kanstroom, Daniel. 1993a. "The Shining City and the Fortress: Reflections on the Euro-Solution to the German Immigration Dilemma." *Boston College International and Comparative Law Review* 16:201–43.

————. 1993b. "Wer sind wir wieder? Laws of Asylum, Immigration, and Citizenship in the Struggle for the Soul of the New Germany." *Yale Journal of International Law* 18:152–211.

Kapteyn, Paul. 1995. *Market without State*. London: Routledge.

Katzenstein, Peter. 1984. *Corporatism and Change: Austria, Switzerland, and the Politics of Industry*. Ithaca: Cornell University Press.

————. 1985. *Small States in World Markets: Industrial Policy in Europe*. Ithaca: Cornell University Press.

————. 1987. *Policy and Politics in West Germany: The Growth of a Semisovereign State*. Philadelphia: Temple University Press.

————. ed. 1997. *Tamed Power: Germany in Europe*. Ithaca: Cornell University Press.

Kay, Diana, and Rob Miles. 1992 *Refugees or Migrant Workers? European Volunteer Workers in Britain, 1946–1951*. London: Routledge.

Keating, Michael. 1988. *State and Regional Nationalism: Territorial Politics and the European State*. London: Harvester, Wheatsheaf.

Kellenbenz, Hermann, and Jürgen Schneider. 1977. "Les investissements allemands en France, 1854–1914." In *La position internationale de la France*, edited by Maurice Lévy-Leboyer. Paris: Editions de l'Ecole des Hautes Etudes en Sciences Sociales.

Keohane, Robert O., and Stanley Hoffmann, eds. 1991. *The New European Community: Decisionmaking and Institutional Change*. Boulder, Colo.: Westview.

Kern, Stephen. 1983. *The Culture of Time and Space, 1880–1918*. Cambridge: Harvard University Press.

Kitzinger, Uwe. 1963. *The Politics and Economics of European Integration*. 2d ed. Westport, Conn.: Greenwood.

Klausen, Jytte. 1995a. "The Contested Origins of Swedish Wage Policy in the 1930s: Swedish Socialism as a National Road to Capitalism." Unpublished paper, Center for European Studies, Harvard University.

———. 1995b. "Social Rights Advocacy and State Building: T. H. Marshall in the Hands of Social Reformers." *World Politics* 47: 244–67.

———. 1996. "Citizenship and Social Justice in Open Societies." In *The Rationality of the Welfare State*, edited by Erik O. Eriksen and Jørn Loftager. Oslo: Scandinavian University Press.

Klusmeyer, Douglas B. 1993. "Aliens, Immigrants, and Citizens: The Politics of Inclusion in the Federal Republic of Germany." *Daedalus* 122:81–114.

Knauf, Diethelm. 1993. "Germany: From Emigration to Immigration? Reconsidering the Importance of 'Migration' in English Language and History Teaching in Secondary and Higher Education." Paper presented at workshop on the "Importance of the Migration Factor in History Teaching at Secondary Schools in Europe," International Institute of Social History, Amsterdam, September.

Knechtel, Erhard F. 1992. *Die Bauwirtschaft in der EG: Unternehmen im internationalen Vergleich*. Wiesbaden and Berlin: Bauverlag.

Kohlmann, Dr. 1911. "Die neuere Entwicklung des lothringingischen Eisenerzbergbaues." *Stahl und Eisen* 31:413–24.

Körner, Heiko. 1993. "Die neue Ost-West-Migration: Eine neue Völkerwanderung?" *Wirtschaftsdienst* 2:79–85.

Kornai, Janos. 1990. *The Road to a Free Economy*. New York: W. W. Norton.

Korpi, Walter. 1983. *The Democratic Class Struggle*. London: Routledge and Kegan Paul.

Koslowski, Rey, and Friedrich V. Kratochwill. 1994. "Understanding Change in International Politics: The Soviet Empire's Demise and the International System." *International Organization* 48: 215–47.

Krasner, Stephen D. 1983. "Regimes and the Limits of Realism: Regimes as Autonomous Variables." In *International Regimes*, edited by Stephen D. Krasner. Ithaca: Cornell University Press.

Krupp-Archiv. N.d. WA 43/307–320, WA41/2–185,FAH II B 100. Essen.

Ksiezopolski, M. 1993. "Social Policy in Poland in the Period of Political and Economic Transition: Challenges and Dilemmas." *Journal of European Social Policy* 3:177–94.

Kulczycki, John J. 1994. *The Foreign Worker and the German Labor Movement: Xeno-phobia and Solidarity in the Coal Fields of the Ruhr, 1871–1914*. Providence: Berg.

Kulischer, Eugene M. 1948. *Europe on the Move: War and Population Changes, 1917–47*. New York: Columbia University Press.

Kunz, Josef L. 1968. *The Changing Law of Nations*. Columbus: Ohio State University Press.

Kupferberg, Feiwel. 1972. "Byggnadsstrejken 1933–34." *Arkiv för Studier i Arbetarrörelsens Historia* 2:36–60.

Kvapilová, Eva. 1993. "Social Policy in Independent Slovakia." *Czech Sociological Review* 2(Summer):173–183.

Kynaston, David. 1976. *King Labour: The British Working Class 1850s–1914*. Totowa, N.J.: Rowman and Littlefield.

Labor in the Treaty of Peace. 1919. Boston: Houghton Mifflin.

Labour Party. 1944a. *Full Employment and Financial Policy*. London: National Executive Committee, Labour Party.

———. 1944b. 1945. 1946. 1947. 1948. 1949. 1950. 1951. *Report of Annual Conference*. London: Labour Party.

Lancelot, Alain. 1985. "Introduction à la première partie." In *Explication du vote*, edited by Daniel Gaxie. Paris: Presses FNSP.

Landes, David. 1970. *Prometheus Unbound: Technological Change and Industrial Development from 1750 to the Present*. Cambridge: Cambridge University Press, 1970.

Langan, Margaret, and Ilona Ostner. 1991. "Gender and Welfare: Towards a Comparative Framework." In *Towards a European Welfare State?* edited by Graham Room. Bristol: SAUS.

Lange, Christian L., and Auguste Schou. 1954. *Histoire de l'internationalisme*. Vol. 3. Oslo: H. Aschehoug.

Lange, Peter. 1984. "Unions, Workers, and Wage Regulation: The Rational Bases of Consent." In *Order and Conflict in Contemporary Capitalism*, edited by John H. Goldthorpe. Oxford: Clarendon.

———. 1992. "The Politics of the Social Dimension." In *Euro-Politics: Institutions and Policymaking in the New European Community*, edited by Alberta M. Sbragia. Washington, D.C.: Brookings.

Lange, Peter, and Louise K. Davidson-Schmich. 1995. "European Elections or Elections in Europe? The European Electoral Consequences of European Economic Integration." Unpublished paper available from the author.

Lanzalaco, Luca, and Philippe C. Schmitter. 1992. "Europe's Internal Market: Business Associability and the Labour Movement." In *The Future of Labour Movements*, edited by M. Regini. London: Sage.

"La percée des Vosges." *Journal des De'aabats* 1909. 222:1.

Laurent, Pierre-Henri. 1989. "Historical Perspectives on Early European Integration." *Journal of European Integration* 12:89–100.

Lazard, Max. 1911. "Notre programme." *Revue Internationale du Chômage* 1:10.

Lazonick, William. 1991. *Business Organization and the Myth of the Market Economy*. Cambridge: Cambridge University Press.

Lecher, Wolfgang. 1993. "Perspektiven europäischer Kollektivverhandlungen." In

Tarifpolitik und Tarifsysteme in Europa, edited by R. Bispinck and W. Lecher. Cologne: Bund Verlag, 401–19.

Leibfried, Stephan, and Paul Pierson. 1992. "Prospects for Social Europe." *Politics and Society* 20:333–66.

———. 1994. "The Prospects for Social Europe." In *Social Policy beyond Borders: The Social Question in Transnational Perspective*, edited by Abram de Swaan. Amsterdam: Amsterdam University Press.

———. eds. 1996. *European Social Policy: Between Fragmentation and Integration*. Washington, D.C. Brookings.

Lepsius, M. Rainer. 1991. "Die Europäische Gemeinschaft: Rationalitätskriterien der Regimebildung." In *Die Modernisierung moderner Gesellschaften*, edited by W. Zapf. Frankfurt am Main: Campus.

Lequin, Yves. 1988. *La mosaïque France: Histoire des étrangers et de l'immigration*. Paris: Larousse.

Leroy, Maxim. 1913. *La coutume ouvrière*. Vols. 1–2. Paris: Girard et Brière.

Levinson, Charles. 1972. *International Trade Unionism*. London: Allen and Unwin.

Lévy-Leboyer, Maurice. 1980. "The Large Corporation in Modern France." In *Managerial Hierarchies: Comparative Perspectives on the Rise of Modern Industrial Enterprises*, edited by Alfred D. Chandler, Jr., and Herman Daems. Cambridge: Harvard University Press.

Lewin, Leif. 1967. *Planhushållningsdebatten*. Stockholm: Almquist och Wiksell.

Lewis, Jane, ed. 1993. *Women and Social Policies in Europe: Work, Family, and the State*. Cheltenham, England: Edward Elgar.

Lidové Noviny. 1996. Vol. IX, May 10, "Základní makroekonomiké ukazatele zemí CEFTA" (Basic Macro-Economic Indicators of the CEFTA Countries).

Liebert, Ulrike. 1996. "A Gender Gap in the European Union? Exploring Patterns of Female Support to European Integration." Unpublished paper, Government Department, Cornell University.

Liepmann, H. 1938. *Tariff Levels and the Economic Unity of Europe*. London: Allen and Unwin.

Lindberg, Leon N., and Stuart A. Scheingold. 1970. *Europe's Would-Be Polity: Patterns of Change in the European Community*. Englewood Cliffs, N.J.: Prentice-Hall.

Linden, Marcel van der. 1988. "The National Integration of European Working Classes, 1871–1914." *International Review of Social History* 33:285–311.

Lipset, Seymour Martin, and Stein Rokkan. 1967. "Cleavage Structures, Party Systems, and Voter Alignments: An Introduction." In *Party Systems and Voter Alignments: Cross-national Perspectives*, edited by Seymour Martin Lipset and Stein Rokkan. New York: Free Press.

Litvak, I. A., and C. J. Maule. 1972. "The Union Response to International Corporations." *Industrial Relations Journal* 11: 62–71.

LO (Landsorganisationen). 1946. *LO Kongress-Protokoll 1946*. Stockholm: LO.

———. 1951. Fackföreningsrörelsen och den Fulla syssellsättningen. Betänkande och förslag från Landsorganisationens organisations Kommitte. (The Trade Union Movement and Full Employment. Report and Proposals from the National Organization's Organization Committee.) Stockholm: LO.

————. 1953. *Trade Unions and Full Employment*. Stockholm: LO.

"L'alliance provisoire franco-allemande-luxembourgeoise contre les grèvistes métallurgistes de l'Est." 1906. *L'Ouvrier Métallurgiste*. 16:2.

Lorwin, Lewis L. 1929. *Labor and Internationalism*. New York: Macmillan.

————. 1953. *The International Labor Movement*. New York: Harper and Brothers.

Lowe, Boutelle Ellsworth. 1918. *International Aspects of the Labor Problem*. New York: Columbia University Press.

————. 1935. *The International Protection of Labor*. 2d ed. New York: Macmillan.

Lucassen, Jan. 1987. *Migrant Labour in Europe, 1600–1900*. London: Croom Helm.

Lucassen, Leo. 1996. "The Great War and the Origins of Migration Control in Western Europe and the United States, 1880–1920." In *Regulation of Migration*, edited by A. Böcker, Amsterdam.

Luebbert, Gregory. 1991. *Liberalism, Fascism, or Social Democracy: Social Classes and the Political Origins of Regimes in Interwar Europe*. Oxford: Oxford University Press.

Luxembourg. N.d. Archives de l'État. Ministère de la Justice, J 76/70.

Lyons, F. S. L. 1963. *Internationalism in Europe, 1815–1914*. Leiden: A. W. Sythoff.

Lyttelton, Adrian. 1993. "The National Question in Italy." In *The National Question in Europe in Historical Context*, edited by Mikulás Teich and Roy Porter. Cambridge: Cambridge University Press.

Maclennan, Malcolm, Murray Forsyth, and Geoffrey Denton. 1968. *Economic Planning and Policies in Britain, France, and Germany*. New York and Washington, D.C.: Praeger.

Mahaim, Ernest. 1912. *Le droit international ouvrier*. Paris: Recueil Sirey.

————. 1933. "The Principles of International Labor Legislation." *Annals of American Academy of Political and Social Science* 166:11–13.

Maier, Charles. 1975. *Recasting Bourgeois Europe: Stabilization in France, Germany, and Italy in the Decade after World War I*. Princeton: Princeton University Press.

Majone, Giandomenico. 1993. "The European Community between Social Policy and Social Regulation." *Journal of Common Market Studies* 31: 153–70.

————. 1994a. "The European Community as a Regulatory State" Lectures given at the Academy of European Law.

————. 1994b. "The Rise of the Regulatory State in Europe." *West European Politics* 17:77–101.

Mancini, Federico G. 1991. "The Making of a Constitution for Europe." In *The New European Community: Decisionmaking and Institutional Change*, edited by Robert O. Keohane and Stanley Hoffmann. Boulder, Colo.: Westview.

Mann, Michael. 1986. *The Sources of Social Power. Vol. #1*. Cambridge: Cambridge University Press.

————. 1988. "Ruling Class Strategies and Citizenship." In *States, War, and Capitalism: Studies in Political Sociology*. Oxford: Basil Blackwell.

————. 1993. "Nation-States in Europe and Other Continents: Diversifying, Developing, Not Dying." *Daedalus* 122:115–39.

Marginson, Paul, and Keith Sisson. 1994. "The Structure of Transnational Capital in Europe: The Emerging Euro-Company and Its Implications for Industrial Relations." In *New Frontiers in Industrial Relations*, edited by R. Hyman and A. Ferner. Oxford: Blackwell.

Marks, Gary. 1992. "Structural Policy in the European Community." In *Euro-Politics: Institutions and Policymaking in the New European Community*, edited by Alberta M. Sbragia. Washington, D.C.: Brookings.

———. 1993. "Structural Policy after Maastricht." In *The State of the European Community*, edited by Alan Cafruny and Glenda Rosenthal. New York: Lynne Rienner.

Marks, Gary, Liesbet Hooghe, and Kermit Blank. 1994. "The Changing Role of the State in the European Union." Paper presented at the conference on "The Politics and Political Economy of Contemporary Capitalism," held at the University of North Carolina at Chapel Hill and Duke University.

Marks, Gary, François Nielsen, Jane Salk, and Leonard Ray. 1994. "Regional Mobilization in the European Union." Unpublished paper, available from first author.

Marks, Gary, Fritz W. Scharpf, Philippe C. Schmitter, and Wolfgang Streeck. 1996. *Governance in the European Union*. London: Sage.

Marsden, David, ed. 1992. *Pay and Employment in the New Europe*. Aldershoot, England: Edward Elgar.

Marshall, T. H. 1950. *Citizenship and Social Class and Other Essays*. Cambridge: Cambridge University Press. *Class, Citizenship, and Social Development*. Westport, Conn.: Greenwood, 1973. Reprint, (page references are to reprint edition).

Martin, Andrew, and George Ross. 1995. "Labor and Europe: European Institutions and the Precarious Construction of Interest Representation to Confront Globalization." Unpublished manuscript, Center for European Studies, Harvard University.

Masters, Ruth D. 1932. *International Law in National Courts: A Study of the Enforcement of International Law in German, Swiss, French, and Belgian Courts*. New York: Columbia University Press.

Mayes, David 1995. "Introduction: Conflict and Cohesion in the Single European Market: A Reflection." In *Behind the Myth of European Union: Prospect for Cohesion*, edited by A. Amin and J. Tommaney. London: Routledge.

Mazey, Sonia, and Jeremy Richardson, eds. 1993. *Lobbying in the European Community*. Oxford: Oxford University Press.

McCarthy, William. 1992. "The Rise and Fall of Collective Laissez-Faire." In *Legal Intervention in Industrial Relations*, edited by William McCarthy. Oxford: Blackwell.

McDonnell, John. 1920–21. "International Labour Conventions." *British Yearbook of International Law* 1:151–222.

McLaughlin, A. M., G. Jordan, and W. A. Maloney. 1993. "Corporate Lobbying in the European Community." *West European Politics* 17: 31–52.

McMillan, James F. 1988. "World War I and Women in France." In *Total War and Social Change*, edited by Arthur Marwick. New York: St. Martin's.

Meehan, Elizabeth. 1991. "European Citizenship and Social Policies." In *The Frontiers of Citizenship*, edited by Ursula Vogel and Michael Moran. London: Macmillan.

———. 1993. *Citizenship in the European Community*. London: Sage.

Meier-Braun, Karl-Heinz. 1995. "40 Jahre 'Gastarbeiter' und Ausländerpolitik in Deutschland." *Aus Politik und Zeitgeschichte* 35 (August) : 14–22.

Melling, Joseph. 1983. "Employers, Industrial Welfare, and the Struggle for Work-Place Control in British Industry, 1880s–1920." In *Managerial Strategies and Industrial Relations: An Historical and Comparative Study*, edited by Howard F. Gospel and Craig R. Littler. London: Heinemann.

Melucci, Alberto. 1976. "Actions patronales, pouvoir, organisation: Règlements d'usine et contrôle de la main-d'oeuvre au XIXe siècle." *Le Mouvement Social* 97: 139–59.

Merrheim, Alphonse. 1908. "L'organisation patronale en France." *Le Mouvement Socialiste* 200:5–25, 81–95, 178–97.

Merriman, John. 1985. *Red City: Limoges and the French Nineteenth Century*. Oxford: Oxford University Press.

Mill, John Stuart. [1843] 1949. *A System of Logic: Ratiocinative and Inductive*. London: Longmans, Green.

Miller, David Hunter. 1921. *International Relations of Labor*. New York: Alfred A. Knopf.

Miller, P. 1993. *Práce, mzdy a sociální věci*. Prague: Consus.

Miller, Susanne. 1986. "The SPD from 1945 to the Present." In *A History of German Social Democracy: From 1848 to the Present*, edited by Susanne Miller and Heinrich Potthoff. Leamington, England: Berg.

Milner, Susan. 1990. *The Dilemmas of Internationalism: French Syndicalism and the International Labour Movement, 1900–1914*. New York: Berg.

Milward, Alan S. 1984. *The Reconstruction of Western Europe 1945–1951*. Berkeley: University of California Press.

———. 1992. *The European Rescue of the Nation-State*. Berkeley: University of California Press.

"Mines et fonderies de zinc de la Vieille Montagne." 1915. *Recueil Financier.* 22:563–67.

"Mines et usines á Zinc de Silésie (Schlesische Aktien-Gesellschaft für Bergbau und Zinkhütten-Betrieb)." 1915. *Recueil Financier* 22:852–54.

Minkin, Lewis. 1991. *The Contentious Alliance: Trade Unions and the Labour Party*. Edinburgh: Edinburgh University Press.

(MNS), Migration News Sheet (Brussels). 1995. 6.

Moch, Leslie Page. 1992. *Moving Europeans: Migration in Western Europe since 1650*. Bloomington: Indiana University Press.

Moine, Jean-Marie. 1989. *Les barons du fer: Les maîtres de forges en Lorraine du milieu du 19e siècle aux années trente*. Nancy: Editions Serpenoise.

Molinari, Gustave de. 1893. *Les bourses du travail*. Paris: Librairie Guillaumin.

Molle, Willem. 1990. *The Economics of European Integration: Theory, Practice, Policy*. Aldershot, England: Dartmouth.

Mommsen, Hans. 1979. *Arbeiterbewegung und nationale Frage*. Göttingen: Vandenhoeck und Rupprecht.

Mommsen, Wolfgang. 1981. "Nationalism, Imperialism, and Official Press Policy in Wilhelmine Germany, 1850–1914." In *Opinion publique et politique extérieure*. Vol. 1, *1870–1915*. Rome: Ecole Française de Rome.

Moravcsik, Andrew. 1991. "Negotiating the Single European Act: National Interests and Conventional Statecraft in the European Community." In *The New*

European Community: Decisionmaking and Institutional Change, edited by Robert O. Keohane and Stanley Hoffman. Boulder, Colo.: Westview.

————. 1994. "Why the European Community Strengthens the State: Domestic Politics and International Cooperation." Paper presented at the American Political Science Association meeting, New York.

More, Charles. 1980. *Skill and the English Working Class, 1870–1914.* New York: St. Martin's.

Morgan, Kenneth O. 1985. *Labour in Power, 1945–1951.* Oxford: Oxford University Press.

Mörner, Magnus, and Harold Sims. 1985. *Adventurers and Proletarians: The Story of Migrants in Latin America.* Paris: UNESCO.

Morokvasic, Mirjana. 1984. "Birds of Passage Are Also Women . . ." *International Migration Review* 18:886–907.

Moss, Peter. 1993. "Conciliation of Professional and Family Life for Women and Men." In *Comissao para Igualdade e para os Direitos das Mulheres: Actas do Seminario Construir a Igualdade.* Lisbon: Comissao para o Igualdade e para os Direitos das Mulheres.

Možný, I. 1993. "An Attempt at a Non-Economic Explanation of the Present Full Employment." *Czech Sociological Review* 2:199–210.

Müller, Bertrand. 1992. "'Problèmes contemporains' et 'hommes d'action': A l'origine des *Annales*: Une correspondance entre Lucien Febvre et Albert Thomas, 1928–1930." *Vingtième siècle* 35 (July–September): 78–91.

Murphy, Craig. 1994. *International Organization and Industrial Change: Global Governance since 1850.* Oxford: Oxford University Press.

Murray, Gilbert. 1921. *The Problems of Foreign Policy.* New York: Houghton Mifflin.

Myrdal, Gunnar. 1960. *Beyond the Welfare State.* New Haven: Yale University Press.

Nocken, Ulrich. 1983. "Das Internationale Stahlkartell und die deutschfranzösischen Beziehungen, 1924–1932." In *Konstellationen internationaler Politik, 1924–1932,* edited by Gustav Schmidt. Bochum: N. Brockmeyer.

Noiriel, Gérard. 1988a. "Du 'patronage' au 'paternalisme': La restructuration des formes de domination de la main-d'oeuvre dans l'industrie métallurgique française." *Le Mouvement Social* 144: 17–35.

————. 1988b. *Le creuset français: Histoire de l'immigration XIXe-XXe siècle.* Paris: Le Seuil.

————. 1991. *La tyrannie due national.* Paris: Calman-Levy.

————. 1993. "L'identification des citoyens: Naissance de l'etat civil republicain." *Genèses* 13:3–28.

————. 1996. *The French Melting Post.* Minneapolis: University of Minnesota Press.

Nord, Phillip. 1986. *Paris Shopkeepers and the Politics of Resentment.* Princeton: Princeton University Press.

North, Douglas C. 1991. "Institutions." *Journal of Economic Perspectives* 5: 97–112.

Northrup, Herbert R., and Richard L. Rowan. 1979. *Multinational Collective Bargaining Attempts: The Record, the Cases, and the Prospects.* Philadelphia: Industrial Research Unit, Wharton School, University of Pennsylvania.

Nye, Joseph S. 1972. "The Strength of International Unionism." In *Transnational*

Industrial Relations: The Impact of Multi-National Corporations and Economic Regionalism on Industrial Relations, edited by H. Günther. London and Basingstoke: Macmillan.

Oalid, William. 1923. "L'immigration ouvrière en France et l'organisation du marché du travail." In *Assemblée générale de l'association internationale pour la lutte contre le chômage*. Geneva: Association Internationale pour la Lutte contre le Chômage.

OECD (Organization for Economic Cooperation and Development). 1990. 1991. 1994a. *Employment Outlook*. Paris: OECD.

————. 1992. *Trends in International Migration: Annual Report, 1991*. Paris: SOPEMI, OECD.

————. 1994b. *Trends in International Migration: Continuous Reporting System on International Migration: Annual Report, 1993*. Paris: SOPEMI, OECD.

————. 1995. *Trends in International Migration: Continuous Reporting System on International Migration: Annual Report, 1994*. Paris: SOPEMI, OECD.

Offe, Claus. 1981. "The Attribution of Public Status to Interest Groups: Observations on the West German Case." In *Organizing Interests in Western Europe*, edited by Suzanne Berger. Cambridge: Cambridge University Press.

————. 1991a. "Capitalism by Democratic Design? Democratic Theory Facing the Triple Transition in East Central Europe." *Social Research* 58:865–892.

————. 1991b. "A Non-Productivist Design for Social Policies." Paper presented at the Anglo-German Conference on "Social Justice and Efficiency," Nottingham.

Offe, Claus, and Helmuth Wiesenthal. 1980. "Two Logics of Collective Action: Theoretical Notes on Social Class and Organizational Form." *Political Power and Social Theory*, 1:67–115.

Offerlé, Michel. 1985. "Mobilisations électorales et invention du citoyen." In *Explication du vote*, edited by Daniel Gaxie. Paris: Presses FNSP.

————. 1988. "Le nombre de voix." *Actes de la Recherche en Sciences Sociales* 71/72: 5–22.

————. 1993a. "L'électeur et ses papiers: Enquêtes sur les cartes et les listes électorales." *Genèses* 13:29–59.

————. 1993b. "Le vote comme évidence et comme énigme." *Genèses* 12:131–51.

Olivi, Louis. 1897. "L'émigration au point de vue juridique international." *Annuaire de l'Institut de Droit International* 30:413–44.

Olsen, Johan P. 1995. "Europeanization and Nation-State Dynamics." Working Paper no. 9, ARENA, University of Oslo.

Olson, Mancur. 1984. *The Rise and Decline of Nations: Economic Growth, Stagflation, and Social Rigidties*. New Haven: Yale University Press.

Olsson, Lars. 1992. "Labor Migration as a Prelude to World War I." Paper presented at the Conference of Europeanists, Chicago.

Orenstein, M. 1995. "The Czech Tripartite Council and Its Contribution to Social Peace." In *Social Reform in East-Central Europe: New Trends in Transition*, edited by S. Ringen and C. Wallace. Prague Papers on Social Responses to Transformation, vol. 3. Prague: Trevor Top.

Orloff, Ann S. 1993. "Gender and the Social Rights of Citizenship: The Comparative Analysis of State Policies and Gender Relations." *American Sociological Review* 58:303–28.

Orth, John V. 1991. *Combination and Conspiracy: A Legal History of Trade Unionism, 1771–1906.* Oxford: Clarendon.

Overturf, S. F. 1986. *The Economic Principles of European Integration.* New York: Praeger.

Panitch, Leo. 1976. *Social Democracy and Industrial Militancy: The Labour Party, the Trade Unions, and Incomes Policy, 1945–1974.* Cambridge: Cambridge University Press.

———. 1981. "Trade Unions and the Capitalist State." *New Left Review* 125:21–43.

Pedersen, Susan. 1990. "Gender, Welfare, and Citizenship in Britain during the Great War." *American Historical Review* 95:983–1006.

———. 1993. *Family, Dependence, and the Origins of the Welfare State: Britain and France, 1914–1945.* Cambridge: Cambridge University Press.

Pelkmans, J. 1990. "Regulation and the Internal Market: An Economic Perspective." In *The Competition of the Internal Market*, edited by J. Siebert. Tübingen.

Pelkmans, J., and A. Winters. 1988. *Europe's Domestic Market.* London: Royal Institute of International Affairs.

Pelling, Henry. 1968. *Popular Politics and Society in Late Victorian Britain.* London, New York: Macmillan.

Perkins, J. A. 1981. "The Agricultural Revolution in Germany, 1850–1940." *Journal of European Economic History* 10:71–118.

Pflung, Fritz. 1940. "Die Internationale ARBED." *Deutsche Volkswirt* 33:1719–22.

Phélippeau, Eric. 1993. "La fabrication administrative des opinions politiques." *Revue Française de Science Politique* 4:587–611.

Phillips, Angela, and Peter Moss. 1988. *Who Cares for Europe's Children?* Report of the European Childcare Network. Brussels: European Commission.

Phillips, Ann. 1991. *Engendering Democracy.* Oxford: Polity.

Piehl, Ernst. 1974. *Multinationale Konzerne und internationale Gewerkschaftsbewegung.* Frankfurt am Main: Europaische Verlagsanstalt.

Pierson, Paul, and Stephan Leibfried. Forthcoming. *Multitiered Institutions and the Making of Social Policy.* Washington, D.C.: Brookings.

Pillinger, Jane. 1992. *Feminising the Market.* Basingstoke: Macmillan.

Piore, Michael J. 1979. *Birds of Passage: Migrant Labor and Industrial Societies.* Cambridge: Cambridge University Press.

Platzer, Hans-Wolfgang. 1991. *Gewerkschaftspolitik ohne Grenzen? Die transnationale Zusammenarbeit der Gewerkschaften im Europa der 90er Jahre.* Bonn: Dietz.

Poggi, Gianfranco, 1990. *The State: Its Nature, Development, and Prospects.* Stanford: Stanford University Press.

Poidevin, Raymond. 1969. *Les relations économiques et financières entre France et l'Allemagne de 1898 à 1914.* Paris: Armand Colin.

Poitrineau, Abel. 1985. *Les Espagnols de l'Auvergne et du Limousin du XVIIIe au XIXe siècle.* Aurillac, France: Malroux-Mazel.

Polanyi, Karl. 1957. *The Great Transformation.* Boston: Beacon, 1944. Reprint, Boston: Beacon, 1957 (page references are to reprint edition).

Pollack, Mark A. 1995. "Creeping Competence: The Expanding Agenda of the European Community." *Journal of Public Policy* 29:123–63.

Pollard, Sidney. 1981. *The Economic Integration of the European Economy since 1815.* London: Thames and Hudson.

Pontusson, Jonas. 1988. *Swedish Social Democracy and British Labour: Essays on the Nature and Conditions of Social Democratic Hegemony.* Ithaca: Center for International Studies, Cornell University.

Pontusson, Jonas, and Peter Swenson. 1996. "Labor Markets, Production Strategies, and Wage Bargaining Institutions: The Swedish Employer Offensive in Comparative Perspective." *Comparative Political Studies* 2:223–50.

Poole, Michael. 1986. *Industrial Relations: Origins and Patterns of National Diversity.* London: Routledge.

Potůček, Martin. 1993. "Current Social Policy Developments in the Czech and Slovak Republics." *Journal of European Social Policy* 3:209–26.

————. 1994. "Quo Vadis: Social Policy in Czechoslovakia." In *Societies in Transition: East-Central Europe Today,* edited by C. Wallace and S. Ringen. Prague Papers on Social Responses to Transformation, vol. 1. Aldershot, England: Avebury.

Powell, Walter W. 1990. "Neither Markets nor Hierarchy: Network Forms of Organizations." *Research in Organizational Behavior* 12:295–336.

Powell, Walter W., and Paul J. DiMaggio. 1991. Introduction to *The New Institutionalism in Organizational Analysis,* edited by Walter W. Powell and Paul J. DiMaggio. Chicago: University of Chicago Press.

Preuss, Ulrich. 1993. "Citizenship and Identity: Aspects of a Political Theory of Citizenship." In *Migration in Europe. Challenges and Opportunities.* The Stanford Berlin Symposium on Transition in Europe.

Reconstruction in War and Peace: Interim Report of the National Executive Committee of the British Labour Party. 1943. Approved by the Party Conference under the title "The Old World and the New Society." New York: League for Industrial Democracy.

Reder, Melvin, and Lloyd Ulman. 1993. "Unionism and Unification." In *Labor and an Integrated Europe,* edited by L. Ulman, B. Eichengreen, and W. T. Dickens. Washington, D.C.: Brookings.

Reid, Donald. 1993. "The Politics of Immigrant Workers in Twentieth-Century France." In *The Politics of Immigrant Workers: Labor Activism and Migration in the World Economy since 1830,* edited by Camille Guerin-Gonzales and Carl Strikwerda. New York: Holmes and Meier.

Reim, Uwe, and Stefan Sandbrink. 1996. "Die Werkvertragsabkommen als Entsenderegelung für Arbeitnehmer aus den Staaten Mittel- und Osteuropas." ZeS-Arbeitspapier no. 12/96, Zentrum für Sozialpolitik, Universität Bremen.

Rhodes, Martin. 1991. "The Social Dimension of the Single European Market: National versus Transnational Regulation." *European Journal of Political Research* 19:245–80.

————. 1995. "A Regulatory Conundrum: Industrial Relations and Social Dimension." In *European Social Policy: Between Fragmentation and Integration,* edited by Stephan Leibfried and Paul Pierson. Washington, D.C.: Brookings.

Riding, Alan. 1993. "France, Reversing Course, Fights Immigrants' Refusal to Be French." *New York Times*, 5 December.

Robertson, David Brian. 1993. "The Return to History and the New Institutionalism in American Political Science." *Social Science History* 17:1–36.

Robson, Peter. 1980. *The Economics of International Integration*. London: Allen and Unwin.

Rogers, Joel, and Wolfgang Streeck, eds. 1995. *Works Councils: Consultation, Representation, Coordination*. Chicago: University of Chicago Press.

Rogers, Rosemarie. 1985a. "Post-World War II European Labor Migration: An Introduction to the Issues." In *Guests Come to Stay: The Effects of European Labor Migration on Sending and Receiving Countries* edited by Rosemarie Rogers. Boulder, Colo.: Westview.

————. ed. 1985b. *Guests Come to Stay: The Effects of European Labor Migration on Sending and Receiving Countries*. Boulder, Colo.: Westview.

Rokkan, Stein. 1975. "Dimensions of State Formation and Nation-Building: A Possible Paradigm for Research on Variations within Europe", in *The Formation of National States in Western Europe*, edited by Charles Tilly. Princeton: Princeton University Press.

Rosanvallon, Pierre. 1988. *La question syndicale*. Paris: Hachette.

————. 1992. *Le sacre du citoyen*. Paris: Gallimard.

Rose, Michael. 1987. "Economic Nationalism versus Class Solidarity: The Perspective of Active Trade Union Members." In *Trade Unions in a Changing Europe*, edited by George Spyropoulos. Maastricht: PIE.

Rosenau, James N. 1990. *Turbulence in World Politics: A Theory of Change and Continuity*. Princeton: Princeton University Press.

Rosoli, Gianfausto. 1985. "Italian Migration to European Countries from Political Unification to World War I." In *Labor Migration in the Atlantic Economies*, edited by Dirk Hoerder. Westport, Conn.: Greenwood.

Rothstein, Bo. 1992. *Den Korporativa Staten*. Stockholm: Norstedt.

————. 1996. *The Swedish Model and the Bureaucratic Problem of Social Reform*. Pittsburg: University of Pittsburgh Press.

Rousiers, Paul de. 1896. *The Labour Question in Britain*. London: Macmillan.

Rueschemeyer, Dietrich, Evelyne Huber Stephens, and John D. Stephens. 1992. *Capitalist Development and Democracy*. Chicago: University of Chicago Press.

Ruggie, John. 1983. "International Regimes, Transactions, and Change: Embedded Liberalism in the Postwar Economic Order." In *International Regimes*, edited by Stephen D. Krasner. Ithaca: Cornell University Press.

————. 1993. "Territoriality and Beyond: Problematizing Modernity in International Relations." *International Organization* 47: 139–74.

Rust, Michael. 1973. "Business and Politics in the Third Republic: The Comité des Forges and the French Steel Industry, 1896–1914." Doctoral dissertation, Princeton University.

Rütters, Peter, and Kurt P. Tudyka. 1990. "Internationale Gewerkschaftsbewegung: Vorbereitung auf den europäischen Binnenmarkt." In *Gewerkschaftshandbuch*, edited by M. Kittner. Cologne: Bund Verlag.

Ruyseveldt, Joris van and Jelle Visser, eds. 1996. *European Industrial Relations in Transition*. London: Sage.

Salt, John. 1992. "Migration Processes among the Highly Skilled in Europe." *International Migration Review* 26:484–505.

Sandholtz, Wayne. 1996. "Membership Matters: Limits of the Functional Approaches to European Institutions." *Journal of Common Market Studies* 34:403–29.

———, and John Zysman. 1989. "1992: Recasting the European Bargain." *World Politics* 42:95–128.

SAP (Swedish Social Democratic Party.) 1944. *Protokoll: Sveriges Socialdemokratiska Arbetarepatis 17:e Kongress i Stockholm, 18–24 Maj 1944*. Stockholm: SAP.

Saraceno, Chiara. 1993a. *Child Poverty and Deprivation in Italy: 1950 to the Present*. Innocenti Occasional Papers, no. 6. Florence: UNICEF/ICDC.

———. 1993b. "The Feminization of Poverty as an Outcome of the Gender Division of Labor." In *Comissao para Igualdade e para os Direitos das Mulheres: Actas do Seminario Construir a Igualdade*. Lisbon: Comissao para o Igualdade e para os Direitos das Mulheres.

Sargent, Jane A. 1985. "Corporatism and the European Community." In *The Political Economy of Corporatism*, edited by W. Grant. London: Macmillan.

Sassen, Saskia. 1995. *Transnational Economies and National Migration Policies*. Amsterdam: Institute for Migration and Ethnic Studies, University of Amsterdam.

———. 1996. *Losing Control: Sovereignty in an Age of Globalization*. New York: Columbia University Press.

Sassen-Koob, Saskia. 1980. "The Internationalization of the Labor Force." *Studies in Comparative International Development* 15:3–26.

Sbragia, Alberta M. 1992. "Thinking about the European Future: The Uses of Comparison." In *Euro-Politics: Institutions and Policymaking in the New European Community*, edited by Alberta M. Sbragia. Washington, D.C.: Brookings.

———. 1993. "The European Community: A Balancing Act." *Publius* 23:23–37.

Scharpf, Fritz W. 1992. "Europäisches Demokratiedefizit und deutscher Föderalismus." *Staatswissenschaften und Staatspraxis* 3:293–306.

———. 1994. "Community and Autonomy: Multi-level Policy-Making in the European Union." *Journal of European Public Policy* 1:219–42.

Schendelen, M. P. C. M. van, ed. 1993. *National Public and Private EC Lobbying*. Aldershot, England: Avebury.

Schmitt, Hans. 1962. *The Path to European Union: From the Marshall Plan to the Common Market*. Baton Rouge: Louisiana State University Press.

Schmitter, Philippe C. 1974. "Still the Century of Corporatism?" *Journal of Politics* 36:85–131.

———. 1996. "Imagining the Future of the Euro-Polity with the Help of New Concepts." In *Governance in the European Union*, edited by Gary Marks, Fritz W. Scharpf, Philippe C. Schmitter, and Wolfgang Streeck. London: Sage.

Schmitter, Philippe, and Gerhard Lehmbruch, eds. 1979. *Trends toward Corporatist Intermediation*. London and Beverly Hills: Sage.

Scholz, Arno, and Walter G. Oschilewski, eds. 1953. *Turmwächter der Demokratie: Ein Lebensbild von Kurt Schumacher*. Vol. 2. Berlin: Arani.

Schöttler, Peter. 1982. *Die Entstehung der "Bourses du Travail": Sozialpolitik und Französischer Syndikalismus am Ende des 19. Jahrhunderts*. Frankfurt am Main: Campus.

Searle, G. R. 1971. *The Quest for National Efficiency, 1899–1914*. Oxford: Oxford University Press.

Seideneck, Peter. 1996. "Trade Union Integration in Europe: Remarks on the ETUC's Policy on Eastern Europe." In *European Trade Union Yearbook, 1995*, edited by E. Gabaglio and R. Hoffman. Brussels: ETUI.

Self, Peter, and Herbert J. Storing. 1963. *The State and the Farmer: British Agricultural Policies and Politics*. Berkeley: University of California Press.

Shalev, Michael. 1992. "The Resurgence of Labour Quiescence." In *The Future of Labour Movements*, edited by M. Regini. London: Sage.

Sharp, Alan. 1991. *The Versailles Settlement: Peacemaking in Paris, 1919*. New York: St. Martin's.

Sharpe, L. J. 1988. "The Growth and Decentralization of the Modern Democratic State." *European Journal of Political Research* 16:365–80.

———. 1989. "Fragmentation and Territoriality in the European State System." *International Political Science Review* 10:223–38.

Shklar, Judith. 1991. *American Citizenship: The Quest for Inclusion*. Cambridge: Harvard University Press.

Shonfield, Andrew. 1965. *Modern Capitalism: The Changing Balance of Public and Private Power*. New York: Oxford University Press.

Shorter, Edward, and Charles Tilly. 1974. *Strikes in France*. Cambridge: Cambridge University Press.

Siegfried, André. [1913] 1979. *Tableau politique de la France de l'Ouest*. Paris: Armand Colin.

Siim, Birte. 1991. "Welfare State, Gender Politics, and Equality Politics: Women's Citizenship in the Scandinavian Welfare States." In *Equality Politics and Gender*, edited by Elizabeth Meehan and Selma Sevenhuijsen. London: Sage.

———.1993. "Gender, Power, and Citizenship: The Interplay between Women's Social and Political Citizenship in Scandinavia." Paper presented at the seminar on "La citoyenneté sociale des femmes en Europe," organized by the International Research Group on "Etat et rapports sociaux de sexe," Paris.

Silverman, Dan. 1972. *Reluctant Union: Alsace-Lorraine and Imperial Germany, 1871–1914*. College Station: Pennsylvania State University Press.

Simmel, George. [1908] 1983. "Die Kreuzung sozialer Kreise." In *Soziologie*, edited by G. Simmel. 6th ed. Berlin: Duncker und Humblot.

Simon, Herbert A. 1991. "Organizations and Markets." *Journal of Economic Perspectives* 5:25–44.

Singer-Kérel, Jeanne. 1991. "Foreign Workers in France, 1891–1936." *Ethnic and Racial Studies* 14: 279–93.

Sisson, Keith. 1987. *The Management of Collective Bargaining: An International Comparison*. Oxford: Blackwell.

Sledziewski, Elisabeth. 1992. "Conseil de l'Europe: La democratie paritaire." In *Quarante années d'activitè du Conseil de l'Europe: Actes du Seminaire du 6 et 7 novembre 1989, Strasbourg*.

Slichter, Sumner H. 1919. *The Turnover of Factory Labor*. New York: D. Appleton.

Slomp, Hans. 1990. *Labor Relations in Europe*. New York: Greenwood.

Snyder, David. 1975. "Institutional Setting and Industrial Conflict: Comparative

Analyses of France, Italy, and the United States." *American Sociological Review* 40(3):259–78.

Söderpalm, Sven Anders. 1976. *Direktörsklubben: Storindustrin i Svensk Politik under 1930– och 40–talen*. Stockholm: Zenith-Rabén Sjögren.

Solano, E. John, ed. 1920. *Labour as an International Problem*. London: Macmillan.

Sorge, Arndt. 1976. "The Evolution of Industrial Democracy in the Countries of the European Community." *British Journal of Industrial Relations* 14 (3): 274–94.

Sorlin, Pierre. 1966. *Waldeck-Rousseau*. Paris: Armand Colin, 1966.

Soysal, Yasemin N. 1994. *The Limits of Citizenship: Migrants and Postnational Membership in Europe*. Chicago and London: University of Chicago Press.

Spencer, Elaine Glovka. 1984. *Management and Labor in Imperial Germany: Ruhr Industrialists as Employers, 1896–1914*. New Brunswick, N.J.: Rutgers University Press.

Stalker, Peter. 1994. *The Work of Strangers: A Survey of International Labour Migration*. Geneva: ILO.

Standing, G. 1994. "From the Minimum Wage to Income Security: The Challenge." Paper presented at the Third Central European Forum, "Labour Market Changes in Central Europe: Lessons for Social Policy," Vienna.

Steil, Raymond. 1992. "'Einer für Alle, Alle für Einen!': Der Deutsche Metallarbeiter-Verband in Luxemburg, 1904–1918." In *75 Joër frai Gewerkschaften: Contributions à l'histoire du mouvement syndical luxembourgeois/Beitrage zur Geschichte der luxemburgischen Gewerkschaftesbewegung*, edited by Jacques Maas. Esch, Luxembourg: OBG-L.

Stephens, John D. 1986. *The Transition from Capitalism to Socialism*. Urbana: University of Illinois Press.

Stöckl, Ingrid. 1986. *Gewerkschaftsausschüsse in der EG*. Kehl a. Rh., Germany: N. P. Engel.

Stovall, Tyler. 1993. "Color-Blind France? Colonial Workers during the First World War." *Race and Class* 35:35–55.

Strange, Susan. 1995. "The Limits of Politics." *Government and Opposition* 30: 291–311.

———. 1996. *The Retreat of the State: The Diffusion of Power in the World Economy*. Cambridge: Cambridge University Press.

Straubhaar, Thomas. 1988. *On the Economics of International Labour Migration*. Bern and Stuttgart: Klett.

Strayer, Joseph R. 1970. *On the Medieval Origins of the Modern State*. Princeton: Princeton University Press.

Streeck, Wolfgang. 1982. "Organizational Consequences of Neo-corporatist Cooperation in West German Labour Unions." In *Patterns of Corporatist Policy-Making*, edited by Gerhard Lehmbruch and Philippe C. Schmitter. Beverly Hills: Sage.

———. 1993. "The Rise and Decline of Neocorporatism." In *Labor and an Integrated Europe*, edited by L. Ulman, B. Eichengreen, and W. T. Dickens. Washington, D.C.: Brookings.

———. 1994. "European Social Policy after Maastricht: The 'Social Dialogue' and 'Subsidarity.' " *Economic and Industrial Democracy* 15:151–77.

———. 1995. "Politikverflechtung und Entscheidungslücke: Zum Verhältnis von zwischenstaatlichen Beziehungen und sozialen Interessen im europäischen Binnenmarkt." In *Reformfähigkeit von Industriegesellschaften: Festschrift für Fritz W. Scharpf*, edited by R. Schettkat, K. Bentele, and B. Reissert. Frankfurt am Main: Campus.

———. 1996. "Neo-voluntarism: A New European Social Policy Regime?" In *Governance in the European Union*, edited by Gary Marks, Fritz W. Scharpf, Philippe C. Schmitter, and Wolfgang Streeck. London: Sage.

Streeck, Wolfgang, Josef Hilbert, Karl-Heinz von Kevelaer, Friederike Maier, and Hajo Weber. 1987. "The Role of Social Partners in Vocational Training and Further Training in the Federal Republic in Germany." Discussion Paper no. IIM/LMP 87–12, Wissenschaftszentrum Berlin für Sozialforschung (WZB).

Streeck, Wolfgang, and Philippe C. Schmitter. 1991. "From National Corporatism to Transnational Pluralism: Organized Interests in the Single European Market." *Politics and Society* 19:133–64.

Strikwerda, Carl. 1990. "Corporatism and the Lower Middle Classes: Interwar Belgium." In *Splintered Classes: Politics and the Lower Middle Classes in Interwar Europe*, edited by Rudy Koshar. New York: Holmes and Meier.

———. 1991. "Interest Group Politics and the International Economy: Mass Politics and Big Business Corporations in the Liège Coal Basin, 1870–1914." *Journal of Social History* 25:277–308.

———. 1993a. "France and the Belgian Immigration of the Nineteenth Century." In *The Politics of Immigrant Workers: Labor Activism and Migration in the World Economy since 1830*, edited by Camille Guerin-Gonzales and Carl Strikwerda. New York: Holmes and Meier.

———. 1993b. "The Troubled Origins of European Economic Integration: International Iron and Steel and Labor Migration in the Era of World War I." *American Historical Review* 98:1106–42.

Sturmthal, Adolf. 1943. *The Tragedy of European Labour, 1918–1939*. London: V. Gollancz.

———. 1953. *Unity and Diversity in European Labor*. Glencoe, Ill.: Free Press.

Sundhausen, Holm. 1992. "Deutschen in Rumänien." In *Deutsche in Ausland/ Fremde in Deutschland: Migration in Geschichte und Gegenwart*, edited by Klaus Bade. Munich: C. H. Beck.

Svedberg, Peter. 1978. "The Portfolio-Direct Composition of Private Foreign Investment in 1914, Revisited." *Economic Journal* 88:763–77.

Swaan, Abram de. 1988. *In Care of the State: Health Care, Education, and Welfare in Europe and the USA in the Modern Era*. Cambridge: Polity.

Swann, Dennis. 1988. *The Economics of the Common Market*. London: Penguin Books.

Sweden. 1944. SOU (Statens Offentliga Utredningar) Folkhushållningsdepartementet. *Statsmakterna och folkhushållningen under den till följd av stormaktskriget 1939 indträdde krisen, Juli 1943–June 1944*. Stockholm. 1944: 11.

———. 1952. SOU. Handelsdepartementet. *Kristidspolitik och kristidshushållning i Sverige under och efter andra världskriget*, by Karl Åmark. 2 vols. Stockholm, 1952:50.

Swenson, Peter. 1991. "Bringing Capital Back In, or Social Democracy Reconsidered." *World Politics* 43:513–44.

Tapinos, Georges. 1983. "European Migration Patterns: Economic Linkages and Policy Experiences." In *U.S. Immigration and Refugee Policy*, edited by Mary M. Kritz. Lexington, Mass.: Lexington Books.

Teague, Paul, and John Grahl. 1992. *Industrial Relations and European Integration*. London: Lawrence and Wishart.

Tenfelde, Klaus. 1977. *Sozialgeschichte der Bergarbeiterschaft an der Ruhr im 19. Jahrhundert*. Bonn: Verlag Neue Gesellschaft.

Thelen, Kathleen. 1994. "Beyond Corporatism: Toward a New Framework for the Study of Labor in Advanced Capitalism." *Comparative Politics* 27:107–21.

Thelen, Kathleen, and Sven Steinmo. 1992. "Historical Institutionalism in Comparative Politics." In *Structuring Politics: Historical Institutionalism in Comparative Analysis*, edited by Sven Steinmo, Kathleen Thelen, and Frank Longstreth. Cambridge: Cambridge University Press.

Thomas, Clive S., ed. 1933. *First World Interest Groups: A Comparative Perspective*. Westport, Conn.: Greenwood.

Thorpe, Wayne. 1989. *"The Workers Themselves": Revolutionary Syndicalism and International Labour, 1913–1923*. Amsterdam: Kluwer.

Tilly, Charles. 1975a. "Reflections on the History of European State-Making." In *The Formation of National States in Western Europe*, edited by Charles Tilly. Princeton: Princeton University Press.

———. 1985. "War Making and State Making as Organized Crime." In *Bringing the State Back In*, edited by Peter B. Evans, Dietrich Rueschemeyer, and Theda Skocpol. Cambridge: Cambridge University Press.

———. 1989. "Cities and States in Europe, 1000–1800." *Theory and Society* 18:563–84.

———. 1995. "Globalization Threatens Labor's Rights." *International Labor and Working-Class History* 47:1–24.

———. ed. 1975b. *The Formation of National States in Western Europe*. Princeton, NJ: Princeton University Press.

Tilly, Chris, and Charles Tilly. 1992. "Capitalist Work and Labor Markets." Working Paper no. 153, Center for Studies of Social Change, New York.

Timmesfeld, Andrea. 1994. *Chancen und Perspektiven europäischer Kollektivverhandlungen: Zur Bedeutung nationaler Interessendivergenzen für die kollektive Handlungsfähigkeit europäischer Fachverbände*. Baden-Baden: Nomos.

Tinbergen, Jan. 1964. *Central Planning*. New Haven and London: Yale University Press.

Tingsten, Herbert. 1973. *The Swedish Social Democrats: Their Ideological Development*. Totowa, N.J.: Bedminster. Stockholm: Aldus/Bonnier, 1967. Translation of *Den Svenska Social Democrat ins Ideuveckling*. (Page references are to translation.)

Titmus, Richard M. 1950. *Problems of Social Policy*. London: Her Majesty's Stationery Office.

Tracy, Michael. 1964. *Agriculture in Western Europe*. New York: Praeger.

Treue, Wilhelm. 1966. *Die Feuer verloschen nie: August Thyssen Hütte, 1890–1926*. Düsseldorf: Econ-Verlag.

Tsebelis, George, 1994. "The Power of the European Parliament as a Conditional Agenda Setter." *American Political Science Review* 88:128–42.

Tubben, Willi. 1930. *Die nationale und internationale Verbandspolitik der Schwerindustrie vor und nach dem Kriege.* Würzburg: Buchdrukerei Popp.

TUC (Trades Union Congress). 1944. 1945. 1946. 1947. 1948. 1949. 1950. 1951. *Report.*

Turner, H. A. 1962. *Trade Union Growth Structure and Policy: A Comparative Study of the Cotton Unions.* London: Allen and Unwin.

Turner, Lowell. 1992. "Prospects for Worker Participation in Management in the Single Market." In *Labor and an Integrated Europe*, edited by L. Ulman, B. Eichengreen, and W. T. Dickens. Washington, D.C.: Brookings.

Tyszkiewicz, Zygmunt. 1991. "UNICE: The Voice of European Business and Industry in Brussels: A Programmatic Self-Presentation." In *Employers' Associations in Europe*, edited by D. Sadowski and O. Jacobi. Baden-Baden: Nomos.

Ulman, Lloyd. 1975. "Multinational Unionism: Incentives, Barriers, and Alternatives." *Industrial Relations Journal* 14: 1–31.

Ungeheueur, Michel. 1912. "Die wirtschaftliche Bedeutung der ostfranzösischen Erz- und Eisenindustrie." *Technik und Wirtschaft* 5:11–15.

———. 1916. "Die wirtschaftliche Bedeutung der luxemburgischen Erz- und Eisenindustrie." *Schmollers Jahrbuch* 40:2, 211, 273.

UNICEF. See Saraceno, Chiara.

United Kingdom. 1948a. Cmd. 7321. *Statement on Personal Income, Costs, and Prices.* London: H. M. Stationery Office.

———. 1948b. Cmd. 7572. *European Co-operation: Memoranda submitted to the Organization for European Economic Co-operation relating to Economic Affairs in the Period 1949 to 1952.* London: H.M. Stationery Office.

———. 1949. Cmd. 7647. *Economic Survey for 1949.* London: H. M. Stationery Office.

Upham, Martin. 1992. "The Role of Peak Employers' Organizations in Collective Bargaining." *Bulletin of Comparative Labour Relations* 23:255–70.

Večerník, J. 1993. "Escaping from Socialist Paternalism: Social Policy Reform in the Czech Republic." *Czech Sociological Review* 2:149–72.

Vignes, Maurice. 1913. "Le bassin de Briey et la politique de ses entreprises sidérurgiques ou minières." *Revue d'Economie Politique* 27:1–40.

Visser, Jelle. 1989. *European Trade Unions in Figures.* Deventer, Netherlands and Boston: Kluwer.

———. 1990. "In Search of Inclusive Unionism." *Bulletin of Comparative Labour Relations* 18.

———. 1991. "Trends in Trade Union Membership." In *OECD Employment Outlook, 1991.* Paris: OECD.

———. 1992. "The Strength of Union Movements in Advanced Capitalist Democracies: Social and Organizational Variations." In *The Future of Labour Movements*, edited by M. Regini. London: Sage.

———. 1996. "Internationalism in European Trade Unions: A Lost Perspective or a New Agenda?" In *The Lost Perspective? Trade Unions between Ideology and Social Action in the New Europe*, edited by P. Pasture, J. Verberckmoes, and H. deWitte. Vol. 2. Aldershot, England: Avebury.

Visser, Jelle, and Bernhard Ebbinghaus. 1992. "Making the Most of Diversity? European Integration and Transnational Organization of Labour." In *Organized Interests and the European Community*, edited by Justin Greenwood, Jürgen Grote, and Karsten Ronit. London: Sage.

Vogel-Polsky, Eliane. 1993. "La démocratie paritaire: vers un nouveau contrat social." In *Comissao para Igualdade e para os Direitos das Mulheres: Actas do Seminario Construir a Igualdade*. Lisbon: Comissao para o Igualdade e para os Direitos das Mulheres.

Wall, Richard, and Jay Winter, eds. 1988. *The Upheaval of War: Family, Work, and Welfare in Europe, 1914–1918*. Cambridge: Cambridge University Press.

Wallace, William. 1982. "Europe as a Confederation: The Community and the Nation State." *Journal of Common Market Studies* 21:57–68.

Walzer, Michael. 1970. *Obligations: Essays on Disobedience, War, and Citizenship*. New York: Clarion.

Wautelet, J. M. 1975. "Accumulation et rentabilité du capital dans les charbonnages belges, 1850–1914." *Recherches Économiques de Louvain* 41:3–79.

Webb, Sidney, and Beatrice Webb. 1902. *The History of British Trade Unionism*. London: Longmans, Green.

————. 1920. *The History of Trade Unionism*. New York: Longmans, Green.

Weber, Max. 1958. "Capitalism and Rural Society in Germany." In *From Max Weber: Essays in Sociology*, edited by Hans H. Gerth and C. Wright Mills. New York: Oxford University Press.

Wee, Herman van der. 1986. *Prosperity and Upheaval: The World Economy, 1945–1980*. Berkeley: University of California Press.

Weidenfeld, Werner, and Olaf Hillenbrand. 1994. "Wie kann Europa die Immigration bewältigen? Möglichkeiten und Grenzen eines Einwanderungskonzeptes." *Europa-Archiv* 1: 1–10.

Weill, Claudie. 1978. "Le débat sur les migrations ouvrières dans le deuxieme Internationale." *Pluriel* 13:55–73.

Weir, Margaret, and Theda Skocpol. 1985. "State Structures and Possibilities for 'Keynesian' Responses to the Great Depression." In *Bringing the State Back In*, edited by Peter B. Evans, Dietrich Rueschemeyer, and Theda Skocpol. Cambridge: Cambridge University Press.

Werner, Heinz. 1994. "Regional Economic Integration and Migration: The European Case." *Annals of American Academy of Political and Social Science* (July): 147–64.

White, Harrison. 1981. "Where Do Markets Come From?" *American Journal of Sociology* 87:517–47.

Wihtol de Wenden, Catherine. 1991. "Immigration Policy and the Issue of Nationality." *Ethnic and Racial Studies* 14: 319–32.

Williams, Ernest E. 1897. *Made in Germany*. London: Heinemann.

Williamson, Jeffrey G. 1995. "Globalization, Convergence, and History." Working Paper no. 5259, National Bureau of Economic Research, Cambridge, Mass.

Williamson, Oliver E. 1985. *The Economic Institutions of Capitalism*. New York: Free Press.

Wilson, Francis G. 1933. "The Enforcement of International Labor Standards." *Annals of American Academy of Political and Social Science* 166: 95–102.

Windmuller, John. P. 1975. "The Authority of National Trade Union Confederations: A Comparative Analysis." In *Union Power and Public Policy*, edited by D. B. Linskey. Ithaca: Cornell University Press.

————. 1980. *The International Trade Union Movement.* Deventer, Netherlands: Kluwer.

Windolf, Paul. 1992. "Mitbestimmung und 'corporate control' in der Europäischen Gemeinschaft." In *Die Integration Europas*, edited by Michael Kreile. Opladen, Germany: Westdeutscher Verlag.

Winkler, Heinrich. 1972. *Mittelstand, Demokratie, und Nationalsozialismus.* Cologne: Kiepenheuer und Witsch.

Woleková, H. 1994. "Reform of Social Security System Is Complicated by Changes in Labour Market." Paper presented at the Third Central European Forum, "Labour Market Changes in Central Europe: Lessons for Social Policy," Vienna.

Women of Europe. 1992. No. 36, supplemental issue ("The Position of Women on the Labour Market: Trends and Developments in the Twelve Member States of the European Community, 1983–1990").

Wright, Gavin. 1990. "The Origins of American Industrial Success, 1879–1940." *American Economic Review* 80:651–68.

Wright, James D. 1981. "Political Disaffection," in The Handbook of Political Behavior. (vol. 4), edited by Samuel Long. New York: Plenum.

Yarmie, Andrew H. 1984. "British Employers' Resistance to 'Grandmotherly' Government, 1850s–1880." *Social History* 3:141–69.

Yücel, A. Ersan. 1987. "Turkish Migrant Workers in the Federal Republic of Germany: A Case Study." In *Migrants in Europe: The Role of Family, Labor, and Politics* edited by Hans Buechler and Judith-Maria Buechler. New York: Greenwood.

Zelizer, Viviana A. 1988. "Beyond the Polemics on the Market: Establishing a Theoretical and Empirical Agenda." *Sociological Forum* 3:614–34.

Zolberg, Aristide. 1987. "Wanted but Not Welcome: Alien Labor in Western Development." In *Population in an Interacting World*, edited by William Alonzo. Cambridge: Harvard University Press.

————. 1993. "International Migration." In *The Oxford Companion to Politics of the World*, edited by Joel Krieger. New York and Oxford: Oxford University Press.

————. 1995. "Response: Working-Class Dissolution." *International Labor and Working-Class History* 47:28–38.

Zolberg, Aristide, Astri Suhrke, and Serio Aguayo. 1989. *Escape from Violence: Conflict and the Refugee Crisis in the Developing World.* New York: Oxford University Press.

"Zur Änderung des Asylrechts: Debatterbeitráge und Hintergründe." 1993. *Der Tagesspiegel*, May: 5.

Index

About the Authors

Bernhard Ebbinghaus is a senior researcher at the Max Planck Institute for the Study of Societies, Cologne (Germany). He is a coauthor, with Jelle Visser, of *The Development of Trade Unions in Western Europe, 1945–59: A Data Handbook* (Frankfurt: Campus Verlag, forthcoming).

Thomas Faist is a research fellow at the Institute for Intercultural and International Studies, Bremen University (Germany). He is the author of *Social Citizenship for Whom? Young Turks in Germany and Mexican Americans in the United States* (Brookfield: Avebury, 1995).

Michael Hanagan teaches history in the Graduate Faculty, New School for Social Research. He is author of *The Logic of Solidarity: Artisans and Industrial Workers in Three French Towns, 1871–1914* (1980) and *Nascent Proetarians: Class formation in Post Revolutionary France, 1840–1880* (1989). He is currently completing a third book manuscript, co-authored with Miriam Cohen, "Families, Reformers, and the State: The Emergence of the Welfare State in Europe and the United States."

E. J. Hobsbawm is Professor Emeritus of Economic and Social History, University of London, and Professor Emeritus at the New school for Social Research. He is Fellow of the British Academy, the American Academy of Arts and Sciences, and author of numerous historical works; most recently *The Age of Extremes: 1914–1991* (1994) and *On History* (1997).

Jytte Klausen is an assistant professor of comparative politics at Brandeis University and a fellow at the Bunting Institute of Radcliffe College, Harvard University, and the Minda de Gunzberg Center for European Studies, Harvard University. She is the author of *In the Image of War: European Capitalism after 1945* (1998).

322 About the Authors

Christiane Lemke is a professor of political science at the University of Hannover (Germany). She is the author of *Die Ursachen des Umbruchs; Politische Sozialisation in der ehemaligen DDR* (Opladen: Westdeutscher Verlag, 1991) and a coeditor of *The Crisis of Socialism in Europe* (Durham: Duke University Press, 1992) and *Frauenbewegung und Frauenpolitik in Osteuropa* (Frankfurt: Campus Verlag, 1996).

Gary Marks is Professor of Political Science at the University of North Carolina Chapel Hill, and Director of the UNC Center for European Studies. His publications include *Unions in Politics: Britain, Germany, and the United States in the Nineteenth and Early Twentieth Centuries* (1989, Princeton UP), *The Crisis of Socialism in Europe* (1992, Duke UP) co-edited with Christiane Lemke, and *Reexamining Democracy* (1992, Sage) with Larry Diamond. His most recent books are *Governance in the European Union* with Fritz Scharpf, Philippe Schmitter, and Wolfgang Streeck (Sage, 1996) and *Continuity and Change in Contemporary Capitalism*, co-edited with Herbert Kitschelt, Peter Lange and John Stephens (Cambridge UP, forthcoming).

Leslie Page Moch is a professor of history at Michigan State University. She is the author of *Moving Europeans: Migration in Western Europe since 1650* (Bloomington: Indiana University Press, 1992) and *Paths to the City: Regional Migration in Nineteenth-Century France* (Beverly Hills: Sage, 1983). Moch is the editor of *European Migrants: Global and Local Perspectives* (Boston: Northeastern University Press, 1996), with Dirk Hoerder.

Gérard Noiriel is a director of research at the École des Hautes Études en Sciences Sociales (EHESS-Paris) and the director of the graduate program in social sciences at the École Normale Supérieure. He is the author of *The French Melting Pot: Immigration, Citizenship, and National Identity* (Minneapolis: University of Minnesota Press, 1996) and *Workers in French Society in the Nineteenth and Twentieth Centuries* (Oxford: Berg, 1990).

Michael Offerlé is a professor of political science at the University of Paris I (Pantheon Sorbonne). He is the author of *Les Partis Poitiques* (Paris: PUF, 1987) and *Sociologie des Groupes d'Intérêt*.

Martin Potůček is the director of the Institute of Sociological Studies, Faculty of Societal Sciences, Charles University, Prague (Czech Republic). His publications include *Nejen trh (Not Only the Market)* (Prague: SLON, 1997), *Sociální politika (Social Policy)* (Prague: SLON, 1995), and *The Formation and Implementation of Social Policy in the Czech Republic as a Political Process* (Prague: Foundation for Research on Social Transformation, 1995).

Chiara Saraceno is a full professor of family sociology at the University of Turin, Italy, Faculty of Political Science, head of the Department of Social Sciences. The Italian expert in the EC Observatory on Policies for Combating Social Exclusion from 1990 to 1994, she is member both of the Italian Poverty Commision at the Prime Minister Office and of the National Observatory on Families. She has written extensively on family changes and family policies, on poverty and social policies, on gender and women issues. At present she is coordinating a project on the evaluation of income support policies at the local level funded by the EU under the TSER program and is a member of a European Network on Gender and Citizenship.

Carl Strikwerda is an associate professor in the Department of History and the chair of the European Studies Program at the University of Kansas, Lawrence, Kansas. He is the author of *A House Divided: Catholics, Socialists, and Flemish Nationalists in Nineteenth-Century Belgium* (forthcoming) and co-editor of *The Politics of Immigrant Workers: Labor Activism and Migration in the World Economy since 1830* (New York: Holmes and Meier, 1993).

Louise A. Tilly is Michael E. Gellert Professor of History and Sociology and Chair of the Committee on Historial Studies, Graduate Faculty, New School for Social Research, New York, NY. She is the coauthor (with Joan Scott) of *Women, Work, and Family* (1978, 1986), and coeditor of *Women, Politics and Change* (1990) and *The European Experience of Fertility Decline* (1992). She is author also of *Politics and Class in Milan, 1881–1901* (1992).

Jelle Visser is an associate professor of sociology at the University of Amsterdam and an associate guest researcher at the Max Planck Institute for the Study of Societies. Cologne (Germany). His publications include *European Trade Unions in Figures* (Deventer: Kluwer, 1989), *In Search of Inclusive Unionism* (Deventer: Kluwer, 1990), and *European Industrial Relations in Transition* (London: Sage 1996) (coeditor).